*Studies in the
Anthropology of North
American Indians Series*

FOUNDING EDITORS

Raymond J. DeMallie

Douglas R. Parks

The Dakota
Way of Life

Ella Cara Deloria

———

Edited by Ramond J. DeMallie
and Thierry Veyrié

Afterword by Philip J. Deloria

University of Nebraska Press ‖ Lincoln

Published by the University of Nebraska Press, Lincoln, in cooperation with the
American Indian Studies Research Institute, Indiana University, Bloomington

The University of Nebraska Press is part of a land-grant institution with campuses and programs on the past, present, and future homelands of the Pawnee, Ponca, Otoe-Missouria, Omaha, Dakota, Lakota, Kaw, Cheyenne, and Arapaho Peoples, as well as those of the relocated Ho-Chunk, Sac and Fox, and Iowa Peoples.

∞

Library of Congress Control Number: 2022011707

Set in Merope.

Contents

Illustration

Acknowledgments

Many anonymous Dakota people should be credited for having shared their knowledge of Dakota social life with Ella Deloria, and they can only be thanked collectively. Deloria wrote to Hiram Beebe:[1]

> I should like to add your name in the preface to those of all friends who have helped, either by encouragement, material aid, information, or whatever. I am not trying to name individually the literally scores–into the hundreds–of Dakota people I have talked with and from whom I have obtained not only plain facts but–and more especially–the psychological background that motivated action and behavior in the old camp circle life. (December 2, 1952)

Since she never formally completed her manuscript, this quote is the only testimony of Ella Deloria's gratitude toward and acknowledgment of the many people who made this work possible.

We know that Ella Deloria received precious guidance from Franz Boas, Ruth Benedict, Margaret Mead, and, in secondary roles, Alexander Lesser, Will Robinson, and Inez Adams at Columbia University. Several other institutions should be mentioned for providing stipends, travel funds, and money for gifts that made fieldwork and typing possible. The Penrose Fund of the American Philosophical Society supported her fieldwork before 1944. The Viking Fund of the Wenner-Gren Foundation, the Institute for Intercultural Studies, and Hiram E. Beebe sponsored Deloria's editing of her manuscripts after 1944.

Ella Deloria's family, over four generations, was integral to the materials comprising *The Dakota Way of Life*, beginning with Reverend Philip J. Deloria and Mary Sully Deloria, her parents, who were undoubtedly the first sources of her knowledge of Dakota culture and language. Vine V. Deloria Sr. and Mary Susan Deloria, her brother and sister, were companions throughout the preparation of this manuscript. Vine V. Deloria

Jr., with whom DeMallie maintained a long friendship, correspondence, and collaborative study, introduced him to his aunt's work and unpublished manuscripts. The fourth generation of Deloria scholars, manifested by Philip J. Deloria, also deserves mention for his suggestions and for authoring the afterword to this volume. We express our deep gratitude to the Deloria family.

Our admiration for Ella Deloria's life and commitment to the description of her Native culture and language is immense, and we are proud and grateful to bring this manuscript to the public. DeMallie also had the privilege to enjoy conversations with Deloria in 1965 and 1970. Many people have helped or informed DeMallie's research on Deloria's life and work and cannot be listed exhaustively. We should, however, make mention of her biographer, Janette Murray, who was most helpful in diving into Deloria's life.

In the final stage of the editorial work on this book, students and colleagues have been a precious help. Douglas Parks, Della Cook, David Miller, Erik Gooding, Christina Burke, Carolyn Anderson, and David Posthumus all provided scholarly expertise and improved the manuscript in some way, be it by copyediting, adding diacritics, or providing additional sources and context. Travis Myers has also been of invaluable assistance. We also want to thank Emily J. Levine for her insights and attention given to the manuscript.

Lastly, we wish to thank Matthew Bokovoy, Heather Stauffer, Ann Baker, and Emily Shelton at the University of Nebraska Press for taking on this book project and guiding us through the process.

Presentation of Ella Cara Deloria

Ella Cara Deloria, who devoted much of her life to the study of the language and culture of the Sioux (Dakota and Lakota), was born on January 31, 1889, on the Yankton Sioux Indian Reservation in southeastern South Dakota, near the present town of Lake Andes. She was the firstborn child of the reverend Philip Joseph Deloria and Mary Sully Deloria and was named *Ąpétu Wašté-wį* 'Beautiful Day Woman' in commemoration of the blizzard that raged the day of her birth. Her parents, members of the Yankton Sioux tribe, were both descended from Yankton Dakota (Sioux) and Euro-American ancestors. Her father's Dakota name was *Tʻípi Sápa* 'Black Lodge'; her father's father was François des Lauriers (known as *Saswé*, the Dakota pronunciation of François), a Yankton chief who was the son of a Frenchman and a Yankton woman. Deloria's mother, Mary Sully Bordeaux, the granddaughter of the artist Thomas Sully, was also of mixed heritage, being of Irish and Yankton descent. Both of Deloria's parents had had children by previous marriages. As a young man, Philip Deloria had converted to Christianity and renounced his claim to chieftainship; ultimately he became one of the first two Sioux to be ordained priests in the Episcopal Church.[1] In 1890 he was placed in charge of St. Elizabeth's Church and Boarding School, near Wakpala, South Dakota, on the Standing Rock Reservation. There Ella Deloria was raised with her younger sister and brother, Susan and Vine. Her childhood memories of the big tipi her mother would put up during the summers, which served as the children's playhouse, and of the families of Chief Gall and other local Hunkpapa and Blackfeet Lakotas, are warmly recalled in her writings.

None of this made for a carefree childhood. Ella Deloria wrote that she and her siblings were not completely at home in Indian society, where social restrictions of gender and respect circumscribed the children's play, and, in the context of the mission they were the minister's children, always called on to "set an example." Being the eldest of her siblings, she started acting as caretaker early in her childhood and was called upon for farm work. At twelve she was driving a team of horses that accidentally got scared, tipped the wagon, and caused the loss of her right thumb, handicapping her for life (Deloria 1998, xi). Then they were sent to boarding school at All Saints in Sioux Falls, where Deloria studied from 1902 to 1910. That year she entered Oberlin College, after which, in 1913, she enrolled at Columbia University Teachers College in New York City, where she received her bachelor of science degree in 1915. During her last semester in New York, she was introduced to pioneer of American anthropology Franz Boas, who was pursuing a study of the Dakota language. Boas hired her—Deloria's first paying job—to come to his class and work with him and his students on translating portions of the texts written by Lakota scholar George Bushotter in 1887. It was her first realization that her skill in her Native language was valued outside Sioux Country. This experience introduced her to the formal study of American Indian languages and cultures, thereby setting in motion the course of much of the rest of her life. After graduation Deloria returned to All Saints, where she taught for four years. In 1919 she took a job with the YWCA as health education secretary for Indian schools. In 1923 she returned to teaching, this time as a physical education instructor at Haskell Institute, an Indian boarding school in Lawrence, Kansas.

Her letters from Haskell reveal Ella Deloria's strong identity as a Dakota and as an Indian—an identity fostered by a network of educated Indian friends and acquaintances. While at Haskell she was particularly proud of her accomplishments in writing and staging pageants, modeled in part after tableaux performed by the students at All Saints. In 1928 she copyrighted "The Wohpe Festival," a day-long celebration of traditional Dakota religion for schools and summer camps that celebrates Indians as children of nature: "The great lesson is taught that life in any form is precious . . . all children, regardless of race, need to learn it at some time during their lives." Based on the Sun Dance, the directions for the festival give invocations, prayers, dances, and ritual movements.

In 1927 Boas's student Martha Warren Beckwith happened to meet Philip Deloria while recording Sioux folklore in South Dakota. From him she learned of Ella Deloria's whereabouts and wrote to tell Boas. Anxious to continue their collaboration, Boas visited her in Oklahoma to propose that she resume the Dakota-language studies she had begun with him in New York. That June, in Lawrence, they continued their work on the Bushotter translations and finalized the writing system for the Dakota language, Boas reinforcing in Deloria's mind the necessity of distinguishing aspirated, unaspirated, and glottalized consonants. Before leaving Boas drew up a formal agreement to pay her to continue work during the summer. She readily agreed and spent the summer translating written texts, including those by George Sword, a reservation policeman who wrote for Lakota newspapers. She also recorded texts on her own. In a letter to Deloria in January 1928, Boas referred to the writing system they developed in the summer of 1927 as "the alphabet as we designed it."

Ella Deloria continued translating the Bushotter texts that Franz Boas mailed to her at Haskell. Writing to Bishop Hugh L. Burleson, her spiritual advisor and temporal benefactor, in August 1928, she explained it this way:

> Dr. Boas of Columbia, with whom I did some work in recording Dakota phonetically, when I was in school, came to see me and we worked out some more material. He is most interested in getting the language recorded accurately for future reference in comparative languages of primitive peoples, and wants me to work with him . . . I am finishing up now some revision of the Bushotter Dakota texts from the Smithsonian Institute. Also I am writing a course of study in physical education for the Indian schools. . . .
>
> I always have the feeling that this (whatever I am doing) is temporary—that ideally I would be doing church work. I feel a constant pull towards that. I wish there were a position in the Church in South Dakota involving traveling for the woman's auxiliary. I don't brag, but I know that I have been fortunate enough to have the natural ability of getting people to do things, and that with my Dakota, and knowledge of Church affairs, and of changing customs among the white people, I can make a success of such work, helping women to take their place in the Church and also interpreting white people to them, so they can adjust themselves better than they have till now. I am very thoroughly convinced that you can not really get at the heart of a people without knowing their language. I think my knowledge of Dakota is a big asset there. And then, pageantry. I have been putting on things [pageants] down here, and made each one better than the previous one.[2]

Deloria so enjoyed the linguistic work that at the end of the fall semester she precipitously resigned her teaching position in Haskell, even before Boas could guarantee her full-time employment. At age thirty-nine, she found teaching physical education to be too exhausting and was looking for another line of work. In November 1927 she wrote to Boas by hand in an exhilarated tone:

[I] am considering resigning . . . I have in view two things, —a position in a book company, or church work at home. But of course that is in case you have nothing for me. I am wondering—you once said that for a time you might have me come to live in your home and do work on the Dakota. Would you care to offer me such a thing at this time? I could come the first part of January . . . I should have to have a salary, and whenever an opportunity came from a high school or organization, to tell Indian customs and demonstrate dances, as used to come when I was in New York, I would like to be able to go. The rest of the time I could give to any work you would want me to do. . . .

P.S. You spoke of a possible fellowship. If that should materialize, I could come back to the Sioux Country in June. I would like that better than teaching gym work any more.

Boas was guardedly optimistic about being able to provide support for Deloria and proposed a salary of $100 per month, with Ella to live with his family. She preferred a higher salary that would allow her independence in New York. On Christmas Day, 1927, she wrote to Boas again, assuring him that there was nothing she wanted to do more than work with him on the Dakota language. The following month, on January 18, 1928, Boas wrote her that he had obtained funds for her to revise the Riggs dictionary of Santee (1890), recording the equivalent forms in Teton Dakota, or Lakota. Finally, on January 28, Boas was able to guarantee her regular employment for eighteen months, which began a decade of collaboration supported by Columbia University.

Her funding permitted to employ her under Otto Klineberg, a friend of Boas's, to work on a project to study Dakota psychology, "the habits of action and thought" of children and adults. However, Boas used this as an opportunity to further their collaboration on Dakota language and culture. When, in January 1928, he asked her to write the Dakota forms in the Riggs dictionary, he noted that, "from an ethnological point of view, the whole study will, of course, have to know all the details of everyday life as well as of religious attitudes and habits of thought of the people."

Boas asked Deloria to come to New York to receive directions and assist in the classroom, but she delayed her trip until February, when her brother could come to South Dakota to stay with their father and assist him, as his health was precarious. Philip had retired from missionary work and moved back to the Yankton Reservation. The $200 a month Boas now provided allowed her to rent her own lodgings and to bring her sister to live with her; as neither Ella nor Susan Deloria ever married, the two would be lifelong companions. At the end of April 1928 she wrote to her bishop that she had completed the work on the Riggs dictionary, having written the Lakota forms in the margins. Boas's objective was to reorganize the dictionary according to verb stems. Deloria was also teaching two classes: one on her own (presumably devoted to Dakota culture and society), and the other a linguistics methods class, "where I do not teach but answer questions put to me by the students who are trying to learn methods of getting at a new, primitive language."

During the summer Deloria returned to South Dakota to continue field study. Upon her departure Boas provided directions about the comparative psychology project to Deloria in a letter:

> The principal object of your trip is to supplement your knowledge of the general culture background of the Dakota for the purpose of assisting in the preparation of psychological tests that will fit their culture. . . . If you should find any kind of games among children that train activities, with which our own children in the cities are not familiar, these will be of particular value. . . . At the same time, you will obtain as much information as possible on the ethnography and language of the Sioux. (Whitten and Zimmerman 1982)

Deloria was to develop a comparative performance test. Two years later the test, which was based on beadwork, proved adequate for showing that Lakota children performed better than children from the city in an activity with which they were familiar, unlike the tests that were commonly imposed on them.

In addition to collaborating with Boas and Klineberg, Ella Deloria was to collect song texts for ethnomusicologist George Herzog. He recorded 192 songs, which she translated, and Deloria herself collected an additional 240 Dakota song texts. Her ethnographic studies were carried out under the supervision of Ruth Benedict, a cultural anthropologist who was Boas's assistant and colleague.

The second project Deloria undertook for Boas in the summer of 1928 was the translation of a Native-language text on the Sun Dance, the most important traditional Lakota spiritual ceremony. A long and detailed account, it had been written in the early 1900s by Sword, who was a religious leader among the Oglala Lakotas on Pine Ridge Reservation, in southwestern South Dakota. Deloria read the text aloud to several Oglala elders and, with their guidance, edited and retranscribed it. The text, printed in both Lakota and English, was her first professional publication (Deloria 1929).

This first experience with anthropological fieldwork was not without difficulties in working with language consultants. In a letter to Boas, written from Rosebud in August 1928, she expressed frustration: "I am getting along all right. There are some discouraging features—one of them, the temperament of some of my informants. It is the old man or woman who is most valuable, but unfortunately is apt to be vague and indefinite. I do not see how non-Dakota-speaking workers get along as well as they do."

Searching for someone who would talk about traditional spiritual beliefs and practices, Deloria was led to an old medicine man, a diviner, said to be the only man capable of providing the kinds of information she needed. As a half-brother to her father, he was also father to her, but "he hates my father because he considers him disloyal to the teachings and practices of their father." Another old man was a possibility, but his son was married to one of Ella Deloria's half-sisters, making her his daughter-in-law, and kinship custom forbade direct communication between them. In short Deloria's status as an insider seemed a mixed blessing.

Deloria intended to be back in New York by fall, but her father suffered a stroke, and she went to be with him. She continued working for Boas by writing texts, doing interviews, and correcting dictionary cards as he sent them to her, but she stayed with her father on the Yankton reservation. Klineberg also sent her questions for investigation. Most comfortable working with the people at Wakpala, Deloria decided to move her ailing father back to Standing Rock, over the bishop's protest, to facilitate her work. She made three trips there during the summer, then moved her father in the fall.

Not until the spring or early summer of 1930 was Deloria able to return to New York. There she worked with Boas on language and organized her field data. By the fall she was back in South Dakota. In November she started collecting Lakota men's vision experiences on Rosebud. The pattern of field study with periodic visits to New York continued.

By 1932 Ruth Benedict had taken over direction of her ethnographic work, and Deloria came to develop a close relationship with her. She also continued working on the Dakota languages with Boas as a research mentor. Deloria's field study involved working with Native consultants, which required knowledge of Dakota etiquette. In a letter to Boas in July, Deloria outlined her field work methods:

> I can not tell you how essential it is for me to take beef or some food each time I go to an informant—the moment I don't, I take myself right out of the Dakota side and class myself with outsiders. If I go, bearing a gift, and gladden the hearts of my informants, with food, at which perhaps I arrange to have two or three informants, and eat with them, and call them by the correct social kinship terms, then later I can go back, and ask them all sorts of questions, and get my information, as one would get favors from a relative. It is hard to explain, but it is the only way I can work. To go at it like a white man, for me, an Indian, is to throw up an immediate barrier between myself and the people.[3]

In the summer of 1933, Ella Deloria conducted field study among the Assiniboines in Montana. While she had difficulties at first finding informants, she used the mediation of a Teton Christian missionary named Red Door, whose daughter Deloria had adopted as a cousin at Haskell. One time an elderly Assiniboine man came to visit the Red Doors and addressed Mrs. Red Door as younger sister. When he stepped up to Deloria and said, *Háu, Nakʿóta* 'Hello, Indian', Mr. Red Door said, "She is my niece." Deloria immediately addressed the elder as "father," at which he was much pleased. She commented: "When I asked questions in a general way, I prefaced them all with *Até* 'father', and so immediately he opened up to me." The elder turned out to be *T'até Hųká*, a traditional spiritual leader. Deloria wrote, "From my relationship with him, I became related to many others of the people. And I had an entrée that was definitely denied me until this happened" (Deloria [ca. 1933], 16–17). During her time with the Assiniboines, Deloria began to contemplate writing a study of contemporary Sioux social life to complement the reconstruction of traditional culture that was the main goal of her studies.

Deloria continued doing fieldwork throughout the 1930s. She worked among the Santees of Prairie Island, Minnesota, in 1934, which resulted in a manuscript called "Santee Legends," comprising twenty-one texts with literal and free translations. With the Santees she began studying colloquial Dakota, which she continued on Pine Ridge throughout 1935 and into 1936, regularly sending manuscripts to Boas.

While continuing her fieldwork, Deloria worked by correspondence under Boas's supervision on translating and checking manuscripts. In 1936, during her only trip to New York in this period, she resumed and finished translating the Bushotter texts. From 1937 to June 1938, she worked on the Sword manuscripts and, at Boas's request, attempted to confirm with her informants some of the details of James R. Walker's mythological cycles, recorded at the turn of the century at Pine Ridge.

At last, in May 1939, Boas wrote that there was no more money to continue the work. The grammar they wrote together was accepted for publication, bringing closure to their long collaboration, which had culminated with *Dakota Grammar*, a classic of American Indian—language description (Boas and Deloria 1941). Final corrections and proofing continued through 1940.

Ill, lacking funds, and facing the specter of world war, Boas wrote in November 1942 to Deloria, who was then in New York: "It will take such a long time before I can get your Dakota manuscripts published that I should feel much safer if I could have the two copies in different places, but for that purpose the second copy ought to be provided with diacritical marks." Boas died less than a month later.

Benedict continued to provide support for Deloria's sustained work, when possible, and helped her prepare her manuscript material on Dakota social life for publication, a manuscript that would become *The Dakota Way of Life*.

Ella Deloria helped to support her sister, Mary Susan, an artist known professionally as Mary Sully, who did the artwork for Deloria's *Speaking of Indians* (1944a), which was intended to introduce American Indians to a broad popular audience. In this book, with great insight and empathy, Deloria succinctly summarized her understanding of traditional religion. She considered the Lakotas before they had learned of Christian teachings to be naturally religious, "always subconsciously aware of the Supernatural Power. Before it they felt helpless and humble" (51). She exemplified this with an account of the Sun Dance, making the esoteric ritual comprehensible to the general public.

With support from the American Philosophical Society, Deloria completed a first draft of the manuscript about Dakota social life in 1947 and sent it to Benedict for reorganizing, writing conversationally with the expectation that her manuscript would be heavily edited. Deloria worried about her writing style; in February 1947 she confessed to Benedict: "It is distressing to find it so hard to do this writing in any detached, professional manner! It reads like a chummy book on travel, rather than like a study. That bothers me terribly. I try to keep out of it, but I am too much in it." Worse, she began to have doubts about its relevance: "With times so changed, I sometimes wonder who cares what the Dakotas were doing and thinking, and what good, if that was known" Benedict completed her work, and Deloria planned to consult with her on the final editing in September 1948. But when Deloria arrived in New York, she learned that Benedict had died unexpectedly. After Benedict's death Deloria struggled to continue her work on the manuscript and received a number of grants for studies of language, religion, and social life.

Writing to Hiram E. Beebe, a benefactor who provided money for the typing of a later version of the Dakota social life manuscript, in December 1952, she described her purpose in the following terms:

This may sound a little naive, Mr. Beebe, but I actually feel that I have a mission: To make the Dakota people understandable, as human beings, to the white people who have to deal with them. I feel that one of the reasons for the lagging advancement of the Dakotas has been that those who came out among them to teach and preach, went on the assumption that the Dakotas had <u>nothing</u>, no rules of life, no social organization, no ideals. And so they tried to pour white culture into, as it were, a vacuum, and when that did not work out, because it was not a vacuum after all, they concluded that the Indians were impossible to change and train. What they should have done first, before daring to start their program, was to study everything possible of Dakota life, and see what made it go, in the old days, and what was still so deeply rooted that it could not be rudely displaced without some hurt. . . . I feel that I have this work cut out for me and if I do not make all I know available before I die, I will have failed by so much. But I am not morbid about it; quite cheerful, in fact. And I can afford to do on it, each day, and put [it] aside to earn a bit, now and then, only so I can get back to it again.

Deloria published a collection of short translated Dakota texts, including conversations, in 1954. She also continued to work on the book about Dakota social life with the aid of a grant from the Bollingen Foundation, but in 1955 she responded to a plea from the church to return to Wakpala and run St. Elizabeth's, where she had been a student, by now reduced to a mission home for Indian children. She remained there until 1958, when she returned to the University of South Dakota to continue her linguistic studies of Dakota. At that time she interviewed Yankton elders in support of the Yankton land claim, as well as elders at the Cheyenne River Reservation, in conjunction with the Doris Duke Oral History Project. Later she worked briefly for the Sioux Indian Museum in Rapid City and served as assistant director of the W. H. Over Museum at the University of South Dakota. There, as a member of the new Institute for Indian Studies, Deloria received a National Science Foundation grant that supported work on a Lakota dictionary from 1962 to 1966. The material she had prepared under Boas and Benedict had been transferred from Columbia University to the American Philosophical Society in Philadelphia, together with Boas's personal papers. She used a microfilm copy of the Lakota dictionary material she had prepared many years before under Boas's direction, but she lacked the support that would have been necessary to complete her dictionary. During her later years Deloria worked under many disadvantages. Her constant traveling had taken its toll in lost notes and manuscripts. At the end of her life all of her major works were left unpublished.

Her concern with communicating to the public motivated Deloria to write an ethnographic novel, *Waterlily*, that told the story of three generations of women before the reservation period. It masterfully summarizes the important themes of her study of Lakota culture and is the only written source that explores the spiritual life of Lakota women. When she completed the book in 1948, she could not find a publisher; it was published posthumously, in 1988 and rapidly became the most widely read of her works.

After retiring Deloria continued to live in Vermillion, South Dakota, and to go on field trips to isolated communities on different reservations (Deloria 1998, xviii). She suffered a stroke in the summer of 1970 and died on February 12, 1971, in Tripp, South Dakota, of a pulmonary embolism.

As a member of a prominent Episcopal family, Deloria initially had little familiarity with traditional Lakota religion, but she became interested in it. She recorded a large number of myths and sacred stories, many of which have been published in Lakota and English (Deloria 1932). While recording the autobiographical texts of elders, she learned a good deal about the individual's role in religious ceremonies, about visions and other supernatural experiences, and about conflicts between traditional beliefs and Christianity. Benedict pressed her to interview medicine men and record their visions, but this forced Deloria into a personal dilemma. Her father was a prominent missionary, and her younger brother, Vine, had followed in his footsteps and begun his career as a missionary at Pine Ridge. Showing undue interest in traditional religion jeopardized the family's reputation, and, in any case, traditional religious leaders were not comfortable sharing their sacred knowledge with a devout Christian, who they feared might ridicule them. Deloria focused instead on the forms of ceremonies, starting with the Sun Dance. She hypothesized that all the Sioux groups shared common ceremonies, but that each performed them in different ways. For years she collected material for a study that would document the variations from group to group, but failed to complete it. Her unfinished manuscripts contain important materials of relevance for the understanding of Dakota culture.

Today Ella Deloria's manuscripts are being systematically edited and published. To appreciate them it is important to know how they originated. In the field Deloria worked cautiously, through kin networks. She was concerned about her reputation; as an unmarried woman she had to always be above suspicion, as gossip about her could have hurt her brother's ministry. Vine had followed his father's wishes, become an

Episcopal priest, and served the churches in Bennett County, on what until 1911 had been the east end of the Pine Ridge Reservation. During much of her fieldwork she lived in Martin in order to be near her brother and his family. To some degree these constraints restricted her contacts, but at least she knew well the people whom she interviewed and had a clear sense of the value of the material they gave her.

Deloria's finances were always insecure. She was supported by small research grants, the proceeds from speaking engagements, writing and consulting work, and the generosity of friends. Her correspondence with Boas reveals a continuing conflict between her commitment to work and deeply felt sense of obligation to her family.

Deloria was the most prolific Native scholar of the Dakotas, and the results of her work (much of which is still unpublished, archived in the American Philosophical Society and the Dakota Indian Foundation, Chamberlain, South Dakota) comprise an essential source for the study of Dakota culture and language. Her studies provide some of the best material ever recorded on Sioux culture and are the fullest accounts in the Native language. Her work is also important in emphasizing an understanding of the culture from women's perspectives, which is lacking in most studies of American Indian cultures. Her research had three main goals: first, to translate and to edit linguistic texts that had been written or dictated by Sioux people in the various dialects of the Native language; second, to record a detailed description of traditional Sioux social and spiritual life; and, third, to compile the data for a thorough grammar and comprehensive dictionary of the Lakota dialect of the Sioux language. Deloria was a perfectionist who worked slowly and cautiously, rewriting many times and attempting to be as objective as possible. As a result she published relatively little, but her work is invaluable.

From her papers we know that Ella Deloria recorded material during interviews in oversized, coarse wood-pulp paper notebooks, then transcribed her notes on a typewriter. Late in life, in April 1967, she characterized these notes: "There is no attempt at smooth and 'stylish' writing because that isn't the primary object in note-taking, but rather to transfer the thought of the informant himself." Indeed her notes seem simultaneously transcription and analysis; her English translations are free enough to be characterized as paraphrases. Each set of notes from a particular individual was prepared as a discreet text; most are in English, recorded for

Benedict, but the stories, conversations, and other speech events recorded for Boas are transcribed in Dakota with literal and free translations. To what extent the Native-language texts represent actual dictation as opposed to Deloria's subsequent remembering of a text and writing it down is presently unknown, given the lack of evidence in her papers.

Deloria's ethnographic manuscripts rely heavily on her own life experience and incorporate her field interviews anecdotally to validate more general points. Her manuscripts freely mix material from such historical manuscripts as those of Bushotter and Sword with her own field material. The concept of culture that emerges from her writings is a decidedly normative one; traditional culture is presented in terms of broad generalization, bolstered by narratives of events. Perhaps following Boas, she was not content with information from a single individual; she wanted corroboration from multiple sources before accepting anything as true. Consequently, she only occasionally named the sources of information in her writings, preferring to leave her informants anonymous.

Deloria assumed an essential continuity in Dakota culture, which she understood as disrupted not by the end of warfare and buffalo hunting, or by the introduction of Christianity, but by the moral degeneration that she began to see on the reservations in the 1930s, marked by the use of alcohol and the sudden proliferation of unwed mothers. Her writings could have the practical value of educating missionaries and teachers about traditional Dakota values. In this sense her detailed cultural descriptions were intended less for purposes of cultural preservation than for practical application; the Sioux knew their own values — they only needed the support of church and school to live up to them. By the 1930s, she felt, very few still believed in the old Sioux religion; the people had become Christians. She herself had never interviewed a man who had gone to war, and buffalo hunting was nearly as distant from the collective Sioux memory. Cultural continuity was best expressed in the kinship system, though she bemoaned the degeneration of extended families. Her concept of culture as the core of Dakota life was normative and collective, not individual.

As an individual Ella Deloria was secure in her conception of a stable, normative culture to serve as support and guide. She herself could move easily between social contexts — church life, secular reservation life, academic life. Thus she could, without contradiction, speak contextually of *we Indians* and *those Indians*. In speech, behavior, and dress, she was alternately insider and outsider, both welcomed and resented. She exploited kin networks and was treated with the respect required by custom. But among the Tetons she was always a Yankton, with all the baggage that befalls a familiar neighbor and rival, a subcultural boundary that may have been harder to cross than that between Indian and white. In academia she was always the Indian—as she characterized herself to Ruth Benedict in a letter of February 1947, "the glorified (?) native mouthpiece," lacking a degree, at the periphery of the profession.

Ella Deloria was a scholar through and through, yet she never let her dedication to scholarship overwhelm her sense of responsibility as a Dakota woman, with family concerns taking precedence over her work, nor did she ever lose her deep faith in Christianity. She was a warm and gracious individual, whose kindness and personality were inspirational. Her constant goal was to be an interpreter of an American Indian reality to other peoples. Her studies of the Sioux are a monument to her talent and industry.

In 1967, at the fifteenth annual meeting of the American Society for Ethnohistory, held in Lexington, Kentucky, Ella Deloria delivered a paper on Yankton place names that derived from her land claims work. Her style of delivery, total mastery of the material, and level of excitement to share information with the audience set her presentation apart from all the others. As an undergraduate student, already committed to a life as an anthropologist, I listened to her with rapt fascination. At the end of her talk, she explained the significance of the name of the Vermillion River, where the Dakota used to dig *wasé* (Indian paint), but her time was up. "There's so much left to tell," she said, breathlessly, "so invite me back next year, and I'll tell you more!" Her writings go on telling generation after generation. Whatever the personal costs of her life as a transculturalite, today we are all the richer for it. And enormously grateful.

Editorial Note

The Dakota Way of Life was a project long in gestation and has had several editors. Ella Deloria first elected Ruth Benedict, with whom she entertained a passionate correspondence and friendship, to edit her manuscripts, including this one. In a letter dated April 7, 1947, she provided Benedict with clear guidelines to direct the editorial work that it needed:

> Of course I want you to edit it! I don't know who else could, with the understanding and sympathy it cries for. . . . When you read through, you will find that the repetitions abound, and that much is dragged in that can easily be omitted. I wanted <u>you</u> to understand what I was trying to explain from all angles, but did not truly intend it should all appear. The problem of selection also is an art—and I don't have it, I guess. I think you know better, from your experience and also from "ringside seat," what must go in and what can be cut out. I just wrote on and on. . . . Please cut ruthlessly, and also change my wordings for better clarity. If you think an expression sounds absurdly affected, or I seem to be straining too desperately for effect, change it. You can't insult me. . . . P.S. . . . I think if the [American Philosophical Society] turns it down it will be because it isn't scholarly. No scores of footnotes, bibliography, references to previous works, all that. Maybe you better add some of those? Or give them some excellent arguments as to why this m[anuscript] does not have them.

In her last letter on July 19, 1948, Benedict invited Deloria to retype "the Philosophical Society M[anuscript]" after she had "been over it carefully and tried to delete the sections that seemed repetitious or unnecessary." This work was continued by subsequent editors, but Benedict was the first to help Deloria shape her manuscript, which was at that time unnamed. In their correspondence Benedict had suggested "Dakota Home Life" as a title (March 26, 1947), and Deloria referred to this manuscript as the

"Dakota Family Life" (April 26, 1947) and the "tiyospaye study" (July 17, 1947). The *t'iyóšpaye* is the traditional camp group, the fundamental unit of Dakota social life.

When Benedict unexpectedly passed away, Margaret Mead took over the manuscript, along with many other projects of Benedict's. Together Deloria and Mead settled on *The Dakota Way of Life* as a title, and Mead continued the editorial preparation for sending the manuscript to the American Philosophical Society for publication. Although, as noted earlier, Deloria expressed concerns about her style in the manuscript, Mead offered the following remarks in her letter of transmittal about its value and the authentic character it brought to ethnographic writing: "I have gone over the manuscript with care and have paid special attention to the problem of more idiomatic English that still conveys the Dakota manner and meaning. . . . The manuscript is written with a very rare feeling for Dakota life and style."

While the manuscript was edited for and reviewed by the American Philosophical Society, Ella Deloria continued to conduct research well into 1953. In a letter to Alexander Lesser, from whom she hoped to receive input, she wrote: "At VERY long last, my [manuscript] is about ready. It has taken a lot of time because every time I talk to Dakotas I get more and even better angles on the subject." Deloria's manuscript originated from fieldwork that had been supported by the American Philosophical Society, and much of her typing and editing work on it was financed by grants from Wenner-Gren and from the Institute for Intercultural Studies.

But the manuscript needed more work. To Beebe, who was supporting her during the typing, she wrote in February 1954, "The [manuscript] was read and I was told to reorganize it again, and add some Appendices [to the text]. This is what I am trying to do now." By necessity Deloria nonetheless moved on to other projects, including one to prepare a book on Dakota religion for which Mead had obtained funding. As a result Deloria was unable to dedicate sufficient time needed to reorganize her manuscript for the American Philosophical Society to publish it.

All the different versions and typed copies of *The Dakota Way of Life* started to form an editorial maze. The following manuscripts each derive from one another in a chronological fashion:

1. The first version of the manuscript was completed in 1945, and
Deloria continued to revise it for several years. She gave it to Ben-

edict and received feedback on it just before her death. This early
version is less stilted in style and includes more Dakota words. Its
introduction was largely different from subsequent versions, and,
unlike other versions, its first half included handwritten diacritics
on Dakota words; in fact it is the only copy that includes such diacritics, in accordance with Franz Boas's advice. It is archived at the
South Dakota Historical Society in Chamberlain.

2. In 1953 Ella completed a second revision. This manuscript was
edited by Margaret Mead, with handwritten ink annotations consisting of word additions and stylistic improvements. It is archived
at the Dakota Indian Foundation and is also available online at the
Ella Deloria Archive. Another version of the 1953 manuscript was
typed for Beebe and had a different title, "The Sioux Indians." The
Beebe manuscript is incomplete.

3. The "Pierre" or 1954 version of the manuscript is the one that
was submitted to the American Philosophical Society and
included Mead's edits. Its table of contents mentions a preface originally planned by Margaret Mead and also includes an
abstract of Alexander Lesser's dissertation, "An Analysis of the
Dakota Kinship System," listed in an appendix. It has some word
additions by Ella Deloria and is archived at the American Philosophical Society.

4. A version of the 1954 manuscript, edited by Joyzelle Gingway
Godfrey, a relative of Ella Deloria, with Margaret Mead's foreword
and a preface by Godfrey, was published in 2007 by Mariah Press.
It was minimally edited, omitted some repetitions, and "up-dated"
some of the language (vii).

5. Raymond J. DeMallie started preparing *The Dakota Way of Life*
in the 1980s and accumulated copies of all of the versions mentioned above, as well as all the Deloria correspondence with Boas,
Benedict, Mead, Lesser, Beebe, and Burleson. On April 26, 1988,
Vine V. Deloria Sr. wrote a formal letter to DeMallie endorsing
his research at the Dakota Indian Foundation, the South Dakota
Historical Society, the Southwest Museum, and the Vassar College
Library. DeMallie combined the style and Dakota language of the
first manuscript with parts of the additions found in subsequent
versions.

This new manuscript was typed on a computer in 1994 and included the diacritics from the first manuscript, but this draft was not in Unicode, and, as a result, the diacritics were lost in subsequent versions. Also, it was copyedited again by several of DeMallie's doctoral students. Then, due to a series of unforeseen health issues, and other priorities, DeMallie's attention became distracted from the manuscript, and eventually a stroke suffered in 2014 made it impossible for him to work on the manuscript on his own. He then enlisted Thierry Veyrié to assist in finishing it, help prepare the prefatory materials and annotations, and guide it through publication. At this stage the diacritics in the second half of the manuscript that did not exist in any of the previous versions were added either by comparison with DeMallie's previous notes or by using the *New Lakota Dictionary* (2011).

Following the spirit of the guidelines quoted earlier that Ella Deloria had given to Benedict in 1947, Raymond J. DeMallie and I excised some of the repetitions, reduced the excessive length of some of the prose, selected chapters that were appropriate to incorporate the appendices and endnotes, revised some of the wording to improve clarity, mitigated some of the stylistic excesses, and added footnotes and scholarly context. This edition is the result of the long history of Ella Deloria's ethnographic manuscript on the Dakota social life.

Pronunciation Guide

a	like in father	*k*	like in skip	
e	like in bed	*kᶜ*	like in ba**ck h**ome pronounced fast	
i	like in pit			
o	like in no	*k'*	like in ki**ck** it	
u	like in moon	*p*	like in spin	
ạ	like in can't	*pᶜ*	like in punish	
ị	like in sing	*p'*	like in sto**p** it	
ụ	like in don't	*t*	like in still	
b	like in baby	*tᶜ*	like in si**t h**ere pronounced fast	
l	like in light			
m	like in me	*t'*	like in til**t** it	
n	like in no	*s*	like in so	
g	like in go	*š*	like in she	
ǧ	like in red	*z*	like in zero	
h	like in he	*ž*	like in pleasure	
ȟ	like in Oaxaca	*w*	like in we	
č	like in church	*y*	like in yes	
čᶜ	like in chin (aspirated)	*'*	like in oh-oh	
č'	like in pit**ch** (followed by a pause)			

Kinship Terms

These terms were recorded by Ella Deloria with Alexander Lesser in New York City in the spring of 1928. They were published in Lesser's dissertation *Siouan Kinship* (1958, 17–65). They are presented here in the orthography that Deloria elected. The first name of any pair is for a female; the second is for a male.

Blood Relatives

Grandmothers, grandfathers	*Ųčí, Tʿųkášila*			
Aunts, uncles, mothers, fathers[1]	*Tʿųwį́, Lekši*		*Iná, Até*	
Cousins, older siblings, younger siblings[2]	Woman speaking	*Čépʿąši, Šičʾéši*	*Čʿuwé, Tʿibló*	*Mitʿą́, Misų́*
	Man speaking	*Hąkáši, Tʿąhą́ši*	*Tʿąké, Čʿiyé*	*Tʿąkší, Misų́*
Children of siblings of different sex; children	Woman speaking	*Mitʿóžą, Mitʿóška*	*Mičʿųk̓ši, Mičʿįk̓ši, Mičʿįča*[3]	
	Man speaking	*Mitʿų́žą, Mitʿų́ška*		
Grandchildren		*Mitʿákoža*		

Marriage Relatives

Fellow parents-in-law, mothers-in-law, fathers-in-law	*Omáwahitʿų*		*Ųčíši, Tʿųkáši*

Sisters-in-law, brothers-in-law, wife, husband, cowife	Woman speaking	*Čyép'ąn, Ši'č'é*	*Mit'áwin* (address) *winya mit'áwa* (reference),	*T'éa*
	Man speaking	*Hąká, T'ąhą́*	*Mihígna* (address) *wicása mit'áwa* (reference)	
Children-in-law			*Mit'ákoš*	

1. By "aunt" and "uncle" is meant "father's sister" and "mother's brother." "Father's brother" and "mother's sister" in Dakota kinship are referred to with the terms for father and mother.
2. By "cousins" is meant children of a father's sister or mother's brother (crossed cousins). Children of a father's brother or mother's sister are referred to with the terms for elder sister, elder brother, younger sister, and younger brother.
3. *Mič'įča* is not marked with gender.

THE DAKOTA WAY OF LIFE

Introduction

This book is about the Dakota-speaking Indians of the Plains, and all its material comes directly from them. One of the largest tribes in North America, the Dakotas have sometimes been referred to as the Dakota or Sioux Nation. Perhaps "nation" is not the most apt designation, since it was not as a single and unified greater tribe that the Dakotas made their impact on neighboring tribes, but rather as three tribe-size distinct peoples who occupied separate regions, had their own traditions, and spoke a particular dialect of the common tongue. These three component peoples are: (1) the Santees, or Eastern Dakota; (2) the Yanktons, or Central Dakota; and (3) the Tetons, or Western Dakota. In terms of language, there is no "pure" or classical Dakota apart from these dialects; each of them is equally valid and acceptable as long as they are not confused, or fused, into a hybrid Dakota, as has sometimes been done by non-Dakota unaware of the finer distinctions among them.[1]

Although all Dakotas consider themselves as one single people, under the surface universality of language and of a social system based on kinship relationships, variants of custom and dialect, of habits, skills, and arts, tend to set the three peoples apart from one another and to give a recognizable character to each. Because of this an account that lumped the three peoples together as if they were exactly alike in behavior, custom, speech, and traditions would be too general to be completely satisfactory. On the other hand, it would not be feasible to treat them separately, sorting into neat piles the material pertinent to each. How to discuss Dakota culture as a whole and still retain an awareness of the distinctiveness of the three peoples was my first problem. Out of the inchoate mass of Dakota data I had accumulated, I cast about for the right approach, and, after some false starts, I saw that the simplest way was the best: to take one people for a focus and work out from there.

Consequently I have written these chapters with the emphasis on the Tetons. Everything said here is applicable to them first, but, the Yanktons and Santees being also Dakotas, it is broadly true of both or either of them as well—except for an occasional minor difference not necessary to dwell on. Only radical departures from the Teton forms as they come to light are specifically pointed out. I may add that divergences from the Teton ways are most likely in the Santee tradition—an understandable fact when it is realized that "Santees and Tetons have always lived farthest apart," as one informant said, "with the Yanktons between them."

I have chosen the Tetons as my focus for two reasons. In the first place, they form the largest division, their number being generally understood to exceed that of the Yanktons and Santees combined. Secondly, because of their location farthest west, they were able to retain their culture for a longer period than could the Yanktons east of the Missouri River, or the Santees still farther east. The tide of modern civilization overran first the Santees and kindred bands speaking the same dialect, and next the Yanktons farther west. Finally, and inexorably, it reached the Tetons beyond the Missouri and forthwith affected their culture also.

Even so, thanks to a geographical accident, Teton lives remained integrated and undisturbed the longest, so that this investigation is most rewarding among that people. Among the Tetons a very satisfactory number of old people were still alive who could tell me about their people's old life out of personal experience and knowledge. A scant dozen Yanktons still lived who could do this, too, and only a handful of Santees, who were remarkably reliable informants despite their extreme age. Such eyewitnesses were priceless because they could say, "I saw; I did." Without exception they gave conscientiously only what they had personally known: nothing secondhand, nothing from hearsay. And if they must illustrate with a myth or legend, they carefully added the indefinite quotative *keyápi* 'they say; it is said'.

More numerous and often as valuable were those middle-aged to elderly men and women who, even if they could not clearly recall the camp circle environment of early childhood, had nevertheless grown up well imbued with the flavor and feel of it from their parents and grandparents. When they could not say "I saw; I did," they could do the next best thing—name someone they had known and trusted as their authority ("My mother said this"; "I heard my grandfather tell"; meaning, "and so I know that it was true").

When asked about the *yuwípi*, an ancient divining rite wherein the seer was first blindfolded and tightly bound, Little Moon, a *Húkpap'aya* Teton, did not hesitate: "Yes, I do know something about that *from my father*."[2] So he described the procedure step-by-step and ended with the following:

> When my father was sitting in on a *yuwípi* one night, something struck him in the chest so forcibly that it stunned him. Yet he managed to grope for the thing and felt it to be the thong rope with which the holy man was bound before he was brought into the dark sweat lodge. It was looped and bound in a tight roll, as long as his forearm. And my father, though only a curious and skeptical boy, knew that "It" [the Power being invoked] had punished him for his disbelief.[3]

If there was a time when all Dakotas lived together and spoke the same language, what was that mother tongue? Was it like Santee, Yankton, or Teton? Or did those dialects, those divergences, occur after the people separated into three groups and moved independently? How long a period was that, before they finally remained in the regions where the white man found them — Tetons west of the Missouri, Yanktons east of it, Santees still farther east in what is now Minnesota?[4]

To these and other such tantalizing questions the people offered no authentic answers, not even hopeful clues. The one informant who spoke of "Seven Council Fires" admitted that he had read of them in a book. Zeneas Graham, a Santee, did date the event he was relating by saying, "They say it was while our people were dwelling near what is now Dulut [Duluth, Minnesota]." Yankton informants insisted on a traditional affinity with the Missouri River:

> Always our people traveled along its course and never abandoned it. If they roamed for a season over buffalo country, they always returned to their home tipis in its valley where those who had stayed behind kept up the homes, cared for the children, and tended the gardens. Our people did not rely on meat alone, you know, corn and squashes were also necessary to them. Upstream, northward and then westward, the Yanktons migrated slowly throughout the years, always as it were with one hand grasping the river for support and guidance.

His word, *įkduzeze* 'to cling to', was a well-chosen metaphor, suggesting that the winding Missouri River was a steadying bannister to which the Yanktons clung for support and reassurance as they moved along. Its nearness gave them their bearings; its sameness through ever-changing terrain their sense of security. Perhaps it is no accident that all the Yankton-speaking Dakota finally settled in detached colonies along that river.

The usual Teton reply to my inquiry about the origin of the tribe is exemplified by Fast Whirlwind, an Oglala, who delivered the following assertion with supreme certainty: "Why, we have always lived here!" With a wide sweep of his arm he proceeded to delimit a great expanse that was "the Tetons' hunting range." He said: "From the *Mníšoše* 'Roiled Water', the Missouri River westward to the foothills of the *Ȟeská* 'White Mountains', the Rockies, and from *Ų́čiyapi Tʿamákʿočʿe* 'Grandmother's Land', Canada southward to the *Pʿ̇ąkéska Wakpá* 'Musselshell River', the Platte River in Nebraska, our people roamed and hunted, and sometimes went beyond these boundaries. . . . Many tribal reunions took place in the Black Hills, they being central."

However, he conceded at the same time that the Dakota country was earlier occupied by alien tribes, a fact generally inferred from the reminiscent place names still heard: *Šahíyela Wóžu* 'Cheyenne Plantings' is the name of the agency and reservation known as Cheyenne River; *Pʿaláni Tʿawákpa* 'Rees' [Arikaras'] river' is the Grand River in South Dakota; *Pʿaláni Tʿíohe* 'Abandoned Homesites of the Rees' are large circular depressions on the flats overlooking the Missouri, across the river a few miles upstream from Mobridge, South Dakota. Another Ree village site, called *Tʿítʿąka Óhe* 'Remains of Large Dwellings', is now under the waters of the Oahe Dam, north of Pierre, South Dakota.

It remained for *Makʿúla*, an Oglala Teton who was perhaps the best informant of all, to give the only vivid and plausible legend to account for his people's arrival west of the Missouri. He was the last of the professional raconteurs among the Oglala who knew the old culture from personal participation.[5] But this story was an ancient tale in his youth; he dated the alleged event by saying, "My grandfather told me this when I was a boy. His grandfather told him when he was a boy." How much further back it began, he could not say. He himself was in his middle eighties when he told it to me. He knew the tale was legendary, and so, by way of disclaiming all personal responsibility for its authenticity, he punctuated the telling of it rather frequently with *keyápi* 'so it is said'.

Long ago, all the Teton-speaking Dakotas lived in *čʼúwąča* 'wood-continuous'; that is, forest land, far off in the direction of the sunrise, so it is said. From time to time a party broke out into open country to hunt buffalo. Once they did this again but never went back. Instead they roamed over the trackless prairies for an indeterminable number of years, ever in search of food. But at last, and not without design, all Tetons found their way to this country, and here they have lived ever since. It is probable that whenever a hunting party of several parties failed to return to their forest home, others went out after them, until all Tetons were in habitual migration.

If this became a mass migration, it could not be likened to a planned invasion of new territory, with the intention of wresting it from its occupants in the Old World manner. Without plan or organization, out of touch with the others—and perhaps not even aware that all the other Tetons were also roaming over the same trackless land—those fragments of the one people moved fortuitously, each at its own pace, each going here and there, as necessity dictated.

The legend tells how and why a group of Tetons crossed to the west side of the Missouri, to live there permanently. Unconsciously *Makʼúla* kept saying "the Oglalas," though he could not say when that name was fastened on his particular band of Tetons. But he speculated that if those roving groups that broke out of forest country and reassembled west of the river as one people were seven in number, perhaps were they the beginnings of the seven bands of Tetons as we know them today. A trim theory, but who knows?

At any rate each group eventually reached the Missouri and crossed over on the ice to the west river country at some advantageous point. It was enough for *Makʼúla* that he could account for the Oglalas and describe the occasion of their crossing and give the specific site of it. "It was where a little stream flowing westward empties into the Missouri, where that river starts to bear eastward, somewhere north of the [Wheeler] bridge," he said. He did not name the stream, but it could have been the one marked

Platte Creek on the map, which empties into the Missouri not too far north of the Wheeler bridge, roughly forty miles south of the present town of Chamberlain, South Dakota. As a child I heard my grandfather refer in the Yankton dialect to a place in that region as *Pté Kdíyąka* 'Buffalo Return on the Run', which would seem to indicate this alleged crossing by the Teton. Perhaps the Yanktons knew the legend, too. The legend told by *Makʿúla* follows:

> The Oglalas were camped for the winter at the mouth of a creek that flowed westward into the Missouri. One day at dawn a cry went up throughout the camp: "Get up! Get up! A herd of buffalo is arriving on a run from the north; a blizzard is driving them down!" Buffalo were welcome at all times but now they were hailed with special joy, for the people were close to starvation. So the men hastily organized and forced the herd onto the river by waving blankets and branches and shouting in concert to create a general din. The terrified beasts stampeded and were soon sliding and falling on the slick ice, many breaking a limb. Unable to run fast or to rise when down, they were easy prey.
>
> Their flesh was hastily dissected and dragged by loads in their own slippery hides to the nearest point of land, which happened to be on the west bank. And thither the Oglalas moved their camp for a few days while they cared for the meat and feasted with one another, which was always their delight. Unaware that the unseasonably warm winds were thawing the ice, they woke one morning to see the river flowing and bearing great hunks of ice along. "We are trapped," they said. "Well, no matter. We can hunt buffalo on this side of the river just as well."

Makʿúla concluded by saying, "My people made that crossing in the 'Sore Eyes Moon', *Ištáwičʿayazą Wí* 'March'," so named because hunters and scouts were blinded by the strong sun on the late snows. Each moon of the year had its own descriptive name.

From then on the Oglalas roamed and hunted over large areas of the western plains. One day—the legend does not say how long after that crossing—two strangers appeared, "sitting on novel beasts that bore them along." Clearly, they were peaceful visitors, but their alien speech was not understandable. At last in desperation one of them dismounted and made a rude drawing in the dust; then the two rode off, gesticulating and jabbering earnestly, and pointing northward again and again until they disappeared over the horizon.

The wise men studied the drawing and decided it was an invitation: "Two sleeps on the way. Come!" So next day the Oglalas struck camp, and after two nights on the way they came to a vast encampment in a wide pleasant valley, close to a beautiful river that might have been the White River, or farther north, the Cheyenne River. Here they were warmly welcomed and feasted many times and given fine presents. From the hills where countless horses were grazing, their leading men were given some choice ones. These non-Dakotas who welcomed them so generously were Cheyennes, and those "novel beasts" on which their messengers brought the invitations were "the first horses those Tetons ever saw," *Makʿúla* said. He remarked that in his youth he sometimes heard the old men haranguing the people say, "Let us never forget. It was the *Šahíyela* [Cheyennes] who first disburdened our shoulders of the wearisome travois."[6]

Makʿúla also said that the Oglalas regarded the Northern Cheyennes and their companion tribe, the Arapahos, as their traditional friends. Naturally, intermarriages were not infrequent, and there are Oglalas today who claim part-Cheyenne descent. "They have always been our friends," many informants said of the Cheyennes. I have to explain here that "always" and "never" are not invariably used in their absolute sense. Often they signify "as far as anyone knows."

When *Makʿúla* finished relating the legend to me, he said, "We Oglalas have had horses for two hundred years." Historical records indicate that the Tetons were mounted by 1742, or thereabouts.[7] Informants readily agreed that the horse drastically altered and improved the people's capabilities and quickened the pace of Dakota life to an unbelievable degree. *Makʿúla* commented, after dwelling at some length on the lavish giveaway and feasting customs:

Ah, but you must not imagine that it was always like that. For when our people were on foot, nothing was easy to obtain. The custom of relatives honoring one another might be from of old, but before the coming of the horse, gifts and feasts were much simpler. Our people were very poor, you know, in those times when it was difficult, even in fair seasons, to kill enough buffalo to meet the demands of all the families of the village. And when the snow was very deep, hunting was out of the question. An exceptionally hard winter brought famine without fail, unless the people had enough food preserved from the preceding summer to tide them over until spring. Famine and cold were their real enemies.

As far into the past as anyone would dare to say, certainly within remembered times, the three Dakota peoples lived and moved over a vast uncharted territory, though each one kept generally to a chosen area where it felt at home. The Yanktons and kindred bands lived generally on the prairies east of the Missouri River, and the Tetons west of it. The Santees and related bands meanwhile lived mostly in what is now Minnesota until their dispersion following the so-called Minnesota Uprising in 1862. But one band, the Sissetons, whose reservation occupies the northeast corner of South Dakota, is said to have lived in and around that region for many generations.

These areas were not without certain boundaries, of course; there were intervening bands of wild country, a kind of no-man's-land, where danger lurked; danger from wild beasts, danger from chance encounters with enemy war parties passing through, danger from becoming lost in unfamiliar terrain. One must therefore suppose that visits from one tribe of Dakotas to another were uncommon. Only the most daring would take the risk. But, after the horse made long journeys less arduous, it is thinkable that a few related families sometimes went visiting for an indefinite stay and were sure of a welcome. Usually such visits took place at long intervals because they involved difficult traveling over a wide expanse of no-man's-land before reaching Dakota country again. Travel was never without its risks.

But, whatever the difficulties, there was always room for romance and courtship resulting in an occasional intermarriage. Every such marriage, say of a Teton and a Yankton, a Yankton and a Santee, or a Teton and a Santee, automatically brought all relatives of the marrying pair into specific kinship relationships. For, as will appear in later chapters, Dakotas shared all relatives of marriage with their relatives of birth, and still do, at least in theory.

Yet the fact is that, despite such alliances, the Yanktons, Tetons, and Santees never mingled together freely or permanently but continued to keep with their own people in the region where their own familiar habits and dialect prevailed, so they never lost their identities or their distinctive dialects. A Teton and a Santee could converse all day, each in his own dialect; a Yankton woman and her Teton husband could live together a lifetime without either one's compromising a single item of their respective dialects.

At the same time, a sense of oneness held them together, an attitude of laissez-faire, a tolerant, casual allowance for the "oddities" of "those other Dakotas." The idea seemed to be: "That is their peculiar way—so let them have it; this is our cherished way from of old and we will keep it." To this day each people from habit continues certain inherited practices and techniques even while openly admiring the superiority, ingenuity, or practicality of some feature of another's way, without thereby adopting it. A melody sung, tale narrated, or art form borrowed was conscientiously attributed to its source: this is a Santee melody, a Yankton story, the Teton cut and style of moccasin.

There was universal interest in the deeds of Dakota warriors, whatever their tribe, and their names enjoyed fame among all the Dakotas. Yet the three peoples carried on their warfare independently. Even had there been no differences of dialects, customs, or ideas, they were not situated near enough together for one people to be either a help or a hindrance to another. The three peoples had their own special enemies, too—those non-Dakota-speaking tribes within their range—with whom they carried on intermittent warfare, except during truces. At such times they welcomed their erstwhile foes as friends, feasted them, and showered them with fine presents at the ceremonial giveaways. The Sun Dance, for example, by its very character as a religious event demanded peace between tribes. At other important though secular festivals during the year, visitors from enemy tribes were also welcomed as friends. "When the Crow came to sue for peace" and "When the Omaha came to sing" are incidental references to such occasions in the life stories of informants.

Certainly it cannot be denied that the Dakotas and their enemies fought viciously, but I find no sign that they hated one another with an unremitting hate, on general principles. After all, war, cruel and primitive as it might be, was primarily a game, but it could not be dispensed with. It was considered essential to both sides as the proving ground for manliness, courage, endurance, cunning, and such-like attributes; and it was the arena in which honors and tribal prestige could be won. I could almost say that the Dakotas rather treasured their enemies as worthy opponents who, like themselves, dauntlessly accepted the challenge to fight—and to die if need be. I feel quite sure of this because as a child I often listened with fascination to war stories told around the campfire, where the old men unstintingly praised all deeds of outstanding valor, be the warriors Dakotas or aliens. Also I heard them scorn the coward, for cowardice in any man was unforgivable.

Returning to the mutual attitudes of the Tetons, Yanktons, and Santees, from all reports it seems unlikely that any one of them ever tried to subdue the other two, in order to exercise lordship over them. Today rivalry and hostility are singularly absent, and perhaps it was always so. Normally each of the three Dakota peoples minded their own affairs, like respectful peers, or like adult siblings with family responsibilities who were ready to make common cause against a common threat if necessary, but were otherwise content to leave one another to live in their own way.

There was light ridicule back and forth, no doubt, and even open irritation at another's poor judgment or unseemly show of vanity, but nothing serious enough to call for interference or advice. *Íš iyépik'e čį!* is a key idiom here; it is untranslatable, except by a lengthy paraphrase: "If that is what they want, let them go ahead! It is entirely their affair, their responsibility; no one but themselves is responsible for the consequences." In the students' slang at Haskell Institute, one might say "It's their own ups!" It amounts to a regretful shrug from helplessness to avert a possible bad outcome. In that spirit internal peace and amity were possible to maintain—no taking up arms by one people against another or by one camp circle against another camp circle, for they were all of one kind, one people.

The single instance to the contrary in all my material was something quite minor and local. A mere handful of unhappy men once joined a Crow war party and attacked their own *Húkpap'aya* Teton village because of resentment over some real or fancied injury to them. But those were frenzied men and renegades, not sane and responsible Dakotas, who would never turn against their own people or village. All such traitorous behavior was everlastingly reprehensible, no matter the exciting cause.

The old men preached: *Hóč'oka kį wak'ą yélo; kiksúya pó!* 'The center of the circle is hallowed ground; remember!' Hence there was no glory in taking the scalp of another Dakota. The two terms for killing a human convey a contrast: *t'ilwíč'aktepi* 'killing within home' is plain murder, a crime against society and therefore punishable; *t'ók'akte* 'slaying an enemy' is alone legitimate and honorific.

So the distinction between "our kind" and "not our kind" was sharply drawn between all Dakota-speaking people, and all others who spoke alien tongues. At first meeting the latter must always be approached with inner caution until their intentions could be discerned as friendly, for aliens, being potential enemies, might more likely have sinister motives. Always the language barrier was the deterrent to immediate understanding, without which no association could be wholly free and safe. Undoubtedly an outsider's approach was equally tentative and for the same reasons. Without mutual understanding friendliness was impossible and association was unsure.

By the same token, only a Dakota climate was reassuring. The individual Dakota could feel completely at ease only among other Dakotas, where he was on familiar ground; where he knew what to expect and what was expected of him, because the prevailing viewpoint, speech, and standards were the same as his own. If he came to a strange camp circle of Dakotas, all that he needed was a valid kinship relationship with at least one person there. Any plausible connection, however tenuous, would do. Failing that, he could resort to the time-honored custom of establishing social kinship with someone convenient, and he was in. Once in he belonged and was surrounded by relatives, for automatically all the kinsmen of his new relative became his, too. He was then able to start functioning at once as a bonafide member of the community, with the smoothness of one who knows his way around. Wherever there were Dakota people, there potentially was home. He knew the password for entry: the kinship term of address.

From this point on, kinship will be the recurring word, for one cannot describe Dakota life fully and omit what was its very heart and substance. Kinship law was tribal law in fact. Abstract, yet both compelling and impelling, it was in complete control of society. Through its specific rules of attitude and behavior in every relationship it made for amiable group living. Particularly stringent were the rules for siblings and cousins of opposite sexes, which must be obeyed until death. Other kinship situations also had rules suited to them. All rules were to be sedulously kept. It had always been the way to do, and few would want to neglect them. But why? Because the stakes were high. They were what all self-respecting citizens wanted: social prestige and a good name.

To the end that kinship law might be universally effective, all persons who had regular association together must be specifically related. This arrangement served to bind the people in a common social responsibility. If they were not already relatives of birth or marriage, establishing social kinship was the answer for bringing even newcomers into the circle of relatives. Within the *t'iyóšpaye*—the name for the larger family composed of related family units—kinship law knit the generations even more tightly, both laterally and lineally.

To understand this we have to see each generation of siblings and first cousins of both sexes, from here on to be called *collaterals*, as a unit, an integrity, rather than as independent individuals who would be at liberty to accept this member and reject that one according to personal mood or whim, or to bother or not bother with this or that child of the next generation according to like or dislike. Tribal structure depended heavily on two principal factors: a strong cohesion of the collaterals, and their corporate acceptance of a common responsibility for their collective offspring—nieces and nephews no less than daughters and sons. All obligatory responsibility was forward-looking, on behalf of the next generation. This was so generally obvious that children sensed it early and turned as confidently to uncles and aunts as to fathers and mothers for help and comfort.

It was this, the kinship system and its particular workings, by which all Dakotas lived. It was the one bond beside the common tongue that made Yanktons, Santees, and Tetons feel at home together. There might be a slight variation in the interpretation and observance of some rules, an occasional word same in form but with different, though closely related, meanings, or same in meaning but varying in sound or form. For example, the word for sister-in-law (woman speaking) is *Šép'ą* in Yankton, *Ščép'ą* in Teton, and *Ičép'ą* in Santee. At a glance one can see that the three forms are fundamentally the same word. In the days when Dakota culture was all there was and Dakota the only language, any visitor to another people could quickly accommodate to such minor local modifications in a speech and a social system familiar in the main.

It is only within recent times, as Dakotas get away from tribal society and as the young people speak more English than Dakota, that the kinship way of life is threatened, and the observance of kinship obligations tends to slacken. As the native terms of address are substituted for by English proper names, their concomitant rules of attitude and conduct grow dim, and finally disappear altogether. The old courtesies go as the language goes. For example, schoolchildren become accustomed to calling both father's and mother's sisters "aunt" when speaking English, but when they address these relatives in Dakota, they make no distinction between them and call both by the aunt term, *t'ųwí*, whereas that term only designates the father's sister, the mother's sister being *iná* 'mother'. *Lekší* 'uncle' also is improperly applied; only the mother's brother is *lekší*, father's brother being *até* 'father'. Thus in little ways a disintegration of the old culture sets in, not entirely, but partially, due to an unconscious disregard for the niceties of Dakota terms of address that were meant to teach Dakotas good manners. This disintegration of speech and manners is destined to become increasingly general as English inevitably displaces Dakota more and more.

This book would have been easier to write fifty years ago when the culture still had stability enough. Today it is impossible to fit all its parts into a neat, static frame. Even as I write, the old life is rapidly changing under the steady impact of the dominant culture closing in on it. When the subject is so fluid that I am conscious of it—when it is something formerly believed, but not anymore; or still going on, but to a lesser extent; or is true of some Dakotas, but no longer true of all of them—the simple question of which tense to use in writing about it ceases to be simple. To present in their fullness certain rituals, beliefs, or customs that ate on their way out or have long since been dropped, or that are current only here and there but are no longer general and then not always seriously regarded, should I write "It is thus" or "It was thus"?

As one example the actual functioning of the avoidance rule or the joking sanction becomes more immediately plain if it is explained in the present tense as though it were still true in every respect. Yet the fact is that today many of the younger generation pay scant attention to the rules—if indeed they know them—and treat even respect relatives with the casualness customary in only certain family relationships, and sometimes joke about any relative, indiscriminately, in the flippant tone permissible only between brothers- and sisters-in-law. However, here and there among these moderns one finds some who prefer to live by the old rules that dictate correct attitude and behavior, because they were carefully trained by conservative parents to be as correct in their kinship manners as were all Dakotas fifty years ago to respect the values inherent in the gracious old ways.

Throughout the text I have used such Dakota words as seemed apt, even at the risk of slowing down the narrative. Most words are pronounced with stress on the second syllable. This is the rule, but there are exceptions where the accent is moved forward to the first syllable. All kinship terms are given in their vocative form, "my . . ."

Unless the speaker quoted is a Yankton or a Santee—in which case he would be speaking his own dialect—all native words are in the phonetics of the Tetons, except the tribal name. This is *Lakʿóta* in Teton, and *Dakʿóta* in Yankton and Santee. In Assiniboine, the Siouan tongue closest to Dakota, it is *Nakʿóta*. Dakota, as an anglicized term, is more familiar generally than is *Lakʿóta*, which is my reason for using it. The term "Dakota" will be used to comprehend the entire tribe and the language, irrespective of internal groupings by dialects.

The position of an outside investigator looking at an alien scene with cool objectivity did not seem altogether becoming or desirable for one such as myself, speaking from within the culture. Such a position might not be entirely impossible to maintain, though only with considerable artifice. But since the effort to remain convincingly impersonal for page after page would be too preoccupying—whereas the important thing was to tell what must be told—I chose the less exalted role of plain mouthpiece for the numerous Dakotas who gave this material, and have tried to write it simply and directly, and, I hope, lucidly enough.

It further seemed that if I was to make any distinctive contribution toward a deeper understanding of the Dakotas, it must consist not only in describing what went on in their life but also, and more especially, in explaining just why it went on in that precise way, and how and to what extent the nature of Dakota education and the social milieu conditioned and compelled the people to feel, think, and act as they did in each given situation. In attempting to do this comprehensibly, I have not hesitated to give instances out of my own experience wherever I thought they might throw further light. This I have done with a total disregard for and lack of characteristic Dakota reticence, for which I hope to be forgiven.

Even if it had been possible, it was not feasible to account in detail for all the many sources of each item and to report exactly who said what, and when, and where. Too many subjects and problems had to be discussed from too many angles, and checked and rechecked at different times and with informants scattered far and wide among the three Dakota peoples. In the interest of space and word economy, those findings on each subject were best brought together in single digests. I am alone responsible for such digests of my copious notes.

Lest some valuable archaic word or some new idea escaped me, I listened to numerous versions of past events generally known as if it were for the first time, and observed how the same story was colored by each speaker's viewpoint, for that was also of value. Then, stripping the different versions to their essentials where they were in reasonable agreement, I made my own composites of them. As one example, the story of the little girls who stole brown sugar from the chief is a typical digest. I was not there, and, anyway, it happened before my time. I learned all about the "theft"—how it was received and how dismissed—only because I inquired about it in exact detail from several old informants who were on the scene when it happened. The story seemed important as illustrating one facet of Dakota education. Sundry items of local interest such as this one were general knowledge, and I could not escape hearing various versions of them as I went about in any given community, and had to make one composite of them.

In quoting Dakota informants who spoke their language with intelligence and skill, I saw no reason to limit or otherwise alter my own vocabulary, no reason to translate grammatical Dakota into broken English. My single purpose was to transfer their thought content as accurately as possible with the best English tools at my command. Nor have I tried to translate into English the many terse idiomatic phrases and graphic figures that pepper the language and give it zest and sparkle. Translated literally, they lose their punch anyhow, no matter how effective they are in the original. However, I have translated certain words not in their absolute sense, but in their idiomatic usage, wherever they were so used in the Dakota language.

Finally, it was not for me to manipulate this source material, to untwine, isolate, and classify its various elements and then give them impressive scientific names. Rather, I have written in simple terms and rigorously avoided technicalities, leaving it to the social anthropologists who, with practiced eye, will immediately spot and label such elements as *tort, crime, polygyny, endogamy, amitate,* and all the rest—for they are all here. It was enough for me to strive to show what specific uses the Dakotas made of many common cultural phenomena by adapting them to the demands of their way of life.

Because the culture is all of a piece and its components are interrelated, intermixed, and interacting all the way, it was impossible to contain each subject exclusively in the chapter assigned to it. This fact made repetition unavoidable, since the same subjects appeared again and again in relation to different sets of factors. Throughout the writing runs kinship and its implications, gluing the whole together. At no point could I get away from that.

1

The Camp Circle

Hóčʼoka is commonly translated as 'camp circle', but the emphasis is not on the circle but on the area it encloses: *hó* 'circle' serves as an adjective, while *čʼóka* 'center' is the noun. Literally *hóčʼoka* means 'center of the circle'. For convenience I will refer to it as the *common*. This was the logical setting for all corporate activities, rites, ceremonies, feasts, and dances. It must be kept harmonious; nothing untoward must take place there. When it did it was a community misfortune. "The camp circle was sacred," said many informants. "Only friendship and mutual good will belong there."

A camp circle was open to all who chose to live there. At any given time, members of a goodly number of the seven Teton bands could be found there, as well as representatives in lesser numbers from the Yankton- and Santee-speaking peoples from east of the Missouri River. These could be there as visitors or sojourners for a season, or as permanent residents drawn there through a marriage alliance.

Each Teton camp circle was loosely called by the name of the band having the largest representation. But since there were a large number of Teton camp circles, it was necessary to differentiate, for example, the various Oglala circles by individual names. Often camp circles were named after chiefs or other prominent men who had lived there. In my time there still remained localities with such place names as "Flying By's Camp," "Red Water's People," "Blue Feather's Settlement," and "White Horse's Camp," indicating places where those camp circles finally settled down. Today there remains only, so far as I know, "White Horse's Camp," now known simply as White Horse, a small village on the Cheyenne River Reservation.

Only for a winter camp did the Tetons dispense with the circle formation and place their tipis in congenial groupings, huddled into the sheltering bends of a wooded meandering stream or at the foot of a high ridge or cliff, out of the reach of the blizzards that swept the uplands. During the remainder of the year they invariably contrived the camp circle as they roamed about, even for overnight camps during long migrations.[1] For the sake of group unity it was important for them to center their life in the protection of the camp circle.

It would seem that there never was a time when the exact number of these mobile communities throughout Teton country was known. Today we cannot tell the size of the average circle since opinions differ. Some informants recalled that "there were over one hundred tipis," while others spoke of moving camps that took "all day" to pass a given point. That would seem like an endless line going at a snail's pace. One thing is fairly certain: the average camp circle could not afford to be too unmanageably large; it must be kept to a maneuverable size, small enough to make a quick getaway in case of a raid and to keep together reasonably well at all times. Also, for a very large circle the wood, grass, and water supply would give out too soon, thus necessitating another camp migration after only a short stay. A new migration was no simple matter.

In such considerations the Tetons probably would have preferred larger circles, for they liked and welcomed all opportunities to be together. It was always a happy thing for two or even three small camp circles to go into winter quarters together in some prearranged site, where wood, water, and grass were abundant. A recurring comment in personal histories is "That was an exceptionally pleasant winter camp — so many people!" For, although the weather might prevent outdoor functions, it permitted constant visiting and feasting, as long as the food held out. This kind of assemblage was also occasionally possible for a few days, during the milder seasons, notably at the Sun Dance and similar reunions, and was enjoyed with the same fervor.

From all indications each camp circle moved independently and at its own pace. However, if two crossed paths by accident, they managed to halt for a few days of conviviality, unless either of them had to hurry on. At such times they camped in what was called *oyáte núpa* 'two-nations' style, wherein each group retained its formation instead of dissolving into one common circle with a common council tipi in the center, as was the case when a reunion was planned for and scheduled.

As a rule the roving Tetons did not maintain a specific home base to which they returned after each hunting trip as the Yanktons did. The latter left their dwellings, gardens, and small children in care of responsible members of their families who stayed at home. However long they might roam over the prairies east of the Missouri and farther into what later became North Dakota, they knew they would eventually go back home. Sometimes they stayed away through the winter and returned in the spring. They took smaller travel tipis along.

If the Tetons constantly roamed, that did not mean that they moved haphazardly over the plains without definite objectives. On the contrary, each camp circle kept more or less to its own customary orbit. While they were on an eternal quest for buffalo, they also aimed to reach certain localities at certain times, for deer hunting, or for gathering wild fruits and vegetables where they would be in season. They depended heavily on these wild fruits and vegetables because both the arid character of their country and the unsettled nature of their lives offered little opportunity for such systematic gardening as the Yanktons were able to practice, combining hunting with planting and harvesting. "We have always had corn," said a Teton informant, and doubtless it was true. But generally it was obtained by them from their Yankton or Santee visitors or from alien tribes during times of friendly reunions. Their friends the Cheyennes supplied them regularly. From "Cheyenne corn" and "Cheyenne squash" the women saved the seeds to try planting, too, as far as possible.

As the Tetons moved about, the men who held the office of *wak'íč'yza*, who were planners and thinkers for the common good whom for convenience I call *magistrates*, led the moving camp. They always knew where they were and whither they were moving, and even if the people did not always know for certain, they could and did rely on their leaders. Individuals or families temporarily going into the wilds, for reasons of their own, might possibly become lost; but the camp circles, never. They moved according to a plan: a rough and elastic plan, perhaps, with only approximate timing, but still a plan.

We find numerous hints of this planning, and of the fact that the people knew that eventually they would return to the same spot, at the same season, after a year or two—or longer—as required for that country to renew and restock itself. For instance, one woman's life story recounts this incident:

Again it was hazy autumn weather, and at last we were going back there. I had lived for this time and yet I was very sad as I hurried to the little hill where we laid my son away, some years ago. Under the scaffold, now a total wreck, with the supporting posts leaning at various slants and the platform all apart, his poor bleached bones lay scattered. I gathered them up tenderly and wrapped them in a handsome calf skin I had prepared and decorated for this purpose, and buried them deep in the earth. And I wept as I told him. "Son, you see that I am doing what I promised you I would do." For that was what I said to him when he laid dead in our tipi. I promised him that if I lived to return, I would take care of his bones.

Talking to a corpse was a Dakota custom.

Before a camp circle started out, the magistrates set up the *čʼą apáki* 'slanting stick' beside the fireplace of the council tipi. It pointed in the direction the moving camp would take, so that anyone who might be absent at the time of departure from the site could follow and catch up with them. An aged Teton of the *Hųkpapʻaya* band told me: "This was never omitted. For should a straggler come back in the night and find the camp circle gone, he could feel the stick in the dark to get his bearing even though he could not see the path of beaten-down grass made by the moving camp."

Every camp circle included the following essential features: (1) the circle of tipis, (2) the common within the circle, (3) the single break for the official entrance into the camp, (4) the council tipi in the center, roughly equidistant to every point in the circle, and (5) the circular track in front of the tipis, which, for convenience, I designate as the *parade track*.

The parade track was only gradually achieved until it became a wide trodden path. The official crier, the errand-goer, the various processions, visitors going to their friends' tipis, hospitable persons carrying courtesy food to a newcomer or comfort food to the bereaved—all these added to the growing distinctness of the track. It remained plain after the camp circle moved away, and its degree of distinctness was one clue to the length of time a people had lived at that place.

Joyriders used the parade track a lot in the early evenings of pleasant days when the sun was low. They were adolescents of both sexes who used their fanciest saddle blankets, bridles, and quirts, wore their better clothes, rode along as strollers walk, and held their ponies in check to keep them prancing prettily. Two or three went together, chatting, joking, and laughing in soft, subdued tones, and all the while making a show of going somewhere for a purpose, though their real object was to see and be seen. The adults condoned this natural desire of youth, principally by seeming unaware of it, while at the same time deliberately sending them on errands to give an excuse for it.

Properly, girls rode with girls and boys with boys, and they all moved in the "natural direction, with the sun"—that is, clockwise. It was a very daring girl indeed who would defy the conventions by riding with a boy—unless he was her very new husband. Even the affianced did not ride together. A girl and her classificatory nephew (male collateral's child) or son (female collateral's child) or a boy with his niece (female collateral's child) or his daughter (male collateral's child) might ride together without disapprobation, since they were relatives of birth and belonged to different generations, so that courtship was entirely out of the question for them. But even though this kind of pairing off was quite legitimate, few in those relationships cared to ride together because it was too commonplace—like baby-tending at home.

Ideally, all dwellings in the circle were regulation tipis. If for some reason a family must live for a time in an improvised shelter such as a dome-shaped hut, they placed it a little back of the circle. All tipis faced the center, as a rule, and "the entrance to the camp circle was always towards the east," but this was largely in theory. The rule had to be disregarded whenever unfavorable terrain made it necessary to do so. The tipis, even though built on the traditional pattern, were far from uniform in size and quality. There were no restricted areas for those with finer homes; sometimes the newest and handsomest tipis stood side by side with smaller and humbler ones. The important thing was that related families live together, whatever the condition of their respective abodes.

Wherever a bridal tipi stood in front of the home of either spouse's parents it interfered slightly with the parade track, but the people felt kindly toward newlyweds, and they gladly detoured enough to get past. When next the camp circle moved to another location, the new couple placed their tipi side by side with the others and became one more household.

Decorated tipis were the exception. In fact, no tipi was decorated without a valid reason. Ordinary people lived in plain tipis. These, being in the majority, provided the background against which the occasional ornate ones stood out conspicuously. The average tipi was usually adequate for the family occupying it and was generally well enough maintained. When it became shabby and dark from smoke—as all tipis grew in time, no matter how well ventilated they might be—it was replaced. Slipshod tipis, old ragged cast-offs, which the needy or the prideless and indolent picked up as soon as a more thrifty family succeeded in acquiring a new one, formed another contrast. Though shiftless people were apparently content to live poorly, they were nevertheless far from slow to preempt a used tipi if they knew that its owners were working for a new one.

Here and there a man might choose to live in a humble and unpretentious way all his life because he shrank from putting on airs. The fact was that, as in a modern town, there were all sorts and conditions of people in the camp circle. The contrast with a modern town in which everyone consistently strives to live in a better and better way as he grows more able was that, in a Teton camp circle, other factors were present that caused a periodic shift between high and low.

If a self-respecting family lived in an inferior tipi it might be that the husband and father was ill and unable to hunt, or that a recent death in the home had caused a temporary dejection as one mark of grief. Such a family would reestablish itself when the mourning period was over and could be living in a fine tipi again.

The relatives of bereaved persons might insist that they not abase themselves overmuch, and give a good reason why they ought not. For example, one woman related the following: "When my nephew died, my brother, himself an invalid, gave everything away including his fine new tipi. So my sisters and I set up another quite as fine and said to him, 'Brother, your own life is precarious. Do not mourn and neglect yourself for you are not equal to [death].'" Ordinarily, however, such an offer would be gently refused. People in sorrow found a balm for acute grief in such self-humbling.

If one were to walk around the parade track one would see here and there a uniquely painted tipi. The symbolic designs would have meaning for only the holy man residing there. They would have mystical reference to his vision experience, which he might share with no man, but with only the particular spirit that came to him in his vision and promised him abiding friendship and supernatural help in times of stress. By those symbols the man identified himself to that spirit.

It was customary to step with caution near a holy man's tipi until one learned the specific rule governing it. For instance, one holy man's rule was that all wood burned within his tipi must be laid on the fire butt end first, to burn toward the tapering end, which of course was the exact reverse of the usual way. Another's rule was that only red cedar must be burned there, while still another forbade his tipi poles' being struck, even accidentally, for "they were sentient and might bleed." In one holy man's tipi only certain kinds of food might be served. In most cases there was only one simple rule, but it was absolute. It was believed that if it should be transgressed, both the holy man and the offender would meet with misfortune and perhaps death.

Such rules as well as the religious decorations on the tipis were mystical, and the rank and file did not understand them; perhaps they were afraid to ask about their meaning because they were *wak'ą* 'sacred', and anything sacred must not be explored curiously.[2] But everyone, including children, knew what the symbols that decorated the tipis of the *heyók'a* meant. They were those unfortunate men and women under temporary bondage to the Thunder Beings.[3] The motif of their tipi decorations was always the same: white dots for hailstones and zigzag lines for lightning. The dots were usually white, but the lines might be one or all of the standard colors representing lightning—red, yellow, black, and blue-green, according to the choice of the *heyók'a* who lived there. Only in the selection of colors and in the design and size of the dots might he display originality, for some private reason. That was not to be questioned.

Without warning a *heyók'a* dream might visit anyone at any time. Both men and women have been *heyók'a*, but no instance is reported of child *heyók'a*. This sinister dream usually came during a daytime nap. An old saying that it is bad to sleep in daylight stems from that belief. "The *heyók'a* spirit was the Thunder Beings' messenger," explained one informant, "and if you were so unfortunate as to meet him in a dream, you were obligated to act out your dream in all its details, in the public ceremony known as *heyók'a-wozápi*."

All the *heyók'a* dreams I have recorded begin in very much the same way. There was a black storm cloud, solid and stationary, across the western sky, and out of it came a series of shrill staccato shouts, "soldier or scout calls." The native term is *akíč'ita-pápi*. Arrested by those calls, the dreamer fixed his attention on a weird drama unfolding before him, with the *heyók'a* spirit as protagonist and a pitiful little man, or woman as the case might be, as his foil. The dreamer watched the two going through all manner of fantastic and sometimes shocking antics, mostly ludicrous. Gradually he realized that that foil was himself, doing things he ordinarily would never do. He might see himself absurdly dressed and made up; he might find himself stark naked.

Upon awaking he was wretchedly unhappy because he knew the meaning of that *heyók'a* visitation: he must put on a public demonstration of his dream, thereon the common for all to watch, and act out his undesirable role, or be struck by lightning and perhaps die. Mercifully, when he did stage his ceremony, he did not have to occupy the scene alone with all eyes on him. All former *heyók'a*, even though they had long since emancipated themselves through their own ceremonies, were obliged to support him. And so, while he was acting out his peculiar dream role, those, his brother *heyók'a*, created an appearance of extreme business all over the foreground, each one doing something different to invite attention to himself, or two might work together on one act. They seemed to be continuously on the run, hither and yon at high speed; or, if stationary, to work with frantic haste at something. With absurdly serious faces they did stupid or ludicrous things that held the spectator's attention and made them laugh. Their clowning especially delighted little children, who were unaware of the tragicomical aspect of the show, which of course the grown-ups felt even while they chuckled. They were sorry for the poor man who had to undergo this ordeal at the same time that they fought down the fear that the same dream might come to them.

The auxiliary players were there to provide a distraction to screen the unfortunate man while he played his humiliating role, so they worked to attract attention to themselves. They did everything in reverse, never in the normal way, and it was for this that ethnographers named *heyók'a -wozápi* the anti-natural ceremony, in early writings.[4] Always the clowns did the illogical thing—for instance, painstakingly erecting an awning, with haste and with great to-do, and then sitting down on the sunny side of it, fanning themselves happily there; or struggling desperately through the smoke vent of a tipi, with the entrance wide open below it.

The name of the ceremony must be paraphrased: "They draw [object not defined] out of liquid, after the manner of the *heyók'a*." It was the final rite that gave the ceremony its name. At a given instant, the star performer reached his bare arms and hands into boiling water and drew out a piece of meat. Incidentally he sprinkled some of the water on himself, with obvious enjoyment, while his fellow actors cheered him on in a pantomime. In accordance to a set ritual he "presented the meat to the thunders," and the ceremony was ended and he was absolved. The meat offering might be buffalo tongue or dog flesh. Yanktons report only the former, Tetons both.

No longer needed that man fear the thunders; he had appeased them in the traditional way, and they were his friends. But in the interval between his dream and his demonstration, while he was making the necessary preparations, he and all his relatives wailed fearfully whenever a thunder storm was gathering, lest the thunder beings strife him dead, impatient over his slowness, perhaps.

It was believed that if a man or woman on whom this course had been laid through a dream, ignored their obligation to act it out before the people, he or she was destined to die by lightning. By the same token, whenever someone was struck by lightning, it was taken to indicate that he had met the *heyók'a* spirit in a dream but had disobeyed it behest.

It was told that, among the Tetons, if the meat offering was to be dog flesh, the animal must not be shot with an arrow and must not be clubbed. A vague analogy might be read into this: the arrow, a dart, might symbolize a lightning shaft, and clubbing, the force that would knock a person down. Nobody so explained it, however. Instead a rope was looped about the dog's neck and two men, standing distantly pulled on each end with a slow, steady pull, until it was dead.

The informant said he knew for a fact that a certain plant with tight clusters of yellow flowers called *pįspíza-t'awóte* 'prairie-dog food' was pounded into a poultice and rubbed on the man's arms and hands before he plunged them into the boiling water, thus rendering the flesh numb to pain. I have not been able to verify this, and perhaps it is too late, but I recall seeing a short-stemmed plant that grew profusely in prairie-dog towns, in my childhood.

Informants generally agreed that the *heyók'a-wozápi* was the oldest of Teton ceremonies "antidating the Sun Dance." It was part of Yankton life as well as Teton, though with certain differences, but I found no Santee informant who would describe its main features. Perhaps the Santees did not have it all. I do not know that.

At the turn of the century, it is said, one man held *heyók'a-wozápi*, but even that long ago it was much too far out of time to be sympathetically received, particularly in the farming community where he staged it. It had no meaning for them; they came purely out of curiosity. Because the mythical *heyók̓a* spirit was no longer generally believed or feared, the demonstration was not a success.

However, for many years after the custom passed from the scene, there lived Tetons here and there who had been *heyók̓a* in their time. They are all gone now. Perhaps the one I saw with my father at the Rosebud celebration in the 1920's was one of the last, for he was very old, though still a remarkably nimble dancer. The twenty or more dancers were dressed and made up in various ways, no two exactly alike since each man's performance had meaning for him alone. As they danced past, my father pointed one man out to me, "There goes a *heyók̓a*." When I asked if he was a real one, my father said certainly. *Heyók̓a* symbols were a dreaded thing in the old days, and no man would presume to use them without a valid reason. I observed that the man had black, red, and blue-green zigzags down his arm and legs, and groupings of white dots of graduated sizes all over his body and his forehead and cheeks.

It is said that most *heyók̓a* became themselves immediately after their ceremony, but that occasionally there was one who, though freed from his bondage to the thunders, still unintentionally continued to behave illogically at times, thus furnishing a comic relief for the community. This was so in spite of the fact that he was harmless and otherwise entirely reliable, and normal in his relationships. The wife and children of such person learned to take his antics in their stride. It is from typical *heyók̓a* behavior that the common simile comes, *heyók̓a s̓é*, 'like a *heyók̓a*', with reference to something that happens contrary to the expected. Within my hearing a Teton woman told her companion, "For days I had had a cold but was losing it at last, when yesterday, I became thoroughly soaked in that rain storm. Not only I looked for a relapse but, instead, *heyók̓a s̓é*, I was suddenly rid of it!"

Aside from the holy men's tipis with their esoteric markings, there were always a few whose upper third was painted solid black, blue or red. "Important men lived there," but what each color signified is no longer clearly defined. However, it is certain that a tipi whose entrance was painted red was the home of a man or woman self-obligated to a life of hospitality over and above the usual. Any wayfarer who arrived hungry had only to walk around the parade track until he came to a "red door," for there he would be fed. If all food was gone, his host or hostess was committed to obtain it from somewhere, anywhere, by asking a relative or by bartering with an outsider, or even by begging if need be, whatever the cost. Only in extreme famine might one have to fail such a guest. "If I have but one morsel remaining, it shall be cut in two. The first piece for my guest, and only what remains for me" was the solemn pledge in this connection. The surname 'Red Door' *T^ciyóp-Šá* borne by a Dakota family living around Poplar, Montana, is significant to those who understand its meaning.

Perhaps the most remarkable character of the Teton camp circle was its complete mobility. The people took it all with them whenever they moved to a new locality, for they were not coming back, at least not for a considerable time. As long as they remained settled in one place—never sure for how long—they achieved a convincing picture of permanency and went about their business of living as though for all time.

But then, often on the shortest possible notice from the council tipi, they quickly dismantled their homes and working appurtenances, and, in no time at all they swung into line and waited for the starting signal from their leaders. Presently the long procession began to move in a slow march—without a backward look, for the most part, although sometimes a family that had lost a dear one and laid him away on some nearby knoll went reluctantly. Sometimes, and especially if the death had occurred very recently, they remained behind for one more cry and final leave-taking there. Various other reasons might hold some persons back for a little while, but eventually they all went. By her own confession in old age, one young girl "hated to leave that spot" because it was where she first fell in love, and was romantic about it.

Arrived at the new site after perhaps several nights on the way, the people promptly restored the entire scene, there to resume their life. They brought in fresh willows and such poles of ash or box elder as were needed for such backyard structures as drying racks for meat, sun shades, and other similar arrangements—and set them up. The lodge poles, lacing pins, anchoring pegs, and certain specially selected stakes of hardwood with hooked tips for guying the windflaps were items of standard equipment carried about from place to place and not cut fresh each time. They were valuable because they had been seasoned and shaped with care for their respective uses.

Without undue fuss the people resumed their life, so accustomed to moving, so eager to be at home again, as though there had been no laborious interruption. The camp circle was the constant, with the same neighbors side by side; only the terrain and scenery had changed. It was as though, with everything in place, the camp circle had been lifted intact with the sod on which it stood in one place, and set down again in some distant place with nothing changed, or hardly anything.

Within the camp circle everything human went right on. Always, here and there, in the tipis, some lay sick or dying or dead, while others were being created and born—in an endless cycle. Social events went on as planned: none stopped because of a camp move. Sometimes a family ceremonial had to be performed in sections, act 1 at the old site and act 2 at the new, and now and again a baby was born on the march. Without rebellion the people accepted those interruptions for the common good, recognizing the camp moves to be as inevitable as rain and weather, so the sick were carried along and sometimes also the dead, if there had been no time before the move to bury and mourn them decently. A dead body in transit was bound in a buffalo robe and strapped laterally to a travois dragged by a gentle pack horse, but dead bodies were rarely necessary to carry on a camp move.

Ordinarily the travois was used for carrying small children or the sick or aged and infirm. Sometimes household goods were piled on it instead, or the tent, folded into a bundle with the lacing pins and anchoring pins safe inside it. An oval platform, made by bending a supple willow into a frame and crisscrossing it firmly with stout thongs in a tight web, was fastened to the poles to support the cargo. Whenever the web commenced to sag from repeated loadings, it was thoroughly soaked in the river and then allowed to dry, shrunken to its original tautness.

In those remote days before the Tetons had horses, everyone must walk when moving camp. Only little children and the very old or the sick might ride on the low travois pulled by a dog, the only beast of burden. Adults were borne along in hammocks, by strong men and women, and sometimes an old grandparent too feeble to walk was carried like a child on the back of some strong male relative. Because moving was hard in every sense of the word in those days, periods of rest along the way were essential. Four stops were regularly made, thus dividing the distance somewhat equally on a long march, the fourth being the final stop, where camp was made.

Gradually the emphasis seems to have shifted from the altogether practical to a religious reason, and the four stops were dedicated to the four sacred directions. As the religious aspect became all-important, even absurdly short trips were portioned into "ceremonial stops," where the peace pipe was offered ritually. After the arrival of the horse, which greatly simplified all transportation, those stops were sometimes neglected, though they were retained in all ceremonial or religious processions. After all visitors had arrived for the Sun Dance, hosts and visitors together made a solemn pilgrimage to the virgin spot selected for the enactment of that great religious festival. This religious use of the four stops was so customary that in the early days of the Church, Christian Dakotas tended automatically and unconsciously to stop four times in their processions, notably in their measured march around the cemetery for the memorial service on Easter Day.

When people traveled on foot, everyone was grateful for the respite at each stop, particularly on hot summer days. The women hastened to pass out some lunch to their families and attend to their children's bodily needs, while here and there men settled on the grass in groups to smoke the pipe together.

As recently as twenty years ago, men still lived who liked to sit down together in a cluster to smoke the common pipe socially. Each man carried his own blend of smoking material, as in olden times, in a long buckskin pouch fringed at the bottom and often highly ornamented with porcupine quill work or beads. Inside, along with his kinnikinnick mixture was his red catlinite pipe with its long stem sticking far out of the top. A short stick of hardwood pointed at one end for cleaning out the residuum, and blunted at the other and for tamping, was also a standard equipment. The blend was mostly the inner bark of certain variety of willow, dried slowly and then out very fine and mixed with enough tobacco to suit the owner's taste. To this some men added for flavor and aroma, a bit of mint, laurel, or aroma leaf, possibly other things too. Each man had his own recipe that he preferred and that was known by his friends.

Correct social smoking etiquette was important, and it was automatically followed. A man filled his pipe quietly with his own blend of tobacco, while the talk went on. Then he handed it to his neighbor on his left. The neighbor lit it and smoked leisurely, two to four puffs, before he handed it unhurried to the one on his left—and so the pipe went. When it was burnt out, it was passed back to its owner, who cleaned it and laid it down. Meanwhile, someone else began to fill his pipe and started it going, by handing it to the man on his left to light and smoke it before sending it on. In a large circle, the first man's pipe would go out before it could get around to him, but he got his smoke from the second man's pipe. During a long talk-feast everyone smoked several times on different men's pipes, for they took turns in offering smoke to the company. They did not assign turns to each other in any precise way, but instead the matter was managed naturally and as if randomly. The two rules were that the owner did not light his own pipe after filling it with his own blend of smoking material, and that the pipe always traveled clockwise while burning and counterclockwise when burnt out. Incidentally, when Dakota men sat smoking a long time, the air did not reek with tobacco odor, because only one man smoked at a time, and then just two to four puffs, deliberately, like sipping wine.

Social smoking is now definitely a thing of the past. The few old men who once took pleasure in it are now too scattered and frail to foregather. They find cigarettes more convenient but admit that they miss the social aspect. Old and middle aged women smoked, too, but they did so within their tipi, generally sitting alone there. They used miniature pipes of red stone, with shorter stems. If you entered unexpectedly, they explained, *Išé č̓uwí osníwakiyįkta č̓á* ... 'Only that may cool off my *č̓uwí* ...' The native word means the breathing area of the body (i.e., the thorax). There was no sentiment against women's smoking, but young women and girls considered it an old woman's pastime and would have none of it. Nowadays, however, many of them smoke cigarettes, some even rolling their own, deftly.

In winter the people avoided moving, unless they were driven forth by enemy attack, or the threat of it. The people carried fire with them when moving camp. An aged *Sič̓ą́ǧu* Teton learned the following from his grandparents:

> In the very, very long ago, the magistrates always carried a slow-burning log on camp moves, and when the camp circle was again in place, the people hurried to the council tipi with tinder and a bundle of sticks for a light from that eternal fire, for warming their lodges and cooking their food. Because the obtaining of fire was neither easy, nor sure, nor quick, it must be carefully guarded and nursed at all times, so that everyone might benefit from it. Thus the magistrates were also the traditional keepers of the fire.

The fireplaces were the focal points of sociability. In winter the family sat around their fire in the tipi. In summer they sat outside with their guests, in a circle around the fire there, to eat the evening meal in the cool of the day and remained talking long afterward. All around the camp circle these rings of seated people might be seen, their shapes opaque against the flaming fires, as night fell, pungent with wood smoke.

In mixed company it was the men who properly carried the stream of conversation, while the women and children sat listening, silent for the most part except to laugh at an occasional joke, but in a low tone, never conspicuously loud. It was extremely rude to interrupt a speaker. Women were not forbidden to speak, but it was customary for them never to snatch the talk away from the speaker. Children were trained not to do so, and women felt it unbecoming and immodest for them to be talkative where men were present. Yet, if a woman had something important to contribute to the subject, she was perfectly free to speak out. Meanwhile, the men sat with bowed heads, listening politely without looking at her, for to look at a woman speaking would be bad manners on a man's part. Old women of a certain stamp were likely to abuse this right, gaining attention by their frequent insistence on being heard. Sometimes a venerable woman of established reputation was politely invited to express herself or to give advice out of her wisdom and long experience, and then men as well as women sat with heads bowed to listen respectfully.

The women always sat together and from time to time talked quietly on the side, imparting a bit of information, asking or answering questions of one another, or exchanging current events of women's interest in an undertone, temporarily away from the general conversation and yet never quite unaware of it. When women sat alone together they might indulge in light talk on domestic matters—the children, fancywork, easier ways of doing things, a pending feast across the common, and similar subjects. If none were in respect relationship, which would require them to observe considerable politeness, they were free to laugh, joke, and gossip inconsequentially as much as they pleased.

The council tipi stood in the center of the camp circle, though the location was perhaps determined by guess only and not paced off. It was the town hall, occupied by the four magistrates during their term of office. It was a lively place most of the time. Men came and went and none were barred from it, though generally one who had committed a crime barred himself. Men of mature judgment and prestige came there to deliberate with the magistrates, or to bring news or obtain it from them, while men of no particular standing, quiet souls who lacked both the capacity and the desire to philosophize, also came and sat on the fringe, to listen and to eat.

For nearly always there was food on hand, brought by women who wished to honor the council tipi. As soon as it was taken from them with expressions of thanks—*Háho! háho! háho!* coming from here and there as more became aware of the gift—the women hurried away. Women did not properly push their way into a company of men, and it was just as unseemly for men to do so in the reverse situation. This keeping out of a group of the opposite sex was by no means due to any rule based on inferiority or superiority of either sex. The very simple fact was that woman had her conventional sphere and man had his.

The Teton council tipi was called *t'ípi iyók'iheya* 'tipi joined onto', the reference being to the method of enlarging the already commodious leaders' lodge by adding other tipi covers to it. These, with the council tipi itself, were stretched out in a circular awning to provide for extraordinary gatherings. A full council of all leading citizens of the camp circle, a mass meeting in the common interest, or a reception and feast for non-Dakotas on an official visit, could be comfortably seated in its shade.

The Yankton council tipi was made and used in a similar way, but was called by the term *akíč'ita ot'í* 'watchers' or 'soldiers lodge'. These watchers or soldiers were the four magistrates who must stay there night and day during their tenure of office and who were expected to be unceasingly vigilant in their people's behalf. No details were reported about the method of their selection.

From all accounts their initiation was more formal and perhaps more solemn than that of Teton magistrates, and they lived by unremitting rule. Two salient points were that they must totally abstain from all carnal satisfactions, so that their thinking might be the clearer and truer, and their wits sharper to detect any incipient danger; and at night they must sleep with their feet toward the center and their heads pointing out in the four sacred directions, in token of their constant alertness to danger from any quarter. However, one Yankton informant was sure that his grandfather said the magistrates slept with their heads toward the center—to confer at any moment—and feet toward the four directions—to rush out instantly in case of trouble. Whatever the symbolism, they apparently formed a cross as they slept, as it were, "covering the world." Such rules could be systematically watched and followed by the generally sedentary Yanktons in a way not always possible for the Tetons, ever on the move.

Santee informants tell me that among the Eastern Dakotas, the Santees, and kindred bands, there were no permanent council tipis where, in their wooded habitat, they were obliged to place their lodges anywhere that the ground was level enough, among the scattered trees. For them the camp circle formation was neither always practical nor essential. But then, whenever it became necessary for the leaders to deliberate on tribal matters, the finest and largest lodge that qualified was requisitioned. A white banner was raised above it, and it stood for a council tipi for as long as the banner remained furled there. Incidentally, as one woman pointed out whose home was once so used, it was a rare compliment for a Santee woman to have her home selected for such a noble purpose; it was something for her to recall with pride in her later years. Definitely it was a coup for her, since only a woman of flawless reputation was considered worthy to lend her tipi. The more handsome tipis of women of lesser character were regularly bypassed for that reason.

The Teton and Yankton council tipi, and doubtless the Santee also, employed the soldier societies, which were composed of young and active men, for carrying out the magistrates' plans. From all accounts the several societies took turns to be on duty and on call. The *T'ok'álas* 'Kitfoxes' are most frequently mentioned in this regard by Teton informants, but the others also served on equal terms with them. They acted as scouts, guards, messengers, and camp circle police; they patrolled the communal hunts; and whenever visiting groups were coming near, they went to meet and escort them in and assign camping places to them in the circle as the council ordered. However, in no remotest sense were they policemen watching individual behavior. Kinship law took care of that quite sufficiently. They merely stayed aware that, during their own society's term of duty, the camp circle's general welfare depended on them, and that therefore they must be ready at all times to move fast in case of emergency. They might not relax or go off on their private ventures while on duty. They had a responsibility. Only if a member's relative was dying or dead was he automatically excused, while the others closed ranks to carry on without him. For death took precedence over any other consideration.

Each society managed its men for routine duty. It sent forth scouts or relieved them at reasonable intervals, as long as it was held answerable. It is probable that this account is oversimplified, but so is this procedure remembered, at least this much is fairly certain. The scouts served by turns according to the societies of which they were members. Thus routine duty more or less regulated itself, without constant oversight or direction by the magistrates.

Only for some special, important errand did the council make a formal assignment, particularly if the mission was a strategic and even dangerous one. For that kind of duty usually two men were chosen, on the basis of their personal qualifications and character, and were commissioned together. In the presence of a few representative citizens the magistrates first feasted the men and offered them the peace pipe, after ritually presenting it to the Four Winds, the Sky, and the Earth. The scouts in accepting the pipe and smoking it vowed to serve honestly and well at whatever cost. Then they set forth on the errand assigned to them.

Any time they returned with a negative report they needed only to notify their society, without going back to the council tipi to report there. Their fruitless return was realized by the magistrates who dismissed the matter by saying, "They found nothing to tell us."

On the other hand, if they had learned something important, they went straight to the council tipi, there to be questioned according to a set form, which is said to be ancient. One might guess that it gave way to faster reports at a distance, after scouts were mounted, for it is common knowledge that certain positions and movements of a scout on horseback conveyed his message unmistakably to those who were prepared to read such signals and were watching for them.

Upon the scouts' return to the council tipi once more they were feasted and caused to smoke the pipe ritually. Then they were ready for the questioning, for again their smoking was tantamount to a vow to report the truth and nothing but the truth. Several aged Tetons gave what they knew of the routine—from hearsay, of course, since it was used before their time. They were accustomed only to smoke, blanket, mirror, and horseback signals.

Since they lived at scattered places and were interviewed singly at different times, it was natural that their recitals varied in some details, but the gist of the accounts was, in my opinion, as obtained from Fast Whirl-wind, the Oglala Teton living at Pine Ridge. I record his version in exact detail as being the most nearly representative of the other versions. It is a composite of them. Note that when the council spokesman, who does the questioning, speaks in the first person singular, he speaks for the camp circle; he is the voice of the circle personified. When the scout replies in the same way he speaks for his companions and himself, representing the mission, personified.

QUESTIONER: Now, *hokšíla*, tell me what you know. Tell me truthfully. Think not to deceive me!

ANSWER: *Wąk'éya, wič'áȟčala* 'Why certainly, why not, old man', you saw me smoke the pipe! Hear me then. I saw . . .

Q. [interrupting] Come, come, *hokšíla*, out with it, ere I grow impatient! Am I safe from enemies? Is there food nearby for my children that they may live and thrive? Come, do not tantalize me. Hold nothing back!

The entire audience of leading men watch the scout with exaggerated eagerness. With quick-moving head and eye they follow his words and rapid gestures, some turning their entire torso as they sit to look where he points. It is all quite unnecessarily lively and even frantic.

A. I hold nothing back, *wič'áȟčala*. Listen, then. Over yonder, I climbed to the top of the land "pushed upward" and gazed beyond over the land "pulled downward" and there in the hollow I saw the land covered with as it were one immense black fur robe!

There are common nouns for hill and valley, but the scout uses symbolic language for them here. The listeners break out with relief and joy. They cry *Háye! Háye!* And many rub their palms together to denote their satisfaction. Not that they are so desperate for meat as to act rapturously over the finding of it. This is plain dramatics. Nor is the questioner so eager and impatient as he seems.

Q. Say what else, *hokšíla*, say!

A. I noticed that they all carried as it were square packs on their shoulders!

At this last the applause is renewed and intensified many times. Each listener exclaims in his own fashion until there is a jumble of utterances and of gesticulation, in keeping with the several moods expressed. Some become so ecstatic that they pat the ground caressingly, murmuring, with cheek close to the earth, "Thank you, Grandmother! Thank you!" And some bend over as they sit and reach out all around them as far as possible, to pat more of the ground, stroking it affectionately.

Q. And now, *hokšíla*, tell finally just where you saw all this. In which direction? Then will I sharpen my knives and hasten to the chase, ere I starve!

A. I saw all this over there!

He designated the direction with his thumb. Why the thumb rather than the index finger is something my informants did not know. In this one situation alone it was traditional.

At last the tension, whether real or simulated, was passed. All the facts were out. The council knew from the start that the scouts had returned with positive news and that the reporter would speak truly. They knew that his news did not have to do with imminent danger from enemies, for then it would have been breathlessly reported, without elaborate ceremony. Thus they expected some other news—perhaps another camp circle beyond the hills, perhaps tracks of many deer at a water hole, perhaps buffalo.

As the dialogue progressed they learned that buffalo had been sighted, and gathered the particulars from the speaker's figurative language. "With as it were square packs on their backs" meant buffalo, specifying the kind of game. "Covered as it were with one immense black fur robe." What else but a closely packed herd numbering maybe hundreds, maybe thousands! It was indeed something to send them into exultant activity. To the chase! For other kinds of reports, other figures of speech were used, often highly original, for the council to interpret.

Because in olden times scouts about to be sent on a difficult mission were first royally feasted, to this day whenever someone is being fed extraordinarily well, he laughingly remarks, "Well! Am I about to go scout to the hill?"—even while he eats with relish. It is an inherited saying, but I have found no one under the age of seventy-five who could say to what it referred.

Before leaving this subject I have to explain the use of the term *hokšíla* 'boy' in addressing the scout. When used in an official or formal way—for instance, by a war chief exhorting his men or a venerable man haranguing on tribal ideals—it has a specialized meaning, to designate the hearers.

Another indispensable assistant to the magistrates was the camp crier, *éyapaha*, a word whose etymology is not known. Usually he was a mature-to-elderly man with a good carrying voice, good enunciation, and—most important—an orderly memory. In the average-sized camp circle one official crier was enough. He stayed in and around the council tipi most of the time, ready to go forth to proclaim whatever must be communicated to all the people.

But during larger encampments of two or more camp circles together, additional criers were needed. These deputy criers might remain at home, until asked to cover their particular sectors. Thus at times there might be as many as four or more criers calling out the news simultaneously, and it is said that this was regularly the case at the annual Sun Dance, when the normal circle was augmented to several times its size by visiting camp circles and other groups.

Orders to move at once, or notice of the proximity of a buffalo herd and instructions as to procedure and chase, news of visitors arriving, warnings of immediate danger from the enemy—such were the matters to be made known at once, and that was the crier's responsibility. Speaking for the council, when visitors were arriving he exhorted the people to bestir themselves and extend hospitality to them. Then, presently, various families might be seen cutting across the common armed with food and gifts for them, and here and there a man might stand outside his tipi shouting an invitation to be relayed to the visitors, while his wife hastily prepared to entertain them.

Normally a crier walked his horse around the parade track and called out the news loudly and leisurely, but there were other times when he must move fast and whisper as he went. In one life story a woman reports: "We knew we were in great danger [of an attack] because the crier whispered as he hurried by for us to smother our fire at once."

The practiced crier gave out the order of the day in a distinctive sing-song, phrasing his words with intervals of silence, while he walked his horse a few steps. This allowed the people to take in his message. In Dakota country west of the Missouri there is nearly always some wind, or at least a light breeze. On this the crier's voice came and went fitfully, so that hardly anyone who did not ride along near him could catch every word in sequence and get the full import of the notice entirely by himself; cooperation was essential. So everywhere women stood halfway out of their tipi entrances and strained to hear. They called to one another, "What did he say just then?" "Well, I heard . . ." "But I thought he said . . ." In the end they would have it intact by piecing together their several fragments to make sense out of them.

Among other functions the crier served to wake the people. He sounded off just before sunrise, telling the people it was time to get up. He was the weather prophet as well, appraising the kind of day the skies promised and thereby warning or delighting his hearers still in bed. Some criers were all business, formal and direct and without any frills. Others, the born criers, put imagination into their work and both gave and got fun out of it. When times were uneventful, they offered amusement along with the more prosaic notices, causing many an early riser to stop blowing on the damp wood of her obstinate fire to chuckle at a witty remark. When telling of his boyhood, an old man recalled a particular crier: "He was a brother-in-law to me [hence a joking relative] and so whenever he went by our tipi he always managed to give a dig at 'those lazy fellows who sleep late to be waited on by women.' This was for my special benefit. He knew perfectly well that, young as I was, I was always up at daybreak to water all the horses of our *t'iyóšpaye* long before he started on his round."

It was normal for the Tetons to live gregariously. They were happiest in company, surrounded by kinsmen. Under ordinary circumstances they would not want to break away from the camp circle and live forever out in the wilds alone, or with only a wife and children. Whenever someone did so, he had his reasons. The variety of reasons I recorded include the following:

1. A man who was consumed with jealousy over his young wife finally took her and their small son to live permanently in the wilds, far from the glances of other men, who, he imagined, looked on her with desire.

2. A family left the camp circle forever because the eldest daughter was pregnant though unwed, and the fact aroused strong suspicions of incest involving her own father, who was generally unprincipled. Such a thing, besides being a crime against kinship law, was regarded as "unnatural," revolting to all decent people. There was no vested authority to deal with such offenders or to order them away, but the mass horror was strong enough to drive them out. It was in such situations that subtle tribal sentiment was in full and effective control.

3. Occasionally, a man who felt impelled to seek a vision through fasting went out alone quietly and remained on some distant peak for a few days. When he was ready, he returned home quietly.
4. During times of famine, individuals, or one or two congenial families, went out to hunt for small game on which to keep alive until better days.
5. A murderer who lacked the courage to face punishment, or one who felt himself unworthy to be among innocent people, went into self-imposed banishment and remained forever in exile from his own camp circle.

Those who left for less serious reasons than this last intended to return to a life with other Dakotas sometime. Those who went forth in shame or to escape mental conflict hoped, when they could no longer stand the loneliness, to enter some remote camp circle where perhaps their story was not known. But since news of all sorts traveled from camp circle to camp circle with amazing certainty, however slowly, theirs was too often an idle hope. Yet to live habitually in the wilds, "like beasts," was both distasteful and unnatural to the Dakotas. A hermit's life was nearly incomprehensible to them.

Upon entering any camp circle not one's own, it was imperative to make oneself known immediately and become related to the likeliest family there, through an assumed bond if necessary. For one who had a bad deed to live down, this was far from easy. Yet, thanks to the social kinship system through which total strangers could become relatives, even such as he could be integrated there eventually. One informant speaking on this point said: "We took the strange young man in and made him our son in place of the boy we had lost. And then after two years, some travelers arrived who reported that he killed a man back home and ran away. But we had accepted him as our son, so of course we continued to treat him as one." Having taken a stranger in and made him a relative, it would be an offense against kinship law to turn him out on any account. People derided those who reversed themselves after accepting social kinship with someone.

By degrees, as more immediate local happenings claimed public attention, a newcomer's offense in a remote camp circle could grow vague. After many years of good conduct, he could conceivably regain a measure of respectability in his new home. However, such a man lived under an eternal shadow. Some day, any day, a malicious person could resurrect his past and throw it up to him in public to shame him. Only the consistently upright could be wholly free.

After all, men seeking asylum in a new camp circle because they could no longer remain in their own were not nearly so numerous as those who came on legitimate business. Often they were looking for relatives they had never met. Such a visitor might say, "I grew up as an Oglala and knew only my father's people. Now I have come to meet my mother's relatives among the *Itázipčo* 'the Sans Arc Tetons', where I also belong." As soon as his maternal relatives heard this, they and their relatives of birth and of marriage would promptly claim him to do him honor. It was always right to extend one's circle of relatives; there was no need to be hesitant about doing so, and indeed it was the expected thing.

But anyone who did not account for himself with reasonable promptness, and relate himself to the community, was mildly suspect. In close-knit communities this is still likely to be the case. On one recent occasion a handsome stranger appeared in a certain Teton community without saying who he was, where he came from, or why. His presence was incredibly disturbing, particularly to the older people, to whom kinship was of prime importance still. They wanted to extend hospitality to him, but were unable to determine how or where to reach him. Yet he stayed around. At all public functions, feasts, or Christian gatherings, there he would be in the background, sitting on his horse and watching the proceedings at a distance, a solitary, taciturn, altogether intriguing figure, a mystery to all.

As it turned out, his mission was a legitimate and harmless one. During the recent celebration at the agency he had been attracted to one of the local girls, and he had come with romance on his mind. He married that girl in due time, and they lived happily together into middle age, with children and grandchildren.

It was only after his reason for keeping aloof was realized that his initial behavior was understandable. It was simply his way of guarding against becoming related to any family through social kinship, lest he thereby place himself in a brother or cousin relationship with that girl, which would of course forbid courtship. So it was safest to remain anonymous in order that, as a total stranger, he might honorably approach her in courtship. He waited until he could find an opportunity to speak to her directly, without kinship restraints.

In olden times especially, and even today among conservative Dakotas, a stranger in their midst was the responsibility of all the people, who felt it incumbent on them to maintain the status quo wherein all Dakotas who had daily association with one another must be kinsmen to one another, since that was *the way* to get along smoothly, with mutual deference and courtesy. Whether the relationship was actual or assumed made no difference.

So they contrived to get to the stranger and say something like this to him: "Being Dakotas, no doubt we have mutual relatives through whom we can become 'something-to-each-other' [*tákukič'iyapi*, i.e., relatives]." In this way they gave him an opening to declare his relationship to some well-known person to whom they might also be related—if not by birth or marriage, then at least in social kinship. Prominent men and women who were well known across the land were invaluable links in such a situation. Of course, a stranger who had a famous relative had no trouble at all in relating himself to any community.

There was a time when kinship was as vital as that, and indispensable in all Dakota social life. Today many who speak more English than Dakotas tend to lose all kinship awareness except toward their immediate families. To them others are as strangers. But in life stories and in the reminiscences of the old people, great emphasis was laid on kinship as the ruling factor in all human associations. Once it functioned in all camp circle problems with complete effectiveness. Examples of its operation must be given in some detail, for everything that took place involving two or more persons was within the framework of kinship. That means everything—except religion. There each person was on his own.

2

Law and Order

Open quarrels among persons of consequence were rare, though they did occasionally take place.[1] Perhaps there is significance in the fact that of all the quarrels reported, those that took place in olden times grew out of resentment and hurt feelings over some kinship slight. Nothing disturbed the Dakotas so much as to be improperly treated by a relative, or for them or their relatives to be the object of malicious talk. Quarrels, in the times after contact with white culture, were in the majority of cases due to drunkenness, which caused men to forget themselves enough to engage in a spirited exchange of bitter words ending in threats to kill each other. Unless relatives interfered and made peace between them, sometimes they carried out their threats. One man remarked, "You might suppose that when they came to their senses they would see their mistake, but even then it was not easy to recant. Their attitude remained, as if to say, 'I spoke those words and they are mine. I stand by them, like a man!'" But at the time those words were spoken, they were not really men.

Whenever two men or two women had a quarrel it could not remain their private affair for very long. It became the concern of the entire community, for everyone was a kinsman, however indirectly or remotely. Not that they all needed to take sides and implicate themselves, but the atmosphere of possible tragedy made for general uneasiness.

At such times, prominent men who were accustomed to peace-making once again decided to interfere and try to restore friendship between the two at enmity in order to extinguish the trouble. *Kasni* means 'to extinguish a flame by striking it down', and is here used figuratively. They did this for the sake of the ones at enmity, and also in the interest of peace within the camp circle. The peacemakers, who could also be women, used an approach somewhat like this:

My relative, I have come to remind you that we Dakotas love peace within our borders, peace-making is our heritage. Even as children we were trained to settle our differences through kinship so that we may live in *Odákʻota* 'in a state of Dakota-ness'. Alas, my relative, now we grieve over your unhappy state. We go about with heavy hearts fearing what this quarrel might lead to. You wrong not only yourself but also your kinsmen and friends. As long as you are at odds with another, we all go about with heavy hearts. Come then, my relative, before it is too late.

If that was not argument enough, the pleader continued, "Ah, my relative, murders have resulted from just such a path as you are taking. I beg of you, turn about. Do not bring tears to helpless women's eyes. Do not orphan your children!" If there was no reply, he went further: "I plead with you in tears, my relative [using the appropriate kinship term]! I even humble myself to beg of you!" So he would talk and then pause between arguments. He might add, "You know I am not a man of property. I have no worthy gift with which to beguile you. But at least I offer you these words of entreaty, a little food, and a little tobacco." Gently, soothingly, he would talk. If, on the other hand, he was able to make a gift, he said, "Out on the hillside a horse is grazing. He shall cool off your heart. Take him, and so live happy in our midst again."

The kinship appeal was supreme. To a people trained through the generations to bow to its rule, kinship was irresistible to all but a maddened man or a born fool. Its claims were reason enough for a man to reverse himself honorably and make friends with his enemy. The conciliator placed squarely on him the responsibility for his relatives' peace of mind, reminding him that no Dakota lived unto himself alone; his life was not exclusively his, to keep or throw away. Since all were inextricably bound together in kinship, one could not harm himself without harming others, too. Such were some of the ideas implicit here.

Reasonable men, unable to ignore such an appeal, in the end smoked the pipe together at a special feast, and so the breach was healed. Then their friends, happy over their reconciliation and the restoration of peace, brought them more gifts, as they were able.

Just as it was wrong for disputants to disregard their kinsmen's anxiety over them, so it was wrong for those kinsmen to take an indifferent attitude toward their quarrel, saying in effect: "To the devil with those two! If they have no better sense than to fight, let them go to it! Let them kill each other if they like!" Instead relatives and friends should bestir themselves to end the strife. To remain a neutral bystander was to be willfully negligent of one's social responsibility. One invited harsher blame for not interfering than did those who were quarreling. "See that? He being sane, he was the logical one to interfere, and yet he did nothing. Small wonder that frenzied men have harmed each other, since he made no gesture to cool off their hearts? How stingy he must be! How fearful of losing a little property!" But the man who did interfere and managed to restore peace was a domestic hero quite as laudable as the warrior who struck coup on an enemy.[2]

If a man who was normally peace-loving and self-respecting had been unwittingly drawn into a quarrel, he might regret his hasty step almost at once. Yet, in order to justify himself, he might determine to see the matter through at all costs, once he was in it. Men have confessed in later years that all the while they were hoping someone would care enough to rescue them in the name of kinship so that they might have a valid reason for abandoning their stand. Said one, "And then he came to me, and asked me to desist, calling me by kinship term. How could I, who have always respected kinship, withstand its appeal?" In another such situation, a man complained, "While I stood mired I yearned for some kinsman to help me, but no kinsman came." From the Dakota standpoint both of these statements were reasonable.

A peacemaker acted on his own initiative, in his capacity as a relative. If also he happened to be a magistrate, that official position had little to do with it. In all interpersonal matters it was kinship alone that dictated attitude and conduct; and it controlled tribal leaders as rigorously as anyone else. It was for their obedience to kinship rules that they were regarded as worthy members of society, and it was because they were worthy members of society that they were selected as leaders.

Broils among irresponsible, heedless, and quick-tempered men were common enough, but such men were of little consequence anyway, and their systematic fights were more or less taken for granted. "What is the use of trying to appease them? Conscientious citizens have tried to help them time and again but it was of no use. It is normal for them to quarrel; they were marked from birth to be so."

If such a character provoked a good man into a fight, that was the time for restoring peace in order to rescue the good man and relieve his relatives of their anxiety. It sometimes happened that a good man in trouble was slow to relent, feeling too outraged at becoming involved with so unworthy an opponent, and wanting nothing but to avenge himself. In that case he might sit unmoved by the most passionate pleader. "No, my kinsmen, I cannot listen to even you. Already you are the second [or fourth, or tenth] to come to me and I am gratified. Whatever may befall me, never let it be said that I lacked relatives who cared about me, but this is something my pride cannot brook."

There were certain preeminent men and women who had it to their abiding credit that no one in trouble was ever able to resist their appeal and were told, "Alas, my relative, why did *you* have to come, too? Already others have pleaded with me and I was able to harden my ears, thinking to remain unmoved. I have succeeded in refusing to hear them, deeply as I care for them, but now you come; and because of you I cannot but listen." Words like these honored the successful peacemaker.

Thus were quarrels aborted as soon as possible, before they led to murder. Even so, murder was occasionally committed, and when that happened, it had to be dealt with just as promptly, before a chain of reprisal killings within the camp circle could begin—an intolerable prospect. When men only quarreled, the conciliators' efforts were prophylactic, but when there was a murder, curative measures were due before further killings could follow. Then the problem ceased to be a simple kinship obligation voluntarily assumed and became a community responsibility to be taken over by the council tipi.

There was a clear distinction between killing in war and killing within the camp circle, between killing an enemy and killing a fellow Dakota. The first was legitimate; the second was a crime against society and hence liable to punishment.[3] From all the material on hand, there appear to have been three principal ways of dealing with murderers: (1) immediate reprisal killing of the murderer by a relative of his victim, (2) trial by ordeal at the behest of the council, and (3) adoption of the murderer by his victim's kinsmen.

The first was the simplest and quickest. Any one of the slain man's relatives might take it upon himself to settle the score at once, by stabbing or shooting down the slayer on sight. Such a reprisal killing was accepted as the inevitable consequence of the first killing: that the murderer had paid a life for a life, and there was nothing for his relatives to do but to mourn his passing. As for the kinsmen of his victim, they were grateful to their member who carried out the reprisal killing. An ugly job had faced them all, and he had taken care of it for them. They were morally obligated to him and said so: "Our kinsman has soiled his own hands to spare us."

However, supposing the murderer he had killed in reprisal had a relative who swore to kill him, saying that there had been enough provocation for the first killing, then a grave situation would arise in the camp circle: two men out to get each other, the one in anger, the other in self-defense. They must be stopped before they could engage one another, and that was the council's problem.

In order to work out a resolution they carefully selected two men of prestige who were likely to command respect and sent them forth to dissuade the angry men. The spokesman handed a filled pipe to each, saying, "Take this to our unhappy relative and ask him to smoke it as a sign of his willingness to yield. Tell him that while there is discord in our midst our hearts are heavy. Remind him that it is every good Dakota duty to keep the peace, for peace is our heritage. It is in our very name." As previously mentioned, *Odák'ota* 'peace' literally means 'in a state or condition of Dakota-ness'. The initial *ó-* is a locative prefix here, signifying 'in', and Dakota, the tribal name, while it cannot be satisfactorily analyzed linguistically, connotes such ideas as friendship, fellowship, alliance, and understanding of the common tongue, usages, and customs.

It was a grave errand, and those who were selected as worthy to carry it out were honored and at the same time challenged to make a success of it. The fact of their being selected was an indication of their influence for good and hence of their worth to the camp circle. Even they sometimes returned unsuccessful because the troubled men were still too madly angry to be reasoned with and would not be placated by anyone at all. Other, equally worthy men went out to try next. Eventually, most men at enmity gave in, on the ground that one had come to them whom they could not ignore. Perhaps another reason was that their anger had abated meanwhile, so they accepted the pipe to signify that they were ready to be reconciled.

At the proper time they were led to the council tipi to smoke and feast together as friends, but still the situation was extremely delicate; the least false note could upset it. Knowing this danger, those who admonished them there had to choose their words carefully and speak without a trace of censure. Again those tribesmen who could afford it took part in the reconciliation by contributing gifts of value to "cool off their hearts" so that the two men might live again in peace. It was not the intrinsic value of those gifts that counted but what they symbolized: that they, the troubled men, did not stand alone. They had relatives who cared for their welfare more than they did for mere property.

The successful mediators expected and received nothing for their services, nothing material in repayment. Their reward lay in the added prestige their success had brought them. Once more they had proved themselves "men to be headed."

The facetious might say that it paid to become involved in strife and thereby to suddenly come into riches, but those who understand Dakota thinking know that a man did not endure such anguish simply for material gain. Only sudden anger, a desire for revenge, family or personal pride, or some such drive could motivate a Dakota into a bitter quarrel. In a milieu where giving rather than getting was glorified, where goods were in constant flux through the formal giveaway practice, where it was regarded as antisocial to amass worldly possessions for self alone, one who did so was immediately suspect. A material consideration could hardly be the reason.

Trial by ordeal, the second method of dealing with murderers, might be carried out in one of two ways, known as *čʼą́-ápsil-kʼiyápi* 'caused to jump over sticks', which I call *the hurdles*, and *wayáka-kíyuškapi* 'captive released'. The second seems to have been a later variant of the first ordeal, since a wild horse was used, and the Dakotas did not have horses until relatively recently.

Unless a murderer was immediately killed in reprisal by the victim's relatives, or ran away into the wild country and hid there, the council resorted to trial by ordeal according to whichever way they decided. Sometimes the council stepped in at the request of the slain man's relatives. As one informant explained it, "If the slain man's relatives were all men of peace who could not kill even in reprisal, they preferred to have the Great Spirit decide the punishment." Contrary to the wide-spread notion that every "Sioux" was per se a cutthroat who thrived on killing, there were actually men who chose life occupations far removed from the warpath because they refused to spill human blood. When asking about some detail of warfare, I sometimes got the reply, "I cannot say, for I do not know from experience. I have always been a man of peace. Ask my cousin [naming him] for he was a fighting man."

At the ordeal, the council included the four magistrates and a large body of worthy citizens drawn there by the gravity of the occasion: men who had right of entry and speech because of their standing in the community and past record. The following account of trial by ordeal with hurdles was told by White Horse, a Brule Teton from Rosebud. I give it in free translation:

My grandfather's grandfather witnessed this when he was a boy. These are my grandfather's words as he told them to me:

At the request of the slain man's relatives, who were all gentle and modest people, and unable to kill, the council decided on the ordeal with hurdles. Four pairs of uprights were set up at reasonable intervals along a runaway in front of the augmented council tipi, where the witnesses sat under its awning. They did not talk, but fanned themselves steadily with their eagle-wing fans, for it was a hot day. The camp police cleared the runway and a considerable space around it of stray dogs and heedless people who might otherwise crowd too close. Horizontal bars were laid on the uprights at a level suited to the murderer's height but they were not secured by tying. It would be possible for him to clear them safely, but only with supernatural help. Lacking that, even the slightest movement of air as the runner jumped would knock them off, they were so light and so precariously laid.

It was an ominous and solemn day, oppressive to everyone, but particularly to the relatives of the man on trial. Without any hope for a safe outcome for him, they were already wailing aloud as they waited in a group. Meantime the slain man's relatives stood all ready to shoot, for they had been instructed to let their arrows go the instant the runner failed, and so to inflict on him together the punishment none wanted to undertake singly.

The people thronged and milled about, children included. Here was something everyone dreaded both to see and to miss seeing. The murderer was led out of a nearby tipi and placed on the starting line. He was stripped except for a breechcloth. His hair hung loose, his face was unpainted, and his feet were bare. He waited for the signal *hóka-hé!* and when it was given he dashed away. In quick succession he cleared the first three hurdles. And then, at the fourth, almost before the eye could follow, he was down flat with many arrows impaling him.

The people took his failure at the fourth hurdle as supernatural judgment. The *wak'ą* could have helped him there but had not, because the verdict was that he must die. If he had cleared that last hurdle it would have been an indisputable sign that he had been exonerated. Let no man presume to condemn whom the Great Spirit had set free!

The alternate method, 'captive released', was used when the council so ordered. The setting was the same, except that instead of hurdles, a spirited horse that had never been ridden was brought there and the man on trial was made to ride it, bareback and without reins. Hitherto accustomed to complete freedom, the horse had to be held fast with the greatest difficulty while the man mounted him. Then, as soon as released, the horse went bucking and rearing and whirling about in a frantic attempt to rid himself of the man, who meanwhile hung onto his mane literally for dear life. It was said that the more callous among the younger males of the camp circle found grim sport in trying to frighten the horse still more, by waving blankets and boughs while screaming and shouting wildly. If and when the rider gave up and fell off, he was riddled with many arrows, as in the other type of ordeal. This kind was said to be even stiffer than the hurdles, the temper of the untamed horse making a fatal outcome all but certain.

I have to make it plain that only a few informants were able to recall ever hearing about trial by ordeal. The majority had never heard of it. Even so I feel safe in recording it because the few accounts obtained were given by reliable men, and, although they did not live anywhere near one another, their reports were in substantial agreement, even if some were scant and some full. I was unable to learn how regularly—and how often—trial by ordeal was necessary, as compared with immediate reprisal killings.

A gruesome variant was also reported, though not satisfactorily. It would seem that if the murderer had committed his crime wantonly, he must be made to realize the enormity of it, even after he passed his ordeal safely, before he could again life among free men. The slain man's corpse was laid out in the honor place of the council tipi, and the murderer was brought there to see it. In the presence of a small group of leading men he was caused to lie down naked on the naked corpse, live limb on dead limb, warm face on cold, the bodies of slayer and slain momentarily in contact entire. This was for impressing on the slayer the awful difference between life and death, and with the fact that he could never restore the life he had impulsively destroyed.

The worst was still to come. Next a piece of boiled meat was thoroughly rubbed over the dead man's mouth, and the murderer was caused to eat it. Then a lighted pipe was inserted between the cold lips, and the murderer was caused to smoke it. At last he atoned fully for his deed. "Few would be too fastidious to go through with this," one man said. "We all want to live — at whatever cost."

This phase differed from the accounts of ordeals in that no informant would take the responsibility for its authenticity. None would attribute it to an exact source and say, "So-and-so's grandfather told him of having witnessed it." The two men whom I heard discuss it were cautious and objective about it. They told it in the way that myths are told, as something remote and incredible, and both ended by saying, *keyápi* 'so it is said'. This is one indefinite quotative; the other, *šk'é*. Untraceable rumors and myths regularly close with either of these quotatives. Perhaps it would be safest to class it with the myths.

It is said that only the brave, the arrogant, or the contrite remained available for punishment. The cowardly murderer ran away to live indefinitely in the wilds. One who did so, who refused to face death for himself, was of all men the most despicable.

A more recent picture of the behavior of murderers was given me while I was working on this chapter by an extraordinarily intelligent man by the name of Josephe Irving. He was far past seventy. He said that as a boy he lived in a typical Dakota community, but conditions there had already begun to change. Ostensibly, the people were still free to live in their traditional way, but they were actually under the government and many old customs had already become a thing of the past. The ordeals were practically unheard of anymore. He related: "Within my memory, if one killed a fellow Dakota, he got away at once even though he might be a brave man, because it was necessary to separate himself from blameless people. Somewhere in the woods or the hills he stayed alone. Every night he wailed pitiably, and then the older people, upon hearing him, got up from their beds and went outside to wail in sympathy with him."

Mr. Irving explained that there was no longer any tribal punishment for murder, but self-banishment was the custom—until the U.S. government's laws were in full operation, and the guilty were subject to the normal processes of the law.

My most complete account of the third method of dealing with murderers, by adoption, was also my first awareness of it. It was given me by Simon Antelope, an aged Yankton who was universally honored for his integrity and still remembered for it. I quote in full, again in free translation:

My uncle remembered a time during his boyhood when a youth was slain by a fellow Yankton. As soon as it was known, his incensed male relatives met in private to decide how best to deal with his slayer. "What shall we do? Shall one of us go out straightway and finish him off? If so, which one of us? Or shall we ask the council to deal with him?" Thus they talked.

"My kinsmen, a great wrong has been done to us. We have been outraged and caused to weep without shame, men though we are. With our family honor at stake, who shall blame us if we go out to avenge ourselves?" Then he paused for a long time and puffed slowly on his pipe. When again he spoke, he had switched to another key.

"But, my kinsmen, there is a better way! And we must take that better way if we are to restore peace between ourselves and the slayer and his relatives. Go home now, and come back here this evening, each of you with the thing he prizes most, be it a horse or robe, weapons or apparel, to be a token of our sincere intentions. For behold, we are going to take the very man who has hurt us, and make him 'something-to-us' [*tákukičiyapi*, a relative], in place of the one who is not here [a common euphemism for the dead]. Was he your brother? Then this man shall be your brother. Or perhaps he was your son, or your cousin? As for me, he was my nephew, and therefore this man shall be my nephew. Our gifts shall be to him the sign that we want him to live among us as though he were our dear one returned to us. Let others take an easier course." And then he challenged them with this: *Okáǧe-ų́ťokečape dó!* 'We are men of a different make!'

If at first his kinsmen regarded this as a wildly impossible course, in the end they saw the wisdom of it. To retaliate in kind might take only an instant, but it would settle nothing. Rather, it would fan the flame of hatred on both sides all the more. The only real remedy was to win the murderer's heart through kinship kindness.

In due time the council was informed of the plan, and the fine presents assembled. And on the appointed day, the tribal leaders and the relatives of the slain man sat in the council tipi. When the murderer was led through the crowds outside and into the tipi, he came willingly. He had done this deed in his right mind and he was ready to pay. Whatever punishment might be meted out to him he was ready to take, like a man, but he did not want pity, so he hardened his countenance and looked neither right nor left. He would not have it said in afteryears, "Yes, I was there and I saw him. And how I pitied him! Like some hunted animal he furtively tried to read mercy in men's eyes!" He would not flinch, but he did not want pity. He was a man!

But when the council spokesman handed him a pipe, saying, "Smoke now, with these, your new kinsmen, for they have chosen to take you in place of the one who is not here. Those gifts yonder are for you, that you may be assured by them that your relatives want you to come and go in peace and safety among them forever. Whatever it was that provoked you to such a deed, forget it from this day on, and have no fear. You have their good will and loyalty forever,"

gradually the hard-set look on the man's face relaxed and tears rolled unchecked down his cheeks. The kinship appeal had trapped him completely. When the pipe was passed around he smoked it with his new relatives, and so he became 'something-to-them'. It was no wonder that he proved himself an even truer relative than many others who were related by right of birth, for the cost of his redemption had come high.

Of the several Tetons I questioned about this kind of adoption, which by its very nature must have taken place very rarely, only two recognized it from having heard of it somewhere, though they had never seen it take place. One was, of course, *Makʿúla*, the Oglala, who knew something about practically everything Dakota. On one point they all agreed: that it was consistent with the familiar pattern of adopting captives in place of relatives lost in battle. It is said that some went so far as to seek out during times of truce the very man who had killed their kinsman, and, if he could be identified, they took him for their relative in place of the one he had slain. In such a case, the relationship was sustained from a distance and gifts and messages between the man and his adoptive Dakota family were carried by travelers to and from the adopted man. His family bent over backward to be the very best of relatives to their generous adopters. If there was an intertribal gathering, adopters and adopted camped side by side in t'iyóšpaye style and extended every kinship courtesy to one another.

There is a further sidelight on this custom in the story of a Teton woman who came upon a Crow scout lying dead near the Dakota camp circle, where he had been spying when apprehended. She was well aware that if he had escaped he would have brought his whole war party back to raid her people. Yet she ululated in his praise and then wailed over him as a mother: Mič'įkši, mič'įkši! 'My son, my son!', she wailed, and then said, half-crying, half-singing, "Ah, why did you have to venture here? Ah, my brave son, just once too often have you been careless of your life! Mič'įkši, mič'įkši!" Real tears streamed down her cheeks as she tenderly stroked the youthful brow.

He was a handsome lad, obviously had standing back home, as indicated by his attire. When it was remembered that this woman's only son, also a mere lad, had been killed in battle by the Crows many years before, her present behavior was instantly understandable. For the moment she had adopted the Crow boy's corpse as a symbol of her son's slayer, whom she might have adopted in his place, had she had the opportunity. In weeping over this Crow, she was in effect mourning once more for her son.

In all the foregoing cases of quarrels and killings there was time to plan how to meet them. The men who merely quarreled were appeased by friends, on their own initiative. Those who threatened each other's life were reconciled through the work of peacemakers when their case was taken over by the council. The ordeals were arranged for, after the council had so decided. The adoption of a murderer demanded preliminary thought and preparation. However, there were still other situations within the camp circle that must be met immediately with preemptory action, because the general welfare was at stake.

For example, during the communal hunt, a hunter who did not wait for the starting signal but dashed out to get his buffalo ahead of the others must be punished at once. The offense was a grave one since it could result in a blind stampede of the whole herd, with a consequent loss of meat for the entire community. Hence the penalty must be swift and sure. Without waiting for orders the scouts patrolling and directing the hunt were within their rights when they inflicted the penalty, since they had sanction to act both from the tribe and the magistrates. Two or more went after the offender and struck him heavy blows, perhaps even knocking him off his horse. They went further; they shot his horse from under him and killed his dogs. They took sharp knives and slashed his tipi irreparably. It is no longer certain to what extent the degree of punishment reflected the severity of the offense. Maybe only when the herd got completely away as a result of the man's selfish and impetuous act was he penalized to the full.

What is quite certain is that this punishment, called *akíčʿita ktépi* 'soldier killed', was a disgrace. Few who aimed to be considered socially reliable at all times would want to incur this stern treatment so damaging to personal dignity and pride. Only a man of antisocial tendencies and without tribal standing would be so willfully disobedient.

Of all tribal activities, the communal hunt demanded the strictest cooperation. This was the one time when the needs of the whole people superseded even kinship obligations, if necessary. The scouts on duty must punish any offender, even if he be a respect relative. With typical directness, a Yankton informant said: "Yes, even if you were in avoidance relationship to the one deserving to be soldier-killed, the fact that ordinarily you owed him kinship respect must not deter you from your duty as a scout. As you struck the blow you could say, *"Hé hé hé! Tʿųkáši!"* 'Alas, my father-in-law!' He should understand by that you regretted your action but that you could not fail as a scout."

On the other hand, one Teton informant took a gentler, more compromising view. He related: "As a Kitfox on duty it was up to me once to penalize a respect relative. I hesitated, from habit, in momentary bewilderment, but then I solved my problem by calling on a fellow-scout to act in my place, which he did." It was an unpleasant duty in any case.

Instead of 'soldier-killing', the Yanktons used the term *akíčʿita apʿápi* 'soldier-striking', and perhaps that is a better term because, or so far as my information goes, no man was actually beaten to death, whatever his wrong. He might be badly bruised and his horse and dogs killed and his tipi ruined, but that would seem to be the whole of it. What he was made to suffer was the insult of being struck by a fellow Dakota. To any but the most obdurate and insensitive that was far worse than physical pain.

Except for soldier-killing, which was sanctioned, it was improper for responsible adults to strike one another under any circumstances. Merely to threaten to strike someone was to insult him: "And she even said she would hit me! As though I were a dog!" That was beyond the pale of human decency. Slapping was also too puerile for adults. Only small children might slap their way out of the restraining arms of a grown-up, and then they were said to "knock their way out." The only legitimate use of k'aškápa 'to slap, clap' was to clap the hands together in praise, for example, over a baby's first steps or attempt to dance. When a child in the government schools was slapped as punishment during the early days of the reservation, it was an unheard-of calamity. Who would strike a child! Mothers warned their friends: "What are we coming to? That white woman strikes children! So keep yours out of school. Our children are not animals"—as though striking children were that teacher's propensity.

Unlike soldier-killing (or soldier-striking), which was the province only of the scouts on duty, anyone might take steps to protect the people in an emergency. As one example, there is the story of a sex-maddened man who was posthumously dubbed Yellow Kettle.

His wife's attractive orphaned niece had not been living in his tipi very long before he began forcing his attention on her. That in itself was highly improper because uncles, whether actual or by marriage, belonged in the category of parental or protective relatives. Among the Dakotas uncles and nieces were no more eligible to marry than were fathers and daughters. When she resisted him in the woods, he stabbed her thighs and lopped off her breasts and then started to march her back to camp at spear's point, crying out to those who saw them coming back, "This evil girl must be punished for making advances to her uncle!"

But when they saw her stagger a few steps and then fall headlong, they set up an alarm that brought indignant citizens running with their guns. The man took refuge in a vacant tipi but they riddled it from all sides until he was dead. They found him lying with his head thrust into a brass kettle such as the U.S. soldiers used. It was from this hideous incident that, on the local winter count, that year was named "When Yellow Kettle Was Killed."

The winter count must be explained. It was the Dakota "calendar of years" in which the years were not numbered but named after their most significant happenings. It was recited backward, starting with the latest year. Events of tribal importance were included on all winter counts, but where something very unusual took place, that year was called by it, locally. Thus there were variations in the winter counts and perhaps no single one was universally accepted. The two records I have seen were on skin, and the small drawings depicting the events that gave each year its name were placed to make an ever widening spiral, with the oldest year remembered in the very center, and the years that followed it in successive order going round and round.

There are other stories, too, about people endangering the camp circle by going berserk from all manner of reasons. At least one man was reported as having gone mad because of his religious experience. When he went out alone to fast, it was the Bear who came to him in the form of a man, in his vision, and promised to help him throughout life as his spiritual mentor. This meant that in times of stress he would not stand alone for the Bear spirit would be with him for superhuman power.

When he reenacted the details of his vision in a public demonstration, as was customary, he so completely identified himself with a grizzly bear that he became violent. "He grew tusks," the narrator said, meaning that he lost all reason and became a bear enraged. With knives drawn he roamed growling about the common, all ready to stab whoever might dare to cross his path. Terrified women pulled up the anchoring pegs in the rear of their tipis and fled from the circle in all directions, many dragging small children by the hand and carrying babies on their backs, their little heads bobbing jerkily behind. It was a humorous performance since, luckily, no one was harmed before some strong men managed to sneak up on him and knock him down from behind and restore him to sanity by dousing him with cold water.

Except for Yellow Kettle's heinous deed the few sadistic instances reported have to do with non-Dakota victims, but there is no reason to suppose that any hardened character would hesitate simply because it was a fellow Dakota who angered him. Without doubt the most brutal was the man who once butchered the body of an enemy scout killed near camp. Those who watched in fascinated horror scarcely heard him explain as he worked: "You think this is bad? Well, so it is. But it is something that I must do; I and none other. So stand back!" Thus even he felt it necessary to excuse his act by attributing it to supernatural compulsion, by implication. He tried to clear himself by blaming it on his destiny.

My informant, Fast Whirlwind the Teton, was a small boy at the time:

He gave orders to send all women and children and 'weak-minded' [squeamish] men back to their tipis. But I wedged my way through the crowd unnoticed until I stood in the very front line where I could watch everything. The man trimmed a willow sapling and rammed it down the dead man's throat, and worked until it came out at the rectum—or so it appeared. Then with a powerful tug he pulled it through, all bloody. After that he painstakingly dismembered the body as animal carcasses were dismembered. That was where I learned that in man there is every organ found in the buffalo.

Fast Whirlwind never saw the "butcher" again but remembered him as a huge, austere man with terrifying eyes. He remembered also that women said: "Oh, is it not enough that the man was dead and harmless? How could one treat a human body so? The whole affair is evil. Even the dogs know it is evil for they will not go near, not so much as to sniff at it."

This kind of flagrant brutality was the mark of men who considered themselves impervious to public disapproval and independent of kinship sentiment, which is to say human sentiment. They might live in the camp circle with their families, but because they were erratic and unpredictable, gentler folk gave them a wide berth lest they be accidentally provoked to violence. If that happened, as in the case of the man who thought he was a grizzly, it would be for the men of the community to take him in hand to protect the people. Nothing was done to the one who cut up an enemy's body because, after all, it was dead and insentient, and it was not that of a Dakota.

Fortunately such men were the exceptions. The rank and file aimed to live innocent of 'killing within home', because the aftereffects of murder were too tremendous to be borne. I have already said that a coward ran away after killing a fellow Dakota and remained hidden in desolate places to escape punishment but that eventually he might turn up in some very remote camp circle. "Perhaps such men could no longer endure the loneliness and remorse," said one. But some did remain permanently in the wilds, and such men were known as *wič̓áša-watʼógla* 'wild, untamed men'. They were feared as though they were wild beasts, although no informant knew of their actually harming anyone who encountered them accidentally. They rather tended to run away or hide, to avoid face-to-face meetings with "good" men.

A brave man was willing to remain within reach for whatever punishment. Even if he had killed in self-defense, he, too, moved off and lived at a distance "for perhaps one moon or longer," though near enough to be reached. He went voluntarily because it was the proper thing to do. Enduring loneliness and deprivation for many days and nights, he at last underwent a sweat lodge purification and burned all his clothing that in any way savored of the foul deed, and only then was he ready to come home.

For the man with conscience, the life of a murderer even under the best of circumstances was an unhappy one. Although he was still and always a relative, since the Dakotas did not disown their relatives, yet all his life he imposed on himself the rules of conduct for murderers. He did not drink from a vessel but directly from the stream, putting his lips to the surface and drawing water in, as horses drink, or he took it up in his cupped hands. He ate only solid foods that could be held in the fingers and refused anything of the consistency of soup or porridge that must be served in a bowl because any bowl he used must ever after remain ceremonially unclean. Above all else he declined the common pipe when it was passed to him, if he found himself in a group. The saying was traditional: "Men with unclean hands do not smoke with others."

Thus, even though a murderer might properly return home after his self-imposed exile, things were never quite the same again. It was natural for people to feel a little uneasy with him. If he could forget himself enough to kill once, then why not again? He was no longer regarded as an altogether reliable member of society. Knowing this to be so, he was exceedingly adroit in his movements so as to avoid attracting attention. He went in and out quietly and spent much time alone. If a friend sought him out to talk with him, that was not his doing; he himself did not seek people out to talk with them.

One woman reported: "I had an uncle who once killed a man. When I was small, my mother seemed always to be keeping me away from him and when I asked why, she said, 'Your poor uncle is a very sad man because he once did a dreadful thing; he killed-within-home, so do not get in his way; he likes to be alone.'"

3

The Family

The Dakota family was not limited to father, mother, and child. Nearly always there were one or more close relatives present as part of the household. Because it hardly seemed natural not to have relatives outside of the nuclear family around, when such was the case it evoked the comment and query "You are living here — all alone?"

Those outside relatives might be the unmarried sibling or cousin of either spouse, or a widowed parent, aunt, uncle, or grandparent. If both parents of either husband or wife lived close by, for help and protection, they regularly preferred their own smaller tipi as long as both lived, but they were as much part of the family as if they lived in the home of their child. Their son or son-in-law, as the case might be, hunted and provided their meat, while their daughter-in-law or daughter looked after their other needs. For their part the old people shared the family responsibilities and made themselves useful in the ways they could. Even after their physical strength gave out, they continued to provide moral support.

The old woman helped by keeping the home supplied with certain necessities, which was her traditional service for as long as she was able. She spent an occasional afternoon collecting fallen dry wood for fuel, which she packed home in a bundle bigger than she by means of the leather packstrap she habitually wore as a belt, unconscious of it until she needed it. Fetching water for household use was also part of her task. At butchering time she jerked the meat for drying, cleaned and cared for the entrails that were used as food. These duties were not left to her exclusively; other women sometimes assumed them, but they represented typical old woman's work, after she could no longer do more minute, more exacting tasks.

Both the old man and woman were especially helpful in caring for the grandchildren, thus freeing their mother for her many duties. The old man did this sitting still, by controlling them at a distance as they played. He used gentle tones of admonition: "Take care, *t'akóža* 'grandchild', or you may hurt yourself!" Or he might say, "Do not quarrel with your playmates!" *Héč'ŭšni, t'akóža; tuwéni héč'a héč'ŭšni yé!* 'Don't do that, grandchild, nobody does so'—meaning, it is not proper. As for the grandmother, she seemed always aware of what went on, and if a child became unmanageable, she might come up from behind, pick him up, fling him expertly onto her back, and take him visiting along the line of tipis to divert him. Grandparents ruled the children admirably well, with only gentle suasion, most of the time. In fact, grandchildren were their happy preoccupation.

As he got older, the grandfather sat around, making useful little things such as toys, arrows, bowls of wood, pipes of catlinite. It pleased him to keep busy in that way. In good weather he sat outdoors, always off to one side, out of the way of the active younger folk. When he tired of his work, he laid it aside and sat idle, smoking and dreaming of the past—but always aware of the grandchildren.

When either mate died, without question the other belonged in the son's or daughter's tipi. Old men readily acceded to this new arrangement as something inevitable and moved in cheerfully, but most old women were reluctant to give up their home. They were usually able to maintain it even without a husband, since the son or son-in-law continued to supply them with meat, and they needed little else if they had that. Perhaps some unattached woman relative came to live with the old widow, in which case she also became part of the household. The more the better.

Young unmarried relatives in the home accepted their share of responsibility without demur. The males hunted and tended the horses, while the females helped with the wife's work or acted as companions for the children. Wherever one found oneself, the rule was to be useful. "Learn to be useful," mothers told their daughters, "so that if someday you are left alone in the world and must join yourself to another family, you will be liked." Even chance callers who dropped in for only a few moments fell to helping at some task while they chatted. If a woman visitor found her hostess shelling corn, for instance, she mechanically finished a few ears while talking before she went on. A poor caller was one who sat aloof, stiffly proud, withholding her hands. Such withholding of hands was proper and indeed, expected, only from specially invited guests seated at the honor place. In that case, it was formal behavior.

Without additional members the average family was not large. Children reaching maturity ranged in numbers from one to four in the home, rarely more, unless the man had plural wives and each had children. Then there might be perhaps six or eight children, and that would be an unusually large family. From all reports infant mortality was always high, and families lost their growing children rather more often than is the case today. In addition to this, there was another reason for small families. The Dakotas frowned on too-frequent pregnancies. Occasionally a family had only one, two, or at most three children, as a matter of principle. An exceptionally large family of lively little ones was regarded with kindly interest, almost as a curiosity, but if they had not been properly spaced, they were something of a reproach to their parents. Since continency was expected of strong men, a child per year was sure to invite whispered criticism of the father among the women.

The basis of the rule requiring proper spacing was a certain origin tale wherein the people were instructed to have their children "four winters apart." This was regarded as proper and admirable in theory. In practice it was not strictly observed, some children being spaced two and three winters apart. Couples who conspicuously disregarded this rule were sometimes loudly berated by some talkative old woman who grumbled, "What is the matter with those two? Have they no control? Do they care not about their poor child that they hasten to displace it—as though it were dead?"

Should an infant die, then it was proper and desirable for the mother to conceive again, as soon as possible. In that case there might be a new baby within the year. If it happened to be the same sex as the one who died they sometimes called it by the same name. "We were grieving— but now we are happy again. Our little one [naming the dead child] has returned!" It comforted them to think and say that. However, it was only in a manner of speaking, unless certain signs indicated to them that the new baby must be the other's separated twin spirit.

The records of thirty Teton families, covering the first decade of this century, were examined in old parish registers. They indicated that by 1910 eight couples over the age of fifty were childless. Of these eight two had never had offspring while the other six had lost all their children. The combined births recorded in these six families was thirty-four, and yet not one child was left alive; and in four of those families, all the deaths had occurred under ten years of age. Eleven babies had died at birth or a few days afterwards.

The other twenty-two families had children living in 1910, coming to a total of fifty-six, but it also appeared that nineteen of those families had lost at least as many children in infancy as had survived, although the records were far from conclusive. Quite possibly the parents did not report fully. When aged persons were questioned by me without warning, they could not always remember instantly how many babies they lost in all, having lost track through failing memory, particularly their babies who died at birth. Some couples did not agree on the exact number. We have to remember that there were no written records in their day, and many babies died soon after birth, still unnamed.

Of those twenty-two families with living children in 1910, only three appeared never to have lost a child. They had two, two, and four, respectively. When the family with four children were baptized together, in the late 1890s, according to the record the intervals between the children's ages were given as five, four and five years, respectively. "She [the mother] was a 'straight woman' and he [the father] was a real warrior," an old woman commented approvingly when we discussed the matter. Her implications were unmistakable. In her warrior husband's absences, the wife remained faithful; and he, a warrior at heart, was possessed of those rare qualities of stability, control, and moderation. The idea prevailed that a real warrior must have himself well disciplined to be stable and moderate in all things, sex included.

A partial check was also made of six families where there had been plural wives. This was not wholly satisfactory, however, because the facts as to the size of the family had to be gotten from conversations with some of their children, who were well along in years when questioned. Plural marriages are now a thing of the past. They could not know definitely the number of babies their parents lost when they themselves were small, or perhaps not yet born. As obtained, the average family with each wife bearing had 7.1 children. In one family there were three wives; in the others, two.

In all these cases the cowives were already sisters or cousins and were therefore "mother" to one another's children, even if they had had different husbands. If one cowife died, there was no question where her own children should go. They remained in their father's home, where, according to the kinship system, the surviving wife was their mother, and her children their siblings. All my informants spoke with gratitude and affection regarding the mother who brought them up. Unless I asked they did not think to separate themselves in a different camp from their half-siblings. They were all brothers and sisters without distinction.

What happened to the family when the cowives were not relatives of birth can hardly be determined by only two isolated cases. Nevertheless, a Sans Arcs Teton woman reported such a situation in which she was involved. "I was bought by a man of renown," she began. That would give her standing and confidence in the tribe; she was the head wife, the wife of his choice. "We got on well together, because I was wise and did not talk too much nor bother him by trying to change his mind on anything. I just let him alone to make his own decisions." After a few good years together, he was offered a beautiful young virgin for a second wife, on the plea that her parents coveted the man's protection and prestige for her. "When he asked my opinion about it, I said, 'This is your affair. You are not a child, so make up your own mind. I am not marrying the girl!'" Yet she hoped privately that he would accept the offer, which he finally did. She said:

Being an only child, I had always longed for a real sister. So now I made preparations for a feast and there I adopted her formally as my younger sister. But before long it was plain that she had ambitions; she aimed to outrank and perhaps eventually drive me away. I never cared for family strife because it was unknown in my childhood. The sense of expecting something to break at any moment was new and very distasteful. I wanted to get away from it, and, anyway, I was too proud to stay and fight with a mere girl over a man.

So she told the man that one of his wives must go and she would willingly be that one if he so decided. He did not answer, but he quietly began amassing some worthy gifts, including two fine horses. Then one day he sent the girl home with them, under proper escort.

Of course, he could have thrown her away publicly, for he was much annoyed with her; and then some man would have been proud to take her, for she was important in her own right and a truly beautiful girl, but he disapproved of that cruel practice of vain men. Besides, the girl had not merited such disgrace, for she had not been unfaithful but only contentious. Still, that made her a threat to the serenity of our household. Fortunately she had no children, though if she did have, they would have gone with her.

Under normal circumstances children belonged with their mother.

The second instance came to my attention by accident, while I was chatting with two sisters at a celebration. They told me that their father had two wives who were not relatives of birth, but who, as cowives, automatically became sisters, as was the custom. They got on well together and the family was harmonious.

But after both women had children, the mother of my two acquaintances died. As soon as the news reached her people in a distant camp circle, her aunt and uncle journeyed cross-country to claim her children. They called the surviving wife their niece, and told her, "You will be busy with all your duties; we will take these two little ones and bring them up." They promised to bring them back from time to time so as to keep them in touch with the brothers and sisters living in their father's home, and they kept that promise faithfully through the years.

Their aim was to forestall possible friction between the mother and the orphaned girls, thus anticipating the possibility that she might not be kind to them "because she was not their family relative," as their mother's own sister would be. This was a typical kinship gesture of loyalty, designed to meet the probable wishes of their dead niece that her children be free of family discord while growing up.

These two women were very pleasant, direct, and easy-mannered. Unbothered by their own frisky children who romped around and over them without fear of being scolded or cuffed, because evidently they had never been, the sisters vied with each other in relating details of their happy childhood with indulgent relatives. It was apparent that they had enjoyed an early life without tensions.

We must now look at the larger family of related households known as the t'iyóšpaye. The single household, composed of parents and offspring, might with average health and industry maintain itself well enough independently, but it was not complete and sufficient unto itself. T'iyóšpaye connections were vital to it, for the t'iyóšpaye rather than the family was the significant social unit.

As a matter of course, related families always pitched their tipis side by side, thus maintaining an inner circle of their own within the larger camp circle. This was the most pleasant and indeed the only arrangement for them, in an outward sense. Beyond their physical togetherness, the really important fact was *t'iyóšpaye* consciousness and *t'iyóšpaye* interaction. That must always exist, whether the related families were together or lived scattered far and wide among the various other camp circles. Their camping together and living cooperatively was only the physical expression of that inner unity.

If related families found themselves anywhere near one another, they automatically gravitated into one group, because they belonged together. If one family removed from the *t'iyóšpaye t'ípi*—that is, 'the group of relatives living', and camped elsewhere within the same circle—it needed explaining. Since it was "abnormal," there must be some reason for it: "We have been asked to assist at a ceremony across the common, that is why we are going. When it is finished we shall return." Without some such explanation, speculation was inevitable. "Why did that family pull out so suddenly? Has there been some trouble? Perhaps they do not get on together as relatives should? Who is to blame?"

At the same time, there was the utmost freedom for any individual or family to come and go at will, without permission or hinderance by anyone. The *t'iyóšpaye* was equalitarian, relying only on generational categories: grandparents, parents, collaterals, offspring, and offspring's offspring. All that held the group together in concord was kinship law, which controlled all interacting relationships there, and it was enough. The titular head was not formally elected from a panel of aspirants as soon as the former head died or became inactive. He gradually found himself in that post by virtue of the fact that the others naturally and regularly turned to him for counsel. He might be one of the parent generation, a father or uncle, or perhaps a youngish grandfather. He might even be one of the collaterals who had marked leadership qualities that gave him influence. And at least one woman is reported as having been titular head of her *t'iyóšpaye*. Natural dignity, wisdom, and tact in a leader were what gave stability to the group, but he did not give orders; he was no dictator. In no sense might he be called their ruler. He merely suggested and advised whenever the need arose, and he was respectfully heeded.

Even the titular head of the *t'iyóšpaye* did not always know which members went or stayed unless the matter came up incidentally, and then there was nothing he could say or do about it. It was not for him to keep tabs on every relative. At any time travelers from a distant camp circle might arrive with a message for someone there. "Your uncle lies sick unto death, but he waits to see the face of his sister's son and only then will he die happy." That was enough to send the nephew on his way, alone or with his immediate family, for an indefinite stay in his uncle's village. Meantime another member who had been living among his wife's people might return to stay, bringing his family. Thus the *tʿiyóšpaye tʿípi* remained at its average size throughout the years despite a slow but steady shifting of personnel in and out.

I may add that the Dakotas did not go about announcing their plans and saying goodbye to all and sundry, although they might make it a point of seeing someone who was gravely ill. They simply left, usually at dawn, and of course they shook hands with those immediate family relatives who were on hand. Otherwise it was quite proper to slip out quietly, and their doing so was accepted as nothing extraordinary. It was no slight in regard to those of whom they did not take formal leave. If they were coming back eventually, there was no making an occasion of leaving. If they were changing their residence and that fact was general knowledge, then as many outside friends managed to say goodbye as convenient. A social round of farewell parties or feasts was unheard of, and would not be approved of, because they would hinder the preparations of those who were leaving. It was no way for Dakotas to honor their friends. The time for such honoring was when a sojourner returned to stay, and was welcomed with hospitality. He was bidden to eat, here and there, or different people carried courtesy food to him. *Wóayapi* 'taking food' was an established custom.

The *tʿiyóšpaye tʿípi* was not made up of relatives of birth exclusively. Each spouse from the outside had a following of his or her own relatives who chose to come and live near him or her. These might be elderly parents, or aunts or uncles, and generally one or more unmarried collateral relatives. Such outsiders formed the affinal group. They did not keep apart in a distinctive camp, but lived scattered throughout the *tʿiyóšpaye tʿípi*, near the particular relative whose marriage had drawn them there. At the start these affinal relatives were like perpetual visitors constituting the periphery of the *tʿiyóšpaye tʿípi*, family relatives constituting the core. As children were born to whom both family relatives and affinal relatives had equal claim, the ties that bound them together became stronger. Some outsiders so identified themselves with their adopted *tⁱiyóšpaye* that in time their own distant camp circle seemed less important to them, although they never actually forgot their relatives there. The Dakotas clung to all relatives of birth. Disowning even the remotest one was out of the question: "It was not Dakota" (i.e., not human).

Five generations were to be found in every *tⁱiyóšpaye tⁱipi*. The middle, active generation would be the collateral relatives, say Ego and his siblings and cousins. Then there would be the parental, protective generation to Ego's, composed of fathers and mothers, uncles and aunts; and still beyond them, in the ascending scale, would be the grandparental generation to Ego's. In the descending scale would be the generation consisting of all the children of Ego's generation, sons and daughters and nieces and nephews. Finally there would be the grandchild generation. The few aged parents of Ego's grandparents were also called by the grandparent terms, *tⁱukášila* 'grandfather' and *uči* 'grandmother'. The terms applied to all ascending generations beyond the parents' generation ad infinitum, until they connoted "forebears." In the same way, the few babies of the oldest grandchildren were also called by the grandchild term, *tⁱakóža*, and that term connoted "offspring" when applied to all who would come later, to all descending generations ad infinitum. The gradations indicated by great- and great-great are not contrastive in Dakota; or at least there are no terms for them. One must explain a great-grandfather by saying, "My grandfather's father," or "My father's grandfather." Quite sensibly, there is only one term for grandchild, *tⁱakóža*, without distinguishing sex, because it cannot be known until the child is actually born whether it is male or female.

In a functioning group, there was a wide range of ages, roughly from around thirty to fifty or more years, depending on the relative ages of their parents. The middle-aged siblings and lateral cousins gradually took over the reins from their parents, who, however, did not automatically all become inactive at once. Many remained active, and they watched to anticipate any possible failures of Ego's generation to gain and hold both personal and group prestige, and tactfully steered them in the right direction.

Rather than the younger generation displacing the older and becoming the mainstay of the *tⁱiyóšpaye* on a prearranged day and with special ceremony, the leadership of the family and responsibility for the surviving parent fell on him or her as each one's father or mother died. By degrees this came about in the various families until all of Ego's generation were taking full initiative and functioning as their parents had before them. It was customary to hold off as long as a reasonable number of the older generation were still active and strong. Always there was reluctance to assume authority until the older generation was entirely through. This reluctance might have seemed an indication that the Dakotas were long inarticulate because they matured slowly; rather, it was that they deferred to their elders. It was proper to do so. The whole process of changeover was a deliberate, continuing cycle.

Even after Ego's collaterals were predominantly in leadership, if a father or uncle or even a grandfather still lived who had exceptional qualities, they wanted him to sit at their conferences because he was needed. Thus he functioned as their elder statesman, to whom the younger men gave heed whenever he chose to counsel them. Such a man often acted as the *t'iyóšpaye* spokesman also. It was such a relative who advised the adopting of the murderer instead of killing him.

I have already said that the family unit was an integral part of the *t'iyóšpaye*, and this relationship consolidated the strength of the group. Nevertheless, the family retained its privacy, integrity, and distinctiveness. Related families respected one another's right to make their own decisions and plan their own course of action; whatever one family wished to do was its own affair. At the same time, it was as components of the *t'iyóšpaye* that the family made its real impact on society. The feasts and gifts they gave cooperatively, the rites and ceremonies they staged with assistance from one another, their correct observance of kinship rules among themselves—all such items were an index of their group character, which earned them their tribal standing. Moreover, each member was personally responsible. Any untoward act, even of a mentally limited person among them, could fasten an uncomplimentary nickname on the entire *t'iyóšpaye*. Examples of such names were remembered.

Wood and water were entirely free to all. A woman needing fuel for emergency cooking went to another's tipi for it. The words they exchanged were casual and few. "Sister, I am taking some wood." "Of course. There it is." If the owner happened to be absent, the other took it anyway, because she would be just as indifferent about her own wood or water, in reversed circumstances.

However, there was a slight difference with regard to taking food supply—meaning buffalo and other meat—although it was proper to be just as liberal in sharing them too. Only in extremity might food be taken without asking. Women respected one another's right to dispense their own food as they liked, always assuming that they would be generous with it. Quite possibly this different attitude was due to the fact that, whereas wood and water were for the mere taking wherever it was found, meat especially was hard to obtain and required a measure of particular skill and sometimes involved danger. It might even require supernatural aid, in which case only the hunter who was en rapport with a spirit-brother could obtain it.

Each man brought his kill to the tipi where he lived. After unloading it outside, he relinquished all right to say how it was to be used, although he might on occasion ask his women folk to prepare a choice part so that he might feast a few friends. Except for that the meat became the property of the wife, mother, sister, or aunt who owned the tipi. A family that shut itself inside the tipi and ate in privacy was behaving extraordinarily, contrary to the custom of hospitality and generosity. Such a family was not admired, because it did not share food. The majority shared as a matter of course. Good-sized pieces of the raw meat were distributed among those families of the t'iyóšpaye where there was a need because there was no hunter. The rest was for the owners, and all that could be spared was promptly jerked for drying. In butchering the Dakotas followed the musculature of the carcass so that each piece was a separate muscle intact.

While sharing some of the raw meat and drying some, the woman of the tipi cooked generous amounts for immediate enjoyment and served it to any relatives who dropped in. They did not have to be hesitant in coming, for it was expected. Some frankly admitted, "I was starved for fresh meat, so here I am!" "Of course, this is the place to come," the hostess said as she prepared to offer the food to them. When they had fresh meat, she would go to them. Meat was served liberally so that they would have something to carry away. It was customary to eat as much as one wished of the portion served and take the rest. To leave any food in the bowl was to insult the hostess. The food so taken was called wat'éča, an idiom literally meaning 'something new'. Many neighbors outside the t'iyóšpaye were also invited to eat, in accordance with the rule of hospitality, but that was not the end of it. The people went out of their way to hail even passerby—not excluding total strangers—"Why do you hasten past? We have meat!"

T‘iyóšpaye loyalty and interdependence were desirable as marks of group solidarity and stability, and consequently were good to foster. They could be demonstrated in various ways, all of which were for honoring one another. A family preparing a feast to memorialize their dead or to honor their child at his huká or other rite, were made proud and happy by the assistance of their relatives, whose gesture was heart-warming to them, no matter how able they might be to stand the cost independently. More than once have I seen this happen: a feast all ready to be served, and a great circle of guests waiting for the inevitable preliminary speeches; and then some relatives arriving with huge kettles of cooked food to add to the menu.

It was not the extra food—there was plenty already—but what it revealed that was important: that the spirit of mutual dependence among t‘iyóšpaye relatives, and of mutual readiness to justify one another's faith in it, was healthily present among them. That lively awareness of mutual obligation to honor relatives was what men were judged by. For, to be generous in behalf of relatives was essential in Dakota society. People were lauded for it: "How well these relatives treat one another! So should all men do. It is the Dakota way!"

Another, even more spectacular way of honoring a relative was not to give him something directly, but to cause him to give to someone else at the giveaway ceremonies. During the festivities there, a man or woman might give away a horse or something else of value with the public announcement: "My relative [naming the man, woman, or child] gives this!" The official drummers and singers immediately raised a song of praise in which they named the one who had been honored, as though he had parted with something valuable of his own. The honor to him was multiple. He had been honored by a relative and he had been praised in song, and presently the recipient of the gift came to thank him by "stroking his face," which was the traditional gesture of gratitude for such a gift. The recipient knew well who had provided the gift, of course; but he had benefited from the one in whose name it had been given. Thus was a feeling of good will spread far around, to include the real giver, the one caused to give, and the one who received.

In explaining the manner in which relatives in the *t'iyóšpaye* expressed loyalty and interdependence, I may have given the impression that honoring was restricted to relatives. That was not always the case. On occasion someone might want to honor an outsider by giving at the formal giveaway in his name, or by some other equally worthy gesture. One woman recalled the following, which bears on this.

A humble little man without sisters to honor him became a father, but the fact, important to him alone, went unnoticed. She felt sorry for him and gave the baby a *p'óštą*, an elaborately ornamented baby cradle or carrier, which was a sister's prerogative to provide for her brother's child, in his honor. When she presented it, she placed the infant in it with her own hands and called its father her brother, and, of course, he was happy to have a sister.

"It pleased me to make this gesture and I supposed that the matter was closed," she said, but evidently the unexpected honor had overwhelmed her adopted brother. He moved away shortly, but about three years later, he led a small girl to her doorway, during a tribal reunion. The child held the rope by which a beautiful bay mare was following. As he caused her to surrender the rope to the woman he explained, "My daughter has wished and intended for three years to honor her aunt."

To give at the giveaway is called *itúȟą*, literally, 'to give in vain, to give aimlessly'. That is idiomatic, of course, for 'to give freely, gratuitously', without prior stipulation—without prior agreement as to what one would get out of it, or when. Perhaps designating the recipient publicly did obligate him somewhat for people would begin to think, "When will he act, in his turn?" The purest kind of *itúȟą*, then, would seem to be the occasional undesignated gift, to the needy, *ničá*. Said one informant:

> My father did not admire the custom of naming the recipient, or giving to him publicly. "That is for show, and is nothing but barter," he would say. "One 'gives in vain' only when one gives where there is no possibility of a return gift."
>
> And so, when the Omahas came to sing, and among them was a wretchedly poor boy, obviously an orphan, he put the bridle reins of his finest horse into my hand and caused me to lead it to that boy, which I did. The Omaha boy was so startled and happy that he left the horse standing and followed me until I returned to my father,

and there he stroked my face, while audibly thanking me breathlessly—in a tongue I did not know. Clearly, the boy was never going to be able to make me a return gift.

In this way that father honored his son, by causing him to "give in vain." To honor another by giving in his name as though he had given was called *itúȟʼąkʼiya* 'to cause (one) to give'.

Even better, because it included an element of happy surprise for the one caused to give, was to give in his name without first notifying him of the coming honor. Then he would learn of it only when the recipient came and stroked his face gently. It would fill him with pride and satisfaction that his relative had so magnificently honored him, without his knowledge. Back of it all, he realized that sooner or later he would be impelled to honor his relative in a return gesture of some sort, and that would be a pleasure. Of course it might entail some difficulty and sacrifice and might even cause him to go into debt, but all that did not detract from his present happiness.

If someone was about to give a feast and needed kinship assistance, his relatives should see that need and supply it unasked, if they were able. This mutual obligation made the average Dakota very observant and imaginative in behalf of others. If it had not been possible to anticipate an occasion where they might properly help, perhaps something like this took place, as told by an Oglala widow: "When my boy lay sick unto death I told him, 'Son, please get well. If you do, I will give a horse to the needy in your name.' This was my vow, and so, when he did get well, I planned a feast. But I needed kinship help, for I had no suitable horse for the major gift. So I sent word to my brother [father's brother's son] that I needed a horse. I knew that when my *hakáta* realized my need he would quickly manage to supply it." The brother did not refuse her, his respect relative, but instead proudly put himself in debt to procure a handsome horse, having none at the time. The term *hakáta* designates collaterals of opposite sexes, who owed each other the highest deference.

Relatives did not systematically pair off for life, each exclusively reciprocating the honoring of the other. One gave now to this and now to that one, as it was timely and convenient. It was the will to give, to show that mere property was nothing in comparison to one's relative, that was important. Nor was this kind of honoring either hurried or frequent. Months, even years, could pass without a suitable opportunity for a spectacular demonstration of this kinship loyalty. The giving was spontaneous and unexpected, without pressure, and it crisscrossed among the different members of the *t'iyóšpaye*.

In such ways did the *t'iyóšpaye* earn good report, which elevated its standing in the tribe. At the same time that the conscientious member helped to raise his group's prestige, he enhanced his own and strengthened his position in the tribe at large. Visiting camp circles heard of his good works and carried his name throughout Dakota land as a man of character and worth, one who could always be relied on; in short, as a "good" Dakota. Because his utterances were "weighted with good deeds" of hospitality and generosity—mere words counted for naught—he earned the right to be listened to whenever he chose to speak. Of such as him was the larger, deliberative body at the council tipi composed.

This is not to say that the standard personal qualities of honesty, truthfulness, fairness and courage counted for nothing; certainly they did, but they must be demonstrated within the framework of kinship. No doubt a man could have those qualities and remain independent of his relatives, but then he would not be a successful functioning member of Dakota society.

Despite their readiness to part with property whenever the occasion appeared, the Dakotas were not disdainful of material possessions. Far from it. Nor were they communistic to the extent of pooling all their goods to be shared by rationing. What a man owned, what he succeeded in acquiring, was his by natural right. Goods, tipis, horses, weapons, and clothing were privately and individually owned, even by small children, and a person was free to withhold them if he chose. There was no authority vested in magistrate, council, or titular head of a *t'iyóšpaye* to pry them from him. Even a father could not command his son to give something away against his will. If the son wished to give something away, even his best, the father could not properly forbid him. Was it not his own?

Kinship alone had that power and it was a compelling power, making an individual give his finest for a relative's sake. Public opinion pressed on him, too. He could not throw off the feeling that people were watching him and he imagined their saying, "Now. Here is his chance to play the man. We shall see!" To withstand such a challenge was more than the average Dakota was able.

Yet there were some who did reject their kinship obligations, and because of it were regarded as inhuman, queer, "lacking a heart." The story is told of one man, who in the early reservation days returned from an eastern school with a firm conviction to copy the white man in his economy. Immediately he separated himself from his *t'iyóšpaye* and went out on his own. He took up land far from the center of the tribe and commenced to live the independent life of a white man.

Ignoring all normal kinship privilege and responsibility, he neither accepted from nor gave anything to his relatives and sneered at the traditional honoring. The old much-vaunted mutual loyalty and interdependence were not for him! When a kinsman's need was pointed out to him he replied: "I am setting out to care for only myself and my wife and children. No one can make me do imprudent things with sentimental talk about our fine old ways! These are new times. Consider how the white man looks out first and only for himself. That's what I am doing, for it is the only sensible way. If all Dakotas would do the same, then everyone would be better off."

He was for a harmony of self-interest that would elevate all, but the people would have none of it. Instead they thought him peculiar and regarded his attitude as vicious and harmful to society. "Going east to school has ruined our relative," his *t'iyóšpaye* members agreed regretfully. "Expect nothing from him. He has lost all loyalties." Outsiders said, "He is freakish—and no longer a man." Though they could see that he was succeeding materially, his example touched them not at all. What a way for human beings to live! He was a bad Dakota; he had in fact outlawed himself by not conforming to the established tenets of society.

His family relatives continued to be loyal, at a distance, and spoke of him still in kinship terms. Because he had failed them was no excuse for them to fail him; that was not the Dakota way. But others dismissed him with the ugly epithet, *hiyáze č'á* 'hair stands on end as it were', an idiom implying that he was no longer a human being, but an austere, hostile, inhuman being; in short, a beast. He became a lonely and cantankerous man, though materially better off than many. Whenever he spoke, he spoke as an agitator.

In contrast is the instance of one who felt his obligations almost too acutely. When one of his women collaterals gave a feast in his absence, without first acquainting him of her plans and giving him a chance to help her as a kinship gesture, he took it as a slight, even though his ignorance of the pending affair had undoubtedly saved him from parting with property, or perhaps going into debt to help her. He looked positively wretched as he talked of it: "I have searched myself carefully many days. I still cannot see what I ever did in the past to make my cousin doubt me. Why did she not give me a chance to help her? Why did she deprive me of the privilege of honoring a respect relative? I have been ashamed and saddened ever since." Ideal kinship responsibility was something like that.

4

The Home

The common term *t'ípi* is a Dakota word that literally means 'they dwell'. Since the passive voice is expressed in Dakota by the third-person plural active voice, *t'ípi* may also mean 'it is dwelt (in)'. Used nominally *t'ípi* means 'home, dwelling'.

In shape the traditional Dakota home resembled a slightly compressed cone of more nearly oval base, the narrow end towards the door. The tipi was not symmetrical from the side view, the distance from top to base being a trifle longer in front than in the back. This gave the correctly erected tipi a proud look: head up, chest high, backbone all but vertical. The smoke vent overhead was directly above the fire inside. The four essentials were (1) the lodge poles, (2) the tent or cover, (3) the lacing pins, and (4) the anchoring pegs.

In olden times the tent was shaped from dressed bullhides cut to pattern and sewed with stout sinew. In later years it was made of canvas. When correctly made it fitted smooth and taut over the pole framework. The poles were preferably of pine because of its strength and slenderness. All women aspired to owning pine lodge poles someday, but not all were ever that fortunate — except those who roamed near the Black Hills. Cottonwood or box elder were satisfactory enough but only until they might be replaced with pine. Doubtless, other woods than cottonwood and box elder were also used, but those were the most usual.

For short trips only the tent was carried, and then willow poles were quickly trimmed of their branches and used without removing the bark. They were a cheap substitute, to be discarded as easily as they had been got, for willows were generally slender without sacrifice of strength. Only certain men were expert at selecting, cutting, and preparing them. Finally the poles were shaped to a point at the heavy or base end, so that they could be planted firmly in the ground for a long stay in one place.

Figure 1 illustrates the manner in which a tipi is set up. The three poles marked X are tied together and set up as the tripod that supports the other

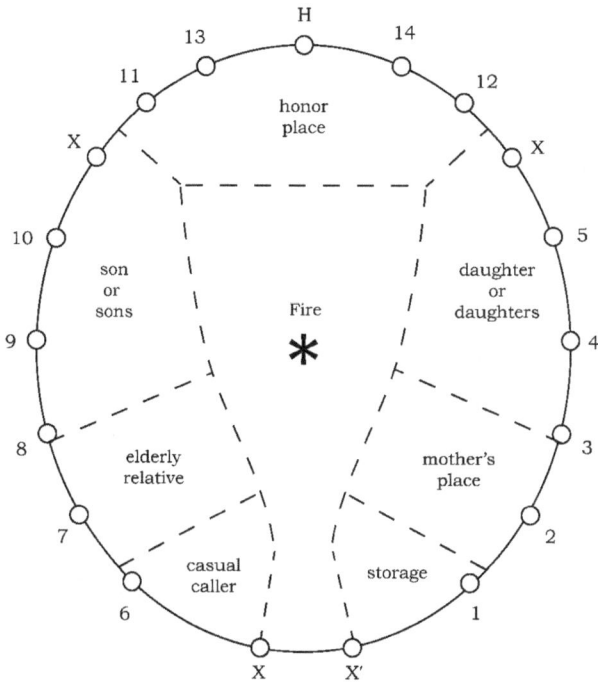

Fig. 1. Arrangement of poles and rough floor plan and space order in a Teton or Yankton tipi. "For the Santees, if my information is correct, 'casual caller' and 'storage', 'mother's place' and 'elderly relative', and 'daughter or daughters' and 'son or sons' must be reversed. 'Storage' refers to space for wood, water, and cooking materials." Rendered by Travis Myers, American Indian Studies Research Institute.

poles. The pole marked X' goes up next, and with front pole X, forms the doorway. Then poles 1 to 5 are laid on in that order. These are set to make a spiral, as though they were twisted on one another. Next, poles 6 to 10 are laid on, and they, too, should make a spiral arrangement, but unless the one who is putting up the tipi is an expert, they will get out of order. At this point the rope hanging downward by which the tripod was tied is carried around clockwise two to four times, and thus it is wound around the cluster of poles. After this, poles 11 to 14 are raised and fitted in wherever there is a good space for them, but these are not included in the wrapping. The tent holds them in place. Finally, the hoisting pole H is set in place with the tent, which is tied to it at the top. Now the two sides of the tent are carried around to meet in front, and there they are laced together with slender wooden pins, usually of chokecherry or plum sticks.

Now the woman who is making the tipi goes inside and works very carefully to set the poles at reasonably equal spaces around the room. She moves them forward and back until they are so placed that the framework is big enough for the tent, until the tent fits smoothly over it. Then she drives the anchoring pins into the ground all around. She puts down the pegs at the entrance way first, then at the other two tripod poles, then at the hoisting pole. After that she anchors the tipi at strategic points here and there until all the pegs are used. This is to prevent the tent from being pulled away, as could happen if she began at pole and drove the pegs in order. Finally she takes the two remaining poles and fits their tips into the little pockets at the tops of the wind flaps outside, and by placing them judiciously with reference to the wind, she braces and guys the flaps into proper position.

Women usually built their own tipis, without the help of men, unless the tipi was an oversize one with heavy and long poles. Then men had to help and place the poles according to the owner's directions. Tipi building was a feminine art; no man who was self-respecting would care to be an expert at it, but men were very agreeable when helping, and took instructions tractably from their wives or mothers.

When the finished tipi stood with both flaps extended at an angle of around forty degrees, on a sunny day the effect was that of a boat in full sail and as beautiful a sight against the blue. A perfectly designed tipi perfectly erected was pretty close to a work of art.

One other feature in this connection should be discussed here. Since a tall tipi must be laced far above normal reach, at the top, some youth or small man who was accustomed to "climb the *tʿičʿéška*" was called in. He began at the bottom by inserting the lowest pin above the entrance way, then the next and the next. When he could no longer reach, he began to climb as he worked, making his own ladder and bracing his feet on the pins already in, as if they were rungs. *Tʿičʿéška*, or *wičʿéška*, is the name for the part of the tipi that must be laced together, the part between the wind flaps and the doorway. *Čʿéška* means 'chest'; hence *tʿičʿéška* is the 'tipi chest'.

Ceremonial and bridal tipis were made in such a way that they overlapped below the entrance and were pinned together with two lacing pins exactly as in the *tʿičʿéška*. This required stepping higher than normal in order to enter. Sometimes fastidious families who wanted a finished look to their tipi also made theirs with this feature. In that case a special door was made by bending a long, green stick into a half-oval curve, and lashing the ends to a short crosspiece at the top. This frame was encased with the same material as the tent, skin or canvas. Along the crosspiece a wide strip was added, having two holes through which the lowest or second to the lowest lacing pin was inserted, thus fixing it to the tipi. The door, hanging from this fixture, rested over the entrance. For ventilation it was sometimes flung off to one side by giving a twist to the flexible part at the top; then on the underside, now uppermost, could be seen the two double strings that were attached midway and a few inches in. To secure the tipi for the night, these strings were pulled inside through corresponding holes in the tent and tied to the first pole on either side. Such a door was very neat and gave the tipi a trim look.

As a rule, though, most homes used a skin or blanket curtain over the entranceway, attached to the top by a lacing pin, in the same way as the oval door was placed, and allowed to hang free in front of the entrance. Others braced such a curtain crudely with a horizontal stick tied on midway. At night this stick was pulled inside, and the ends were caught between the tent and the two poles on either side of the entrance, although it was not too secure. Dogs could crawl in under it.

It is said that an average "large tipi" required from nineteen to twenty-one poles, including the two outside for controlling the wind flaps. Important families preferred even larger tipis because they needed ample space for their retinue of extrafamilial relatives and their many guests. The largest tipi I ever knew was made for my mother at her request and was of canvas, for skin tipis were by then a thing of the past. Everyone conceded that it was extraordinarily large and high. It was set up in our backyard during the summer months for us children to enjoy. The day it was brought out and erected was to me the official beginning of summer. My mother had the tent made because of pure sentiment, for we did not need it for space. She was troubled, I think, by the fact that already many women were making their tipis without care for details, or not making them at all but using instead the not so picturesque, though admittedly more practical, commercial walltents.

We children slept in it nearly every night on cots placed around close to the poles. It was very high and impressive, but I never knew how wide it was in feet. I remember that there was a great deal of space in the center to play in. Sometimes we counted the stars visible through the smoke vent;

sometimes we made a fire in the center at bedtime and then laid watching the smoke rise and go out through that opening far overhead, in a nearly vertical line, so well was the tipi proportioned. On rainy nights the water-tightened canvas became a mammoth drum on which the raindrops played strange tunes in ever-changing rhythms. The sense of security inside as against the stormy world outside was delicious and comforting beyond words. The memory of it is unforgettable.

It was from that tipi, the only one I intimately knew, that I learned the names of the various parts, the poles and their special functions, the correct way of setting the flaps to the prevailing wind in order to create the proper draft, and the several progressive steps in erecting a tipi. I think perhaps I could do it today. Only much later in life did I see a skin tipi, in a museum.

An aged Teton named Standing Elk described for me the home of his father, a Sans Arcs chief, saying: "It was the largest in our entire band and people even said it was the largest of all time." By his reckoning it must have been a giant of a tipi. He paced off what seemed to me to be twenty feet, which he said was the distance from side to side. It would of course be longer from front to back, but he was drawing on his memory and I was estimating, without a tape measure. He said that the better parts of forty bullhides went into the tent and this made it so heavy that for easier handling it was made in two equal parts—a rare feature and perhaps unique among Dakota tipis, though I cannot verify that.

Because it was in two parts, two hoisting poles instead of one were needed. This accounted for the even number of poles, thirty-two, whereas ordinarily the number was odd. The halves were first laced together all the way up the center back and were then carried around the framework to meet in front. There they were again laced together in the regular way in the section below the smoke vent and above the entrance. The entire tipi made such a heavy load that it took two mules to haul it on camp moves, in two even loads consisting of the two halves of the tent, the poles, the lacing pins and anchoring pegs, and the stakes for guying the wind flaps, all equally divided.

After a tipi was erected, experts could detect the least mistake in tying and setting the poles. If the tripod was incorrectly arranged for tying, or if the other poles were not placed in the proper order, the tipi stood lopsided and the cover hung loose over the framework. This made it weak against windstorms. Such a tipi was said to be tied "left-handed." Left-handedness was often jokingly derided, and a person born with that peculiarity was rather expected to do things a little less than perfectly, although that was not always so. Indeed, some of the most skillful workers in porcupine quill embroidery or with beads were left-handed.

In the camp circle the front of the tipi was kept fairly clear, and even neat in its primitive way. If there was an outdoor fireplace or a drying rack for meat, it was placed a little off to one side and never directly in front, where it would interfere with the parade track. Not much else belonged in front. For a long stay, the fireplace was a shallow trough, shaped like the firebox of a range. For a temporary camp, the fire was laid flat on the ground.

Nobody can say when or how the Dakotas first learned to boil their food. In olden times they boiled meat in the paunch of the buffalo, and after metal kettles were obtainable, it was a common sight for a tripod to stand over the fire with an iron kettle hanging from it directly over the heat.

During a Fourth of July celebration I once witnessed a demonstration of the ancient practice of boiling meat in the rumen of a buffalo. Stout stakes were set in a circle about two and a half feet in diameter, and the rumen was tied to them in such a way that it hung suspended like a huge kettle. While this was being done, small hard rocks "the size of an infant's head" were being heated until they were at white heat. Then they were carried on forked sticks to the "kettle" and dropped into the water inside it. Thereupon the water started to boil, and as it boiled very vigorously, strips of fresh meat were thrown in. Not too long afterward they were speared out with sharpened willow sticks and passed around. I had a piece, which was done to a medium rare. It was deliciously juicy.

The very rich soup was then ladled out to those who came with suitable vessels to receive it, and presently many old people were drinking "real broth" with relish. When it was all gone, the cooks cut up their erstwhile "kettle," now well done, and ate that up. Only a pile of stones below, and the stakes, remained. Dakotas did not overboil their buffalo or cow meat but preferred it slightly rare. Meat that had been cooked a long time to tenderize was tasteless to them. If it must be tough, very well; it was still preferred rare. The juicy flavor was the thing desired.

Boiling in this manner was outmoded when kettles became available. I was told that it was best done by men who learned it on the warpath. At the time I saw this, only men prepared and served the meat.

During the daytime, if the man of the household was not out hunting or busy elsewhere, he might be seen sitting outside the doorway, near the tipi, working at something. When his friends came by, he put it aside to talk and smoke with them, but they would not sit too far out from the tipi. Very soon his wife would appear with food for them.

The real area of activity was the "backyard," especially for the women. There, partially hidden by the tipi from the eyes of passerby, they felt free to lay aside their wraps—which were always worn in public—so that they might work unhampered. They tanned hides for clothing and tipis; they painted rawhide boxes and bags and the parfleches, flat rawhide enve-lopes, for dried meat; and they preserved surplus meat, wild fruits and vegetables for winter use. Sometimes they pegged down a new hide and worked at removing the hair and the pieces of meat or fascia adhering to the other, inner side, with sharp fleshing tools. This kind of work was the most exacting, tiring, and difficult of all women's work, and not everyone was adept at it. If a feast was pending, several women built an elongated fire there and cooked the food in wholesale fashion. Occasionally women friends could sit together back there to chat and do fancy work with a modicum of privacy.

Little tipis and impromptu shelters for various uses stood scattered about, like the outbuildings of a country house. Perhaps a sweat lodge with its pile of stones outside, a retiring tipi for menstruating women, an aged relative's home, a play tipi for the little daughters, and often a little hut for the dog and her litter—such were some of those structures in the backyard.[1]

Most of the dogs were impersonally owned by the family, and only one here and there was somebody's special pet. Cats were unheard of until introduced by Europeans. Magpies and crows were formerly caught young and trained to talk, their tongues first split, so I am told. I never saw this. As a rule, however, the Tetons did not try to domesticate wild animals for pets. Now and then a hunter might bring in a coyote or bear cub during a long encampment at one spot, but such pets usually managed to escape sooner or later, principally because their owners were not bent on hold-ing them in captivity. The coyote particularly never lost its wild look and only lived to escape. It is said that little girls sometimes kept pet raccoons but that such animals in the tipi were a nuisance because they stole food constantly, getting at it with almost human cunning.

I have said earlier that holy men—that is, those who believed themselves to be in league with some spirit-brother and had successfully demonstrated its power in a public ceremony, were justified in decorating their homes with private symbols. Since such symbols had meaning only for the dweller in the tipi, self-expression ran riot here. The tipis of lay people, if decorated at all, were decorated purely for looks, and those decorations must conform to a standard style. A family did not suddenly decide to live in a fancy tipi, and then without further ado proceed to make one. Always there must be some specific reason for doing so; perhaps, for example, a bridal tipi would be needed shortly, or a creditable tipi to house a pending family ceremony. Only after it had served its initial purpose might it be used as a home.

The standard style of decoration consisted of three kinds of items: (1) many small hanging ornaments attached at two-inch intervals along the outer edge of the wind flaps and in pairs down the front of the tipi, one where each lacing pin went in and one where it came out. From a distance they looked like two colorful parallel lines drawn down the front of the tipi, until a breeze picked them up and flipped them awry; (2) three embroidered disks of heavy skin, uniform in size, sewn onto the tipi on each side and at the center back, all at the same height from the base, approximately at eye level; and (3) a single panel of porcupine quillwork, attached to the top at the back, like a little collar for the tipi.

I saw a set of these decorations, tied into a sugar sack, which the owner had removed from an old tipi belonging to her grandmother and kept until she could make a new tipi and use them, but she never did. I examined them and found them to be harmonious as to colors, but the three disks and the panel were badly weather-shrunken, so that they were evidently much smaller than when new. The hanging ornaments were also no longer flat and stiff. The work of these last was very intricate and gave the different colored quills a checkerboard appearance, as though they had been braided. They were wrapped tight around strips of rawhide. A tipi decorated in this conventional manner was called a t'ióskapi. It takes its name from the verb óska, which refers to the wrapping of the rawhide strips. T'í is a classifier and many parts of the tipi have this prefix in their name. Sometimes wí is substituted, which, I am almost sure, is a colloquialism.

Inside the tipi the space across the rear, beyond the fireplace, was called čatkú or t'ič'átku, a word whose exact meaning is doubtful except for the initial t'í. I shall call this section *the honor place*, though that is not the literal meaning of the Dakota name, because especially honored guests were usually seated there, and in certain indoor rites this section was venerated and people tiptoed there much as we do in the chancel of a church.

In the tipi of a holy man, this was the holy of holies, where the tokens of his holiness were regularly placed. For instance, there might be a square of pulverized earth, consecrated by sprinkling it with red ocher powder, or, whenever possible, with down dyed a bright scarlet. The down, being sensitive to every slightest movement of air, as though it were alive, symbolized a Presence, for movement meant life, and life was *wakᶜą́*, a mystery. Onto this altar all libations were poured and all food offerings were cast. The residuum from the pipe after each ceremonial smoking of it must not be carelessly blown out, but carefully spilled there, for it was sacred. The holy man occupied the *čᶜatkú* by himself, and only another holy man who was his guest might presume to approach it.

Always there were those who were satisfied to live carelessly and poorly, without pride, but self-respecting families strove for and attained the best in both interior decoration and practicality, until there was a death in the home, at which time a nicely kept tipi was temporarily bereft of ornamentation as a sign of mourning.

As one entered the tipi, the ground was bare in the vacant spaces on either side of the doorway. The space on the right was reserved for fuel and water, while the space on the left was for the use of anyone who might step in for a moment, perhaps only to deliver a message or make an inquiry, and leave promptly after that. Casual callers sat down there, not caring to be too well ensconced for only a brief visit.

Beyond these bare spaces, a continuous carpeting of fur robes was laid around the room and only the central area was left bare. After the grass was worn down, this part became a hard earthen floor, packed solid by the feet of all who walked around the fire to their appointed places and out again, many times. For a long stay, as in winter quarters, three short thick logs were embedded in the ground for a guard around the fire, one on each side and one in the back. These were for blocking any chance sparks that might otherwise shoot out and fall on the fur rugs and perhaps start a fire, if nobody was at home.

A dew curtain called *óžą* was hung all around and was long enough to be tucked under the carpet. This was made in matched pieces with strings attached for tying them together and to the tipi poles. Many dew curtains were decorated at about two- to four-foot intervals with vertical bands of fancywork in bright colors, or sometimes they were painted in heavy, dashing designs. The dew curtain was tied to the poles at a height of perhaps four feet—proportionately higher in the larger tipis—and hung straight down. With the sloping tipi wall, this created a little circular alley shaped like a lean-to, where surplus foods and robes were stored out of sight. Extra personal belongings all packed in containers were sometimes kept there, too. This storage area also served as insulation, and the inside of the tipi was always noticeably warmer because of it. The dew curtain was usually made of either doe- or calfskin.

The summer curtain was purely for decoration and was only hung across the back of the *t'ič'átku*, like an elaborate dossal. If anything this was more ornate than the winter dew-curtain whose primary purpose was, after all, to protect against the bitter cold outside. Informants spoke of beds made of slender sticks lashed crosswise to two long, heavier logs, like the sides of a bed. This raised the sleeper a little above the ground. They also spoke of mattresses of grass, brush, or sage, but whatever the material, it was simply laid in a pile and then leveled, never enclosed in a cover. Except for the sick, however, or the chronic invalid, the people thought it simpler and just as comfortable to sleep on the ground.

Backrests were used in the more able households. They were made by hitching thin sticks together with thongs, in the manner of venetian blinds. They were loose enough to be easily rolled and carried when moving camp. Narrow at the top and widening towards the base, they were perhaps twelve inches to three feet or more. But I never saw backrests in use, and these figures must not be taken as absolute, for I only guessed at them from the gestures of the informant as he described them. The support was a low tripod set firmly in the ground. "This was about the height of a man sitting," he said. It is not clear whether every member of the family used one; perhaps only the adults.

The fur robe, falling in a drape over this arrangement and lying spread out over the owner's space, had been especially made and decorated for its purpose. When the buffalo cow was killed and flayed, the entire hide, head included, was removed intact and prepared in the usual way to render it soft and pliant. Then the head part was shaped to fit like a hood over the top of the backrest. The whole skin was decorated with tassels and fringes, and the edges, even around the eye holes, were worked with an exaggerated buttonhole stitch with brightly colored porcupine quills or beads.

A regulation Teton pillow was laid across the base of the backrest. It was narrow, more cylindrical than flat, and long enough for two sleepers. One side was plain skin for night use, the other, for the daytime, was ornamented. This pillow was stiff and harder than the feather pillows used by Yanktons and Santees, in whose country ducks and geese were more plentiful than in Teton country. The preferred stuffing for Teton pillows was deer hair because of its resiliency. Failing that, buffalo hair at molting time was gathered, but this was a poor substitute because it very soon packed solid and was hard and clumsy.

The fancy side of the pillow was embroidered with painstakingly fine parallel lines of quillwork running the entire length of the pillow. The lines were spaced less than an inch apart and were most often of red or yellow quills. At regular intervals they were broken by a contrasting color, blue or strong yellow on the red lines, or purple or bright green on the yellow lines, although these were not the invariable color combinations, since every artist pleased herself. These contrasting colors were so inserted that they formed wide bands across the pillow against the longer and finer parallels lengthwise. The very close, fine lines represented a pattern known as "one hundred" work. This name must be taken as figurative only, since there was not enough room either on the pillow or on other things where it was used. It is, however, possible that the name derived from some legendary ceremonial robe with one hundred lines of work, but nobody said so to me.

Against the wall, or, in winter, the dew-curtain, each occupant of a space kept his belongings back of him in two or more pairs of saddlebags, made of soft leather, which were often covered with solid quill embroidery, or, later, with beadwork. Saddlebags were made in pairs and could themselves be folded and packed away in other saddlebags when not in use. Each pair was loosely tied together and both were identical in design. During a camp move they hung on each side of the pack animal, balancing each other, and their display in this manner was an indication of the family's taste for fine possessions. A woman with many fine possessions might have several pairs of saddlebags, each pair differently designed. These designs were purely for beauty and were not the identifying marks for their owners. Other families might have plain bags for their practicality alone.

The spaces around the tipi were used by their occupants for sitting, dining, and sleeping. Backrests served as lines of demarcation between them, but when they were not used, each person's extra robes, folded one on another, were lain beyond the pillow to mark off his space. These were the robes not needed for a pallet or cover. Thus each person had his own specific place and it was always the same; places were not exchanged for variety.

In ordinary tipis there was nothing sacrosanct about the honor place. Children often played there, and sometimes a grandfather or old uncle slept there. The father regularly sat there whenever he was at home — not as the lord of the tipi, but because only there could he be out of the way and receive and talk with his male guests, leaving the rest of the tipi for the women and children. During periods while his wife was pregnant or nursing he even slept there, but if there were guests, they occupied it at night and he slept with his wife or his sons.

Where there were several girls, daughters and daughters of collaterals who were staying with them, the eldest slept nearest her mother and the youngest next to the honor place. On the other side, the youngest boy slept nearest the space occupied by an elderly aunt or grandmother while the eldest son slept nearest the honor place. This arrangement was in tacit compliance with the inviolable rule that all young unmarried persons sleep on the proper side for their sex, and that where the break came, it must be the youngest of one sex who slept nearest an elderly relative of the opposite sex. Thus, little girls slept nearest the honor place, where sometimes an elderly male guest might lie, and little boys nearest their elderly female relative. A young unmarried man slept with the sons and a young unmarried woman with the daughters. An elderly relative who must sleep at the honor place because the appropriate space was already occupied slept nearer the boys or the girls, according to his or her sex.

If a married daughter came with her husband, they slept in the honor place. If it was already in use, they slept on the other side of the youngest girl, with the wife next to her sisters. Similarly, a married son and his wife might have to sleep next to his brothers, with his wife on the farther side. Men did not sleep on their sisters' side or women on their brothers' — even with their spouses — because collaterals of opposite sexes must keep distant from one another, here and always. Even so, the married pair managed to leave a little space between them and the boys or girls, as the case might be.

However, if an aunt (father's sister), an uncle (mother's brother), a father (father's brother), or a mother (mother's sister) spent the night in the tipi with their spouse, it was unimportant which side they took because they belonged to the parents' generation and were parental relatives to the sons and daughters. Yet even they kept apart from the children whose space they shared: always the woman nearest the girls, the man nearest the boys—this time because males and females (except spouses) kept apart as a matter of convention.

This whole matter was quite automatically handled. Everyone knew where they properly belonged with reference to the others in the tipi. It did not have to be taught specifically to each generation, with reasons why, any more than breathing had to be analyzed and taught. Nobody had to ask, "What space shall I occupy in this tipi?" He knew. It was one of the commonplaces of Dakota life; so much so, in fact, that I have never heard anyone explain it minutely. That was how it was.

This same arrangement prevailed in the Yankton tipi. Among the Santees the sides were reversed so that the left side was for females, the right for males. I am not entirely sure how general this reversal was, but all my Santee informants who discussed the topic said so. The Santees have not lived in tipis for a great many years, making the matter remote, whereas the Tetons did until comparatively recent times.

Whichever the arrangement it was the woman of the tipi who, being nearest the entrance, was the first to greet a caller by reaching out to shake hands with him. There she was, with all the tokens of her hospitality within reach—her fire, food, utensils, water, and fuel. In the average-sized tipi she could cook from her sitting position by bending forward and reaching. In an oversized tipi she might have to move closer to the fire, but she would move back to her habitual place immediately after the food was cooked and serve it from there.

Certain rules of order, as in the foregoing, and of correct behavior, as dictated by kinship law, helped to maintain decency and dignity in tipi life. In small families each child might sleep alone in his or her accustomed space, but one such space could also accommodate two or even three boys or girls whenever it was necessary in the case of overnight guests. In many families there were not only actual sons or daughters but other children who were in brother, sister, or cousin relationship to these sons and daughters, and whose parents were dead. There were no such institutions as orphan asylums. Children were happily taken in by relatives when they became orphans.

While the rightful owner of a space was present, another might not usurp it, although if it stood vacant for a time it might be borrowed to sit or work in. However, the occupant's prerogative was respected and his space surrendered as soon as he came in to stay. People sat and laid where they properly belonged and without argument. Because the locations of all members of the family were permanent and invariable, anyone coming in search of a certain person did not have to survey the entire room, scan and peer into every face to find him. If, for instance, he was looking for one of the sons, he looked at once in space where sons properly belonged — and there he would be, unless he was not at home.

When the family slept, they managed to lie with face turned from the possible gaze of others. They arranged robes about their heads or adjusted the cascading folds of their backrest drapes into a tolerable barrier, for the Dakotas had an undefined horror of being watched sleeping. Since this aversion was well nigh universal, there was continuous, nearly unconscious cooperation to prevent its happening. To look unduly long at a face, even that of the dead, was unfair, something like invading another's privacy while he was at a disadvantage.

That this aversion still holds is evidenced by the following incident. After an all-night ride in a day coach, a Teton complained of drowsiness so his companions asked, "Well, at least you had an outside seat. Why didn't you turn to the window and sleep?" With a sheepish grin the man replied, "Because I did not care to be stared at by all the Norwegian farmers waiting on station platforms beside their milk cans. They might *makát'apa* 'snap their fingers out at me', an insult, and I wouldn't know." The sleepy Teton said this to get a laugh but also out of a deep-seated dislike of being taken unaware, which his friends understood well.

Closing the fist, then snapping out the fingers at someone or something, was a gesture of ridicule, disgust, or disparagement. Some informants believed it to have a coarse origin, and to mean ejecting objectionable matter from oneself. Its precise origin has long since been forgotten. Today it is no more than a gesture of ridicule or disdain. When so intended it is plain enough and is naturally resented. However, sisters, when in a flippant mood, sometimes snap out their fingers pertly at one another over trivial annoyances, and it is nothing to be resented. When seriously intended, however, it is comparable to spitting on a person—except that the Dakotas were not in the habit of spitting on one another. It simply was not done; perhaps it was unthinkable, but they might turn aside and spit on the ground to indicate their disgust over news of someone's stinginess, or similar shortcoming.

The true Dakota did not lie sprawled out in carefree slumber. He slept but to waken instantly in case of a raid or other emergency. His position might appear tense and cramped but he got his rest. When women napped they lay with shawl partially hiding the face on the side most likely to be visible to passerby. Men lay facing the wall, indoors, or, if napping outdoors on the grass, they chose a spot remote from people moving about, and then, for good measure, they rested a neckerchief or the brim of their hat lightly on the face. Only the entirely unselfconscious slept limp and relaxed, unaware of others, as, for instance, babies and small children and sometimes very old people grown careless in senility. All others normally maintained an attitude of watchfulness, whether asleep or awake.

Many Dakotas still unconsciously keep to their traditional decorum, adapting it to fit their new life in cabin or house. My brother, Vine, while a young Episcopal missionary, observed the following situation objectively and with discernment.[2] He was able to describe it to me in some detail.

When traveling over his extensive field he was compelled to seek shelter for the night in a Dakota home in a conservative region of the reservation because a severe storm was coming. The log house was exceptionally roomy, being twice as long as it was wide. The elongated ridgepole rested on posts at equal distances down the center, thus dividing the room into two long sections. In a line with the posts stood the cook stove and, farther down, the heater. The several beds and an occasional packing trunk were kept close against the walls, and only the tables and chairs were movable. After a bed had been assigned to the missionary, other Dakotas came in out of the storm, and for them pallets were laid in the spaces between the beds.

The congenial host was telling a funny story when the family and guests were ready for bed. Hardly interrupting himself he walked to the table and blew out the single kerosene lamp, thus enabling the company to prepare for bed and lie down in the dark. The laughter and comments in response to his story continued; the getting to bed was nearly noiseless.

Not until daylight did the observer realize with what subtlety and skill the men and women had hung their things—vests, coats, shawls, and broad-brimmed hats—on the long prongs that stuck out spirally from the posts, branches that had been purposely left on to serve as hooks. The owners had hung these articles at exactly the right angles to screen themselves from the eyes of anyone who might waken and lie idly gazing about the room to take his bearings in the strange place. The tables and chairs also were standing apparently helter-skelter, and yet they were in fact placed with studied design in useful positions to the same end.

Purely from habit the adult members of the family as well as their guests had arranged everything individually, without conscious planning, yet as much as to say, "I would not look at a relative sleeping, nor would he look at me sleeping, so I must do my share to avoid our accidentally doing so." One who kept the rules rigidly but did nothing to insure their being kept by others was only half fulfilling his obligations.

One by one the sleepers arose and tiptoed out while the others lay facing the wall in real or seeming sleep so as not to see them even obliquely. Thus everyone had complete freedom to conduct himself inconspicuously.

It was this sort of cooperation and reciprocal consideration that regulated the group living of the Dakotas within the limited confine of the tipi. Privacy was attained mentally, even with many in the tipi. One might retire into one's self and sit silent in thought, and the others would not compel him to enter into the conversation until he voluntarily did so. Everyone did this at some time.

All indoor life was spent in a sitting or reclining position on the ground. Upon entering the tipi one tended to move groundward while advancing to one's own space. Men sat cross-legged or with one knee bent up. Women's correct position in public was always the same: both knees flexed, both feet to the right. Left-handed women naturally sat with both feet to the left, and it was considered modest and acceptable for them. When women sat alone together for a long time to do fancywork or simply to be companionable, they found it relaxing to alter their position by extending both legs straight out, always with the ankles carefully crossed. Even little girls sat as women after they were old enough to understand that cross-legged sitting was "improper for females. But until they understood this they sat cross-legged in the manner of their fathers and brothers, and nothing was said to them."

The family sat in their places forming a circle facing the fire, but far enough back to allow a free passage around it. To get at any personal belongings that might hang from a tipi pole, standing or kneeling momentarily was unavoidable, with face turned to the wall, but promptly one was sitting down again. This left little reason for long standing at full height inside the tipi. An adult who remained standing was sure to draw comment, often from some old grandmother: "Well, when is the enemy attacking? Pray that he stands ready to take flight!" For only so pressing a reason should one be so restless indoors. It was not exactly rude, but it was upsetting to those seated in a unified circle. Either join it or go! Even little children were gently invited to sit down as soon as they came in the tipi, or someone reached out and quietly placed them on his or her lap. So inured were the Dakotas to existence close to the ground that when chairs were first introduced they still preferred the ground, fearful of losing their balance and falling off, at such an unprecedented height. It is said that some did just that. Of course, they were accustomed to riding, which placed them much higher off the ground, but that was something else; they were at home on a horse, and one with it.

The need to move cautiously inside the tipi at all times resulted in an indoor style and position suited to it. One advanced stooping slightly and picking one's way with care. One must avoid being clumsy in the presence of others, some of whom might be respect relatives, but, whether or not any were present, one did this from habit. Only when out alone in the open was it safe to bolt freely about or stride along with complete abandon. The presence of others was always restraining; one became instantly careful of conduct and movement.

Little children soon affected the manner of the grown-ups and moved about in a gingerly way. They stooped immediately upon entering, though they had no need to stoop, and took mincing steps while wearing a determined expression that was comical at times. They were regularly warned against falling over someone in passing and were warned especially against stepping over another's legs or body. One might step over an animal, but never over a fellow human being! I do not know if once there was a religious reason for this rule, but that seems probable from the fact that children were warned so conscientiously that they very soon learned not to transgress the rule, in some cases even before they were old enough to reason. If there was such a reason once, today it is forgotten and only the external form remains.

However tall, probably there never was a tipi with an entrance high enough for an adult to walk through erect. Always he must accommodate to it by bending a little, enough to clear it. On the other hand, no regular tipi had an entrance so mean and low that inmates had to crawl through on hands and knees. When aged persons did so, it was only because of their infirmity. On the whole no undignified or extreme posture or movement was necessary in the tipi, but only such specialized ones as were suited to its shape and size.

Conversation in the tipi was low in pitch, slow, and even. It was not desirable to be heard except by the one addressed, certainly not by people outside the tipi. If one were to walk through a Dakota camp in early evening—and to this day it would be true—one would hear only an undefinable murmur with intervals of silence. Dakotas did not talk on and on over trivialities, in a steady flow, nor accelerate their speech excitedly over nothing. Only if there was need for haste, as in an emergency, might one be compelled to speak rapidly and loudly, though not always then. One spoke in his turn, and sometimes hesitated even then. Dakotas shrink from interrupting a speaker merely to get their word in. Council meetings took a long time because of this trait.

Mingled with the murmured conversation, an occasional low laugh or chuckle might be audible outside, but the general tone was unemotional and indistinct. It was something entirely else for congenial men to assemble for an evening of sociability. Their talk and laughter became hilarious at times, and people in neighboring tipis chuckled with their contagious mirth, though they might not know what caused it. If later the men told their wives, then everyone would soon know what all the laughter had been about. Such foregatherings did not happen every evening.

Babies crying in the night were quickly put to the breast. Older children were held close and soothed, while being reminded, "Nobody makes a disturbance to be heard in other tipis. Be still!" Unreasonable small children were made hasty promises or threatened with "something-to-be-feared," the owl spirit perhaps, anything to quiet them at the moment.

With tipis set rather closely together, and only skin deep, the first essential for peaceful group living in the camp circle was reasonable quiet at all times for the sake of others.

Generally formal meals were served in a family group in the morning, at midday, and in the evening, but without clocks, exact hours were neither possible nor particularly important. The mother prepared more food whenever her family was due to be hungry again, or whenever visitors came, which might be at any time of day.

Within historic times she was able to serve in vessels of metal or crockery, as they became available. It is said that in ancient times foods such as soups, porridges, mush, or stewed wild fruits were served in wooden bowls or tortoise shells. Solid foods were held in the hand—pemmican; cakes of parched corn; boiled, dried, or fresh meat; broiled ribs; corn on cob; and so on.

There were equivalents for modern eating implements—spoons, knives, and forks. The spoon, shaped from ruminants' horns rendered plastic by boiling, were highly prized because they were not plentiful. They were individually owned, although not by everyone. Often their owners carried them about, to use wherever they ate, lending them in turn to friends or relatives sitting near at a meal or feast. All adults carried a knife or two in a special sheath of rawhide painted in bold designs and bright colors. Such knives were not for domestic use alone but were also an essential weapon if one must fight one's way out of a hostile encounter with man or beast. Also, if lost, one must be equipped to kill small animals for food and cut saplings for a temporary shelter and scythe down heavy grass to thatch it. The term *p'eží-wók'eya* 'grass hut' appears in war stories, wherein a wounded man contrives such a shelter for himself, but I never saw one. Therefore the knife-in-scabbard was an important item of standard adult dress, and was worn suspended from the belt on the left side.

In legends of the novelistic type, as related by old people, an occasional reference is made to *mak'á-wakšíča* 'earth bowls', which hints at a possible pottery craft in the past, but no informant could tell about such bowls, much less the process of making them. All that remained of Dakota ceramics would seem to have been clay modeling, particularly of horses and other familiar animals. Up to thirty years ago this was an early spring pastime, and perhaps it still is in localities I do not know about. The finished forms were often remarkable, but without baking they lacked permanency. Small boys owned large herds of clay horses and buffalo or cattle and played happily with them until they were all in pieces. Such fragile items were an inevitable casualty in moving camp.

The equivalent of the fork was a long green stick made on the spot as needed. It was usually of box elder or willow, sharpened at one end for spearing the meat off the coals or out of boiling water. The hot meat was laid on sage leaves or grass to cool off. Then the pieces, already cut in sizes suitable for serving, were again speared and reached out to the diners. For children's portions, the strip of meat was first nicked along one side, in suitable bites, and then cooked. Strips of boiled meat were called *wósoso*.

Long after tined forks were in common use, many families continued to use the sharpened stick, especially when camping. It is still preferred for outdoor cooking on a large scale, as for a feast, and for serving the circle of guests seated on the ground. The ones served must graciously accept the portion held out to them on the stick. It was improper to express a preference, but some who were well acquainted with the server were not above whispering, "Give me a tender piece" or "one with fat."

It was unnecessary and indeed impractical for every guest to hunt out the busy hosts and thank them individually. Their having come and eaten well was a thank-you. When they had had their fill, they simply got up and left, taking with them all the food they were not able to consume there. Each one had brought a sack or other container for that purpose, for, at a feast, many times more food than could be eaten at one sitting was passed around. That was what made it a feast and not simply a meal, and it was rude and ungrateful to leave any of it behind. Food carried away from a feast for eating later is called *wat'éča*, literally, 'new stuff'. Just why that idiom is used, and what it means figuratively, I do not know.

Eating together as a family was orderly. The diners did not close in around a common kettle and pick out their preference without regard for one another. That would be unthinkable. However, sometimes mother and children did gather around one dish in a very intimate group, privately, and that would be the same as our snacking between meals. Or if they must eat hurriedly and be on their way, they might eat snacks in this way.

Under ordinary circumstances food was served with dignity. Just as it must be freely offered, so it must be accepted graciously but without gushing thanks; it must be accepted with a casual restraint. For Dakotas to offer food to one another was nothing extraordinary, so why make a fuss over it? Only small children and sometimes a very hungry old person accepted food with obvious greed. A certain folktale was told to children to teach them that even if one were starving, the cool, controlled approach, keeping in mind the needs of others, was admirable. The tale told of some starving people who, when finally they obtained food, were crazed enough to fight over it with their own relatives—a tragically abnormal scene! Even so, children were always served first, and encouraged to eat.

It was correct etiquette for a guest to say as he returned his empty bowl to the hostess, "Mother [or whatever his relationship to her], take this back." As she received it she murmured, *Hą́* the woman's word of approval, consent, or acceptance. This corresponds to man's *háo*, except that the latter is also used as a greeting, whereas *hą́* is not. With that the function was correctly ended. The words were conventional. They did not contain a word meaning "thank you," but nevertheless that is what they implied.

However, this formality was not observed by the family when they ate in their tipi. A guest must say those words, but not the members of the family. When children ate with only their mother, they sometimes played a visitor's role. With great seriousness they returned their plate to their mother. A boy would say, *Iná, lé ikíkču wó!* 'Mother, take this!' The mild imperative *wó* was used only by males; a girl would say *yé* instead, or omit the terminal particle altogether. In this way children practiced for the time when they would be guests in another tipi. Their mother said *Hą́* with equal formality as she took back the plate, and perhaps expressed her pleasure over the good manners of her "guests." Children liked to play grown-up parts.

The Dakotas had their own ideas of what was clean and what unclean. They were particularly qualmish toward articles that had been used in some other way than was intended for them. Surface dirt was not considered to be unclean if it was the unavoidable result of muddy ground, for example, or of certain kind of work, and was overlooked on that account. A garment stiff with grease and grime from being worn while tanning hides and caring for much meat was an admirable symbol of its owner's industry and skill. The garment was then not called unclean but *slót'a* 'surfeited with grease'. The word was even a popular epithet in olden times to compliment a woman or girl and meant simply that she was, in the opinion of the speaker, possessed of all womanly arts and skill, as well as of character. In this idiomatic usage, now obsolete, the literal meaning was forgotten and *slót'a* meant approval, not dissimilar to our colloquial "she's a number one," or "she's okay."

Food utensils were religiously kept for food only. No matter how well a cooking vessel might be scoured and scalded, once it had been used as an emergency wash basin, it was thereafter too loathsome to use for food again. A woman's menstrual cloth was regarded as unclean in that it was forever permeated with something mysterious and therefore no longer fit for ordinary use. A baby inadvertently diapered in even the most thoroughly cleansed sanitary napkin would be doomed to die young or, perhaps, to live permanently afflicted. Any woman or girl who was not careful to dispose of her cloths was definitely unclean. She should burn or bury them.

Feet, however well scrubbed, must never be directly related to food in any form and great pains were taken to observe this rule. It is said that in the remote past all surplus foods were cached for future use, and that for caching, jerked meat must first be tenderized by a treading process. This softened and even broke the fibers, and squeezed out moisture that could cause spoilage. The process rendered the meat pliable enough to fold away in parfleches.

For this treading healthy and vigorous boys in their middle teens were chosen to "dance" on the meat, but their preparation was no simple matter. They must first swim or enter the sweat lodge, after which they were rubbed down with sage and new moccasins were put on their feet. Only then were they ready to be lifted onto the meat to begin treading it.

The meat, too, was well protected. First a layer of leafy boughs was spread on the ground, then the large sheets of very thinly jerked meat, which had hung in the sun and wind for two or three days, were laid over them, and on the meat a second layer of elm or box elder leaves was spread. Finally, a clean buffalo hide free of hair covered the pile. It was on this skin that the boys' moccasined feet fell hard countless times. Sometimes an old man sat by and sang to keep them from lagging; and occasionally the boys were lifted off and given a rest. "All day they danced," said the informant. Perhaps he only meant the better part of the day, or until experts decided the meat had been treated long enough. Then the meat was again dried many days, until brittle.

This process was most completely reported by Yanktons, but *Makʿúla* said the Tetons used it, too, even though their life, which required periodic camp moves, might have made it impossible to do systematic caching in the Yankton way, but they did make caches whenever they could. Several related families joined together to store their dried meat and other foods, using the same storage hole. The meat was folded almost like cloth to fit the large parfleches and the corn and other foods were poured into small, rectangular boxes or trunks, also made of rawhide. These food cases were made in pairs and permanently tied together loosely. The pairs were painted exactly alike with designs that their owner could recognize. Each woman had her own design and it was generally known so that there was little reason to dispute over them.

It was a Brule informant who described the making of a cache. A hole was dug straight downward to the length of a man's arm and wide enough in diameter for a person to go through. From that depth the hole was widened as it grew until when finished it was a roomy space underground. According to the man's description and gestures, a cross-section of the cache from top to base would suggest the outline of an immense jar set into the ground: a rather squatty jar with a wide mouth and a neck as long as a man's arm.

In cutting out the sod or turf to begin digging the cache, great care was taken to keep it intact and lay it to one side because it must serve as the lid for the hole and must be natural-looking. The cutting was done on a centerwise slant so that it would fit firm and solid and not fall through, much like a keystone. After the turf was back in place, the suture was carefully concealed by scattering leaves and grasses over all, to make it appear natural. Of course, the cache itself was made in an out-of-the-way spot, as a precaution against molestation.

As the diggers loosened the earth, they placed it on bullhides for those on top to pull up and carry away into the tall underbrush, for it would not do to leave piles of telltale dirt by the cache. An agile man jumped into the hole and took the various containers as they were handed down to him. He laid them one on top of another in a spiral arrangement close to the wall, making sure that the containers painted in the same design were kept together. After a good season there might be enough food stored to reach the top of the cache, one informant said. Then the man was helped out of the hole.

If one of the families should be without food and must get what belonged to them, they could open the cache and take out their own. This was sometimes necessary to do. As a rule, however, it was possible to wait until all the owners could go there together.

Santee informants gave me nothing on caching in this way, but they said that treading was also practiced in their wild rice culture and that the boys employed were as scrupulously prepared for their task. The practice was known as *psį́-áwačipi* 'rice danced upon'. The grain was poured into a hole lined with skin and another skin was loosely pegged over it so that the treaders' feet never touched the rice. The purpose of this treading was to loosen the chaff from the rice, to be winnowed out later.

Dishwashing consisted in wiping utensils with fresh sage leaves, using not the broad-leaf varieties but a finer species with very soft, almost feathery barbs. Because it grew practically everywhere and could be easily gathered, women were profligate with it, tossing out a handful after wiping only a bowl or two and reaching for more. The constant wiping with sage, especially on wooden ware, imparted a faint aroma to all foods, like a seasoning unnoticed unless absent.

When commercial towels were first introduced, women were faced with the problem of caring for them. Since they were harder to obtain than sage, they could not rightly be discarded so readily and consequently were used over and over again until in many cases they grew black with grease and grime. If the need of somehow renewing them was realized, the idea of using soap and water was slow in taking hold, unrelated as that was to the traditional method of renewing skins by rubbing with chalk earth and then shaking out, brushing, or buffing.

The bedding on which a birth or death occurred was ceremonially unclean because it was charged with eternal mysteries. No longer proper for other uses in the home, it must be cast out. However, not long after, some poor old woman outside the *t'iyóšpaye* was sure to go by and take it. As she furtively picked up the discarded items she might be heard muttering excuses and rationalizations for her irregular conduct. "My relative died on this," or "My innocent grandchild was born on this, so how can it hurt me who am old and soon to die anyway? I shall take it home and use it." If sheer need compelled her to ignore the stigma she could always obscure it by a declaration of kinship devotion.

Traditional tipi life at its best had decency and order to the extent I have tried to show. Far from being a haphazard affair—any old sticks and any old skins slammed together—the tipi was a carefully designed and pridefully erected structure, in obedience to exact rules of procedure and making, and a safe, kindly place inside. Hospitality being a tribal aim, practically anyone stranded or homeless might seek refuge there and find welcome, with no questions asked. All comers were fed, while food remained. "When the last morsel is gone, then we shall all starve together, with honor" was a stock saying, so often heard that even children knew it by heart before they understood fully its implications.

In the last analysis the tipi was the prerogative of the family living in it. It was their own private residence and could under no circumstances be taken from them. They were satisfied with it and asked for no other kind of abode. It actually seemed cozy and comfortable to a people who knew how to adapt themselves to its limitations and live by its rules.

5

Courtship and Marriage

The Teton term for courtship, *wióyuspa*, literally means 'to catch a woman', and it refers to the custom of catching hold of a girl's wrap as she passed. The purpose was unmistakable, since ordinarily men did not boldly touch a woman except to shake hands. The Yanktons and Santees use another term, *wiók'iya* 'to talk to a woman'. The common term 'to talk, to speak' is *iá* or *iyá*, and such talk might be about anything, but *ok'iya* is more specific: it means 'to confer about something special'. With the classifier feminine prefix *wi-* it means to court a woman. Any time the Dakota youth could 'catch a woman' was legitimate courting time, unless there had been a death in her family and she was in mourning, which would preclude the more or less flippant approach customary in courtship.

However, there was a traditional courting hour, and it was toward evening, when the sun hung low and men took their horses to water and elderly women went out for fuel and water to last the night in their tipis. Then, marriageable girls and young women sometimes went along with their grandmother or elderly aunt, no doubt for the thrill of it, and they generally made a show of being very helpful to her.

All the while they were aware that young men in their best dress blankets and face paint stood behind the trunks of large trees, all ready to step out at the opportune time and block the path when a girl who interested them was approaching. It was proper for a girl to try to dodge him, stepping now to this side and now to that in an effort to get past. But, with the agility of a wrestler, the man would block her every time, until she somehow managed to slip past him, and even then he reached out quickly and caught hold of her blanket—or pretended to miss if he had only been playing. On the other hand, a girl really determined to get free might abandon her wrap and run home without it, but, of course, if she did not want any man to stop her, she could keep close to her chaperone all the time. Few men were so rude as to reach past a chaperone, for she was a potential respect relative and might be an actual one, if the courtship should be successful. Even in the preliminary stages of courtship it was proper to show avoidance respect to a girl's elder relatives.

By their own confession in later life, many girls deliberately lagged behind over something trivial or irrelevant, just for the excitement of escaping, if for nothing else. She did not forget that a certain finesse was proper, that a girl who was too plainly eager to be courted became a laughingstock to other girls and women. The nonchalant manner was considered more womanly and was conventional.

Once caught it was proper to try to get free or at least to put up a token resistance, though perhaps not too spirited, lest it damper the wooer's ardor, in case he happened to be someone pleasing. At last the girl gave up and asked impatiently and impersonally, "Well! If he has anything to say, let him say it so that I may be on my way! Or has he no voice?"

Yet when the man did talk and seemed in earnest, she affected not to hear but stood looking off yonder, showing interest in everything but him, giving an appearance of being bored, hostile, or unimpressed. Thus, young courtship started mostly in parrying as between two opponents—the girl ever on the defensive and alert to escape. A "man's role was to pursue, a woman's to be pursued"—never the other way around, at least in theory. Conforming to that prevailing idea, women created the illusion of continually running away, but of course they did not run forever, else there would be no marriages. The truth is that most Dakota women married.

Many young men played at courtship by detaining any girl they could waylay. Such triflers only wanted to see how many girls would "say yes" to them. They counted those yeses as a warrior might count his coups and told their companions, "She is easy. Why don't you try her next. She will say yes almost at once." Their proposals had been mere pretense.

Sometimes yeses were obtained by fraud. Once a man succeeded in engaging the girl in talk, they might chat about commonplaces but she must be always on guard, for should she inadvertently say yes in agreeing with him on something quite impersonal, he would quickly come to the point: "There! You have said yes to me, to the question I am asking in my heart!" A smart girl said yes to nothing. Instead she might counter with an irrelevant remark to divert him or answer a serious question pertly to tantalize him. If in an unguarded moment she did say yes to anything, he certainly could not compel her to keep her word by marrying him, but he teased her with the idea that she had promised herself to him until she was denying it vehemently and, angered by his insistence, was losing her cool reserve. That suited him; the very thing he wanted to break down was her reserve and her resistance to his charm.

Mature men decried such trifling courtship and admonished their sons against it, even though they may have had their own fun in their youth! If some shy and thoughtful sons did heed, the majority found the game too enticing to give it up, and anyway they knew that it was not unsanctioned. The accepted tribal attitude seemed to be "It is male nature to trifle; woman, look out or you could be hurt and it would be your own fault."

From time to time elder women relatives sounded a warning to their own girls. Elder sisters, especially those who had steered their own way with skill and were now honorably married, spared no words. They might bluntly warn, "Be on your guard, I tell you! Or first thing you know you will bear a fatherless child!"

On the whole girls were wary. Once cornered their first weapon was silence and indifference. When finally they did talk, it was with a deliberate lack of attention to the subject of conversation, a maddening thing to the suitor who happened to be serious. But, serious or not, he tried everything to capture a girl's attention, even resorting to disparaging himself. If she could feel sympathy for him, she might be more amenable.

However, the well-trained girl was not taken in by even that; she only laughed. How did she know but that this was another male trick? One girl told her chum, after a session with a desperate wooer, "Oh, how smoothly he 'made *Iktómi!*' But his act did not fool me!" *Iktómi* was the trickster of Dakota mythology, the spirit of deception. He appeared in many guises that were wholly plausible, as a completely sincere character, but his motive was always the same: to be accepted as a friend that he might quietly work to bring about another's downfall.[1]

On the other hand, a highly romantic girl might not be able to resist such wiles because it was more exciting to take them seriously, and no doubt hopeful. If a man said innocently, "Let's just walk off yonder a little way," she went, forgetting that she had been repeatedly warned against doing so. Too willing for her own good, the indiscreet girl might find herself *maníl-éȟpeyapi* 'left in the wilds', after she had yielded herself. No fate could be worse than that; to be abandoned in the wilds was to suffer the height of disgrace, for it was never quite forgotten by society. Yet that was man's game—to test women to the limit. If perchance a man found his bride was a virgin, his pride in her was boundless. If not, then either the marriage did not last or was destined to remain stormy for years.

While being courted a girl who talked too recklessly and too much was open to ridicule. She should say little and keep the man guessing. If she was reckless enough to commit herself before she was convinced of his sincerity, he might 'sing about her', and that was shameful. For the man might make up a song quoting her exact words and then he and his companions would sing it where the people could hear them. This was the only kind of "love song," and it was no compliment. One typical song is still remembered:

> I came outside barefoot
> So as to trick my aunt.
> So I will go with you,
> So arrive.

It is easy to reconstruct the occasion. A too-trusting girl believed her suitor when he said, "Tonight at midnight I shall clear my throat three times back of your tipi, so listen for me. Then you must come outside for I will take you home" — as his wife, of course. So when he gave the signal she went outside in her bare feet. Her aunt supposed she would be right back.

No sane man dared to make up a song about a girl who was circumspect. That would be libel, and he would be considered a liar or a mad man. Moreover, people sneered at one who sang about a girl and later married her. If she deserved to be sung about — and who should know better than he — then he should not want her for his wife!

Songs about women were called *wii-lówąpi* 'singing about women'. An alternate term, used only by the Tetons, seems more apt: *wiówešte-lówąpi* 'singing in mockery of women'. From the latter term it is clear that not true love, but only ridicule and flippancy, lay behind such songs. A man who yearned deeply after a certain girl was very secretive about her. Until he could be sure of her reciprocal attitude, his behavior was anxious and tentative and in every way guarded. It was not customary for Dakota men to lay their heart open and throbbing for all to see, by bursting into song. Only a born fool would be so unconscious of public reaction as to be that obvious. For the Dakotas there was a legitimate time and place for passion, but that was not all the time, and certainly never in public.

Another song, still generally known, runs as follows:

> My heart is bad [unhappy],
> My heart is bad,
> My heart is bad—
> How can I live on?

This was romanticized in translation some years ago by an American poet to read:

> Breaks now, breaks now my heart,
> Thinking we two must part.
> Hear now what says my heart:
> "Keep me, keep me in thine always!"[2]

That may be very touching, but its premise is all wrong. To a Dakota it sounds downright silly because it assumes the same sentimental mood that European love ballads represent so publicly. The fact is that between the original and the English version there is nothing in common of purpose or character.

Even a verbal promise of marriage, without any intention of doing so, was a man's justification for composing a "love" song. Thus it might be said that the Dakota *wií-lówąpi* was actually a public report on a girl, implying either of two offenses: that she had actually yielded herself without marriage, or that she made a promise to marry but did not keep it. In theory both were comparably serious—or so girls were told. Actually, of course, the broken promise was not so grievous a sin; sometimes it was the only way to get out of a disagreeable situation. The girl's close friends advanced convincing excuses for her: "Oh, but she had to promise in pretense to save herself! He was the kind of character who could harm a woman by force."

If an otherwise irreproachable young woman "fooled a man," the matter was gradually forgotten if she conducted herself in an exemplary manner thereafter. It was best, however, to avoid having to do even that, if possible. Girls from the better families were strictly chaperoned and made to feel that any mistake would impair their reputation forever. Old women sometimes tell me laughingly, "Yes, I did promise in pretense, to free myself from the hold a man had on my wrap. How angry he was!" When girls were young, such a thing was a near disgrace.

Wií-lówąpi or *wiówešte-lówąpi* songs were generally sung in the idle mood of trifling courtship, for a pastime, and as a rule the identity of the girl being quoted was left to be guessed. However, occasionally an earnest suitor who had been treated lightly and rejected vindictively named the girl outright. One Yankton song ends: *Ištá-ǧiwį k'ų hémakiye* 'So the brown-eyed one said to me'. For the normally shy and sensitive girl such publicity was no doubt intolerable. How it was borne is not reported.

On any quiet summer evening a group of youths in devil-may-care mood might be heard singing in the distance as they rode along, or posted themselves atop a hill, sitting on their patient ponies. They sang one another's songs in a chorus, and those in the camp circle who were not otherwise occupied might listen for the words and ask, "Now, who do you suppose they are singing about?" Such songs, ending with piercing shouts of triumph, were once part of the flavor and background of camp circle life, and they have vanished with the society that produced them. No one sings about women in that way anymore, as far as I know.

Nor did behavior of married women escape scrutiny. Their indiscretions, too, were publicly aired—at the Sun Dance of all places! It is said that traditionally the music for that ceremony was grouped into four cycles consisting of four songs each. Being the most solemn and even prayerful of all chants, it would seem that frivolity had no place among them. Nevertheless, during certain rest periods permitted to the dancers, the most sensational of the current *wií-lówąpi* were sometimes desultorily sung by the official drummers, who were also the singers, while they waited for the dancing to resume. If some supposedly staid and settled wife had flagrantly misstepped during the preceding year, they might compose a song on the spot suggesting her offense and introduce it as a startling divertissement.

Yankton and Teton informants have said that, at their Sun Dances, which were very close in procedure and intent, this was the height of reproach. Also, in the manuscript written shortly after the turn of the century by *Míwak'ą Yuhá* 'Sword Owner', an Oglala Teton whose English name was George Sword, there is a reference to this practice.[3] I personally witnessed it, at a reenactment of the Sun Dance in 1928 at Rosebud Agency. The telling words set to an old melody ran thus:

Grey Eagle Woman,
Your tipi stands empty,
Your children are hungry,
Your hearth is cold—
Where have you gone?

It was no invention merely for demonstrating all phases of that ancient festival, for I learned upon inquiry that there was such a person who had left her husband for another man the previous season. Thus even the Sun Dance, that most august of ceremonies, allowed time for calling attention to the improper conduct of women. Nothing was done about men's.

The complete objectivity of the singers was particularly striking. By no slightest gesture or tone did they betray their private opinion of the woman and her highly improper conduct. As they sat singing and drumming, neither smugness nor apology for what they were doing could be read in their placid, sculpturesque faces, but, after all, it was the Sun Dance that was taunting the woman, not they. Individually blameless and free of all responsibility, they were but its collective instrument; their role was as impersonal as a hangman's.

If indiscreet females must endure public disgrace, all too often the man responsible became something of a popular hero good at a sport, especially if he was consistently successful in luring even the most guarded young women to their ruin. Why blame him, just because they had no better sense than to take his trifling seriously, knowing his reputation? Had they not been warned? "Be careful of that one especially. There is something about him." That "something" was an inexplicable charm that could only be supernatural. Surely it could only be the elk spirit operating through the man and imparting a power no woman could resist who exposed herself to it! It was safest to keep away from him.[4]

A Santee legend tells of a boy who was a "nobody" but who nevertheless longed vainly after the proud daughter of the chief. When she laughed at him and called him cruel names he decided to go off and die. So at dawn he shot an arrow northward and followed it all day. At dusk he found it, impaling a deer. It diverted him to cut up the animal and feast on the tenderloin broiled over his campfire. Then he fell quickly asleep, in spite of an aching heart, being exhausted from his day-long walk. Next morning he shot another arrow and found it that evening again impaling a deer.

Four times this happened. Then on the fourth evening he discovered that he no longer felt so poignantly about the girl and that perhaps he would better go home and not die after all.

While he sat thinking things over calmly, he heard men's voices coming through the woods. As the men neared they were saying to each other, "You give it to him"; "No, but you give it to him." Then, "You explain it to him!" "No, but you!" And then they entered the circle of light from his fire, two unbelievably handsome young men. Never had the poor boy seen such male beauty as this! They seemed to emanate supernatural masculine charm, visibly and lambently.

One of them handed the boy a lover's flute—the original from which later flutes were copied—and taught him how to play on it. The notes were sweet beyond words. Then they said, "Boy, you have been hurt, but we have come to help you. Go home tomorrow, and walk through the village at midnight blowing music like this. We will be with you and you shall see that no one will be able to resist your music." The flute was in the form of the gar fish. The two men were elks in human guise.

The boy went home endowed with all their attributes of beauty and allure. When at midnight he walked through the village, his music literally drew the girls from their beds and brought them swarming out after him. He continued on, ignoring them. His music so filled his ears that he did not hear the chief's daughter when she whispered, sidling up to him, "Remember me? I am the one you wanted." It was sheer delight to spurn even a chief's daughter. Only one girl stayed in her bed and did not go out after him, and she became his wife. That boy was the first elk.

Many men with this imputed power appeared disappointingly unpretentious in public, making it hard to believe that they were such a threat, but now and then one could be swaggering and arrogant and not above making cruel fun of the man who married one of his "discards." "He ought to be grateful to me. Didn't I blaze the trail for him?" Naturally, such talk embarrassed a husband and caused him to blame his wife bitterly.

But sometimes a philanderer, even with the elk spirit, was finally trapped for keeps. It is told of one who reputedly had been the terror of mothers with marriageable girls, that he stayed permanently married to the ninth or tenth—and the homeliest of all the women he had courted. So, naturally, the community was in an uproar and gossip was rife. What possible attraction could there be? What power stronger than the elk spirit? Perhaps a rare love potion, but, if so, where was it obtained? Tetons and Yanktons thought the Santees had such medicine, and that they might have got it from their Chippewa neighbors.

The gamut of speculation ended with "Well, whatever the potion and wherever it came from, it must have rendered the man blind!"—a sarcastic reference to the girl's excessive plainness. Whatever the attraction it is said that the former trifler became a changed man overnight and remained a docile and devoted husband to the end of his days.

When girls were being warned by careful and anxious women relatives about courtship pitfalls, they often listened with an affected dread, even though they did not actually feel it. Such warnings were a spur to their curiosity, and challenged them to prove that they could take dares and come through unscathed. When sisters and cousins were alone together they sometimes joked quite freely about the "dangers," and some flirted surreptitiously where no staid elders could observe them. The timid and tractable girl enjoyed a good reputation to the day she married by a literal obedience to the elder relatives' warnings. Spirited and independent girls took them as a dare and might allow themselves to be courted, at the same time managing to keep their wits about them and thereby avoid a bad reputation.

Certain proud feminine names reflect a defiance of the threat and a successful coping with it. There is *Kúpi* 'Coveted One', *Č̣atíheyapiwį* 'Woman Yearned For', and *Íyakč̓unipiwį* 'Invincible Woman'—a name that hints at men's futile efforts to break down her resistance. The legendary name *Č̓aktéwį* 'Heart Killer' comes under this category. Not many years ago, I was shown a tiny baby girl wrapped in a bundle in the old-fashioned way. When I asked whether she had a Dakota name, her grandmother proudly said, "Yes, I have named her *Asčúpiwį*." The name must be paraphrased, since there is no equivalent English term for the stem *sčú*. It means of 'self-possession'. Sometimes, as in this case, such a confident name was conferred at birth to memorialize a woman relative of blameless reputation. Occasionally a girl later belied her high-sounding name by her own conduct.

Outside the family of birth, the *t̓iyóšpaye*, it was improper for a woman to give a present to a man. Nevertheless, a young woman who fancied herself much in love secretly made a pair of moccasins or some male costume accessory and slipped it to the man of her choice. That was plain man-buying, and, if it became known, it would evoke cruel ridicule and suspicion among the women. "If she can do that, how much more might she not do?"

Men were proud of a gift from the girl they were in love with and kept it secret out of loyalty to her, but if the gift came from one they had been courting only for fun, they were indifferent enough to let it be seen or to give it away openly. A secret gift was made by such a girl with the slim hope that the recipient would care enough not to reveal its source.

In presenting a secret gift, it is said, the girl might whisper, "Take this, and remember me." One overeager young woman is reported to have shaken hands with a man who acted totally unaware of her existence, and, leaving a small gift in his palm, said, "Perhaps this will help you to think!" *Wíyukčą* means a little more than merely to cerebrate. The term may be analyzed as *wá* 'indefinite object, something'; *í* 'over, about, or by'; *yukčą* 'to appraise, judge'. As a whole it means to look thoughtfully at something, to see it from all sides and angles, and then to arrive at a fair estimate.

One day a callow youth who spent his time going to different homes to eat appeared at our house wearing exceptionally beautiful moccasins. He lived with only an aged grandmother, and his clothes were always shabby, which made the flashy footwear immediately noticeable by contrast. When my mother praised them, he explained with disarming candor, "These? Oh, they were a secret gift to my cousin. He didn't want them—he gets them all the time—so he threw them at me. So-and-so's wife made them for him!" He named the husband outright, a man of high prestige in the community. It was well that no one else heard the name. Unused to such elegance, the youth had worn the moccasins so carelessly that the exquisite work was caked with mud.

An unscrupulous would-be-suitor might obtain a lock of some girl's hair by trickery and parade it off to his male companions as a secret gift. In more recent times a pocket handkerchief or hair ribbon might be filched for the same purpose. It was never safe to drop one's handkerchief for a man to pick up: he kept it. If his friends got the ambiguous impression that perhaps it was such-and-such girl's ribbon or handkerchief that she had given him, he let them imagine what they liked. Wary girls generally saw that their personal items did not get into men's hands.

Frank competition in courtship was considered undignified and even shameful. This fact drove some girls to strive for attention by means of secret gifts, regardless of the saying "It is unwomanly to pursue." As for men, who preferred to appear casual about their courtship, it was unbecoming for one to be so openly wistful over some unattainable girl that other men must pity him at the same time that they were disdainful of his behavior. It was best to act as though courtship and women were an incidental and indifferent matter.

Of an evening the suitors of a popular girl sometimes joined together to await her coming out of her tipi, and meanwhile they lay in the tall grass side by side, talking of irrelevant matters in entirely friendly fashion. While one man was detaining her to plead his cause, the others waited their turn to detain her next before she could elude them. Sometimes, it is said, one who had finished his courting kept tight hold on her blanket and consigned her to the next man! Such cooperation reflects proper behavior between brothers or male cousins. Ideally they were, first and always, loyal to one another, and that loyalty superseded all other considerations — even women.

It was regarded as laughable to show resentment because the girl of one's choice married another man. Instead one assumed an air of nonchalance, saying, in effect, "Well, women are everywhere! There is no scarcity of women!" In a like situation a woman might say with a laugh, or a sneer, "Is he the only male alive?" Nevertheless, for some it was not possible to hide disappointment. It is said that men were known to kill each other over the woman they both wanted, and a jilted lover might take his revenge by incapacitating his rival's best horse, severing the tendons of its hoofs. I found no informant who knew of this at first hand, but several had at sometime heard the remark concerning a successful rival: "He would do well to guard his horse now!"

It is also reported that traditionally a jilted lover might punish the girl who accepted another man after she had promised to marry him by throwing dirt in her face, but only one old woman informant ever saw it happen, and only once. The girl, a recent bride, was in the crowd watching the dancing when a man stepped up from behind and called her name. When she turned he tossed a handful of dirt in her face, blinding her temporarily. My informant said, "She pulled her blanket over her head and cried softly where she stood, but no woman was very sorry for her. She had it coming!" However, the informant did admit that not every girl who deserved it got such treatment because men were usually ashamed to air their hurt.

A jilted girl could be vicious, too. There is the story of one who, in a rage, hurled a sharp-pointed knife at a man because he had deceived her. She aimed it so accurately that it put out one of his eyes. I knew that man in his later years, because he was a member of our church and came every Sunday. If he had been something of a ladykiller in his time, that fact was no longer believable. To me as a child he seemed the most innocuous and prosaic of family men.

Nor was it unheard of for two women rivals to cast dignity to the winds and engage in bodily struggle over a man. The Dakota place name for Choteau Creek, a stream in southeastern South Dakota, is said to have derived from such an occurrence. It is *Nawíži Kčížapi* 'The Jealous Ones Fight Each Other'. Women in combat generally resorted to hair-pulling rather than slapping or striking with an instrument. "I shall pull her hair!" was a not-infrequent threat, sometimes spoken in jest, though not always.

The deer spirit was the female counterpart of the elk spirit, and as such it was believed to impart supernatural allure to certain women. Thus not only were women in fear of those terrible elks; men were themselves at the mercy of women with this alleged power to lead them to ruin. Men warned one another, "Watch out for that one. On the surface she is quiet and harmless, but underneath she is *wič'ášašni*. She could wreck you!" The native word means, literally, 'not man', hence not human. As an idiom, which is its common use, it means 'tricky, unreliable'; behaving unpredictably; not under the same moral and social codes governing ordinary folk.

Consequently a strange woman with excessive charm was to be regarded with a measure of tentative caution. This is borne out by a familiar legend, which I condense here.

Once upon a time a man walking in a lonely wood was met by a very attractive young woman. She lured him on until he had relations with her. Actually he was unknowingly mating with a deer in human guise. This he discovered too late when, as they sat talking together on a bank, a dog came out of some bushes and barked at them. The woman sprang instantly up and dashed away with superhuman speed and disappeared in a distant thicket, only to reappear in the form of a deer, mocking him. When he reached home the man vomited and became dizzy and lost his mind. After a short while he died.

There are numerous variants of this tale, some with much elaboration. One I recall says that while the deer sat in the form of a woman, the man observed many rings on her fingers and bracelets on her arms, but when she ran off she left only a pile of spiral tendrils from the grapevine where she had been sitting. Another says that the man was growing uneasy even before the dog disturbed them because she cast a shadow with long ears that revolved continuously. Imaginative narrators could dress up the simplest story in such ways.

I do not wish to give these beliefs too much emphasis, for they were not well defined, apparently. Far from being dominant in the minds of people, they were only elusively and chaotically present as background stuff, hinted at by such casual comments as "He must be an elk!" or "She must be a deer!" — stock sayings among adults. I knew a woman named *Tʼáȟčawį* 'Deer Woman', but I was ignorant of the connotation until I grew up into an awareness of it. The woman had been named for an aunt who, in spite of excessive feminine charm, refused to exploit her *wakʼą* power, and was respected because of that. Nor did I immediately catch the point when the village wag, old Striped Face, came into a room and saw the picture of an elk on the wall and exclaimed, pretending kinship with it, "Take that down! It recalls to me my self!" He meant that once he was irresistible to women because he was endowed with the elk spirit, but now, alas, he was old.

With or without help from these spirits, some women were naturally more venturesome than the majority and liked to take risks just for the sport of it. Once, it is told, a young woman dared take a shortcut through the woods by herself, when a man stepped in front her out of nowhere and caught her wrap to detain her. She knew that she had no business out there, and that, if seen, she would be criticized severely. So she stopped short and said to the man, coolly and directly, "What is it you want of me? That I marry you?" He said, "Yes." She replied, "Very well then, I will! But later."

The man was so astounded by her extraordinary directness that he believed her and let go his hold, but when she was beyond his reach she called back over her shoulder, laughing: *Iyé tuwá heyá škʼé čʼų́!* 'As they say someone once said!' She had quoted from a legend; the words were not her own. The completely nonplussed young man could only shout back in frustration, "You *Iktómi!* You trickster!" She had been resourceful enough to gain the advantage, and it shamed him too much to have been so neatly outwitted by a woman that he dared not make up a song quoting her.

If a girl gave her promise to marry without first consulting her parents, there was nothing they could do about it, usually. "She has given her word, so what is there to say?" This being the prevailing attitude, a girl would not ordinarily give a glib promise. For, in the last analysis, most Dakota women with good sense aimed to conform to the standards, being all too aware of the penalty for those who did not conform, and of the fear of a bad reputation that dogged their sex.

Courtship for the mature was expected to be consistently dignified and mutually respectful. A man asked a serious question and a woman answered it in the same way. There was no preliminary sparring. A mature man did not go out with the boys at the courting hour to waylay a woman and struggle with her for her wrap while she tried to escape him. Instead he managed to drop in when she was at home alone or at work outside, and talk with her. Aside from normal pleasantries, and perhaps an exchange of news and comments quite apart, mature people dispensed with the flippant approach. Both behaved cool and emotionless. He might say, "I have something important to say to you. If it should not be agreeable, you have only to say so. We are no longer children, so I shall not try to change your mind." If she listened on, he might finally say, "You seem to me to be the kind of woman I could live with harmoniously." When it was plain that a mature man came to court, the woman's relatives drifted away to other places to give him room, as though they did not know what he wanted. They were very tactful and delicate about this.

Neither would dream of eloping; that would be sheer madness and would invite nothing but ridicule. It would be inconsistent with their ages. Thus, whether they had been married before or not, for mature persons the impetuous marriage was unbecoming. Romantic love was reserved for youth; it was becoming to them. Older people afflicted with it must conceal it under a calm exterior so as not to excite comment. The Dakotas as a people aimed at all times to act their age, in courtship perhaps most particularly. Even if mature men and women were actually romantic about each other—and they could be—they managed to become engaged and start living together with a minimum of fuss. Marriage for the mature was a serious, matter-of-fact business all the way.

They always gave a very practical or altruistic reason for their step. "My tipi needs a woman who can help me offer hospitality as I should like" — that was a most laudable reason for marrying. All men should wish to be hospitable! Or, "My children need a mother's care," "My daughter is nearing the time when a mother's training and companionship are essential." A woman might say, "My father is sick [or, I have no brothers] and no one hunts for us." Or, "I will not let my sister's [or cousin's] children risk life with a strange woman for their mother." If the dead mother had been her sister or cousin, the marrying woman would already be their "mother" and they would be used to her. Friends and relatives repeated these noble and quite sensible reasons to their friends, with sober faces. Who would question them since they were so admirably right?

In discussing marriage from here on, I will refer only to the first marriage, the marriage of youth. There were three principal ways to marry: by elopement, by mutual agreement, and by purchase. Only the last two ways were proper, sanctioned by the tribe. There were at least two other ways reported, but they were not the usual, and need not be discussed in detail. One was that sometimes a girl's parents, or if she was an orphan, her closest relatives, offered her to some man of ability and standing in the tribe because they wanted her to be safe in his protection. If he had a wife already who was the girl's sister, and she accepted the offer of a cowife in the home, the girl was doubly safe, in her care. The second way is legendary and by its very nature it must be regarded as something extremely rare. If a youth of low station and a chief's daughter were deeply in love, she told him to ask outright for her, while she secretly made her father understand that she had suggested the step since he had not the means to buy her as she should be bought.

Elopement has already been considered. It was highly improper, and to the girl's disadvantage, because it threw all the blame on her for taking the supreme risk with her honor. If the man was only trifling with her she might find herself *manil-éȟpeyapi* 'left in the wilds', which was the worst fate that could befall a girl. Sometimes the man brought the girl home to be received formally by his family, only to send her home when he was no longer enamored.

Very rarely it happened that a man found himself truly in love with the girl who had eloped with him, and kept her. Yet even she was the object of disfavor among the people, unless her parents had opposed her choice after she had given her promise, and she had run off with the man to make it good. If her marriage proved a success, it gradually enjoyed a retroactive if reluctant sanction. It was usually the women who openly discussed such matters, and they might gloss over her initial misstep when they were feeling very generous. They would then rationalize it by saying, "Well, after all, she had given her word. And, anyway, did not the first man she knew become her husband? It wasn't as though she had been promiscuous."

To "know" but one living man was an admirable ideal—not always attained, but, as a matter of principle, certain women did remain single forever after they were widowed. I have to add that this was not always out of pure loyalty to a dead mate; for most women it was a personal satisfaction to live up to a vow made to the deceased husband. "When he laid dead I told him I would never know another man. I stand by my word." So said a widow who was being urged to marry a fine man who had proposed to her. It was a serious thing to make a promise audibly to a corpse and go back on it. People sneered at one who did so. "She is not reliable," they said.

Women with strict standards did not care to have several men whom they had known intimately. It was shameful to meet a former husband, much less chat familiarly with him. Former spouses could not dissolve their marital relationships into simple friendship; unless they lacked all sense of delicacy, they avoided one another, like strangers.

The commonest way to marry was by mutual consent, and that meant parental approval. This was the way of the mass of respectable people. There was nothing showy about such a marriage; the pair started unostentatiously living together. It was no secret, and it was entered into deliberately and sanely—nothing like the impulsive elopement. No marriage was forced at the point of an arrow. Before reservation law was in operation, there was no obligation to marry in the event of a premarital pregnancy "to give the child a name." There were no surnames.

Although there was no rule determining first residence, in a marriage made by mutual consent and planning, the girl's family usually provided the bridal tipi near their own. Later, if the young couple chose, they went to the man's family to live, or to visit for a while. In the case of an elopement, however, the man took the girl to his home, never the other way around. Then his people made hasty preparations to insure the newlyweds privacy. This arrangement was a merciful one for the girl, who was doubtless ashamed to face her own relatives and parents but could recover her dignity, somewhat, among relatives of marriage who were obligated to show their respect for a daughter-in-law by avoiding her. There, unobserved and not made self-conscious, she could perhaps better grapple with her situation privately.

I have already discussed the girl's prolonged evasion and her seeming indifference to her suitors. This was in turn a testing of them. Those who were only trifling soon got bored and weeded themselves out. If one came back undaunted, until she believed that he was serious, and if she decided that she cared for him, then it was time to tell her parents that she meant to accept him. If there was what seemed an insurmountable objection, she either gave up the idea of marrying that particular man, or eloped with him. Otherwise the marriage by mutual consent and with parental approval could take place.

Her relatives bestirred themselves to prepare for it. After the two began to live in their own tipi, some of the relatives of the bride and groom gave presents to them and to one another as they were able, although that was not obligatory. Many fathers of the girl tried to give some significant gift, usually a horse, to their son-in-law, and mothers gave ample presents to their daughter-in-law. The mothers of boys planned this long in advance. They carefully examined each new item that came into their possession from time to time, and if it seemed a worthy gift for a future daughter-in-law, they put it away, saying, "I have a son; this shall be for his wife." The son might still be a mere child or even a baby. However, the Dakotas did not pledge their children in marriage. Articles so earmarked were legitimate to withhold if meantime an occasion arose to "throw things away" because of a death in the family. Thus one might say that "hope chests" were kept for boys and girls in many families, not by their parents but by their future parents-in-law, who did this without any inkling as to just who the recipient would be, and not worrying about that.

Giving was a lordly gesture not to be denied to the humblest Dakota. It was everyone's right to give personal expression of the tribal ideal of generosity. No matter how poor he might be, his gift might not properly be refused. To refuse it would be tantamount to saying, "No. You keep it. You are too poor to give," and casting a supercilious glance of appraisal over the giver's person. That would be the unpardonable insult—but I have never heard of it. It was a deep-seated Dakota habit to give.

When I visited the Mandans some years ago, my hosts told me of an old Dakota woman who lived alone in a walltent on the edge of town. Years ago she had married into the Mandan tribe and had become so thoroughly at home there that after her husband's death she stayed, saying that her Dakota relatives were all dead and she had no one to whom to return. I went to see her at once and found her quite destitute and nearly blind, but she was so happy to converse in Dakota once more that she could hardly stop talking. All the while she felt all around her for a pillowcase filled with her belongings and fumbled a long time through it.

At last she brought out a Turkish towel with a fifty-cent piece tied into one corner of it. This she presented to me. "You are of my people and have come far to visit me, but this is all I have to give you, grandchild," she said. I took it and thanked her, knowing that it was her all. There was nothing else to do, but the next morning, since I was leaving shortly, I made my return gift promptly. It consisted of some fresh beef and other grocery items that I was sure she needed and wanted. We had already adopted each other as *ųčí* 'grandmother' and *tʿakóža* 'grandchild', and because we were social relatives we enjoyed a pleasant, homey visit. I was sorry to leave her, although I had never seen her until the day before. We had conformed to the Dakota rule perfectly: be related; give to relatives.

The third type of marriage, by purchase, called *wičʿípi*, was the glamorous way to marry. A woman felt gratified at being bought because it showed that she had been wanted at any cost; that she had properly held her own in the approved way against the smooth wooers who tried to sway her, until at last one of them had made a public bid for her. If she was still very young, the offer of marriage showed her to be so desirable that some man was preempting her before the triflers could get to her. The girl who could keep her head in courtship was one to be admired and respected.

Thus, to be bought did not make a woman mere chattel. Rather, it showed her up as virtuous, upright, and unattainable. An old Teton at Rosebud by the name of *Tʿašíyak-Núpa-Ská* 'White Meadowlark' cleared up some points that were doubtful and mentioned a detail that had entirely escaped me before. If a girl's parents refused to give her up and offered plausible excuses to the would-be wife buyer, saying, "She is too young," or, "She is not well enough to be married," ordinarily that ended the matter, but if a man was determined to have that particular girl for his wife, he might come back again and again, with more and better gifts. At last in desperation, he carried a live coal for some distance in the palm of his hand and offered that to her parents as his ultimate gift. Usually this left nothing but for the parents to relent, for by that time all the tribal sympathy was on his side. A woman who was married by purchase in this manner was said to be *p'éta ų op'ét'ųpi* 'one bought with fire'. The proof of her worth was the scar her husband carried all his life.

In theory, and for the most part in practice, girls were allowed to make the final decision to marry. "She must decide, since she must do the marrying" was a common saying despite the sprinkling of known cases wherein the girl was privately coerced into accepting a wife-buyer — for her own sake or for the sake of her family in need of help.

Even though both parental urging and parental objection were in tribal disfavor, a girl sometimes made her decision with the needs of her family in mind. Thus it was reported of one girl that she agreed to marry because her father was an invalid and unable to hunt for his family; and of another because her brother could use the horses offered for her, but the latter reason was a dubious one. It raised the immediate question "Did the brothers say so, and thereby influence her?" That would be wrong. Any brother who would urge his sister to marry to meet his own needs would be breaking a kinship law that collaterals of opposite sexes must never take advantage of one another for their own benefit. In one life story I recorded, the girl's little brother cried, "Oh, I hope our sister accepts this man! Such fine horses — I'd take the bay!," to which his elder brother answered haughtily, "We in this *t'iyóšpaye* do not sell our sisters. When we need horses, we go to war for them!"

It was no special achievement to marry off a daughter at an early age for the glory of having her become a wife. Since any woman could marry, and most of them did so, it would be a quaint notion for a mother to glory in such a commonplace. Mothers were in no way upset to have an unmarried daughter — on the contrary, they and other women relatives sometimes boasted about an attractive girl who took her time and kept her head in spite of an apparently large array of suitors. With ill-concealed pride a mother might explain as she introduced her daughter to a visitor, "She is past twenty years — yet thus she remains." Yet when finally she decided to marry, they happily prepared her bridal tipi and welcomed her spouse respectfully. If she was bought, that was better yet and it gave them more to glory in. Didn't they raise a daughter who could singly win out against a host of pursuers?

Even if some mothers did privately encourage their daughters to marry, for whatever reason, ideally both mothers and aunts must refrain from discussing any individual suitor, with an eye to his looks, his ability, or his faults. Because any husband of their daughter would be their avoidance relative, toward whom their attitude and behavior must be faultless, they wanted to maintain the correct position in relation to any potential *t'akóš* 'son-in-law', the term used both by mothers and aunts. This they could do only if from the outset they avoided any subject that might lead into channels of thought unsuitable toward a respect relative, so that they could assume their role spontaneously and sincerely when the proper time arrived.

In deference to a girl's natural sensibilities, all males in the family of birth avoided commenting on her courtship. Certainly none of them would dream of teasing her about her suitor or turning critical attention on him. That simply was not done. Rigorously they made her romance none of their business. When she planned to marry, her approaching sex life must be kept entirely outside their area of curiosity and speculation. To grandfathers, fathers, and uncles, she was a child; to brothers and male cousins, she was not one to be thought of in terms of her femaleness at any time.

On the other hand, parents had no hesitancy in urging a son to marry. That they did so was not secret. The father said he would like to see his boy marry and assume a man's responsibilities normally "while I still live." The mother might go so far as to select some girl and praise her in his son's presence. "She would so please me as a daughter-in-law. How I should like to carry her babies on my back!" If happily the son's final choice coincided with hers, she was overjoyed and felt uniquely responsible for her daughter-in-law. Then she gave her not only the respect that convention demanded but affection and devotion as well. Some wives who were not specifically picked by the mother-in-law did in time earn from her this extra regard by their own pleasant personality, ability, and consistently correct kinship behavior toward relatives-in-law.

The girl who eloped was already enamored; the girl who married by mutual consent knew what was ahead for her, but the girl who was bought, especially if she had been pressed by her family to accept, or if the glamour and glory implicit in the offer had overswayed her, might find the idea distasteful at last and run away from her marriage bed. This was most likely to happen if the wife-buyer was a total stranger, whose very appearance was unfamiliar. One girl, it is reported, walked out of her bridal tipi before her husband came in, and kept on walking across the common until she reached her own home, but since such a repudiation was sanctioned by society, a girl was within her rights and could neither be pursued nor forced to return. This rare practice was called *p'iláśni* 'to not appreciate'. The word is specifically used for this situation alone.

A girl who thus rejected a wife-buyer was at liberty to resume her former status without reproach and was reckoned a maiden still. Even though the rejected man's sisters and female cousins might feel insulted on behalf of their respect relative, and bear her secret malice, they could hardly berate her simply because she did not want to marry him, so long as her subsequent conduct was exemplary. But let her misstep just once! Then these were the women most likely to publicize her offense vociferously to shame her. However, wife-buying was no daily event and repudiating a bridegroom was rarer yet. Most girls were cognizant of a woman's marital role and had the good sense to refuse an offer at the outset if the idea was repugnant to them.

From numerous accounts it is possible to piece together the fragments obtained regarding wife-buying, and arrive at a synthetic picture that cannot be too far from the truth. After selecting his future wife, the buyer — or his parents if he was a shy youth — sent a trusted friend to present the idea privately and try to determine the reaction the girl's parents would have to it. If the messenger's report seemed fairly auspicious, a cousin or brother of the suitor led one or more horses to the girl's tipi and tied them to a stake outside the doorway. Then he left without saying a word to anyone. He did not have to, for by tacit consent all the girl's relatives managed to be inside or elsewhere, to spare him. Until the offer was accepted, the wife-buyer was too jittery to take an active part. The horse gifts were delivered in the daytime when everyone might see what went on, for wife-buying was a public affair.

A married man who had agreed to speak to a girl on behalf of a friend or relative went about it with dignity and directness. He made it very clear at the outset that he was only a proxy "for the fine young man who wants very much to marry you but is afraid to speak for himself," and then he set forth all the man's good points for her to consider.

Certain young unmarried men were not so scrupulous. They went about their errand in a playful way, caring less for a successful outcome for their friend than for the sport of courting for fun. There is a classic tale about one charming but unprincipled young man who went on such an errand. He talked so convincingly, as though in his own interest, that the girl accepted him on the spot and promised to elope with him at midnight. When his less-favored cousin came all wrapped up in his courting blanket, she was ready. They traveled all night and she did not discover the hoax until daylight, but by then it was too late and they were too far away for her to go back.

When the writing of Dakota was a fascinating new accomplishment, proxy wooing by letter was the fad. Since only a few had as yet mastered the art, they were in demand as letter writers. I can tell of my own slight involvement in proxy wooing by letter, for, very briefly, I was once a carrier of love notes.

A married man with two girls in our mission school came up to me while I was playing by myself and extended his hand in greeting. He had been in the house talking with my father and had seen me around but paid no attention to me. Now he wanted to shake hands, belatedly. I was puzzled, but I shook hands anyway and found remaining in my palm a piece of ruled paper wrapped tightly around a coin. "The money is yours," he said, "if you will take the paper to 'Helen' (not her real name) and give it to her without being seen." A quarter was well worth the trouble, so I delivered the note, without mishap. Its contents did not interest me, perhaps because I could not read yet.

The news of my skill in dodging the mission school teachers—who most certainly would not approve—must have traveled fast among the young men who were interested in the schoolgirls, for soon others were sending notes, too. Thus quite by accident I was in a paying business, for they all gave me quarters. But my mother investigated me when she realized that I was buying more than my small allowance should bring, and promptly put an end to it.

She was thoroughly displeased that a man old enough to be my father would involve me in a chain of adult activities and encourage me to be secretive about it. Nor did his wife's bland explanation satisfy her, though it sounded reasonable to me. The wife said that, with her approval, "John" was only helping a courtship along for his shy, backward brother "Francis," and that he had to send the note by me because I knew my way around the mission plant. Incidentally, they never got Helen, even with my help.

The family went about their business without "seeing" the gifts, while the girl remained in seclusion to make up her mind. She might say yes, and give a reason. "I want my brother (or uncle, or father) to own these horses." If she remained undecided for very long, she might possibly be wheedled into accepting "for her own good" or for her family's good. One informant who was bought explained why she accepted: "I had seen the man and remembered him as pleasing enough, but when my mother reminded me, 'Daughter, since your father's death your little brothers have often been hungry,' then I hastily said yes, for I cared about my family, especially my little brothers." Thus sometimes a desperate family need drove a girl to consent.

If her decision was yes, the girl's uncle or father immediately untied the horses and led them to water and grass. Then, almost at once, the news was flashed around the camp circle, from tipi to tipi, "The wife-buying is a success!" If not, the horses stood tied until sometime in the night the suitor's brother or cousin slipped in and took them away without a word. Shortly after the acceptance, over across the common or wherever the man's family lived, a bridal tipi went up in front of his parents' home, and women relatives bustled about bringing handsome robes and other furnishings and laying them in place there.

It would be unrealistic to claim that every family was able to provide a special bridal tipi for their child and set it up in front of their home. When such a tipi was used, that was where it was placed for the honeymoon, but many families were too poor to do this. Often enough the best they could do was move in with their various relatives and leave their tipi to the newlyweds, especially when a bride came without any warning, having eloped. On the other hand, a proud and able family, with many cooperating relatives, could provide a tipi easily. When they would honor their child's marriage to the nth degree, they took their own tipi down and reerected it to face the rear of the camp circle for the time being, so that the tipis stood back to back. This was an added expression of their respect for a new avoidance relative, in order to permit the bashful spouse a still wider scope.

Meantime the girl was being readied at home. Her hair was washed ceremonially in yucca root lather and then oiled and carefully braided in two shiny braids, in the customary way for women. There was no difference in hairstyling to set the matron apart from the maiden. Even tiny girls wore their hair that way, if there was enough of it to braid. The oil was scented with pulverized *waȟpé-waštémna* 'sweet-smelling leaf', which was the Dakotas' favorite perfume. Sweetgrass, known as *wač̇ą́ǧa*, a word of doubtful etymology, was another popular scent. It was a spicy aroma from a certain species of grass.

Men used sweetgrass, too, mostly as a braid attached to their fancy costume. I might add that such a braid was fastened to gift items such as tobacco pouches, saddlebags, feather fans, and so on. Hospitality and generosity were sometimes spoken of as "sweet-smelling deeds," but whether that was the reason I have not heard specifically. Both *waȟpé-waštémna* and *wač̇ą́ǧa* were chewed to sweeten the breath; and certain men preferred them, pulverized, in their own smoking mixtures rather than laurel leaf, sumac, or something else. All such flavors were for adding pleasantness to the smell of tobacco smoke.

The part in the hair was painted with red ocher from mid-forehead to the occipital hollow, thus dividing the hair exactly in two sections. A thin film of the red paste was carefully spread over the entire face, as for all formal occasions. If the girl, beloved of her parents, had been raised to *hųká* status at some earlier time, that fact was indicated by the proper markings of tiny parallel lines of deeper red down her cheeks.

The *hųká* ceremony was an elaborate honoring rite, which taught hospitality and generosity.[5] Candidates were carried to the tipi of preparation by the four escorts sent to bring them in. A child was carried on the back by one escort and the others followed behind. An adult was placed in a sitting position in the center of a bullhide and was borne along, with the four escorts holding the four corners of the hide. Incidentally, the name of the Big Dipper or Ursa Major is *Wič̇á Ak'íyuhapi* 'Man Carried along by Several Sharing the Load', named with reference to the *hųká* practice of carrying adult candidates. The four stars are the escorts; the blank space they describe is the bullhide. The man seated there is, of course, invisible from below.

The bridal gown of white doeskin was elaborately decorated, as were the matching accessories, and the moccasins were covered with solid quillwork, the soles included.

Moccasins completely covered with fancywork were not for walking. Formerly the work was solid porcupine quill embroidery, and in later times it was beadwork. They were for a bought bride, for a candidate in the *hųká* ceremony, or for babies not yet walking. Now and then they were put on the dead.

Coming back to marriage preparations, the bride was placed on horseback, but she did not hold the reins to guide her horse. One of her relatives walked ahead and led the horse. She sat passive on it, with a blanket pulled up over her head to screen her face completely, for she was intensely shy and modest. Even if she were not, it was still conventional to hide the face.

The one who led the horse was in a sense giving the bride away. My impression is that he or she must be from the ascending generation, perhaps a parent, aunt, uncle, or grandparent, but it is not unlikely that a much older collateral might fill that role, lacking an elder relative, or he might demand the honor because he had been his sister's or cousin's guardian. This I infer from something I heard in my childhood, long after wife-buying had become obsolete. With reference to a very attractive and well-mannered young woman, an elderly man said, "I value that cousin so highly that unless a man brought me a span of mules I would never give her away!" It was simply his way of estimating the girl's worth, and it was the supreme compliment, for when mules were a rarity and novelty, they were more highly prized even than horses.

One or more pack horses, or a mule if it could be had, came after and carried the bride's belongings and such gifts as her people were presenting to the new relatives of marriage. These were led by various relatives, mostly women. Other people might follow on foot with portable gifts in their hands. All in ceremonial dress, they walked unhurried across the common in a quite flashy procession, toward the bridegroom's *tⁱiyóšpaye tⁱípi*. The entire camp circle paused to watch distantly, calling softly to one another's attention the *wiáyapi* 'woman taken along', which was the special name for such a procession. It was bad form for adults to crowd the scene or join the line, but children did so, and were not forbidden, unless they should block the way. If adults could not see well at a distance, they could learn nearly everything about the affair later on from their observant children, who hardly missed a detail.

As the *wiáyapi* drew near, the groom's relatives came out in a body to meet them. The bride's horse was halted in front of her new tipi and women relatives-in-law lifted the bride gently off her horse and led her inside. There they seated her comfortably before they went out. In all marriages it was women who dealt directly with the bride; men kept aloof after shaking hands with her, but stood ready to help indirectly as needed.

Outside the tipi soft-spoken exchanges of the new kinship terms punctuated the polite conversation that the new affinal relatives carried on with dignity and sober good manners. The bride's relatives were offered food before being allowed to depart. If, as was more than likely, a public wedding feast was planned, it would come later.

The time element remains unclear. For instance, after the acceptance, did the marriage take place immediately? If not, how many days elapsed while both families prepared for it? Was the bridal costume made hurriedly, or did she own a handsome enough outfit already, or was it obtained from friends? Was the very handsome bridal tipi, as required in a marriage by purchase, made while the negotiations went on? Or was it obtained from someone who had just made it for some future need? Not every instance of wife-buying could be as elaborate as this account. Sometimes a girl from a poor family was bought, too. None of this much matters now, but for the record I wish I could be more explicit.

After so much ceremony the bought wife was simply a wife. Aside from the satisfaction of having married in the most admired way, she claimed no particular status above other women. She worked just as hard to maintain her tipi and care for her family as they did. If she had relatives who were able to assist her, well and good. Such assistance was one more expression of kinship devotion. Since all were relatives, the Dakotas did not employ fellow Dakotas as servants in the European sense. All were workers together.

Despite this surface equality, the bought wife must be outstandingly faithful to her womanly duties and kinship obligations, and must maintain for all time the virtue that had won her the title of *opʻétʻųpi* 'one bought'. It would be fatuous to assume that every bought wife lived up to the standard expected of her, but perhaps exceptions were conspicuously rare. In all my data I have no story about a bought wife who proved herself unworthy of her honor.

Very old women, given to reliving the past, sometimes recalled boastfully that their husband bought them; and for them it was excusable, but for younger women to keep reminding others that they had been bought was unbecoming and rather laughable. There was no need; they could well afford to play down the fact that they were *opʻétʻųpi*, since the people never lost sight of it anyway. Indeed, it was the manner of a woman's marriage that visitors liked to know first and their hostesses were eager to tell them. "She was bought"; "That one married quietly, by mutual consent"; "There's one who eloped!" It was only the last who was looked on askance. "You don't say! Tell me about it."

But almost as questionable, or perhaps even more so, was the woman who married into a forbidden category, for by doing so she proved herself an unstable, unreliable member of society. Two persons who considered marriage across the lines dividing the generations had this to consider: the intolerable embarrassment such a step must cause their relatives, even if they cared so little about their own standing as to permit an improper mutual attraction to develop in the first place. For what they did by marrying was to throw out of balance the whole delicate kinship machinery that controlled social life. Inevitably it rocked the entire community, and affected everyone.

If terms of address and reference had been mouthed as a mere formality, the question of changing them would have been quite simple, but it was not a perfunctory matter. A person who all his life had religiously observed the specific rules of attitude and behavior required in each kind of relationship could not but feel unnatural in having to change them overnight. By changing them he would in effect be changing his established character toward those relatives. Imagine a jocular brother-in-law suddenly turned into a respect relative! Why, one could hardly remember to what extent one had bantered words with him, or how. Too flippantly? Too rudely? Even ribaldly? Such registers were permitted in the joking relationship for any who were so inclined. Then should one put on a sober face, turn into a respect relative on the spot and begin saying "brother" to him with convincing sincerity? For a people to whom kinship matters were the prime consideration, this made a nearly impossible situation.

Yet even from this predicament there was a way out, however distasteful. The kinship scheme must be preserved, somehow; its torn fabric must be mended, even though the stitches might show. After the first shock over the news, the close relatives of the new couple set out to "mend kinship" in the most plausible way.

I knew of one such unsanctioned marriage in my childhood. A woman of fifty married a man of thirty-five whom formerly she had called her nephew and had behaved as an aunt toward him. Since both were widely related and had formerly lived as reliable people, their sudden step upset many; it upset even me. For before I could address them again, I too must make some changes. I avoided them for years; it made me feel strange and foolish to call by different terms those I had always known as other kinds of relatives. They were the same people, and yet I had to change toward them and they toward me. I hated it.

One confused woman told my mother how she worked out her own case: "It was very awkward for me. You see, she is my aunt and he is my brother-in-law. However, fortunately, I never knew him well enough to talk informally or joke with him. He is a stranger, you might say, but she has always been very close to us in social kinship. So I have decided to keep her as an aunt and call him uncle." She laughed queerly as she stated her decision.

Any solution was upsetting to those who must mend kinship. Nor could they discuss or even think about the marriage without wondering about the improper steps that must have led to it. As a matter of fact, the pair had been only social relatives, not relatives of birth. Even so, however, since they had been aunt and nephew so long, which meant they represented different generations, it took their kith and kin a considerable while to cast off the unnatural feeling, the embarrassment, whenever they must address or refer to them with entirely new terms.

Perhaps the worst hit were the couple's own children by former marriages. After having been differently related all their lives, they must have been bewildered by their new sibling status—before it became a huge joke. They grinned when they said "my brother" or "my sister." However, it was not funny at school, when quarreling playmates hurled insults at them: "You *t'ųwį́ču glúža!* You *t'oškáku hįgnákiya!*" These nominal phrases might be translated as 'aunt-marrier' and 'nephew-marrier'. *Yúža* means 'to take a wife'; *hįgnáyą* means 'to take a husband'. Here they are inflected to indicate the possessive—*own* aunt, *own* niece are ideas implied to emphasize the impropriety of the parents' union. The elements denoting possession can not be instantly detected in these two verbs because they are not the same; the verbs themselves belong to different classifications, and form their possessives differently.

Since children quickly pick up what is said at home, the nature of these shouted abuses was an unmistakable clue to their families' opinion of the unsanctioned marriage. Though it was the newlyweds who occasioned those abuses by their daring step, it was their children who became the vicarious victims, they being in no way to blame.

A marriage that cut across the generations, like this one, was sneeringly referred to as an *Iktómi* marriage. Only *Iktómi*, who had no respect for decency, would be expected to do such a thing; as indeed he did, according to one myth. To summarize it in a paragraph, when *Iktómi* saw the three mothers of his bride, he fell in love with the youngest and prettiest. But this was improper, so, without venturing to speak with her, he pretended that all men had been ordered by the council to take a mother-in-law with them on the warpath. His wife said, "Why don't you go with my eldest mother?" and offered them in turn, but he objected to the first two. When she said, "What about my youngest mother?" he replied, painfully and very regretfully, *Wą̇ . . . Hóye!* 'Oh, no, that is out of the question . . . Oh, very well!' He stayed away for years and finally returned with the "mother-in-law" and all their countless children. What happened then is illustrative.[6]

An elderly male informant discussed in detail the value of kinship rules of attitude and behavior, and explained why it was imperative that they be scrupulously kept. I translate freely as to language but with care to transmit his exact thought:

It takes two to sin against the sex taboo imposed on all those relatives for whom marriage is eternally out of the question . . . The case is lost only if both dare to change attitude and behavior from the prescribed ones. Granted a mutual attraction, there is always a chance to conquer it, as long as the rules are equally respected; as long as the controlling mechanism does not give way for both. One's temptation can be checked by the other's strength. But should both be equally weak, then, alas, they will allow themselves improper thoughts about the other, and thereby alter their attitude. When that happens, it is not long before their inner laxity is betrayed in overt acts, since the will to prevent such acts is no longer working. Inevitably there follows an exchange of signs of mutual interest. It may begin with a seemingly accidental look, or casual gesture or touch, and gradually lapse into a deliberate informality permissible in only the joking relationship—and the bars are down. And now, the secretly shared desire is ready to reach sexual intimacy. What is left to prevent it?

I have digressed and must go back. The average Dakota marriage—whether by purchase, mutual and open consent, or even elopement—was never characterized by boisterous and confusing celebration. No wedding party of jovial, noisy well-wishers was needed to insure its success. It was neither a particularly happy nor a particularly sad occasion; it was, rather, a sober, tentative time, since what lay ahead was unsure. Public speeches with glib wishes or sly innuendoes about the marital role would be completely out of order, and were indeed unthinkable. If a crazy person or a natural fool ventured to speak offensively, he would be led away before his remarks could be heard generally, but they would not be held against him, because he was irresponsible and devoid of kinship regard—as an uninstructed child might be. Tact, delicacy, and good sense marked the general attitude toward marriage.

As is the case among any people, there were those who were given to carnal joking, but a marriage was not the place to indulge in that. If any of the collateral relatives of the bride or the groom were that kind, they must indulge in such joking somewhere else by themselves: male collaterals of the groom, or female collaterals of the bride, in separate places, never together! That such joking would be grossly offensive will become clear because it contravenes to the *hakáta* relationship.

Relatives helped with marriage preparations according to their abilities, wanting to make the occasion a credit to their *t'iyóšpaye*, as well as honor the relative who was being married. Afterward they stepped aside and left the newlyweds to themselves as far as possible, almost seeming to ignore them while they must get used to one another. For, after all, it was their day; and what they might make of their life together in the years ahead was entirely up to them.

6

Wedded Life

On their wedding day, bridegrooms behaved in various ways according to age and temperament. If he was a very young man, and especially if a wife had been selected and bought for him by doting parents who were disturbed at his lack of normal interest in courtship, he acted with complete indifference, as though he were in no way involved. He stayed away all day, riding with his male companions as usual, and marriage seemed to be the last thing on his mind. His friends did not remind him by teasing him; that was not done. Only long after dark he stole in unobserved, to find his bride waiting alone in their tipi.

Older men, who were more poised and dignified, remained on hand to meet their bride, and this was true particularly of those who had bought a wife on their own initiative, knowing what they wanted, but even a mature-minded bridegroom did no more than shake hands wordlessly with his bride. He would not embrace her in front of other people—not then or ever. It would be no compliment for the girl, either, to be embraced and greeted effusively; it would only embarrass and worry her. Could he not wait? Was she marrying a fool? For conventional Dakota people, delight in a spouse was not properly for public display.

What a girl felt while being taken to her husband, or thought while she waited alone in the tipi, are things extremely difficult to probe. Dakotas would not understand why anyone would want to know such intimate matters about others. They were especially inarticulate about their own reactions to marital experience and would resent the questioner for his undue curiosity, and look on him as a little crazy. "Marry—and find out for yourself!"

However, from many idle reminiscences of old people, who grew less reticent with years, it must be assumed that the average Dakota was cautious toward his new bride. If she could sit indefinitely quiet and controlled, then he could match her. All day long the pair sat in their tipi, side by side, but almost as complete strangers. She was very shy, and it was like a sickness with her, and he would not force her out of her shyness with any clumsy means. When he did finally venture to address some ordinary remark to her or ask her a simple question, she took a painfully long time to reply, having first to gather her forces against the awful timidity that paralyzed her throat. Almost after he had forgotten his question—which was not so important anyway—she might answer it in a word or two, whispered with tremendous effort. If she could not reply at all, he was content, but in time she managed a smile over something he said or did, and then perhaps she would let an occasional chuckle escape her. Days might pass before she would initiate a conversation. His role was one of patience and control until she was more relaxed.

A very young bridegroom was just as shy. In any case most newly-weds were not immediately talkative, although occasionally there was one who was naturally so, one who was "born that way." Young brides were expected to be more or less inarticulate until there was a child to be soothed and quieted. Then the presence of others did not keep them from talking and humming to their infant, as though no one existed but them and their child. Bridal reticence, it might well be imagined, was likely to be more pronounced and sustained longer if the newlyweds lived first in the husband's t'iyóšpaye t'ípi, where his relatives were new to her and many had to be properly avoided, and who avoided the bride in turn, according to custom.

Regardless of the particular place of their first residence, however, newlyweds did not like to have other people's attention concentrated on them. This feeling was respected, and they were allowed to get used to each other privately, and with a minimum of outside interference, how-ever well meant. Except to take food to their tipi from time to time, for the bride to serve to her husband and herself, relatives left them strictly alone and even called off the children from a distance if they went near there, lest they be a nuisance. Very small children, however, toddlers, strolled in and out as they pleased. A bride might talk more easily to them than to her husband, and find amusement in their lisping replies. Very shy young couples together were inclined to make undue fuss over them, to take the other's attention from themselves. In that respect the little ones were a welcome and useful diversion in the bridal tipi.

Since it was customary for everyone to be up and fully dressed by day, the married couple did not loll about half-clad even in the privacy of their tipi. That was an impractical luxury—if luxury it was. I rather think it was not, because there was no taste for it as there was none for eating in bed. Breakfast served in bed would seem quite silly, since one must get up afterward, unless one was sick. For everyone had to remain literally on the balls of the feet at all times, ready to run in case of an enemy raid at any unexpected moment. Alert preparedness was the prime necessity for the old-time Dakotas. Consequently, even the honeymooners were ready to go at any time, and to admit anyone who came in. Even though other people aimed not to thrust their presence on them so early in their married life, while they were getting accustomed to each other, it was not inconceivable that someone might come there at any hour with a message or a gift. However, gradually, as the days passed, those relatives who were not in avoidance relationship to either bride or groom began dropping in under one pretext or another. The bride got acquainted with one at a time, or at most two, and that was for her the easiest way.

The new husband came and went, often leaving at dawn to hunt all day or ride out on some distant errand with his companions, or simply to be with other men. He did not spend the day posturing around his wife and ogling her and telling her how much he loved her. Such things must be assumed to be so. His admiration and delight in his bride must be more subtle. This left her alone for long periods, while she busied herself with the socially important gifts that a bride properly made with her own hands for her husband's parents. She made handsome moccasins for both, and sometimes in addition she made an elaborate tobacco pouch for her father-in-law, if she had the rare skill required to wrap colored quills around the strips of rawhide that formed the base of such pouches. A man's parents were inordinately proud of whatever his wife made for them, and were reluctant to give them away. Many mothers-in-law kept those moccasins against their burial, even though they might live many years after those were presented to them. Far from feeling neglected and deserted, the bride worked contentedly, and welcomed those intermittent opportunities to take her bearings and plan for her new life.

The nature of their society permitted Dakotas to be used to many people and feel at home with them, as relatives, yet no normal person was lonesome in solitude or afraid to be left alone for a time. At no time did a woman claim the whole of her husband's attention. She expected to share it with his many relatives and friends, from the beginning of their life together. Possessiveness, expressed in a demand for the spouse's exclusive interest, was hardly possible. Each was a person and both had their right to be independent and both still had their precisely prescribed obligations to their many relatives and always would have. Any exception to this customary behavior of married couples was considered childish and ridiculous.

Early in the honeymoon period, at a time when the new wife was alone, her sisters-in-law came in and gave her the traditional ceremonial dressing of the bride known as *wišáyapi* 'to paint a woman'. They put a handsome gown on her and dressed her hair, as a formality, and painted her face affectionately with a fresh film of red ocher. It was this last feature that gave this honoring ceremony its name. They did this primarily to honor their brother, whose bride she was.

After a while the bride slowly overcame her bashfulness enough to be seen. She stole out and stood in the open for short periods, a silent figure alone. It took time to master herself and mingle with her affinal relatives, and they did not rush her by speaking to or approaching her prematurely. She had met different ones singly and by twos; now she was able to meet them in a group that no longer seemed so formidable.

When both bride and groom were in a crowd together, one could not know without being told which two were recently married to each other. All through life married couples did not keep close together where people gathered, as though literally tied together. Each moved independently of the other, among those of their own sex. Nor did they slip away at any time with the obvious desire to be exclusively alone. Outside the privacy of their tipi, they aimed not to exclude others from their normal and necessary activities. If they must confer privately, they withdrew from the crowd to one side for a moment. Quickly they returned to the group. A man and wife who suddenly, and for no reason anyone could see, strolled off together away from their friends would be acting most extraordinarily indeed.

Although in one legend a new husband says to his wife, "Let us hunt in the wilds, where we can swim together," under normal circumstances man and wife did not swim together, but with members of their own sex, out of sight of bathers of the opposite sex. Once I saw the following scene when the caravan of wagons stopped at noon beside the Cheyenne River: the men came swimming around the bend and swam far out in deep water, and at the same time their womenfolk sat in the shallow water, washing clothes and keeping an eye on the children splashing about, but they kept their calico dresses on. At no time did the men come out and stand exposed. In due time they again swam around the bend before coming out.

The paramount aim of adult married behavior was to appear practical and plausible at all times, and to conceal all signs of amorous thought about the opposite sex. That was the proper way to behave in company.

All this is not to say that others contrived, amid titters, to keep newlyweds apart in order to plague them. That was unthinkable. It was what they themselves preferred because anything else would be unconventional and even peculiar and would earn unfavorable report: "Are they crazy that they are so obvious?" Only a naive and half-foolish person would be openly eager to get his mate alone. There was a constant and consistent striving for moderation and control of all emotions save grief over death, and perhaps in marriage this striving was most pronounced.

Someone who was there told me the following incident, which illustrates the shyness of the new bride. About 1920 a young Teton couple was invited to afternoon tea at the mission school, following their marriage rite at the church; and for both, this was ordeal enough. When the white teacher who was pouring asked teasingly, "Mary, how does your husband like his tea?," the simple question so flustered the bride that she turned a deep purple and could not reply.

How should *she* know how her husband liked his tea—or anything else about him! Dakota girls ought not to know such personal things about any man until he became their husband, and then only gradually find out. In those days it was still a fact that—theoretically, at least—the one person in the world who knew least about one was that one's new spouse. Discovery began with marriage.

All through life the tendency was to be cautious regarding a spouse's feelings and wishes. The man said: "Ask the woman. It is up to her, whatever she likes." She said: "He has not told me what he prefers about that. Why don't you ask him?" Neither seemed disposed to take the initiative and lay down the law for the other; or at least that was the usual pattern, but always there are exceptions.

One notoriously determined old woman who must always have her way was heard to say at a gathering, "I said I wanted to go home early—and I am going! But where is he? Grandchild, call your grandfather away from that cluster of smoking old men. What a man! Wherever men are smoking and talking, there he remains, as though pegged down!" She added, "He forgets where he came from!" While this habit of bossing is irregular, it is expected of women more than of men. For a quick-tempered and domineering husband it was considered petty, and consequently most men gave at least an appearance of being easygoing and impervious to petty annoyances, so as to be taken for "real men."

Men's working tools were exclusively theirs, but wives and even children owned certain horses or cows individually and these ran in the family herd with the man's. They were designated as "mother's cow" or "son's horse." Properly, wives did not interfere with their husband if he chose to give away his saddle, harness, any particular horse, if he lent a plow or other implement. "I do think he was foolish—the borrower will never return it. But, then, it was his own!" Thus, for the most part, man and wife did what they would with personal possessions.

Women owned and controlled everything pertaining to the home. Dakota men were contemptuous of one who supervised his wife's cooking and dispensing of food. He should provide it, and there his authority should end. One who was exacting with the food and minutely occupied with women's business in general was a stingy man, and stingy men were in general disfavor. Nor was it proper for a husband to dictate his wife's personal belongings. If he showed an abnormal interest in them and said what she should or should not give away, he was dubbed *wįyą* 'woman', a term men did not care for.

Men's activity laid outside and beyond the home, while women's was inside as well as in the yard around where she carried on part of her work. Properly, each spouse kept out of the other's area. A woman who arbitrarily made her husband do her work was laughed at by other women. "Has she no hands that a man must neglect his own work for hers?" Likewise, the husband who meekly submitted to his wife's orders was the object of other men's muttered ridicule: "He does women's work"; "He is bossed by women." Ideally, marriage was a partnership where each must do his own stint fairly. Of course, if one spouse was ill, then the other had an understandable reason to do his work for him. Otherwise, there should be no pampering nor peremptory ordering about of one spouse by the other. Under no circumstances was a wife her husband's "baby." She was from the start his peer. The relationship in marriage started and remained on that basis.

While it is true that married people separated and formed two groups according to their sexes, if a couple was formally invited they were seated side by side in the honor place of the tipi. Immediately upon finishing the elaborate meal, the wife lost no time in getting nearer the hostess for pleasant conversation with her. This left her husband to talk and smoke with the host and other men friends present. A woman who lingered among the men would be acting most peculiarly. "She is someway" meant that she was not normal; perhaps "something" had come over her to make her forget what was proper.

If the couple went calling together, he walked a little ahead "to clear the path," and upon arriving, each of them sought out the proper persons, the group they belonged with — men with men and women with women. To this day there is a men's side and a women's side at all meetings, public feasts, and church, reminiscent of the seating arrangement of the past, in the tipi. Modern young people are more and more tending to occupy a church pew with spouse and children, but they still generally separate for public feasts and meetings unless man and wife are seated at the table, instead of in a circle on the ground. Then they keep close together to be sure they are unquestionably distant from those seated next to them, who might be of the opposite sex or who might be respect relatives.

It was, as I have said, highly improper to stick closely to, or behave amorously toward, one's spouse in public, or wherever they might be observed. Even joking relatives did not normally see that kind of behavior. If the married couple had such sentiment for each other it was privately shared, not foisted on others. Only someone who was naturally foolish might so behave and might even so speak, and bring at least a smile of amusement at his naivete, and at most a word of ridicule, both of which he was unable to sense. If a simple-minded couple did not carry it too far, they were even tolerated for the amusement they unconsciously afforded. They were like "children who do not know any better."

Husbands and wives were not kinship relatives. Usually they omitted the formal terms meaning "my wife" and "my husband," and managed smoothly enough without them. They addressed each other as "you," and that was correct. In reference, if they said, "He is coming," or "She said this," there was no question as to just whom they meant. I have to use the English *he* and *she* to designate the husband and wife, but there are actually no pronouns denoting gender in Dakota. *Iyé* 'self', the third person singular, answers for both woman and man, but it is not used except for emphasis or contrast; the form of the verb indicates the person—for example, *Iyé héč'ų; miyé héč'amųšni* 'He did that; I didn't'.

Spouses did not take each other too much for granted, too obviously "for life." Rather, they seemed to accept marriage with a cool, tentative air, as if to say, "Come what may, I am braced for it! I shall play my part; we shall see if he (or she) will"—that is, that they would accept trouble or bliss with dignity, and with the same exterior calm. Marital battles were by no means absent, yet most spouses were able to adjust to one another without undue or prolonged friction. Men of high principle aimed to avoid trouble in all their relationships.

Because they regarded any vow audibly spoken as a religious matter, when they came with their wives for a belated Christian marriage after many years together, their spoken words were to them a binding oath that would be disastrous to break. "The Great Spirit has heard it," said one.

At one such wedding service during early reservation times, everything progressed smoothly as the native clergyman, the groom's nephew, read and the old couple repeated after him in their turn, until he came to that line in the old marriage office, "And with all my worldly goods I thee endow," which, incidentally, no longer appears in the later editions of the *Book of Common Prayer*. Right there the old man stopped short and bowed his head in earnest thought. The minister repeated the line in case the old man had not heard it, and waited quietly, but at last he looked up and said, *Éyaš it'ó t'ųšká, šúk-hįžila k'ų hék'eš ópaktešni yé ló.* In free translation this would be 'But wait now, nephew, at least that little old buckskin horse is not to be included'. Taking every word quite literally, he felt he must first qualify his vow to fit his intentions. He needed that pony for getting about or he would have to walk. She could have everything but that.

Swiftcloud, another fine old man with these inexorable standards, once came to the subagency and pretended to file a complaint against the woman he personally selected and bought nearly fifty years before. "Alas, that I must do this," he began soberly. "I want a divorce. Something has finally upset my marriage and I cannot bear to go on. At noon each day she goes out on the hill and sits there to wait, while I go hungry."

In his own way he was being facetious. That "something" that threatened their union was the new extension of the Milwaukee Railroad, whose fast trains cut thunderously across the startled reservation four times daily, following the stream below his home. Each day at high noon when the bright yellow flyer streaked by on its way to Seattle, Mrs. Swiftcloud's heart went with it, and Mr. Swiftcloud was jealous—of a train! But, of course, this was his way of amusing the Tetons waiting around the office before stating the real purpose of his call there. At the same time he was indulging in double-talk to indicate his distress at the rapidly increasing number of divorces among the younger folk over just such petty reasons.

It is reported that in former times the husband of an unfaithful wife might cut off her nose, although no informant could say he had ever seen it done. I doubt that it was a regulation, though it might have been done in rare cases. Kinship loyalty being what it was, it is hard to imagine such mutilation of even the most unfaithful wife without her brothers and male cousins rising up to avenge it. Perhaps it was borrowed from another tribe; perhaps it is something out of a myth; and yet, whatever the allusion, the saying persisted. One informant told me that in her childhood she heard the remark made concerning a woman who had been found guilty of a sex offense: "Her husband should cut off her nose!"

Not the eyes but the shape of the nose was the most important feature in judging womanly beauty. Perhaps this playing down of even beautiful eyes can be attributed to the fact that eyes were only for seeing, when necessary. They were not used freely. One who "talked" with her eyes was said to be crazy-eyed, and she was not admired for it. "Nice" women did not look boldly into others' eyes. The ideal feminine nose was shapely and small, and not too long. In profile it should show no bumps and should dip slightly at the bridge. The high "Grecian" nose was undesirable because it gave women a "mannish look." For a man a long nose was acceptable, though preferably smooth in profile. The beaked or broken outline was not conducive to beauty. However, that was not too important for a man. It was better, at any rate, than a too-dainty nose, a "woman's nose."

It is a true that some men indulged in wife-beating, over reasons no doubt valid enough to them. The reasons given me were that the wife was inhospitable, ugly-tempered, flirtatious, actually unfaithful, mean to her stepchildren—all faults that she could correct if she would. Physical plainness or handicap, natural stupidity or lack of womanly skills were not given. Apparently these were not valid reasons; a husband could put up with them if only his wife was easy to live with. Sometimes wife-beating was a form of third degree, when a man suspected his wife of infidelity and meant to beat the truth out of her.

I have the story of Little Crow, a Santee minor chief, who used to punish all his nine wives whenever any two of them quarreled. Incidentally, that is a prodigious number of wives. Four cowives are generally reported as being "many." The man had his reasons. He beat his wives for the sake of maintaining—of all things—harmony in his family. "I will not have it," he would storm. "I must have peace and tranquility in my home." So he would beat them all, innocent and guilty alike, going systematically from one wife's tipi to the next wife's. Soon there would be loud wailing that grew in volume as each wife added her voice to it in her turn, until one would suppose that somebody had just then died and women were wailing as the news went from tipi to tipi. After a while someone would say, "Oh, it is only Little Crow beating up his wives again!" The ultimate result was that whenever two wives began to argue angrily, the other seven did everything, even bribery, in order to appease them in self-defense. "Stop it, or he will beat us all!" The late Reverend Amos Ross, a Santee, told me this story, but he did not say whether this Little Crow was the chief who figured in the Minnesota Uprising of 1862 and I did not think to ask him.

Too great a disparity of ages between husband and wife sometimes caused misunderstanding. It was best for them to be nearly the same age, and even better for him to be a few years older than she. However, if an elderly man took a very young wife he was laughed at a little. An old man who forgot his age enough to behave amorously around young girls was always an object of derision at the same time that he was pitied for his dotage. A woman who married a much younger man also invited mild ridicule. She was said to *hokšíla hįgnáyą* 'marry a (mere) boy'. It was not actually forbidden to marry someone younger, if no kinship rules were broken, but such a marriage was bound to stir talk and arouse mild ridicule, often meant good-naturedly. Even so, such remarks were uncomfortable.

The trouble caused by too widely different ages for mutual accommodation was easily solved. The pair separated, and that ended it, without blame to either mate. Otherwise the most likely conflicts were due to a woman's bad premarital record. A husband given to jealous fits could not forget that fact and must punish his wife from time to time, though he need not have married her in the first place. On the other hand, many a second marriage proved happy where the man was big-hearted, with sound judgment and sense of values. Such men were more forgiving and might marry a woman, no matter her past record, because of her other qualities, of which a pleasant disposition rated highest. It was the first marriage wherein the young man hoped to marry a virgin and was proud if he did.

When a couple quarreled, their relatives and friends might be sorry for them, but it was strictly their own affair. If their disagreement was over some ordinary matter, the husband's parents protested mildly a few times in defense of their daughter-in-law, and her parents in defense of their son-in-law, for that was the conventional gesture for affinal relatives. Yet not they, and not even the council, had any authority to resolve a marital problem caused by unfaithfulness or a bad premarital past that the husband could not bring himself to overlook.

It was quite another thing when elderly couples gradually developed a habit of desultorily scolding the other. Such scolding fell on deaf ears because each knew that the other felt no real animosity. One old man, upon realizing how much junk his wife kept around the house, repeatedly urged her to "burn up all your old and useless things." With feigned impatience she turned on him finally. "I am not deaf, so why repeat? Very well, then, all my old and useless things, you included; you first!" He walked away unimpressed. Sometimes they vehemently blamed the other for some alleged blunder or stupidity. This kind of mock disgust was harmless, the result of a seasoned union marked by mutual tolerance and understanding, even affection, throughout their years together. They were so used to each other and so at home that they could afford to say anything, idly, without fear of wounding the other. Their grown-up children understood and accepted this pastime of their parents, but sometimes their grandchildren rose angrily to the defense of whichever grandparent seemed to be getting the worst of it, until it was explained that they were only pretending.

Young married couples could scarcely afford to treat each other so roughly if they wanted to nourish their new life together. They began by being very formal and so cautious of the other's feelings that both were likely to be touchy. One young husband committed suicide because, as he confided to his male cousin before going off to do away with himself, "She spoke to me as though she despised me. I want to get out of her way." Another, who had always prided himself on his riding skill, was so hurt when his young wife publicly doubted that he could stay on a certain outlaw horse—even though she spoke laughingly—that he went off and was never seen again.

It sometimes happened that a young wife who did not like her husband's attitude and conduct toward her sent for her own relatives and went home with them. This constituted divorce. To stay on and try by tricks to win him over was beneath her pride. "If he does not want me, I do not want him." A man could not compel his wife to stay with him against her will, thus her going home with her people—without saying for how long—was in practice a divorce. However, she did not then resume her former status, unlike the girl who repudiated a wife-buyer before a consummated marriage. The latter situation was comparable to an immediate annulment.

In a good marriage it was the wife who generally made the decisions in the home. Most men let it be that way, perhaps because they preferred to remain on neutral ground. *Nihŭ iyókipʼišni čʼá!* 'Because your mother is not pleased by it!', or *Nihŭ hečʼíyota waštékta iyúkča čʼá!*, 'Because your mother thinks that way will be best!', were typical explanations to his children, and they were enough. To his friends he might say, "It was what she decided," or "It seems to be unfavorable in her opinion." Husbands thus succeeded in staying out of possible minor controversies while at the same time complimenting their wife's efficiency in taking over the responsibility. It may have been their way of passing the buck. If, rarely, a husband made a decision and stood firm on it, his wife accepted it as something that must be extraordinarily important to him. Still, many wives appeared to defer to their husband's wishes by referring even minor matters to him, thus giving him a chance to say again, "Whatever you think best." Each gave in to the other upon occasion.

In rare cases a wife did seem to dominate in the home where the husband was of an easygoing disposition, and she a born manager. She did most of the talking and made quick decisions, she was usually right, and she gave orders immediately and noisily, without waiting for him. Because it was her nature to take the initiative, she was no doubt unaware of her overbearing manner. A woman like that could not keep from shouldering all responsibility instead of sharing it with her husband or of letting him take over certain problems entirely, which should be beyond a woman's scope. A wise husband did not resent such a wife but was instead content to let her handle in her energetic way the petty annoyances and occasional big ones, too, that beset the family.

Still, it would be inaccurate to say that such a man was "hen-pecked." No matter how positive her nature, the Dakota woman was not generally given to nagging her mate from pure viciousness. Marriage was too loose and terminable a relationship for either spouse to tolerate a willful arrogance in the other. In olden times no one was bound by oath to stay with any spouse if conditions were not right. If a man wished to keep a wife who had some annoying habit but was otherwise a good wife, he was wise to take her shortcoming in his stride and make of it an advantage for himself.

For a whole winter I once had an opportunity to observe just such a couple at close range, almost daily. It was in their latter years together, after a long married life. Mr. Brown Elk was a congenial, friendly, soft-spoken man with a subtle sense of humor. He had long since worked out a philosophy for living with his wife, who, though likeable and well meaning, and as hospitable to his guests as he could wish, had the habit of snatching nearly every topic literally out of his mouth. When she did so, he readily let her have it while he relaxed. Often he seemed not even to listen as he sat back with eyes shut, a hint of a smile on his face, while he puffed leisurely on his long-stemmed pipe. The smile seemed to say, "There she goes again—but it's all right." For he was very tolerant of her habit.

Only occasionally he teased her gently by boasting within her hearing about how lucky he was that he did not have to do more than introduce one subject after another, for there his responsibility stopped. At once she bit on it and shook it to shreds and never let go until she had completely exhausted it, but he boasted thus only when his brothers or male cousins were present because they were his wife's joking relatives. "It must be great to have so capable a wife," they would comment, "for it releases you for more important things—like smoking and meditating and taking your ease."

In describing his wife's handling of a topic, the graphic language he used suggested an energetic puppy with a rag in its mouth, to which it clung tenaciously. The rag would have to be torn away before it would let go of it prematurely. Of course the old man did not call his wife a puppy, but he certainly implied that picture by a clever choice and arrangement of words. He was unusually good with words, but his wife appeared neither to hear what he said nor react to the good-natured ribbing of her joking relatives. They had no effect at all on so fixed a habit.

When there were men guests who sat with him in the honor place beyond the fire, Mr. Brown Elk talked entertainingly and with more freedom, because women did not properly interrupt such conversation. Nevertheless, from her own space near the entranceway, Mrs. Brown Elk kept up a steady stream that I might liken to a running commentary down the margin of the printed page. From long association both of them were familiar with practically every subject or story, so that she hardly needed to correct him or ask questions. She had a different interpretation and opinion, the woman's perspective, which she volunteered in an endless muttered accompaniment, low in tone but yet loud enough to excite interest in her version, too. One was hard put to follow both "text" and "commentary" at the same time. Despite this habit the Brown Elks were a happy and congenial couple.

One of the criteria by which married couples evaluated one other was the concern one displayed over the other's kinship obligations to his own relatives. Wise spouses delighted each other from time to time by encouraging and aiding the other in their respective duties in this regard. A sensible wife did not resent her husband's filial devotion or his assistance to a sister in need, on the ground that he thereby neglected her. Instead, if he was not alert to such opportunities, she prodded him to act. Perhaps he purposely seemed a little slow, to see how concerned she actually was over his people. This worked both ways. For no special reason, the man might say, "Why not give that fine new horse I recently obtained to your eldest brother? It would make him happy, and I notice you have not done anything for him in a long time." The wife gave her husband's horse to her brother, and it was a magnificent gesture because of all its implications. A woman was proud to have a husband so thoughtful about her people. In each case they delighted each other by showing their awareness of the fact that obligations toward family relatives were everlastingly important and could not properly be neglected because of marriage.

Adultery affected any union. Both spouses had the right to expect faithfulness. Ideally, a woman's premarital record must be without flaw; no such demand was made of a man's. In any case, once they were married they should be faithful to each other. If the wife proved false, the husband might overlook it on account of their children, first demanding that she mend her ways at once. With a show of brave generosity some men said, "I pity her. After all, women are to be pitied." But even they could not forgive a wife's habitual unfaithfulness forever. A man of stature and prominence within the tribe might conceivably escape criticism for enduring such a wife; by doing so he would express his characteristic indifference to all the annoyances of life, but a lesser man was liable to the other men's jibes. "*Úšika* 'poor thing', how he hesitates to let her go! Does he distrust his ability to get another wife?" The prideful at least affected stoicism, but a vain or short-tempered man might go so far as to "throw away" his wife at a public gathering, and send the children to his womenfolk to be cared for. This sanctioned but unpopular practice was called *wií-hóyeyapi* 'calling out, regarding a wife', meaning, "Let anyone have her who will!"

A wife, on the other hand, did not necessarily leave her husband because of his clandestine affairs. She might be hurt and shamed, but as long as she herself was above reproach, she could ignore his behavior and justifiably hold up her head. Some faced the problem frankly, saying to their friends, "If he wants to behave in that way, what is it to me? My record is clear!" At least one wife was reported to have been rather proud of her man because other women could not resist him. Thus she put the blame on them while glorying in her husband's natural allure.

In such ways did women solve their problem with a philandering mate, but occasionally there was one who made of his weakness an excuse for her own extramarital affair. If she went off with another man and left children behind—and such a woman was not above doing that—then tribal sympathy went toward the neglected children, and perhaps a little of it even swung toward the husband, despite his own faults, on the theory that a wife and mother should be faithful no matter what.

It is reported that a married woman said to her dead cousin's husband, "Even while she lived [her cousin] I desired you secretly. Now that she is gone, I will leave my husband and children if you will have me." But the widower, an upright man, did not want such a woman for his next wife, nor did he take her offer as a compliment to himself. Since male collaterals shared such matters, his younger brothers and cousins promptly quoted her in one of those taunting "love" songs, naming her at the last: "Thus said so-and-so to me!" Of course they could do that, because she could not and would not make an issue of it by denying it. Men were as unscrupulous about discussing a woman of questionable morals as they were scrupulous about not discussing a woman of good reputation. In this case it was the woman's proposal to desert her own children that was most reprehensible, although her readiness to leave their father for another man was irregular enough.

Widows of advanced age continued to live in their own home, usually with a woman relative for companionship, or one or more children old enough to help them, but a young widow was expected to break up her home. With no husband she had in effect no home, but her parents' home was hers always. Without acceptable companionship she would not dream of living apart from them. The idea of an independent unmarried girl was nonexistent. A young widow who preferred to remain with her husband's parents rather than her own was acting abnormally, unless she had no family relatives anywhere and her husband's relatives were naturally agreeable people.

In former times a widow immediately put on her oldest and most unbecoming dress and hacked off her braids. In rare cases she even nicked her legs and arms to induce a flow of blood, but I am given to understand that only relatives of birth did that, ordinarily. Such extreme signs of mourning adopted by a widow were to show her grief, but also perhaps to discourage male attention to herself, lest she seem to bid for that, in thinking of her appearance.

All mourning garb was voluntarily assumed, because that was conventional. For instance, a widow was not forcibly made to cut her hair off. That she wanted to mourn in the usual way was a sign of adult responsibility. A girl widow did not always mourn in the usual way, seemingly unaware of any social compulsion to do so. In her case it was pardonable. People said: "She is still but a child . . . How can she be expected to think or act or feel in a mature way?" If she married inside the year, again, it was not too surprising.

A widower was likely to remarry within a year. He rationalized his step by thinking or saying, "I was faithful, dutiful, and kind to her, and we had a good life together; but it is ended now, so what else should I do?" As a rule the Dakota man did not pledge himself to eternal singleness after his wife died. For him to live on alone forever, with only a memory for companionship with the constancy and devotion attributed to some white men, would be as odd as it was unusual. Most widowers remarried—unless no other woman would have them—largely because it was the only practical thing to do, aside from any romantic reasons not generally revealed. For one thing it was nearly impossible for a man to maintain himself, keep up his clothes and cook his own meals, and of course there was no equivalent of the restaurant or club. Living singly was out of the question, especially for a mature man with a social following, as was remaining indefinitely with parents unless they were helpless and needed him.

To the "manly" Dakota, then, the married state was normal and human; a home and hearth, where he could entertain and thereby uphold his share of hospitality, were essential. Such considerations superseded any wish to remain faithful to a deceased wife. I knew only two Dakota men who never remarried after losing a good wife. The one I knew well had been a professional warrior who could do everything for himself from long practice on the warpath.

Even if, in the first throes of grief, a man decided to be loyal to his mate's memory for a longer time than average, there were sure to be well-wishers, both men and women, who came to comfort him and urge him to take another wife: "Ah, it pains our hearts to see you so dejected and alone." Subtly they pointed out reasons for his remarrying, which, as he thought them over in his lonely hours, seemed entirely acceptable and right. Some friends might go so far as to enumerate suitable women who were free, and those he found himself considering in turn: "How would she do for a wife?"

An elderly man told the following incident from his own experience as an illustration of the difficulty in keeping persistent ideas out of the mind. At the same time he also meant to amuse his audience. When he was a widower the first time, in his early youth, he caught himself glancing down the line of women mourners across the open grave of his girl-wife and weighing the relative merits of the single ones. From time to time the solemnity of the occasion brought him back to the present, and shamed him, but again and again the insidious notion fastened itself on him, he said. He had had three subsequent wives, for this incident had happened a great many years before, and his current wife, a jolly old woman who obviously knew the story by heart from many retellings, kept up a running commentary—like Mrs. Brown Elk's—which was a series of jibes at her husband, good-naturedly meant. "So then, I suppose, all those unmarried women jostled to get to him first!"

The stock criticism of the able man who was slow to remarry was that he was stingy. Old men were exempt. Of a certain widower who lived permanently in his son's home, people said: "He likes it that way because he can dodge the obligations of hospitality. The lack of a wife to maintain his tipi is his excuse for not entertaining or supplying his share whenever we čʼéȟ-gláwa 'count our kettles'." This was the idiom for pooling kettles of cooked food from the various families for a community gathering.

If a man remarried shortly after his wife's death, it was not too much of a shock, though, figuratively speaking, eyebrows were raised: "Well! It certainly did not take that one long to recover from his grief!" But, after all, that was the way of the male. Presently the matter ceased to be news. However, a widow who remarried too soon created more of a stir in the community: "Well! So that is how stable she is!" The female collaterals of her deceased husband were especially resentful, for a widow should mourn until after the year's anniversary memorial feast for her husband. Men should not approach her in courtship as long as she was wearing mourning.

It goes without saying that this rule was not invariably observed. From time to time, even if rarely enough, a woman went off with another man, still wearing her mourning garb, and that was as culpable as it was aberrant behavior. One who was heedless of convention, by so doing, was classed with the witkótkoka 'crazy, foolish, naive'. Incidentally, the stem tkó always arouses my suspicion that it is the same as któ in Iktómi, the trickster. I have no convincing examples to prove this theory, yet metathesis does occur in a few Dakota words. Compare itkópʼu 'to come out to meet, to come in the opposite direction from that of the one approaching'. Contrariness seems to me to inhere in both tkó and któ.

To marry only once was most admirable for a woman. Twice was acceptable, but one who married more often was privately derided as hignátʼusʼa 'habitual marrier'. Generally, or so it seems, women rather than men made such critical comments about a woman's morals and marital behavior. Men kept above participating in "women's talk," and were disdainful of one who stooped to petty matters. However, there is little doubt that they also took note of such things and that women's records promptly went into their mental files.

The widow in mourning must be circumspect, because any careless though innocent act could be interpreted by gossips as a premature bid for male attention. Ideally a woman should wait at least a year before ending her mourning; the longer she waited the more stable she was thought to be. Perhaps it was, in part, to discourage the gossips that widows in olden times deliberately dressed in the meanest of garb and were careless of their appearance, as a sign of mourning. This was voluntarily done. No one could compel a widow to mourn in a certain way, but each conformed to the conventions for mourning in her own way.

Since a widow properly returned to her own people, and since her affinal relatives were often in another camp circle, as a rule it was her own people who helped her to terminate her mourning by giving a memorial feast. At that time they publicly slipped a new gown over her drab one and braided her loose-hanging hair. Her parents, aunts, and uncles cooperated in doing this because it was their obligatory honoring of a son-in-law, her late husband. However, if his people lived in the same camp circle they might give the feast, and thereby remove all signs of mourning from his widow. If she had been an exemplary wife and daughter-in-law, they were especially happy to do this, although they must do it anyway, for convention's sake. If they could say it sincerely, they said: "Put this on; take that off. It is enough, tʿakóš ['child-in-law'; or sčépʿą 'sister-in-law', if her husband's sisters and female cousins were speaking]. It is enough. You have fulfilled your role well. Now let us dry your tears." By then she was weeping and they literally placed the base of their palm on her cheeks and wiped away her tears. The Dakotas were more likely to fit the base of the palm into the eye socket to wipe their tears than to use their fingers.

There are stories indicating the very real appreciation of a man's family when his widow mourned even longer than a year, in deference to their feelings. One woman related the following in her life story:

As a child it seemed to me that my mother was always sad, and wore poor clothing. Her hair hung loose and uncared for, while the mothers of my friends wore theirs in trim braids. One day she went off with some people and left me with my grandmother [mother's aunt as well as mother's mother was ųčí 'grandmother']. When she returned, she looked beautiful and young. Her hair was nicely oiled and dressed and her face was carefully painted. Her gown was new, with much bright beaded decoration.

I learned, only after I was older, that she went to pay a visit to my father's family and show them a letter from a man who wanted to marry her. That man became the only father I really knew, and he was good to me.

She went on with something else, but it is significant in its own way and worth reporting, and said:

Once when my [step]father returned from Fort Pierre he brought me a small rocking chair and a tiny pack of playing cards, the first rocking chair and the first playing cards in our village. I did not know how to play with cards but I liked to lay them all out in a row and look at them. The faces were the most interesting. They were beautiful. Then I always put them all back in their case carefully, so that they remained new. After a while, a strange man brought me a gray horse and said that his invalid son wanted my cards to amuse himself with them. So I gave them up.

Such uneven trading was not unusual. A father was paying not only for the cards but also, and more important, for the satisfaction of pleasing his dying son, whose every whim should be his command. He was thus, in fact and effect, buying release from the poignant regrets he would most surely feel had he allowed his boy to die wanting in vain something he had the means to get for him. The Dakotas, to whom kinship sentiment was the controlling force in life, were often dominated by that kind of grief and unable to shake it off easily.

Because my informant's mother had not planned on remarrying without first consulting her parents-in-law, her consideration of them was taken as such a compliment that they welcomed the idea gladly and prepared her to become another man's bride. They offered the usual objective reasons: "It is well that our daughter-in-law is marrying again. We had been troubled about our grandchild, but now she will have a father to provide for her."

They went further. Perhaps to win his goodwill for their granddaughter's sake, they adopted the new husband in their son's stead and showed him every honor due a son. In addition, his new sisters and female cousins gave the woman a ceremonial dressing of a bride *wišáyapi* for the second time, the first as their own brother's wife and now as their adopted brother's.

After a marriage had lasted a lifetime, those two, who started out together so cautiously, willing and ready to be good partners as long as nothing untoward arose to part them, in the end came to understand and care for each other simply as two human beings. Then they were *k'olá* 'friends', in the realest sense, for sex had long since become an irrelevant thing.

As one faculty after another failed them, their mutual compassion grew deeper. Said an old woman, "I pity him so! Poor thing, he can take only soft foods and soups now. Your grandfather has no teeth at all, and has grown very thin because he can no longer chew the meat he once loved dearly."

Another old man said, "Do you know, your grandmother can scarcely see now? Why, even when she steps outside only long enough to urinate, I must lead her lest she trip over a gopher hole and break a limb."

A woman who was camped on a hillside south of Rapid City sat gazing at her lifelong mate and then sighed: "Oh, but he was handsome in his youth, eager and alive to everything! Now, alas, he must follow me with only his eyes since he cannot walk, and must watch my lips when I speak. He is quite deaf, your grandfather." Every old informant was my grandfather or grandmother. And so, with their proverbial patience with grandchildren, they painstakingly answered my questions and explained whatever I did not understand.

With the end in sight, death and parting are the preoccupations of old people, though they do not fear to die. They have long since withdrawn from the bustle of tribal society, and its activities do not concern them. Values alter. Any possible indiscretions of the wife in her youth seem trivial or have faded into nothing. If she has been a faithful wife and a good mother, correct in all her kinship dealings, and courageous and cheerful through adversity, what more could a man ask of a companion? A husband does not say, "Of course, she did blunder, being very young, but then . . ." and so excuse his wife. A wife does not first recount a husband's faults, even to forgive them. Everything falls into proportion at last.

This is the stage when old people can see clearly through the conventions and formalities to the real issues of life, and are able to sift the real from the artificial. Seeing, they cannot but tell, talking on and on, uninvited and unheeded. Old women sit muttering their thoughts and observations and the young pause only long enough to sigh: "Poor grandmother, her mind wanders!" At public gatherings, for no reason that anyone can see, old men struggle to their feet and begin speaking, declaiming desperately on such tribal ideals as hospitality, generosity, and kinship loyalty, lest the young lose sight of them. They admonish the girls to treasure their virtue, the young men to abstain from making of courtship a cruel sport. Some may heed them but others do not, and things go on much the same as ever.

Once I watched a very old man haranguing the crowd in this manner. He moved slowly to and from behind the great circle of people seated on the ground. By turns he shouted feebly into the distance and then rested in silence, leaning heavily on his staff, his withered seer's face set in a futile determination to warn while he still had time. Everyone was too busy feasting to pay him the slightest attention—until a brassy youth of mixed blood, who was plainly out to impress the school girls with his wit and swaggering cowboy dress, called out smartly in English: "Give that calf more rope!"

A full-blood youth, who had been well trained in kinship with its network of cross-obligations, could never have made such a remark. Even of the most ludicrous or eccentric character there was universal reluctance to make careless fun. Even though he were a stranger and one felt no particular sympathy toward him, one had still to consider the people nearby. Maybe he was their relative; one must not offend them.

7

Death and Burial

In Olden Times

Death was never personified as either "friend" or "foe," but accepted as one more phase of human existence, balancing birth. If one was born, one must die. Hence there was no wisdom in shrinking from the inevitable and the right. Death was dreaded for others, not for oneself. Its intolerable feature was that it took away a dear one and left desolation in its wake. For themselves the Dakotas were indifferent and even flippant about dying. Children died without realizing what was happening to them. Adults sometimes quipped with their last breath.

The story is told that a visitor said to a sick woman, "Sister, what may I do for you? If there is something you particularly want, name it." And the woman replied, indicating the visitor's fine team, and buggy tied to the hitching post outside her window, "Why don't you give men those greys?" Then she smiled with great effort—and the next instance she was gone. She had made a last-minute joke that was a gentle jibe at the sister who, as everyone knew, was inordinately fond of possessions and only talked generosity.

Another story, now told like a legend, relates that when the Yankton chief Swan lay dying, his brother-in-law, named Sunrise, one of his society members who came to watch through the night beside him, suggested to Mrs. Swan, his sister, that she lay down and get some sleep. She answered: *Ibdút'įkte* 'I will try', but the term also means 'to test, to measure', so Swan deliberately "misunderstood" her meaning and said, "No doubt she wants to measure the nose of Sunrise." It was a double thrust: at Sunrise, his joking relative, whose nose perhaps suffered by comparison to his own shapely one; and at his wife, "for considering such a thing!" Was she critical of her own brother's looks? Had she been scanning his face and admitting to herself that the nose was ugly? Or too big for his face? Such were the implications of Swan's remark. The humor stems from the fact that the proper attitude between brother and sister was the ultimate in respect. Swan was only teasing his wife a little, and with that remark he turned to the wall and expired, leaving his companions chuckling. This incident is still remembered as an example of admirable casual adult dying.

A death in the home was frankly faced and the young were not excluded from any discussion of it. To keep them ignorant of it would be needless since, while they were still unable to grasp its meaning, they would not be affected anyhow. So the dead were laid out for all to see, with the result that everyone was accustomed to death from the beginning and took it in stride. Few could tell just when they first saw a corpse, but only that they "always knew" it was well to be respectful and quiet in its vicinity.

Everyone who was able visited the dying. While the patient was still aware, conversation in his presence must be about commonplace and even amusing matters, spoken in a normal tone. Tears must be controlled, for it was unpardonable to break down in front of the sick and dying. Those who could not keep from premature wailing must wail elsewhere. "He is still knowing and able to follow general talk" meant that the patient was not yet in the final stages — stages expected in a more or less regular progression.

As long as the patient remained rational there was hope. The visitor took the limp hand and asked gently, "My son [or whatever the relationship], do you remember?" He meant, "Are you aware?" There was a ray of hope for recovery if the sick man could say yes, and added that he was glad his father So-and-so had come — naming him for further assurance. But if he took no notice of the visitor and instead perhaps talked irrelevantly in delirium, the sorrowful report must be released: "Alas, he no longer remembers." *Kiksúya* 'to remember' also means 'to be conscious; to feel, to be sentient'. To express "He has no feeling in that hand" as in paralysis, one literally says: "He cannot remember in that hand." In this instance the report would mean: "Alas, he is no longer conscious."

Sooner or later might come the next report: "For days he had laid unconscious and unable to swallow, but now he asks for food and eats heartily." Everyone would know what that was — his *ɣwéya* 'his last meal'. As a sign of pending death, *ɣwéya* would correspond to viaticum. When used commonly it means 'food, provisions'.

Then there might come a startling change reported thus: "Without assistance, he who could not so much as lift a finger sat up briskly last night and engaged in happy conversation with his dead relatives who seemed to surround him invisibly." Ah! So now he was far enough along to see beyond the borderline! The welcoming hands held out to him had given him superhuman strength for the moment!

This was final. None who saw beyond the border ever came back. Even then his friends still tried to keep the atmosphere natural by making light of this new development, however saddened by it.

"Well, well! So they are after him already? How eager they must be to lure him from us!" This, whispered, was in affectionate chiding of the spirits of relatives.

After that fact nearly superfluous was the final report. It was inevitable that "now the death odor fills the sick room." This was described to me as "kind of musty," like damp clay perhaps. *Makʻámna*, the term for death odor, literally means 'earth scent'. Now nothing remained but to wait while holding the hand of the dying. Those in attendance whispered to one another, "His feet are like ice"; "His hands grow cold"; "Only the rattle in his throat goes on." All feigned light-heartedness for the patient's sake is no longer necessary. Finally someone soberly announces: "He is truly gone, for he no longer breathes." Cessation of heartbeat and respiration were the certain signs of death, and whether the pulse was also a sign is no longer known.

Immediately after this pronouncement the women started to wail, and as the news spread throughout the village, the wailing grew louder until the air was filled with it. The quavering death songs of old men and the occasional howling of dogs only intensified the general gloom: a relative had departed, never to return.

The eyes and lips must be held shut as much as possible, but sometimes this was neglected because in the first outpouring of grief no one thought of it in time. Many corpses had to be buried with eyes half open and mouth agape, unless later a band was tightly fixed about the head and under the chin to hold the lips together. In more recent times, as money became available, a silver dollar was placed over each eye to weight down the lids. When the coffin was about to be nailed shut, these were removed and given to certain ones, usually some poor, old people. Small coins, half-dollars or quarters, were given to children because they had been placed on the eyes of a child. That I have seen done.

It was admirable to endure pain or anger in silence, to gratify the appetites casually and indifferently without any show of avidity. Even ecstatic joy must be controlled. As a people the Dakotas do not laugh continually over trivial things. Children who laughed too loud were told: "Be careful or you will cry." Whether this meant that they would lose control and become hysterical or that the obverse of joy was inevitably found to be grief, I cannot say. At any rate, moderation was the ideal in all personal expression.

Grief over the death of a relative was the one emotion not to be denied. Women wailed, loud and long, and stopped only when they felt emptied of grief—for the moment. Their wailing was the melody for an impromptu wording of their sense of loss: *Tᶜewáȟila kʼų́* 'How I loved, treasured him, my own'; *Waȟpánima-kí-yé* 'I am impoverished by your leaving'; *Wasáswa- kí-yé čį́ kʼų́* 'I cherished and humored him as my own'; *Tókᶜel waų́kta hųwó* 'How shall I live on?'; and suchlike sentiments, in cadence. Loud wailing by men was not forbidden but it was rare, because they tried manfully to contain even their grief. If one broke down and sobbed momentarily, sympathetic women began wailing again, to "help" him, respecting him for caring so much. There was no virtue in concealing sorrow behind a stony manner; hence the one who did that was assumed to have no human sentiment. Even while controlling their tears, men looked sad. Old men began by singing a dirge and ended by wailing in the manner of the women. Young persons still shy cried softly and without words.

Sometimes men were driven to despair by the untimely death of a dear one and wanted to die, too, so they went on the warpath with the aim of being killed. To that end they took deliberate risks and some achieved posthumous glory. If in spite of careless exposure to danger one returned miraculously unharmed he was dissatisfied—unless in the process he had worsted an enemy. "Be killed or, failing that, kill!" would seem to have been the aim.

Over the death of a dear child some parents so far forgot themselves that they no longer felt physical pain. An old man showed me his left hand with the little finger missing and explained that he chopped it off and "never knew it" after his first child died. A woman related how frantically she prayed for her sick child's life; and how, when he died, she jabbed a sharp pointed knife around a troublesome molar; and then, crying bitterly not from pain but from grief, she jerked it out.

Traditionally, in this mood, scarification was sometimes resorted to. Called *hú-káǧo* 'leg-gashed', the flesh was nicked in rings around the leg from knee to ankle deeply enough for blood to flow. It trickled down in tiers until it coagulated and dried, to wear off in time. Some say that the arms, too, were cut in this fashion, but the details are not clear and none could say she or he had been so scarred. With bleeding legs the mourner went wailing around the parade track and again many women upon seeing her started to wail with her, "helping her."

This style of mourning, it is believed, was done usually by women. Some years ago I had the opportunity to examine the scars on the legs of an exceptionally tall woman. The cuts had been made about an inch or more apart: six scarred rings on one leg and seven on the other. The lack of uniformity suggested an indifference to detail while grieving excessively.

Scarification was not compulsory, nor was everyone moved to it over every bereavement. Some—the majority, I may say—never mourned to this extent for anyone, no matter how dear. Those who chose to scarify themselves generally performed their own hasty operation, for this was entirely voluntary. If they wanted another to do the procedure for them, they would not pick a novice, but one who had herself known this pain.

It is not clear as to whether men scarified themselves in this precise way, but it is certain that they also caused themselves to suffer. A man at Cannon Ball, North Dakota, told me that as a boy he saw a man sharpen green willow into skewers and pin them through his flesh "all over his body" until he stood a veritable pillar of blood while he wailed a dirge over his son's corpse. Occasionally, also, men made themselves suffer by dragging one or more buffalo skulls fastened by long ropes to the flesh below the scapulae, again with wooden pins. The more or the heavier the skulls and the more uneven the ground, the more successful the plan to cause physical pain to oneself as, perhaps, a counterbalance to the inner grief.

Bereavement could even drive a mourner into a kind of temporary insanity, not violently but numbly, until he was passive to all material and mundane considerations. In that state it was easy to carry to excess the Dakota imperative for group living: relatives come first. The unuttered reasoning was somewhat as follows: Since he can no longer live to be happy, why should I? Why hold fast to mere things, having lost him? Why dress myself well and look attractive? Everything seemed pure vanity and futility. The mourners gave away their best things with blind abandon, to be placed at some distance from the home for any passerby to take. It was proper to take them since their owners did not want them back. The term is *wíȟpeyapi* 'things thrown away'. Then, as if that were not enough sign of the mourners' self-abasement, they cut off their braids and donned their meanest garb and appeared utterly dejected.

Without a doubt the following incident of long ago was in a class by itself in that the mourning went so far as to violate the cardinal rule of personal modesty. This was when two ordinarily reticent young parents lost complete sight of its importance because of grief over their little son's death. Their family being important and their *tʿiyóšpaye* an able one, a tipi burial was arranged for their child. When, two days later, the camp circle removed to a distant site, only the burial tipi remained. There, outside its sealed entrance, the parents tarried for a final cry before following far behind the last in the line of the moving camp.

It was while the people sat around their outdoor fires after the late evening meal that the two entered the camp circle and walked hand in hand around the parade track in search of their own people while wailing aloud. That was unusual enough; persons as young as they were too shy to be heard however much they might grieve and weep softly. It was their appearance that left the people speechless, for both had hacked off their hair and cut their bodies severely, and both were stark naked. As they advanced women pulled their blankets over their heads and wailed aloud with them. Since it was a kinship sin to look upon nudity willfully, all the men, and the women who did not cover their heads to wail, sat bowed, or turned to sit facing the other way. My informant, being a small boy, was able to realize askance that the girl was gracefully slender and about the same height as her husband, and the same build, so that in the deepening twilight they looked to him like two boys striding along. Occasionally a dying fire suddenly sent out lambent flames that lit up their mutilated bodies mercilessly, but they were oblivious. It was in 1936 that I talked with the eighty-year-old informant who saw this extraordinary happening when he was perhaps nine years old. Never before had the people known its like, and never since, he said.

A tipi burial, called *tʿiyókitʿi* 'dwelling in one's own home', was an extravagance that, as a rule, only very able families could afford. It might be for a prominent man or woman, or for a particularly dear child. Occasionally the plan had to be abandoned because an enforced camp move was in order before the proper preparations for the burial and the public feast could be made.

Only a well-made tipi would serve. It was set up very securely, to stand firm against storms. Each pole was planted deep in the ground and individually buttressed inside by a forked smaller pole set at a slant. The windflaps were closed tight and tied down. The entrance was blocked by weighting it with heavy logs. The scaffold stood in the center and the body was laid on it in the manner already described.

The foregoing account comes from the Tetons, Western Dakotas. A later discussion with an elderly Sisseton man, an Eastern Dakota, brought out the fact that sometimes a couch-like arrangement was substituted for the scaffold. It was made in the honor place of the tipi, and the body rested on it. "About a foot and a half high, I'd say," he estimated. "A fire was laid ready to light, and fuel, food, and water were provided as though for a home. This was in case the dead person had only fainted or was suffering from suspended animation [such instances have been reported, too]. Then he could feed and warm himself until he was strong enough to look for his people."

Decades after extreme mourning practices had been dropped, they recurred partially, just once, in a community where the general aim was progress. A youngish woman, perhaps in her mid-thirties, who had been among the foremost in adapting to new ways, impulsively hacked off her long braids when her very congenial spouse died without warning. The astonished community buzzed with the news, hardly believing it of her, but she appeared at the church for the funeral with hair unkept and wearing an old, tattered army blanket that her husband once used as a U.S. soldier. Still in a daze from the shock, and with her customary vivacity gone, she looked completely crushed and lost, a sight to stir anyone's pity. It was strange, too, that she should revert to the ancient ways of her people although she herself had never mourned in that way. Her fellow progressives must have felt betrayed. Some did actually blame her for reverting, but the oldest people were generally sympathetic: "If she needed to mourn in that way, if it was satisfying to her, it was right," they said. "Let no one add to her burden by censuring her; but, also, do not wipe away her tears prematurely. Never stifle sorrow, for that is harmful. Best to let it all come out and so be rid of it." Such was their characteristic reasoning.

A dead human body must be treated with respect and solemnity. The rule was inflexible: women prepared a female body for burial and men a male. If time and circumstance made this unfeasible, burial was accomplished with a minimum of handling.

Somewhere, during the years passing, the custom of sponging off the dead body began. Prior to that the face was painted with a film of red ocher paste, and that was all. The torso and genitals were untouched, and that is still true. A wide band of skin was wrapped tight about the loins of both male and female bodies, all under cover. The sensibilities of the person in life were respected in death. Embalming was unheard of, but had the idea of it occurred, it probably would have been dismissed as useless and even foolish. Natural decay as a consequence of death was too obvious a law to dispute. Why strive to retain the shell of one irrecoverably gone? There was no theory of a physical resurrection, though the belief was universal that the spirits of relatives were reunited after death, somewhere. The phrase "happy hunting ground" is, however, not of Dakota origin. It was never supposed that death was the end; the spirits of dead relatives remained much too real for that.

"The best for the dead—at whatever cost to the living" was only a little short of a rule. Those able to manage it dressed their dead as though for a festival in which they were to star. Those less able must put on their dead the best they could get, and yet they, too, tried to get what they did not have already, often at considerable sacrifice to themselves. The general aim was to dress the dead fully, including footwear, which above all else was important.

Said a woman informant:

I remember my grandmother's burial dress, because I studied every detail of it while she laid in the tipi before a lock of her hair was taken [a detail of ghost-keeping rites]. For an old woman her braids were remarkably long and heavy. The center part in her hair was painted red as also was her face. Her gown of white doeskin was beautifully wrought in quills of several colors and her belt, leggings, and moccasins carried out the same designs. Her knife in its painted rawhide case was fastened to hang from her belt, on the left. Decorated hair ties and ear pendants and bracelets were not omitted. Her moccasins were some of my aunt's [the deceased's daughter's] finest work and were completely covered with quill embroidery, even over the soles. All in all she looked ready for a celebration.

An old person elaborately decked out in death presented a sharp contrast to their appearance in life, for it was not the habit of the aged to dress flashily, or even well. The needy, of course, had nothing else, but even those whose daughters or nieces would want to improve their appearance actually preferred plain clothes. One old woman protested when her gifted granddaughter wished to make something fancy for her to wear: "No, t'akóža, make it for yourself or some young relative. Such things enhance the young but do nothing for the old except to emphasize their defects, making them ridiculous!" Naive old persons were the exception, those who did not discriminate but wore things as they came to hand, even if too young for them. For the majority, if they wore a string of plain beads as a necklace, never removing it, or some simple rings on their ears, that was usually the extent of their ornamentation.

No such detailed description of old-time grave clothes for men was available. However, I was told that if one died at home he was laid out as carefully as were women and children, insofar as his relatives had the means to do that, but warriors laid where they fell, dressed as they were.

For rich or poor, the all-important item was creditable footwear, as I have already said. It was a minor tragedy to be buried unshod or with shabby moccasins, if the dead but knew. Even old people, ordinarily indifferent to finery, managed to keep on hand the best moccasins they could acquire, against their burial. Many carried theirs in a little sack hitched to the belt in the back, under their wrap. "These I shall lie wearing," they said.

I feel compelled to say more about moccasins, for their rating can hardly be overstressed. In all social giving, anything new and good made a worthy gift, but the most valued gifts were horses and moccasins. When a woman wished to honor someone, she asked for his or her foot measure in order to make them fine moccasins that would fit. Both poor and handsome footwear were equally observed at once, and commented on: "My, what beautiful moccasins! Who made them for you?," or "Say, did you notice his feet? A man of such prestige should not be wearing such shabby moccasins. What are his hakáta [sisters and female cousins, who were his respect relatives] thinking about? Have they no pride?" Perhaps such consciousness of feet and consequent emphasis on good footwear might have derived from the kinship necessity of keeping the eyes downcast, as a matter of etiquette. The first thing to see and consider about a person would be his feet.

Neatness was peculiarly important to feet. To go barefoot, even out of preference, was questionable; I might say it simply was not done. If a child teased, he might be permitted to wade in the pools around the tipi after a flash rain, but as soon as he came in he was made to put his moccasins back on. Family pride demanded that the children be properly moccasined at all times. To be accused of carelessness of this detail was something resented seemingly out of all proportion. To this day the average Teton or Yankton family might explain the purpose of their trip to town—especially if it was just before school opening—by saying, "We went to buy shoes for the children." Anything else bought would be subsidiary, to be mentioned incidentally if at all. If a child was given some money by a friend, his mother was nearly sure to say, "Oh, that is good. Now he can buy shoes with it." Living or dead the Dakotas must be properly shod, all ready to go.

A score of years ago [about 1920] when a man died at the government hospital, his body was immediately placed in a government coffin and sent down to the church still clad in the faded shirt and overalls in which he had expired. Many came to the guild hall before the funeral to see his face and wail over him, and several expressed regret over the apparently irreverent treatment of the body, for his head was tilted far back and his feet were bare. Presently a very old woman hobbled in, and everyone made room for her. She was the dead man's only living collateral relative, his *hakáta*. It was her responsibility to see that things were rightly handled.

Thoughtfully, she gazed with squinting eyes and then began to whimper: "Alas, *šič'éši* [woman's term for 'male cousin'], that you should lie without a pillow—and without moccasins!" That was the ultimate of calamity. Dry-eyed, she went to the trading post nearby and returned with some white socks, of the cheapest quality, but marked one dollar, and asked the men to put them on him. She still did not wail, and it was plain that something was on her mind. So on impulse I hurriedly covered a sofa pillow with fresh white muslin, and my sister, always ready with the artistic touch, ripped a luscious-looking pink rose from a summer hat and tacked it to one corner of the pillow. As the men slipped it under the dead man's head so that he looked comfortable, his aged cousin broke into loud wailing, but she was satisfied at last. Her cousin was being laid away with at least a semblance of the attention and respect she wanted for him. It was his bare feet that had hurt her the most.

Anything resembling a wake was impractical and indeed unthinkable. During the day people came to see the face of the dead for the last time, to wail, and to eat the food offered. They did not remain grouped around the corpse far into the night; no making an occasion of it. A body must be handled with dispatch, before mortification could become evident. If possible it was laid away before nightfall. If death occurred too late in the day to allow for preparations, it was kept in an empty tipi guarded by men who remained outside. This was to prevent any stray dog from entering during the night; no person would invade a closed mortuary tipi unless he was a relative who arrived in the night.

Relatives living in distant places were not expected, because it would take too long for a messenger to reach them with the news for them to come, and a burial could not wait. It was one of the hard facts of life that the Dakotas, to whom relatives were indispensable, must sometimes live on in ignorance of a dear one's death until the next annual tribal reunion, as at the Sun Dance. There all significant news was exchanged by the visiting groups, who disseminated it upon their return home, and presently it was known far and wide. In that way would relatives learn of a death — perhaps as much as a year after it had occurred — and go belatedly into mourning.

A dead body was wrapped in a buffalo hide, fur outside, and bound with stout thongs. If there were woods nearby, it was laid horizontal in some large tree and secured to its boughs. This must be at a height sufficient to be out of reach of marauding animals. Only against molestation by animals was the body safeguarded, for no sane person would go near it, knowing that it was an affront to the spirit of the dead to invade his haunt and that he, the spirit, would take his revenge by scaring away any who did so. Many ghost stories are based on this notion.

In one a family or a war party make camp after dark in a strange locality but are frightened away during the night by superhuman disturbances of various sorts. Upon returning by daylight to investigate, the intruders are sure to find that they had unwittingly made camp near a burial scaffold, or perhaps under the very tree where a dilapidated corpse was. This is a familiar pattern.

Another, somewhat distinctive story, runs as follows. Two young boys were walking along the bank of the Missouri River in company with an adult male cousin while their people were slowly arriving and forming a camp circle not far away. Suddenly all together they spied an aged woman sitting high above them, with her legs dangling over the rim of the cliff. The cousins studied her for some time and observed her very elaborate moccasins and bright red leggings and a decoratively painted woman's robe, which was pulled up over her head. But her face was in plain sight to those below: a deeply wrinkled face, a placid, passive face, like a mask. In fact, a dead face! The adult cousin cried: "Look out! There sits *Maní-Tʻí!* 'Dweller in the Wilds!'" All three ran at top speed back to the camp. The old woman's identity was not known, of course, but the spontaneously coined name suited her well. For it was a spot devoid of human habitation where she sat solitary in all her incongruous finery.

"Doubtless that was the costume in which she was buried," people said. "She showed herself to indicate her annoyance at those who had invaded her haunt." When the adult cousin and some others visited the spot where they saw her, all they found was a tumbled-down scaffold, beads of all colors scattered about, and bits of hide and rotting red flannel embedded in the earth and packed solid by many years of rain and snow.

If death occurred on the open prairie, a scaffold was built on a small knoll some distance from but in sight of camp. Four or six forked posts were set to form a rectangle and connected by poles caught into their forks. On these poles small lighter sticks of uniform thickness and length were placed close together crosswise to form a platform. Then the whole structure was lashed together. Many paintings that include a burial scaffold give it too much height. Actually, it was not a great deal higher than the height of a tall man. Perhaps it was never more than seven feet, at the most. It had to be accessible to those who must mount the platform and pull the body up with ropes and lay it in place. One short man spoke of standing on the back of his tame horse in order to mount it. How a corpse was carried to the scaffold before there were horses is not precisely known. It was probably carried on a stretcher, improvised by lapping a robe over two long poles, the two sides brought over the poles and laid one on top of the other, thus making a triple thickness on which the body rested. Hammocks also were contrived in that way, on a double loop of rope. Later the problem of transportation was simple: the body, bound in a skin, was strapped crosswise on the travois seat behind the drag pony.

If possible a cake of pemmican in a parchment-like wrapper was placed like a pillow under the head. The wrapper was a piece of animal stomach or a bladder. There was room beside the body for such articles as the family wished to have buried with the dead. At last a great enveloping bullhide was bound over the whole, body and platform, and tied as securely as possible so that the structure would not give way against the storms for some time. Eventually it would.

Items buried with the body were usually tokens of the dead person's skill or particular interests. More than once it was told to me that a toy or other small article that delighted a child was left with his body. A quiver of arrows and bow for a famed hunter, a war club for a warrior, perhaps a fleshing tool for the woman with exceptional ability to prepare hides, a horn ladle for the hospitable woman, maybe a pipe for a man of peace, and, most certainly, his own exclusive medicine bundle for the holy man — these would be typical items buried with their owners. The medicine man's bundle was always buried, since its peculiar potency had been of use only to its owner. It would be without meaning, and useless, to anyone else. Thus it was true that an unburied bundle caused great nervousness because of whatever mystery might attach to it. It was best to bury it with its owner and have it out of the way.

Personal medicine bundles were not inherited, nor might they be bought or sold, since they would be useless to anyone but their owner. One informant spoke highly of his father's humanly unaccountable power, and of the things he did through it. Then he said, "That *wópⁱiye* 'medicine bundle' was the symbol of his power, so it was placed in his hands before he was buried." When I suggested that he might have kept it in his father's memory, he said, "It would be no good to me, just a bundle. To him only it was all-important; it spoke to him. I know nothing of his *wakʼą́* practices. I only saw the results." Having a holy man for a father did not guarantee a derived power through him. Each man who would have power must seek a revelation through fasting. Only then might he have something significant for his bundle to represent to him. Since every man's vision experience was said to differ from all others' it was not likely that a son's bundle would be made in the same way as his father's. It is true that sometimes a holy man was asked to make a bundle or fetish as a safeguard for a child, but that was a different matter.

Food and sometimes a water bag were left beside the dead, it is said. If this was done with the belief that the spirit could eat and drink, the point seems no longer clear. The "last meal" demanded by the dying was "food for the journey." A more practical reason, and so explained, was that, in case the person had only fainted or was in a coma after all, he could feed himself upon reviving until he was strong enough to go. One legend has such a situation. One wonders, though, how anyone so recently "dead" could have the strength to snap the binding thongs and get free.

Only the few who were to help lay the body away accompanied it to the scaffold. A funeral was no public function; neither birth nor death was attended by set ritual or ceremony. People took leave of their dead when the body still lay in the tipi. The so-called four days of mourning were not compulsory and not invariably observed. It was impossible to do so when a camp move was in order immediately after the burial. But "four days" did figure in the notion that if a widow or widower, or indeed anyone in deep sorrow, did not remain at home that long, he or she would never feel settled again but would be ever restless and on the move, being supernaturally habituated to be always going or wanting to go. It was like a curse or spell.

The Dakotas were realistic about death; since it could not be opposed, it was accepted with resignation. They did not wail, "Come back, come back!" They knew that was senseless. Yet now and then someone was moved to spend time alone with the dead and talk audibly to them. There is a Santee legend about a woman who climbed onto her daughter's scaffold and stayed there night and day until she died, refusing all food and ignoring the pleading of her relatives that she come down. Within historic times a father left his bed at midnight and went to the cemetery to lie beside the grave of his little son the first night, "to help him get used to it." Such instances show that the people were not bound by set rule but were free to mourn as they were impelled.

It was never the custom to dispose of a corpse by burning. It was as tenderly regarded as if still sentient. It comforted the relatives to be able to look toward the rise where the scaffold stood outlined against the sky. It eased them to know that it was still safely there. However, it is also remembered that if the wind was from that direction the odor was at times sharply detectable, even at that distance — "a sickening-sweet kind of smell," said one. Visiting burial places was not a pastime but, nevertheless, the Dakotas felt pulled to the regions where their dead were. When I visited a Santee community south of St. Paul, one woman told me, "We were driven out of Minnesota wholesale, though the majority of our people were innocent. [Deloria refers to the Minnesota Uprising of 1862.] But we could not stay away so we managed to find our way back, because our *mak'ápaha* were here." The term means 'earth hills' and is the Santee idiom for graves. Yankton and Teton have another term, *wič'áhapi* 'human burial', but *mak'ápaha* is understandable, even though unidiomatic.

People did not usually fear their own dead, whose bodies were still dear. Frantic demonstrativeness was and still is out of line, but there was no religious rule against touching a corpse, and it was handled without cringing or distaste. Relatives had no hesitancy in preparing their own dead for burial and burying them, if necessary. However, almost always there were friends to help them or relieve them altogether of that sad duty.

Bodies were buried lying straight and supine, not seated, standing, or prone—as far as any informant now can say. It was unimportant in which direction a body was laid. Today it seems customary to bury the dead with feet toward the east, but I am fairly certain that it is due to Christian usage.

The Dakotas were not far removed from modern psychology in that they did not believe in suppressing grief. "Cry—if you must," they said. "Let it out and be relieved. To hold it in is not healthful." The mourners were allowed to wail as they must and nobody was annoyed by the wailing. To everyone the time came to wail in his turn. Because sensitivity was most acute in sorrow, mourners were treated gently, and comforted with food. If one wailed so continuously as to impair his health, then some friend literally wiped away his tears, after which, out of deference to that friend, the mourner stopped for a while and he felt comforted. The term is *kigná*; cf. *akígna* 'to brood over', which has specific reference to a fowl over its eggs. The idea of gently hovering over, to soothe, to treat cautiously as something fragile, is connoted by *kigná*. Murmured words of sympathy accompanied the gestures of comforting the mourner.

Those who assisted at an illness and death were gratefully remembered with suitable gifts as tokens of the mourners' appreciation. These I may designate as (1) for helping the family during the illness of the deceased; (2) for preparing the body for burial; (3) for building the scaffold, or, in later times, for digging the grave and filling it in at the last; (4) for closing the eyes and mouth immediately and holding them closed until they were set; (5) and for carrying the coffin in and out of the church—again, this is in recent times. Such were some of the tender offices performed by friends, which the family would acknowledge with special gifts if they were able. The order and examples I inferred from typical duties.

Not every family could give a feast, nor was a feast obligatory for every death. Often enough the cost was beyond the means of the mourners unless they had many able relatives to assist them. Most families were satisfied if once, for some dear one, they were able to feast the people creditably. Only the able and influential, with a large family and many cooperating relatives, were able to give a feast again and again, as well as to undertake a ghost-keeping.

This last was an exacting and prolonged series of rites that, informants generally agreed, disappeared well over seventy-five years ago, with the camp circle way of life. At any rate, it is a fact that although the term for it, *wanáǧi yuhápi*, comes up in old tales occasionally, the procedure of ghost-keeping—its purpose and its precise details and inviolable rules—is unfamiliar to the majority today. Even so there persist certain customs that are the end result of a gradual modification of that once vivid ceremony. Perhaps the memorial feast, still common enough, is the last recognizable vestige of it.

It is not possible here to give complete and detailed descriptions of all rites and ceremonies mentioned, but ghost-keeping, since so much has been said about it, may be outlined briefly.[1] When someone important died and his family were reasonably sure of their ability to carry the long and difficult ceremony through to a creditable conclusion, they decided to "keep his (or her) ghost."

A holy man was engaged to officiate at all the rites appertaining to the ghost-keeping, and his first act was to cut off some hair from the dead person before the body was bond for burial. That hair represented the dead; it was his "ghost," and so it must be handled with the utmost reverence at all times. The bundle in which it was buried was guarded for a whole year, or sometimes longer if more time was needed to prepare for the distribution feast that closed the ceremony.

Aside from the holy man, the principal actor in this lengthy rite was the woman custodian of the bundle. The "ghost" resided in its own tipi, which was thereby sacrosanct. Anyone who sat there must show their respect by speaking, thinking, and doing only what was right and agreeable, for anything untoward was out of place in "the presence." All night, and all overcast days, the bundle hung from a low tripod in the honor place. If the day was sunny, it might hang outside from a taller tripod near the tipi. Taking it out and bringing it in were in strict accordance to rule, for no single rule relating to the bundle might be slighted or varied, else the entire ghost-keeping became invalid.

Indoors or out a bowl of food stood below the bundle waiting for anyone who wished to dine there as a guest of the deceased. He sat down and ate the food ritually. Old people sometimes talked familiarly to the spirit of the dead as they ate, calling him by kinship term as in life and thanking him over and over for his habit of hospitality, which even death could not instantly cut short. It was one of the custodian's duties to keep that bowl filled with more freshly cooked food as soon as it was empty.

During camp moves throughout the year the ghost traveled with the people "riding" the horse that had been dedicated to carrying it and to transporting its belongings. So the horse dragged the tipi poles, the rolled tipi cover, and all the necessary pins and pegs and stakes, which were lashed onto the travois platform behind it. Upon arrival at the new site the ghost lodge was erected first, the bundle was hung on its support, and the hospitality bowl was filled and set in place. Only then might the other tipis of the *t'iyóšpaye* go up.

"The horse was marked so that everyone knew it carried a ghost," said one informant. Just how it was marked to distinguish it was a point I failed to determine. It was said that the riderless horses of dead warriors were painted down the face with black earth — which was the silent announcement of those warriors' fate — and were led along in the warriors' return parade around the camp circle. Perhaps the ghost's horse was marked in somewhat the same way, but the point is a doubtful one.

The custodian walked, leading the horse. Sometimes another woman took the rope for short periods to relieve her, but this responsibility was hers. While leading the horse, one maintained the rule of silence. The informant, Fast Whirlwind, said that when he was a boy he saw a horse being led along, not in the line of march but off at one side, moving more slowly. Someone said: *Ká wanáǧi č'á iglák-máni* 'That is a ghost moving camp'. At the time he did not know what that meant.

All through the year the women of the *t'iyóšpaye* worked steadily at turning out gifts for the redistribution feast at the end of the period. Meanwhile, from time to time, their friends brought worthy gifts to be added to the accruing pile so that there was a gift for practically all the guests at the end. The *wakíčˀaǧapi* 'redistribution' afforded the occasion for disposing of all the gifts. The actual feast was the ghost's final act of hospitality; the redistribution was the last symbol of his generosity. It is possible to break down the parts composing the word *wakíčˀaǧapi*, but there is no equivalent for the meaning in English. I am only certain that it does not literally mean 'redistribution', a term given to that feast by earlier ethnographers.[2]

At some time during the public feast outside, a private feast known as *wiyógnak wakíčˀaǧapi* 'they are caused to hold something in the mouth' was held indoors for a few boys or a few girls, depending on the sex of the deceased, as I have already explained. In this most solemn rite, the holy man threw aromatic roots and leaves on the fire and when it sent up a heavy smoke he incensed morsels of pemmican containing "sweet leaf" and placed one on the extended tongue of each of the usually four or eight guests. He said: "This food I deliver to you. This food, mixed with perfume leaf and redolent with incense you shall hold in your mouth while you stop to realize that, in the future, whoever sits in your tipi shall be your concern. For him you shall break your very last morsel in two. So shall you share." He preached such sermon to remind the guests that their host, whose ghost had been kept, had lived a life of extraordinary hospitality and generosity, and that now they must carry on for him by being themselves hospitable and generous. While the attention of all was on the feasting and the redistribution, the holy man, accompanied by three other holy men selected by him, bore the ghost bundle away and buried it in a secret place, then "forgot" for all time where that was, and the ghost-keeping came to an end.

One more traditional practice remains. Sometimes a horse was killed below its owner's scaffold and left there "to go with him." This was done only when the dying man, feeling himself en rapport with his favorite horse, expressed the wish. "I want to take my friend with me. He has undergone everything else with me. Where I went, he went."

A Teton woman included the following in her life story:

Our grandmothers stood in a group and we were on their backs. They waited in silence, but now and then they wiped their eyes and blew their noses. They were sad. After a while the entrance to our tipi was thrown wide open and men carried out a long box covered with a scarlet blanket. As they lifted it into the wagon box, I struggled to get down but my grandmother only tightened the shawl about her to hold me fast and tight under it. Š! Š! 'Sh! Sh!' Be still! She whispered: "Your father is in that box for he is dead. They are taking him far off to lay him away. Be still!"

At four years of age, I was ignorant of the meaning of death, but I still see that wagon commencing to roll and hear our grandmothers break into loud wailing, while our grandfathers chant sad songs, half-weeping. They follow a short distance and stop; gazing after the wagon. I still see a man going behind on a black horse, a gun crosswise in front of him and leading a bay, saddled and bridled, but without a rider. I can see all that, in thinking back, and, at the last, a strip of red crawling along below some low hills far away.

As I grew older, I gradually realized from the conversations of my people that my father's horse was shot and killed in accordance with his dying wish. That was why the man carried a gun across his lap. How I know I was four years old is that my father died one year before the Wounded Knee massacre, when I was five.

The people were using boxes for burials, but still they were putting the dead on scaffolds, so I was told later. When I was perhaps ten or twelve, I saw a dead horse lying stretched out over a mound.

In Historic Times

In the preceding section I tried to bring together the more important of the old-time practices and attitudes regarding death, or at least those best remembered by informants. They have changed superficially with the changing times. Yet every so often some remnant may be detected still. For example, the custom of leaving food with the dead was supposedly abandoned after it became the practice to bury by internment in the ground, but the custom died hard. Whenever the people went to a Christian cemetery, say for an Easter Day memorial service, a few women furtively placed food on the mound of their dead—only to invite someone to take it home. It was their way of still "causing the dead to extend hospitality" in the manner of ghost-keeping. Moreover, it is not improbable that occasionally a mourner went alone to a new grave and there left a morsel as a symbol, to satisfy an age-old necessity.

In early reservation days, when the people began bringing their dead to the mission church for burial, but before they had learned to provide coffins for them, they rolled and bound the corpse in canvas, as once they bound it in a hide; or they brought it in a bulky quilt, padded with cheap cotton and covered with flowered goods usually a fiery red. There were many such quilts around in those days, being part of the government's annuity payments for the people's land.

It was nothing extraordinary for a wagon to back up to the church steps at any hour and men to lift out a body rolled in a red quilt. They laid it on a row of chairs in the vestibule and it rested there until the government carpenter could nail some cheap pine together for a coffin. He provided a lid, to be hammered down at the last. He tacked black muslin neatly over an adult's coffin and white over a child's and, for contrast, a small cross of white muslin on the black coffin and of black on a white coffin.

When homemade coffins were being nailed down, the hammer strokes resounded throughout the house, but the family did not wince at that. Compared with the prospect of permanent separation, it was nothing intolerable. After the body was bound for burial in former times, or the coffin was nailed down in later times, relatives were resigned to never looking on that loved one again. Consequently, when they brought their dead to the church for a Christian burial, it never occurred to them to demand "one more look." Never—until professional undertakers began tiptoeing over to them and whispering the idea into their ear. Literally, they forced on the Dakotas that alien custom of doubtful value. "Viewing the remains" definitely was not a traditional need. In many places the trend is away from it again.

Flowers were not essential to a funeral, but if some white neighbors or the missionary ladies gave a bouquet of geraniums or other houseplant flowers, the friendly gesture was comforting. As a rule Dakotas did not pick flowers simply for decoration. In certain festivals green boughs with heavy foliage were used instead. Isolated instances of the use of flowers were always for a definite reason; perhaps the performer wore them for a religious significance. It is said that one man covered himself completely with sunflowers when acting out his vision experience because in that vision the sunflower came to him in the guise of a man and became his spirit helper in his healing work ever after.

But there was other striving after beauty. If a family could supply them, shiny brass tacks were used to hold the muslin cover smooth over the coffin of their dead. More than one coffin had the cross entirely studded with such tacks. A certain coffin maker, an ex-student of Carlisle, had the originality and daring to outline huge flowers and scrolls freely over the top and sides until the coffin was all aglitter with them. For this added touch he was somewhat in demand.

Yet even he never thought of altering the shape and style of the boxes but made them uniformly long and narrow; and they were quite satisfactory for a time. However, when Weasel Eagle, a high-ranking man in the community, died, they ceased to be so. He had been one of the good men of the old life and was a leader in all good works in the new. It was right, therefore, to honor him by asking the Sioux Falls carpenters, who were building a new school for the mission, to make him a fine coffin. The carpenters outdid themselves. Almost overnight they turned out something very special, and novel—an ample casket with shoulders, and tapering gracefully toward the foot. They had sandpapered it to a glassy smoothness, and then lacquered it until it shone like a black mirror. A beautiful thing—it was a crime to put it out of sight so soon before all the people could admire it enough.

After that no common box would do; one must at least have shoulders. Coffin making thus became a complicated business—an art. When new towns sprang up nearer the reservation—with their undertakers and elaborate caskets and glass wagons for carrying a body to the cemetery—those homemade coffins were out for good.

In many localities it became the fashion to remove the plate inscribed "At Rest" on commercial caskets and return it to the family for a keepsake. One family I visited had screwed two ornamental bronze knobs from their daughter's casket into the corners of the wide opening between their living and dining rooms. These they showed reverently to their guests for many years. To them it was a link with their dead.

For many years now the people have managed to provide florists' wreaths and sprays for funerals. These are removed from the casket and laid on the mound after the grave has been filled in. Close friends sometimes remove a petal or a whole flower to press and keep in memory of the deceased. At one state-wide gathering I sat next to a youngish woman whose Dakota hymnal was full of pressed petals, and she was able to tell me where nearly all of them came from.

One man, so I was told, kept a lock of his son's hair always against his bare breast where his heart beat might lend it motion and life. All such behavior was perhaps an unconscious effort to "keep a ghost," even though out of time and setting, by at least retaining some material object that had been related to the dead. But there was nothing unconscious about the incident that took place in my childhood. Far from unconscious, it was an open and deliberate, if momentary, resumption of that obsolete practice.

Once when we went to my grandparents' farm-ranch for our vacation, everyone up and down the Missouri Valley was talking about a man named *Šiyó Sápa* 'Black Pheasant' who was keeping a ghost as best he could. Since it had been decades since anyone had kept a ghost among those Yanktons of the White Swan community across the river from Fort Randall, this bold step backward was proving more than mildly sensational. Only a few elderly full-bloods, who lived wrapped in the past, entirely understood the man's need to spurn the public cemetery and bury his child in his own back yard, only a few paces from his home. The little boy-ghost intrigued me when I was a child. I was most impressed that the father had built a little frame house of commercial lumber, with a pointed roof and a door and windows, over the mound for the ghost to reside in and was keeping a bowl of freshly cooked food outside the sealed doorway and a house lamp that burned day and night. People said, "Black Pheasant has caused his child to lie *t'iyókit'i* 'dwelling in his own home', in this case not a tipi, but a modern-style house." I have always known that rather uncommon word; perhaps that was the first time I heard it.

At nine I was quite callous about death; funerals and graves were an everyday matter. Back home where the people on Standing Rock—many being remnants of Sitting Bull's recently hostile wanderers—were finding life under new and strange conditions bewildering, tuberculosis was nearly epidemic, and so my father held a funeral at least weekly, and sometimes daily at a stretch. For the people died too fast, and without a struggle, lacking the will to live.

But here was something else. The idea of a lively little ghost, approximately my age, owning his own tiny house, with his own food and his lamp, so fascinated me and stirred my imagination that I could scarcely think of anything else all summer. Once I even saw his lamp plain at midnight, burning bravely in its tall chimney. It was immaterial that Black Pheasant's place was over a mile away, around a bend and therefore out of sight. Somewhat later, I realized I had dreamed this—but how vividly! I can see it now. Then it came time for us to go back home and I never learned just how Black Pheasant terminated his modern ghost-keeping.

After I had become interested in old customs through my study and fieldwork, and had obtained some rather full accounts of ghost-keeping, I attended one memorial feast where I was able to identify many features that corresponded with it. The widow who was giving the feast in memory of her only son was far from well-to-do, but her many relatives stood by her. After my arrival they were still coming in with various items to augment her efforts, some with steaming kettles of cooked food and others with gifts to add to the already sizable pile the widow had accumulated through the year for this occasion. As in former days, the many guests sat down on the grass in a circle, with the food and gifts in the center of it. There were the usual articles of Indian make—moccasins and beaded bags and suchlike things, and also some store-bought articles: a new packing trunk, a tan leather suitcase of excellent quality, and even a round parlor table of light oak stood out in the mass of gifts to be distributed.

The program started with Christian prayers and hymns and ended with speeches in keeping with the occasion. Then the serving began. Both men and women assistants passed the food around in kettles and pans, and put it into the containers brought by the individual guests. The main dish was beef, boiled, broiled, or roasted, to suit every taste. Native dishes were chokecherry and other wild berries cooked to the consistency of porridge, dried corn and dried pumpkin boiled together with beef ribs, boiled jerked beef, fried bread, and, as the crowning treat, *wasná*—pemmican cakes with a meat or parched corn base, mixed with wild berries or store-bought raisins and held together by melted beef tallow that is left to harden. Bakery goods, pies, cakes, and doughnuts, were for the younger folk who had a liking for them. The older people were content and even eager for the native dishes, some of which were fast becoming rare. The tone of the occasion was typically Dakota—no hilarity, no loud talking or careless joking and laughing, which were out of place at solemn gatherings like this one.

As the guests were finishing their meal, the widow came out of her log house for the first time and stood beside the pile of goods to make a speech. She said, "My son, who loved to be hospitable, has now feasted you for the last time." Pridefully she acknowledged the help of her relatives. Next she quietly assigned special gifts to certain individuals and her helpers delivered them, but the recipients did not rush up to get their gifts. They remained seated and only reached out to take what was handed to them—without a smile, without gushing thanks; only a murmured *haó* by men, and *hą́* by women.

The mass distribution that followed was orderly and unhurried. Two men piled the remaining gifts indiscriminately onto a blanket which they then carried around the circle, while a woman walked along to take and hand them out one by one to the guests in their turn, until everything was gone. Since the gifts were given for their symbolic value, not for enrichment, those who failed to get any did not mind. It was enough that they had been feasted. If more guests had come than there were presents, it was understandable that some part of the circle received nothing. *Hehą́yą iyówičˀahišni* 'From that point on, it [the act of giving from the deceased] could not reach them' and that was explanation enough.

During these public activities, certain young men were being privately dined at a long table inside, with special delicacies not served to those outdoors. To each of them went a fine gift in the name of the deceased: "He gives you this."

Then came the climax. A man carried a crayon enlargement of the dead son's picture around the circle and held it a moment before each guest. Upon seeing it women here and there pulled their shawls over their heads and wailed aloud: "My nephew! [or whatever the relationship] How kind you were to me! How I shall miss you!" and so on. The face was purposely indistinct because a veil was tacked over the frame. Once before I had seen this, on another reservation. The two daughters of the family giving the feast were side by side in the picture, but only the living girl's face was plain. The other's was covered with white net in much the same way. I was too young to realize whether gifts were distributed along with the feast. They probably were.

As I have said, this was avowedly a Christian meeting; the guests were all church members, as far as I knew. Even so the program was a natural copy of the redistribution feast that in former times terminated a ghost-keeping period. The boy's hair had not been kept to represent the ghost, to be sure; yet the veiled picture was by way of being a ghost bundle, and was so revered. The foods and gifts assembled with the help of relatives were reminiscent of the group endeavors of a t'iyóšpaye, and the private feast for a select few answered for the previously mentioned rite known as wiyógnak wičʼákʼiyapi 'they are caused to hold something in the mouth'. But at this modern feast this feature was omitted and there was no holy man officiant. The guests simply ate, without being admonished. Nevertheless, their being feasted in the dead son's name was in effect a wordless sermon for them to go and do likewise.

The gifts given to certain ones outside were in appreciation of the kindly favors they performed when the boy died. The mass distribution paralleled the wakíčʼaǧapi, the old redistribution ceremony. The impersonal distribution around the circle of diners could be called a wíȟpeyapi 'throwing away of things' even though it took place a year later and not at the moment of death, and was planned sanely. There had been ample time for the mother's grief to mellow into quiet resignation. Dakota customs modify, and finally wear away, but they do so very slowly. If the frenzied giving in blind abandon at the moment of loss is no longer general, the urge to part with something of value lingers and finds its expression in the modern custom of giving a horse, or similarly valued things, to the church organization of which the dead had been an active member. It is given with the understanding that it will be sold and the proceeds spent for the furtherance of the church's work.

I have also to describe a great corporate giving by an entire community, which I witnessed in the 1930s, because it, too, was a distinct carryover from the past. It took place in an obscure corner of the reservation I was visiting for the first time, and, as it happened, the last. The intent of the truly lavish giving was practically the same as that of an old-time wíȟpeyapi, but the place and manner of giving was another modification. The setting was a Christian cemetery and the event was in memory of the many who were buried there, some for many years.

It being May 30, there was first a Memorial Day service in the church conducted by a Native pastor. Then followed the inevitable feast, for which the various families had "counted their kettles"—pooled their food—as for any community undertaking.

After the feast the people formed a line and moved in an orderly procession toward the cemetery some distance away, many carrying containers filled with things. As they entered the enclosure they fanned out in all directions, until almost at once they were everywhere, standing near the graves of their own dead. The women then began to place their gifts in silence. Oranges and apples were arranged in various patterns over the mounds or in a line around the end. Fancy glass or earthenware bowls of candy and nuts were set on both extremities of many graves. Boxes of store-bought cookies and crackers, cakes of pemmican, cases of tomatoes and other canned goods—and even toys, on little graves—appeared everywhere. At the grave of an old man who, I was told, was unable to walk for many years up until his death, there was a new rocking chair eerily in rhythmic motion, in the light breeze. On a young girl's grave a photograph album of rich purple plush lay open, with her picture in the first window.

Some women had come armed with an entire bolt or two of calico in bright prints, from which they quickly measured enough ells for a woman's dress, and spread the pieces on their graves. Others covered theirs with new blankets or shawls, like colorful palls. Small American flags were aflutter in all directions, especially on former soldiers' and scouts' graves. On a very newly made grave, a woman in black spread out six silk neckerchiefs in as many colors, weeping softly as she worked to keep the wispy material in place. Her loose-hanging hair partly hid her sorrowful face. Some women still wear their hair unbraided as a mark of grief, but the custom of cutting it short is no longer general. I could almost say it is no longer observed, except that there is no telling what a distraught mourner might yet do, reverting to the past.

On one corner of each neckerchief was stamped a rodeo-bronco about to throw its rider; and, over in the airy slogan, in florid script, "Powder River—Let'r buck!" There was nothing funny in this for the woman, assuming she could read, for her only thought was to place on her boy's grave something he loved to wear with his cowboy outfit, thereby causing him to own it for a moment that she might then give it away as though from him.

The total effect was highly colorful, and the cemetery would have been a gay place indeed, were it not for the sudden anguished cries from unexpected quarters as each woman stopped to wail briefly upon completing her work.

Now she was ready to give. She invited various persons to come and remove this or that item from the grave, and it was theirs to keep. Dress goods and shawls went to women; blankets, moccasins and other items of clothing went to old people. The toys and sweets were for the children, who naturally hovered about them from the moment they were placed. The neckerchiefs went to six boys of the same age as the dead "cowboy." An old woman got the rocking chair and a young girl the album.

Only old men and young boys stayed around amid the graves. As was their custom, all other males waited distantly, many sitting in groups together to smoke and talk on everyday matters while waiting for their women. It was beneath them as males to hang around, displaying interest in material things pertinent to women only, but they, too, received gifts and their wives accepted them. Through it all no exultant and happy thank-yous were uttered. This was definitely not the time to be delighted. Gifts were soberly given and soberly received, with only a low murmur of acknowledgment. The reason for such giving and at so solemn a place was never forgotten by either givers or receivers.

Nothing was taken without its being specifically assigned. In that respect this occasion differed from the old-time *wihpeyapi* wherein the owners threw things away, indifferent as to who took what. Rather generally that is no longer done. Still it must be admitted that in some remote sections there are those who rather hope for a real *wihpeyapi* and who, if nothing is forthcoming, are not above taking something belonging to the deceased or the mourners, while the latter are preoccupied with their dead. If seen in the act, they might justify it by explaining, "I just wanted something to keep in his memory." In that case, as far as I know, there is no disposition to recover the article taken. Its loss must be charged to a vanished custom. Anyhow, most Dakotas prefer to let the matter stand, rather than have it said of them that they were "concerned with mere things though their loved one laid dead!" Such criticism only the most practical and modern can take with a shrug.

What I have described was a very local affair. I am not certain whether or not it was an annual custom in that community, or how widespread it may be still. I have never attended anything like it since. I do know that memorial services at the cemetery on Easter Day or on May 30 are held in many places, and that they consist of prayers, hymns, and addresses. Any giving would be quite incidental, perhaps even furtive, and done by only a few; no planned corporate giving as the main feature, to my knowledge. There is a gradual lessening of all ceremonial giving, and in time it must end of its own accord as economic considerations make it too difficult and as newer generations, unfamiliar with the past, feel no need for old usages.

It is still proper to hurry to the scene of death. The more visitors the more of a comfort to the bereaved. All are welcome and are fed if food is available. Unless a family is very poor and lacks relatives, it is usually possible to serve all comers at least a lunch. Some able relative butchers a cow or hog and its meat becomes the main dish. Women visitors remain to help cook and serve, thus sparing the mourners and enabling them to rest.

However, even if great crowds must be fed, they for their part do not come empty handed because they know that if they did, the entire burden must rest on the family. So they bring various items to augment the food supply. After one funeral the following food gifts were listed that friends had brought: bread, cakes, and other bakery products, cans of coffee, small sacks of sugar and flour, tomatoes and other canned foods, chickens, jams and jellies, pickles, and one huge carton of fried bread. There was plenty for all who came.

This was at a very important man's death. The fact that he had made many friends and kept them accounted for both the number of visitors and the amount and variety of food brought. Not many years ago I went to a death where there was no food for even the family and the home was indescribably dismal. The family, being without relatives and having taken no part in the social give-and-take of the community, could look to only the church for help and those who came to rescue them from their predicament acted out of Christian charity purely. Thus do circumstances and situations determine what happens at a death. The extremes are wide apart.

The custom of sitting up late around a corpse is already so fixed in many places that the fact is not generally recognized for what it is: a borrowed custom. It is a wake in English, and a *hakíktapi* 'staying up through the night' in Dakota. If distantly located relatives are coming, and the funeral must be delayed two or three days, it is nothing extraordinary to hold a wake more than one night. Ordinarily, though, it is the night before the funeral that is so observed, but the rule is not inflexible.

It is in most cases an entirely religious gathering. At all events the occasion is marked by a characteristically somber and dignified tone and mood. Visitors arrive as they can, and meantime those already present sit quietly around the room waiting for the minister or his representative to hold a service that consists of many hymns, Bible selections, prayers, and addresses, given by various ones. They speak of the dead reverently, or declaim on death and parting, or harangue on morals and tribal ideals and folkways. Finally, about midnight, a lunch is served to everyone.

Following this everyone leaves for home, planning to return for the funeral. Only a handful remain by the casket until daylight, when they also leave. Thus, after the many have gone away, everything settles down and all life is seemingly suspended—unless relatives arrive after a long journey. They go immediately to gaze on the face of the dead and weep softly, but should any of the family arise to greet them, loud wailing begins again, and all day long this viewing takes place as people arrive. Children drift indifferently in and out and are not snatched away, so long as they are quiet.

Liquor drinking, with its consequent unruliness, has no place at a Dakota wake. To appear there in an intoxicated state is an insult to the mourners and a disrespect to the dead. Occasionally a callous or irresponsible modern person does offend in that way, but he or she is an exception. The average Dakota, even if a habitual imbiber, has the good sense to stay away if he is not wholly sober. It must be admitted, however, that sometimes a member of the mourning family makes the disturbance, believing himself so up-to-date that he must drown his sorrows in drink. That is particularly regrettable.

The feeling persists that the dead must be laid away in the best dress obtainable and that it must be complete—footwear and all. Some families today can ill afford it, but they somehow manage with the help of friends and relatives. One woman was heard to say a few years ago: "They were going to bury her without good moccasins but I gave them the pair I had kept on hand for my burial."

As buckskin gave way to woven goods, the pioneer woman's style was adopted—wide, full skirts that hardly cleared the floor were gathered onto a bodice darted to fit tight. This was lined, as were the long narrow sleeves. Only the very old women rejected this innovation and wore calico or flannel gowns that were cut to the traditional style for buckskin ones. Such gowns were called *ikčé čʼuwígnaka* 'common or ordinary gown'. Both name and gown have long since disappeared with those who could not or would not make the change.

The new style was called *čʼuwí-yuskí* 'gathered at the waist'. It was usually a dress of this style that was put on the dead, in early reservation days.

Two or more full petticoats and a chemise next to the body were part of the grave dress, which was the same as that of the living. Today shoes have in most cases replaced moccasins, and the majority of women—and all children—are buried in store-bought ready-mades. My recent impression is that shoes or moccasins are no longer put on the dead in every instance, but at least socks or stockings. It is still unthinkable to leave the feet bare.

In the period when long checked gingham band-aprons were fashionable, they added an ornamental touch to a woman's grave dress with their elaborate cross-stitching in white across the bottom in the form of flowers, butterflies, birds, and other small animals. In addition, the woman's finest shawl, or a friend's, was laid in the coffin folded narrow and long, or it was spread over the shirt and feet. This custom has been gradually dropped as more and more women have learned to wear coats and no longer feel a blanket or shawl indispensable.

Men's grave clothes were just as complete. I speak now of the recent decades, since ready-mades have become purchasable. Whenever possible, the suit was new, as were the accessory items. The necktie was always a long one, tied neatly in a four-in-hand. In rare instances, in years gone by, both tie and vest were of deer skin ornate with quill- or beadwork in an all-over floral pattern. Trousers of skin, cut after the modern style but worked in the same manner, were also put on the dead. The cut and style were modern but the material and ornamentation were traditional. A man's hat was not placed in his coffin, as was a woman's wrap. It had never been an essential item of male attire in the past but only a recent fad. It had not been part of the man in the sense that a shawl was once an almost inseparable part of a woman.

In days before embalming was known on the reservations, both the inside of the coffin and the dress of the dead were drenched from time to time with something labeled "Hoyt's German Cologne," which was the only brand of perfume carried by the early trader. If the family neglected to provide it, some friend was sure to think of it, and this would certainly be classed with those "tender offices" already mentioned, in appreciation of which the family gave gifts at the memorial feast. As many as four or five small bottles might be emptied in this way, in an obvious effort to counteract any incipient odor of decay, although such a reason was not explicit.

In the past certain behaviors were believed to portend death. The daring young girl who was the first to return home with bobbed hair was in for harsh rebuke: "Your father is none too well; this surely foredooms him. You are killing your father!" her mother said. It was a dreadful thought. Cut hair is cut hair, and there was nothing for the girl to do but to endure the bombardment of ominous predictions from all quarters, wherever women talked together. Not until more and more girls returned from government schools in distant cities did the critics give up. For they, too, all wore neatly bobbed hair. Mothers then asked anxiously: "At least you brought your braids home?" They hadn't, and that was nearly as bad. One should never leave one's hair or nail trimmings to lie where they could be trodden by people's feet. That would dishonor one.

At the beginning the spread of the new hairstyle was interpreted as an epidemical urge to "run wild." This was said by the oldsters, to whom the alien manners and notions of returned students seemed improperly aggressive, not to say odious. They promptly dubbed the new style *witkówį-kaškápi* 'harlot haircut'. It is doubtful if the term is even remembered now, since bobbed hair is a commonplace and long braids are the exception.

There was a time when the arbitrary wearing of black also was regarded as an open invitation to death in the family. Women shied away from any black in their dresses, some from even the little black in their dress prints. The presumed consequences were too certain and the responsibility too great. Then one day some cashmere shawls of fine weave, with long silk fringes intricately tied as on Spanish shawls, were displayed at the trader's. They were what caused the breakdown for they proved irresistible to the Dakota girls, who began to buy them and to "appear in black without a cause," shocking their female elders.

The most perturbed were the old women, who pleaded with their grand-daughters: "*T'akóža*, this is a fearful thing you are doing, you know. Surely you do not mean to cause a relative's death? Or perhaps your own?" They shook their heads in dismay: "Oh, dear, oh, dear!" If it so happened that someone did die, even if a whole year later, women said it was because this or that girl had worn black without reason—and they believed it.

In the end style won out once more. Today the wearing or black for mourning is itself on the wane, partly because of the cost and partly because it was a borrowed custom anyway and hence never well rooted. If the women of a bereaved family attend the funeral in a black or dark dress, that is usually the extent of their mourning. Many do not even do that. Nearly everyone wears black as readily as any other color.

Now I must talk about ghosts, a subject too vague and chaotic to present satisfactorily. I may only explain the general notions about ghosts and alleged ghostly behavior, and the average Dakota reaction to them.[3]

Occasionally it was reported that after a funeral the spirit of the deceased was making its presence realized in the home through various means. Typical is the following report. Unaccountable sounds came from the next room, or from the far corner of the single room where the family was sleeping, but stopped the instant a lamp was lighted—only to recommence shortly after it was put out. In the dark the family heard "a trunk being noisily trundled across the room and a saddle flung against the wall; and the dishes in the cupboard clattered until they must surely be in pieces. But next morning everything was the same as it was the night before, the trunk in place, and the saddle, and not a dish broken."

Explanations of such alleged happenings were confusingly at variance: (1) those articles were sentient, imbued with an emanation that gave them potency; (2) the spirit of the dead person was restive until everything was done to its liking; (3) each person "souled" permanently whatever he once touched, leaving with it something of himself; (4) what was happening was simply wak'ą 'supernatural', hence inexplicable.

The only recourse was to go through everything once more and try to determine what of the dead person's possessions still remained and to whom he might want them to go, and then act accordingly. If the disturbance continued even after that, the perplexed family moved outside and stayed in a tent, or went to live with relatives. A very substantial farmhouse near the highway was pointed out to me as having been abandoned many years ago because the family could not resolve their ghost problem and were compelled to change their residence. A Bohemian farming family had later bought the place and the once "haunted" house was being blithely lived in.

Such happenings were not the regular consequence of each and every death; they were, in fact, the rare exceptions. Where they took place, outsiders might be afraid, but the saddened family were only more saddened by the uneasiness of the spirit of their dead, and yearned to know what exactly was the matter. To prevent its uneasiness, mourners generally disposed of its possessions at once. They wanted their dead to be at peace and not lurk about indefinitely.

Only one contrary attitude was reported. A woman was unhappy because of the absence of any such phenomena that would indicate that her son had not promptly left her. It seemed that even a very disgruntled ghost would be better than none. "I try and try to see or hear him. I lie awake with my ear attuned to the least sound. Alas, I am convinced that my son is verily gone."

The following is the most extreme case of ghostly disturbance I was given. The belongings of a once very positive woman were so full of spirit that even after they had been properly given away, immediately after her death, they continued to protest — to their new owners! They were said to be *naǧí t'ú*. The idiom is ambiguous: *naǧí* 'ghost, spirit, or shadow'; *t'ú*; (1) 'to have on, wear', as a hat, for example; (2) 'to emit, give birth to'. As a noun *t'ú* means 'suppurated stuff', generally pus out of a wound. Thus, whether *naǧí t'ú* means to 'wear spirit' or 'emit spirit', I am uncertain, and perhaps nobody really knows which. "Her things were so *naǧí t'ú* that late at night a woman was heard sobbing softly beside her trunk, though no one was there." Presumably the dead woman's ghost was mourning the loss of her precious possessions.

Another recipient, this time of such finery as she had never dreamed of owning, a beautiful shawl and some dresses of *mniȟúha otéȟika* 'costly goods', as silks and satins were called, was finally forced to give them away. "They were so 'alive' that I could not keep them." Whether their next owner had any better luck with them, or was forced to pass them on, I did not learn. It was remarked, however, that the dead woman had been notoriously self-centered and vain, and that she always demanded the best for herself, first at the expense of her family and later of her husband. "She was stingy, and therefore queer. She cared more for things than for people."

To the living the spirits of the dead remained responsible and cognizant of their kinship duties toward their relatives. "Oh, no, she will not frighten her children, she loved them too much" was said of a woman who had died and whose children were much alone. Thus it was not expected that such spirits would worry their relatives out of pure whim or malice but only out of anxiety over the proper handling of their things. But apparently most spirits were indifferent to material things, even when their family had not disposed of them. Or it might be that some of the living were less sensitive to ghostly manifestations than others. As I have already said, the returning ghost was the exception.

For their part the living also maintained their correct attitude and behavior toward the spirits of their dead. I have two examples. At a wake over the body of a prominent man, three young women who had been joking relatives of his whispered as they mounted the front steps, "Watch out, it is dark here. He [naming the deceased] might cause you to miss a step—still up to his old tricks!" They giggled, holding on to one another in mock fear, but the instant they entered the room of death they assumed a sober mien and were presently wailing with the mourners.

When a man's body rested in the church hall awaiting burial, the next day a young woman was heard to say as she prepared to walk home in the evening twilight, "I'm scared to pass the church. He would be just mean enough to chase me!" As brother- and sister-in-law, they had often exchanged snappy banter, each trying to get the better of the other. Hence this remark was consistently flippant, coming from her. Nevertheless, she was nervous, for she talked on of many irrelevancies until some people were going that way and she could join them.

Quite different was the usual attitude toward stranger-ghosts. However, there was one exception. Among Yanktons and Tetons—and possibly Santees, too, although I could not establish that—the famous *Šiná Sáį* 'Wearer of the Gray Blanket' was in former times a standard ghost, handed down from generation to generation until he was around so regularly that he ceased to frighten and became instead something like a tribal pet. His reported appearances were no great surprise. They were, rather, more or less expected, since they were loosely periodic. Sometimes he sidled up to a late cross-country walker and accompanied him to his tipi entrance— quite likely protecting him from less amiable ghosts! He was unbelievably casual. He might appear in broad daylight, going along in the distance, never hurried, never looking to right or left, always enshrouded in a gray blanket that looked so nearly white that as people stood watching him he would blend into the light of day and be seen no more. *Šiná* 'wrap, blanket, robe, shawl'; *sáį* 'light gray, grayish white'; *į* 'to wear wrapped about the body', as a blanket. Colored fabric that has faded after many washes is said to *kisáį* 'turn white'.

None ever saw his face, he was that elusive. Even while acting as companion, he remained silent and appeared to skim the ground without actually treading it. Dogs never barked at him, and on moonlit nights he cast no shadow. No man who walked with him at night was able to recollect his wits or find the voice to address him. For all that Gray Blanket was a very real character. One superstition attached to him, and it was that one who became terror-stricken upon seeing him was due to die shortly, or to have a death in his family. It was a portend for him only. Others could observe him walking along and not be affected by the sight. Such were the facts about this unique ghost.

On the whole there seems to have been a conceptual distinction between ghosts in the abstract and the spirits of known dead that paralleled the distinction in life between strangers and relatives. Ghosts in the abstract were *wanáǧi*. The prefix *wá-* being an indefinite pronoun, this would mean 'ghost of somebody, identity unknown'. But a closeness with their own dead is indicated in the people's speech.

In my fullest account of a Teton ghost-keeping, the narrator said this:

When my grandfather [a widower] asked my three aunts [his daughters] to examine themselves carefully first, in order to decide whether in addition to their regular duties they felt equal to the demanding role of custodian of the ghost bundle containing my grandmother's hair, they sat silent for a time. Then I spoke up. "Grandfather, I know that many will say I am too young to be trusted with that task. Nevertheless, I want to keep my grandmother." He smoked many long moments in deep thought before saying, "*T'akóža* ['grandchild'], I believe you can do it." So I became the youngest custodian of a ghost bundle. I was not yet twenty years old.

The point to observe here is that the narrator said, "I will keep my grandmother," not "grandmother's ghost" or "bundle." The personal aspect was hardly altered by death.

The *wanáǧi* were ghosts of another order. Shades of unknown people, they were no doubt entities, too. Yet because they made no distinct impression, being stranger-ghosts, they could not be realized and imaged as people. For that reason the attitude toward them was as toward strangers — cautious, tentative, fearful. They might be friendly, but how were the living to know that? Since they were sometimes sinister, or at least mischievous, how could they be relied upon?

The speculations about them were varied: "The *wanáği* are helpful to that holy man, whom they promised to assist when they came to him in his fasting and vision-seeking. He alone can trust them. *Wanáği* are dreaded because whenever they are heard to whistle, it is a warning that death or disaster is imminent. Ghosts know more than we the living, and when they appear, surely death comes to us or ours. But *wanáği* do not bring death, they only warn of it."

If that were all that needed be said, one might suppose *wanáği* were rather more benevolent than not, but they actually also had their malevolent side. "They indignantly ward off those who invade their burial place." "They cause paralysis to anyone who in passing brushes against their invisible form." "They pull people's faces awry—and they remain awry." "Sometimes they plague the living for sport. They whistle in concert." The latter was described as an unearthly jumble of squeaky utterances, as from a frolicsome band intent on confusing some lone wayfarer at night to lead him astray. Instead of whistling they might also appear as lights, for the same purpose. Ignis fatuus was thus interpreted.

This incidental bit is from one woman's life story. "That night our people crossed the river after dark and made camp on the farther side, unaware that an old Ree [Arikara] burial ground was close by. Throughout the camp so much ghost whistling was heard that no one dared to step outside, lest his mouth be pulled out of shape." I may interpolate here that it was the prudent custom to cross at once upon coming to a river while on a camp move, and stop for the night on the other side, so that in case of a flood in the night the journey would not be delayed.

It is clear that what inspired fear of stranger-ghosts was their unpredictable nature. That fact put the perennial Gray Blanket in a class by himself. Unquestionably he was a *wanáği*, since his identity was unknown after his own time. Yet, because his harmless behavior was consistent—as nocturnal escort and afternoon stroller—he gradually became identified as a familiar, a friend, with his rightful place in the tribe. He could be explained.

There was a distinction also between the material and the immaterial. Ghosts were immaterial. Hence they were not usually conceived of in terms of bones, nor symbolized primarily in such concrete form. A skeleton was bones, not a ghost. Of course if one happened upon a skeleton in some lonely spot, one beat a hasty retreat from the gruesomeness of it. An unidentified human skull might be abhorrent or depressing, or even droll, but by its very substance it was not a ghost in itself, although the notion was prevalent that its owner's ghost might be around.

Once I brought home from college a neat skull-and-crossbones arrangement in plaster of paris and thought it pretty daring to keep it on my table, but the reaction was generally disappointing. There was much less fear of it than there was curiosity as to whether it was actual or a copy, of bone or *mak'á sǎ* 'white earth' (i.e., clay). Only a certain playful old woman exclaimed shrilly, with exaggerated dread, "*Yaa!* To think that my poor head must look like this some day! *T'akóža,*" she pleaded in fun, "throw the ugly thing out! I cannot bear to look at it!" *Yaa!* is a woman's expletive indicating amazement or fear, or mock fear.

Very probably it was because the usual reaction to unknown skeletons was thus flippant and heartless that relatives always tried to return after a few years to the scaffold of their dead and gather up the scattered bones and bury them tenderly. They did not want strangers to treat them with dishonor.

In ancient times it was a custom when about to eat some special delicacy to cast the first morsel into the fire, saying in a murmur, *Wak'á, hé yúta yó!* 'Supernatural, eat that!' This was reverently done, like a grace before meals, although the purpose was rather to share food with the Great Spirit. A woman speaker omits the terminal *yó.* I rather believe that not everyone did this, and that it was done only if there was choice meat, buffalo tongue especially. Perhaps only those who lived with an awareness of the invisible world thought to do it. Closely allied to this custom was another, just as rare. An old man about to smoke alone sometimes declared as he smoked the first puff, "I smoke to [or with] the Great Mystery." Both of these rites were religious in nature.

More secular was the incidental ceremony of offering food to one's dead, as a memorial. This was done wordlessly, but in recent years I saw and heard a woman do the following. When she was about to serve *wóžapi* 'wild berry pudding' to her guests, she first threw a spoonful on the ground, saying to herself: *Léč'a waštélakela k'ú* 'How the little one craved this kind [of food]'. Obviously the reference was to her boy, for whom she was in mourning at the time.

The following also is reported. In a facetious manner—though perhaps not without a vague dread—women sometimes offered food to ghosts in general. For illustration, one woman, while cutting up fresh beef, peeled off a bit of sinew and tossed it into the underbrush nearby, called out, *Wanáǧi, hé yútapi ná ečʿáš akʿó ečʿúpi!* 'Ghosts, eat that and then carry on elsewhere!' Maybe it was her way of buying off any malicious or mischievous stranger-ghosts lurking about, lest they molest her for fun, but no informant gave any explanation.

Entirely serious is the next item. During a very long famine, an infant died at its young mother's breast because she could draw no milk from her emaciated body. That woman never forgot her firstborn, or the pathetic circumstances of its death. Though later she had other children to whom she was devoted, still, it is said, to the day of her death as an old woman she religiously fed the little ghost before every meal, her pleading words hardly audible: *Nána, čʿúkš, wóta ná!* 'Here, daughter, do eat!' But this she managed to do so inconspicuously that unless one knew her story and watched carefully, one missed the little ritual.

BELIEFS AND SAYINGS ABOUT DEATH

1. If a clean family is suddenly infested with lice, it is a portent of death.
2. That person will soon die, or be very sick, whose clothing is chewed up by mice while other garments hanging beside it are left intact.
3. One who hears a hen crow like a rooster will hear bad news.
4. If something of the dead is retained by the family without an audible declaration that it is intended to be a memento of him, his spirit will return nightly until it is disposed of.
5. If a normally timid wild animal — a porcupine, for instance — enters a home, it is an omen of death.
6. If a snake enters the tipi, it brings a warning of death or disaster.
7. If a pet suddenly acts strangely, it foretells a death. A dog that whines and barks at nothing visible is aware of ghosts hovering about to take a member of the family away. Allegedly one woman killed her entire flock of guineas and threw them away "because they acted out a funeral while she watched — and in a few days her husband died unexpectedly." Another woman killed her pet dog "because he seemed to 'know something,'" — thinking thereby to avert whatever that might be.

8. If a thunderstorm approaches from a wrong direction (i.e., any but the west), it "returns in angry mood and will kill someone." *Wakíyąktepi* 'to be killed by the thunders' is to be struck by lightening.

9. If a sick person converses with spirits of his dead relatives, he will die. Already he is in the spirit world. Should he in his delirium include someone living, that one also will die shortly. Already he is a ghost.

10. If a person clashes with a ghost, he will suffer a stroke. To have a paralytic stroke is to be *wanáǧi ktépi* 'killed by ghosts'.

11. Ghosts walk abroad on overcast days when the wind is from the south. "To go south" means to die. If one accidentally steps over "ghost-spittle" or cuckoo-spit, one is in even greater danger of ghosts. Despite this saying, people go about as they must, regardless of overcast skies and wind direction.

12. Ghosts are attracted by the odor of boiling prairie turnips and of chokecherry pudding, and perhaps other things, too. They can be repelled by tobacco smoke blown in all directions or by calamus root chewed fine and spewed out in all directions.

13. If one hears a long decisive whistle out of nowhere, one may expect bad news. The ghosts are warning him.

14. If a person dies without having been tattooed, the old woman who guards the *wanáǧi tʼačʼáku* 'spirits' road' (i.e., the Milky Way) will push him overboard to wander bodiless over the earth. This is no longer believed, and people are not tattooed anymore. Even the very old people who presumably once believed it now repeat it with the infinite quotative *keyápi* 'so it is said'.

15. If you kill a cat, you will soon die. A variant is that if you beat him, drown him, or crush him to death, in that way will you die. "No one who knows this will kill a cat." This must be a comparatively recent idea, since cats were an importation. The belief itself could be the result of culture contact, based on the saying that cats have nine lives. A cat wantonly killed would have nine chances to come back for revenge.

16. If a child not yet old enough to reason goes through the motions of a funeral, singing and wailing and jabbering prayers, he foretells a

death. Obviously this also is of recent origin. In olden times there were no funeral rites, and burials were not attended by everyone.

17. If an owl hoots close to the home night after night and sometimes through an entire season, "it always stops when a death occurs there, which it had been foretelling."

18. If a small child cuts his hair off, he will shortly be orphaned. Unconsciously he is announcing a parent's death. If an older person does so without a cause (i.e., not for mourning), he invites a death in his family.

19. If a corpse remains limp and must be so buried, another death will shortly occur in that family.

20. You will be killed by lightning if you kill a spider but neglect to say, *T'uká̠šila, wakį́yą niktépe* 'Grandfather, the thunders have killed you'. Today this phrase is idly repeated, as though no credence were given it. Yet the spider is addressed anyway, just in case, in much the same way that we rap on wood while expressing disbelief in the value of the custom.

21. If one hears human wailing in some commonplace sound, like the wind or the buzzing of insects, one will soon hear bad news. Illustrative incident: "An old man heard wailing, and even caught the words of grief, though he well knew that the sound was being produced by a housefly struggling to free itself from tanglefoot. He lived with a haunting expectation of bad news—and got it shortly. His brother had died on another reservation."

22. If you hear a relative call you by kinship term, though he lives far away, he is in great danger or is dead.

23. A ringing in the left ear portends news of death, and in the right ear good news.

24. Incessant twitching below the eyes means that one must shortly weep over the dead, and above the eyes, the eyelids, one will have glad news or unexpectedly meet a friend. This is further refined as follows: if the twitching is below the left eye, the sad news will affect you vicariously, but if below the right eye, it will affect you personally.

25. If a woman's breasts twitch persistently, her child is dead somewhere or in danger.

26. If a man's arms twitch persistently, his child is dead or in danger.

27. If one's body is suddenly aquiver, particularly about the groin, one's spouse is dead or in danger.

These last three sayings reflect an ancient belief that in whatever you have touched, something of you remains to sensitize it.

28. If one's soles twitch persistently, one must soon attend a burial. This also is of recent origin.
29. If one cannot help weeping when taking leave of a friend, either friend will die before the two can meet again. "Tears should be avoided at parting."
30. If a person cannot control his tears in the presence of the dying, he unknowingly weeps for himself; he too will soon die — *ič'íč'ųža* 'to foredoom one's self'.
31. If a person makes decisive plans without saying, "I shall do this if I live," he will die before he can carry them out.
32. If a woman does not dispose of her black mourning apparel after she no longer needs it, she invites another death shortly. Unconsciously she is remaining ready to mourn again. Again, this is of recent origin; black was not worn in mourning formerly.
33. If a wild creature advances fearlessly, it is well to react to it in a friendly way; it could be the spirit of one's dead wishing to be near. The following is an illustrative incident: "A woman was weeping at her small nephew's grave some years after his death when a tiny garter snake came crawling over the mound. Her companion picked up a stick to kill it but she stopped her. 'Let it be. Perhaps it is my nephew.' The two women withdrew slowly after it had disappeared in the grass, not wishing to rush away as though afraid, or hostile toward it." Today this sort of suggestion is usually made with a smile, as if not taken seriously, but perhaps the possibility is not totally rejected by some.
34. If you make a promise audibly, you are bound to keep it because the Supernatural has heard it. If you fail to keep it, you will bring harm to the one to whom you made the promise. He may die, or be very sick, because *wayákihtani* 'you have sinned on his account', or you yourself may suffer the same for failing him. The following is an illustrative incident: "A woman grew thin and sickly from seeing

her dead boy in her dream every night. One day she confessed to her friend that when her little son laid dead she talked to the corpse, promising a pretty tombstone for his grave, but she had never been able to afford it. She was certain that he kept returning to remind her that she was 'sinning on his account'. It made her ill to keep him disturbed."

This was in the days when tombstones were a novelty, but the story ends happily for that friend to whom the woman confessed told her friends, and together they helped to buy a stone. "And then the woman was not thin and sickly anymore." This comes from one woman's life story; she was that helpful friend.

The foregoing items are nowhere near all the sayings and beliefs; many of them are no longer retained. They are a sampling of the type. Some that are pertinent to one locality might not be generally known, as, for instance, that of the woman who killed off her flock because of their queer behavior and what she thought it portended.

8

Relatives of Marriage

Kinship relationships divide into two categories: the family of birth and the family of marriage, or affinal relationships. Formal and informal behavior occur in both. In the family of marriage, formal behavior is obligatory in the child-in-law and parent-in-law relationship and is expressed through the *avoidance* technique, which shows a respect relationship. Informal behavior is permissible in the joking relationship between all the collaterals of one spouse and those of the other spouse. These two types of specialized behavior in the family of marriage are explained and illustrated below. Then the *omáwahit'u* or *umáwahit'u*, a quasi–respect relationship between the fathers, mothers, aunts, uncles, and grandparents of one spouse and the corresponding relatives of the other, will be very briefly considered.

Avoidance

In all kinship etiquette the respect relationships are the most demanding. When a respect relative is present, one must behave in a dignified and formal manner unvaryingly. Whenever possible it is best to avoid such a relative altogether. The socially responsible Dakota can sense at once when one is present and adjust his attitude and behavior accordingly. Because of the seemingly continuous need of doing this, it used to be my belief that all Dakota kinship had a restraining effect. Not until I had to classify the different kinds of relationships did I see that actually there are very few that are restricted to formal behavior. The reason why the entire network of kinship seemed to be so regulated is that in any given group those whom some persons must respect and avoid are sprinkled randomly.

An unexpected encounter with a formal relative causes one to make a quick change of manner to suit the moment. One does this quietly while still associating with informal relatives, seemingly unaware of that particular one's presence, yet being aware all the time. If talking excitedly in a frivolous mood, one feels oneself suddenly on guard and one's erstwhile exuberance gradually dying down.

To illustrate: a group of women collaterals were lounging about and chatting uninhibitedly, as sisters and female cousins may, when their new avoidance relative, mother of the new brother-in-law, came around the corner. Thereupon, without "seeing" her, they sat up and focused their attention on a cunning child playing near, and so they preoccupied themselves while their mother-in-law passed swiftly out of sight, without "seeing" them. They were not acting in order to deceive their new relative into supposing them to be remarkably poised and quiet women habitually. Nor was she so naive as to suppose that of them. She knew that they had toned down their talk and laughter out of respect for her. She also had made a quick adjustment out of respect to them as soon as she saw them obliquely. Had she known they were sitting there, she would have gone another way so as to spare them any necessity to alter their behavior on her account.

When a certain man narrowly escaped a brawl by walking away without a word from the abuses and vilifications of an angry man, he was no coward. He only refused to show off before a respect relative. As he later told his wife: "I would have knocked him down for his insolence, but my mother-in-law was within earshot." His respect for her had forced him into grim self-control, even at the risk of appearing fearful of his assailant. Dakotas understood and admired restraint for such a reason as he gave.

One more example: some men in informal relationship were having a hilarious evening together in a tipi when an elder man who was an avoidance relative of two youths in the group came in. Those two, with admirable smoothness and subtlety, gradually changed from their sprawling position so that what they did was not noticeable. Sitting upright, they quite casually pulled their broad-brimmed Stetsons a bit lower until their eyes were in shadow. They no longer laughed noisily with the others, and one of them began scraping clumps of gumbo from his boots with so much concentration that he no longer heard the jokes to laugh at them. His unsightly boots had not worried him before. Had a question been put to him just then he would have seemed not to hear it, lest it compel him to take the floor in the old man's presence by answering it. One mark of respect was to efface oneself, as it were, by avoiding any need to claim such a relative's direct attention on oneself.

The rule of mutual respect asks little more of parent- and child-in-law than that they avoid each other in such ways as I have illustrated. However, socially conscious parents-in-law consider a marriage gift part of their in-law obligation, while the child-in-law considers a constant indirect solicitude on their behalf as part of his or her obligation.

Whenever possible the newlyweds had their own tipi, and it was set up in front of the home of either spouse's parents. For the sake of illustration of avoidance behavior in further detail, let us suppose that it was the bride who was living among in-laws. She remained in seclusion and came out only when absolutely necessary, and then always with extreme caution lest she accidentally meet an avoidance relative face-to-face—a dreadful eventuality! This being the tʻiyóšpaye of her husband, he was free to mingle with his family relatives as usual, or he went off with male companions on various errands. The bride waited for his return, for she depended on him to make sure that it was safe for her to venture out. If the newlyweds lived first among the bride's people, this whole situation was reversed, and the groom was the bashful one, but he did not stay in all day. Often he slipped out at daybreak to hunt and stayed away till dark.

If the new child-in-law did come into view unexpectedly, the parent-in-law quickly disappeared, but if that was not possible to do naturally, he or she turned his back so as to leave no doubt that he was properly avoiding his child-in-law.

This mutual avoidance has a specific term, wištelkʻiya 'to be bashful toward'. It is a formal "bashfulness," maintained during the honeymoon with strict adherence. Where opposite sexes are involved, as between son- and mother-in-law or daughter- and father-in-law, the avoidance of head-on encounters never quite ends, although in time it becomes natural from practice, or at least ceases to be a panicky vanishing act. If her son-in-law is present in the group, they are never alone together. A woman sits immobile, with attention fixed on her work or on the grandchild in her lap, and deaf to the general conversation if he is taking part; he in turn shows his respect for her by not intruding where she already is, lest he cause her to interrupt her work and sit motionless or rise and go off to something else, busying herself with that until he leaves.

Demonstrativeness between child- and parent-in-law is out of keeping. Whatever loyalty, love, or "pity" one may feel for the other must be shown only by tangible deeds, gifts, little and big marks of attention because the other may need them for his or her comfort or happiness.

Ų́šila 'to pity' means to feel sympathetic toward, to have compassion for, good will, kindness, and all the rest. The word lacks any hint of scorn or condescension in this usage. To be "pitied" in Dakota is a good thing, for it indicates concern for one.

One daughter-in-law made it her private rule to feed her husband's father first, and that was unusual, since in dispensing food the tacit rule was "children first," or "children only" if there was not enough for all. To this day a widower living in his child's home does not pay board by the week at a fixed rate based on what he eats. That would be regarded as cold, heartless, and too calculating for relatives still bound by old standards, but the conscientious and responsible man feels impelled to turn over what money he may get, from pensions, rents, and so on, keeping only enough for tobacco and other little needs. He says to his son, "Perhaps my child-in-law *t'akóš* fancies something to buy." Or to the small grandchild, "Take this to your mother, *t'akóža*, and let her buy you some *šašá*." The latter is the Teton baby-word for candy, *šá* 'red', *šašá* 'red things'. The first candy known was peppermint sticks, spirally red and white. The real term for candy is *č'ąhápi-šašá* 'red sugar'; sugar is *čą́* 'wood', *hápi* 'juice' (i.e., sap). The term is regularly contracted to *č'ąhápšaša*. No matter how poor the old man may be, how pitiable in the English sense, his gift must be graciously accepted. It can always be made up to him, over and above, in other ways, or by a gift.

Gradually the initial efforts of in-laws of the same sex to keep out of each other's way, out of respect, becomes less strenuous. As they of necessity are together more and more, the tension eases somewhat. They see that they may continue to be mutually respectful while not keeping physically distant. Even at that it is nearly inconceivable for son- and father-in-law to joke unrestrainedly or to connive; and gossips have a field day when mother- and daughter-in-law have words, in open quarrel.

Between avoidance relatives of opposite sexes, however, dignity remains so essential that it is actually preferable to ignore the other's inevitable moments of embarrassment rather than to offer help and sympathy directly. Figuratively at least one must still obliterate oneself and not "know" the other's little difficulties in order to spare his or her dignity. Only if either were in serious danger would the other act fast to avert it. Over anything less immediate or serious, direct dealings and attention on each other are to be avoided.

The following incidents illustrate this behavior. A score of years ago, a party of six or seven male collaterals were traveling across the state with their families, and with them was a quiet little man who was father to the brothers and uncle to the male cousins. His naivete invited kindly teasing, and on this trip the men made the most of it for their amusement. At one midday stop, while the men tended their horses and the wives prepared a hot meal over their common fire, this little man busied himself in straightening out a rope that had dried in kinks after the rain. Careful to keep out of sight of the women—his avoidance relatives—he tied one end of the rope to a wagon wheel and was giving it cautious little jerks when, suddenly, it snapped in two! Over and backward went the surprised little man in a deliberate somersault, until he disappeared into the gully behind him—one dusty moccasin remaining in midair for a long moment before it too dropped out of sight.

The men returning from the water caught the comical performance in its entirety, and of course cheered and jeered noisily, *Wą́! Wą́! Takúku tókʿu só, waná akʿé!* 'Look! Look! What in the world is he up to next!' Despite the commotion, their wives did not so much as glance around for the cause of it, knowing to whom "he" referred. One elderly wife did mutter indignantly, "Have they gone crazy? Nothing could be that funny!" Yet even she did not investigate—and not a woman smiled.

Here was automatic avoidance behavior at its finest. The concerted effort to save a respect relative's dignity and spare him embarrassment was a complete success. The women did not "know" of any mishap, and the men never mentioned it again; no doubt they were roundly scolded in private and ordered to keep still. As it happened all the women were kindly disposed toward the guileless old man, as was everyone who knew him. Even if he had been another kind of person, they must treat him properly because their reputation as correct relatives—which in Dakota society was to be law-abiding—must remain consistently above reproach. The matter is not flexible; who the relative is, whether his own character demands consideration, is not the point. During the rest of the trip the old man stayed behind his wagon and wore a band of white cloth around his head to indicate a headache as his reason for keeping quiet, so the women sent him his meals by the men, and occasionally voiced their sympathy indirectly. "Such hot days as these are! Enough to give anyone a headache. Mine aches this morning!" They gave him room to recover his dignity—and cure the headache he probably had after that fall.

The "miraculous growth" theme runs through Dakota folklore, in various situations. For example, "The Four Brothers," culture heroes, find a baby in the wilds and decide to adopt her as their sister . . . They toss her up through the smoke vent of the tipi and allow her to roll down the sloping side to the ground. Four times they do this, and each time she rises to her feet considerably taller. Finally she stands a beautiful young woman endowed with industry and skill: ready to keep house for them and make handsome moccasins, quivers, and such things for them, so that in time they were the best-dressed men in the land. This is a common version; there are others.[1]

One day an old warrior sat as a guest in a tipi, while the alleged indiscretions of his notoriously flirtatious daughter-in-law were being aired in bald detail outside—by women, of course. His uneasy hosts hesitated whether to stop the gossips or apologize for them, but the old man maintained his composure through the entire visit. Moreover, he ignored the matter permanently because he must be loyal even when loyalty was not deserved. "Those who aim to be noble in kinship behave that way," said the informant who gave this incident. "But sometimes it is not easy."

Since a stringent avoidance could be somewhat relaxed in time between respect relatives of the same sex, a widower was likely to feel more comfortable in a daughter's home than a son's because then his avoidance relative would be a man. A widow found it preferable to live with a son, for a similar reason.

Such arrangements were not always feasible. If a man must live with a son, then he perforce is more distant and formal toward his woman t'akóš 'child-in-law'. With consummate skill he manages to be where she is not, and she also avoids him adroitly. Yet time relaxes even these housemates, especially after there are children. Their initial frantic avoidance is then partly substituted for by a mutual courtesy and deference expressed in indirect solicitude for one by the other. As housewife the daughter-in-law must feed her husband's father, wash his clothes, and look after his other needs and wants. She says, "Tell your grandfather that his dinner is ready," or, "Ask him for his shirt that I may wash it."

Unless her husband is at home, the children are the intermediaries. Small children run little errands to and from without question. Only as they become old enough to observe the various types of behavior in operation between certain kinds of relatives do they see why they are go-betweens, as in this situation.

If husband and children are away, the woman must speak directly to her father-in-law in an emergency, so she approaches him swiftly but halts at a short distance and stands looking off yonder while he sits with downcast eyes, on something he is making. Both speak and listen with equal politeness. Both are brief.

Old women talking reminiscently sometimes boast that they could not describe the facial features of a child-in-law, meaning that as part of their avoidance behavior they never embarrassed such a relative by rudely scrutinizing him or her. It was their crowning achievement as proper relatives.

If a man gives money to his son's wife, through his son or grandchild, a woman honors her daughter's husband occasionally with a gift. In former times this might be a decorated shirt or robe, or some accoutrement of war. Today it might be anything, preferably new, like a neckerchief, suitcase, saddle blanket, beaded belt, or even a horse; it might be a pretty patchwork quilt for his bed. The mother-in-law presents her gift — through her daughter; the son-in-law thanks her — through his wife. All the way direct converse is assiduously avoided between parent- and child-in-law of opposite sexes. This is the heart of the avoidance sanction. Ultracareful relatives in this situation do not even send personal messages to each other, to be delivered verbatim by the carrier, since that would be tantamount to a conversation together.

One day I visited a young couple in their neat home where the following incident took place. The husband was intelligent and well educated in the white man's world, yet he maneuvered himself as a relative of marriage in an irreproachable manner, showing that he was just as well educated in Dakota kinship.

An elderly woman came to the house but stopped outside the screen door upon realizing that her t'akóš, her niece's husband, was inside. The niece went to the door and talked with her, and in the course of the conversation the woman told her: "T'ožą ['niece'], my horses have gone off again. Someone is always leaving the gate open." Presently she left. Then the young man, who had continued talking with me and had seemed unaware of what his avoidance relative was saying, excused himself and went outside. In a matter of minutes the horses were in, the gate was shut, and he was riding back to the house. The reciprocal behavior had been perfect. Indirectly the woman had made her need known; she had not given a request for her niece to repeat to the man, but he had acted to meet that need, first giving her ample time to get home.

Unhappily, many young people are no longer so sensitive to their opportunities to show kinship courtesies. Whenever one plays his role as well as this man had, oldsters are delighted that the old ways are not entirely gone.

There is an example of a virgin who lived next door to her brother-in-law, a respect relative, and his two wives who were her sisters. A virgin was called a wit'ášna-ų, literally 'woman lives single-bodied'. Most Dakota women married, and only a very few remained single. If they had lived carelessly in their youth so that gossip could be started about them, they might be called wit'ášna-ų but they were shams and not wit'ášna-ų-hčaká, a 'virgin in truth', hence, a perpetual virgin. A true virgin had so ordered her life from the beginning that no scandal could touch her. Having proved herself, she enjoyed high prestige to the end of her life. The people would rise as one to her defense if any man were to speak disparagingly of her. But only a born fool would do that.

The perpetual virgin lived circumspectly, in the midst of her family, who practically worshiped her, and consulted her like an oracle. Even her settled and married siblings were influenced by her opinions, and they deferred to her judgment and sought her advice. In short, the Dakota virgin was exactly the opposite of the derided proverbial "old maid." Far from being the dried-up, frustrated, unfulfilled hanger-on apologetically creeping around the periphery of the family, she was actually its center.

Though she chose not to marry, her female collaterals' children were her children, and her male collaterals' were her nieces and nephews, on whom she was at liberty to give free play to her natural instinct to love and protect the young. Children were part of her life. She did not feel alone against the world when in a crowd, since society was so organized that she was not conspicuous without a male companion. Automatically, men and women divided in two groups in any gathering, and she could move with her own kind.

Nevertheless, not withstanding the unique instance cited wherein a man of dignity refused to be flippant toward a perpetual virgin who was his joking relative "because he revered her," most masculine joking relatives furnished what corrective there was for all the prestige a wit'ášna-ų-hčaká enjoyed. Though they well knew her position, they sometimes teased her mildly about "the one you could not get" or "my cousin for whom you still yearn," inventing situations that never existed. The self-assured woman would calmly remind them of their own actual futile courtships, but as time fortified her standing in the tribe and as she remained true to her vocation, those men gradually came to regard her more as a sister to be revered than as a sister-in-law to be guyed. Then any man who joked tactlessly about her was sternly rebuked by his wife, her collateral, or his mother, her avoidance relative. Those women would warn, risking to defend her, "That jest is out of keeping regarding her. Watch yourself!"

The perpetual virgin I once knew had two sisters, one younger and one older than she, and they were cowives. Her brother-in-law was an able and respected man, an ex-warrior with a long record of courageous feats. It was told of him that shortly after he gave up a roaming life and came in to settle down with his family, those who would civilize him made the suggestion that he give up one wife. To which he replied, "I 'pity' them both and have provided for them equally these many years. But now, which one shall I cast out to fend for herself? Which children must leave their father's home? Alas, I cannot say. You must choose for me." There was no satisfactory answer for that, so he kept his family together to the end. "Pity" means compassion.

Each wife had her own home and the virgin sister had hers, three square log houses set in a semicircle with a large leaf arbor cut in front of them where the family spent much time in the fair seasons. The sisters sat there with their fancywork, but if some morning one of them preferred to stay in her house it was her privilege, and the others did not require an explanation. The cooking was done on a sunken "stove," which was a hole in the ground with the square top of a kitchen range over it, the pipe extending neatly above the arbor. The one who cooked sat on the ground beside the stove just as she would have done in former times. The family ate their meals on the large canvas spread on the ground.

I have no clear-cut picture of the virgin's face, but I do remember her as a well-built woman, with complete assurance and poise. There was something masterful about her, but she was by no means "bossy." She had her own stock that ran with the family herd, and was therefore independently hospitable and generous. A contented woman, she enjoyed her brother-in-law's protection and help as much as did his wives and children. Though as polite to her as to a sister, unlike brother to sister, he talked with her freely and informally, but both were too mature to pester the other with incessant joking.

For all her importance she did not sit idle to be waited on but assumed her share of the work in the home and devoted herself to the children untiringly. The man lived in both wives' homes but rigidly kept out of hers, as a matter of principle, even in daytime. Her housemate was always some elderly aunt or a grandmother, and there was no slightest chance for gossip involving her and her brother-in-law. Such gossip would have been as unfair to him, for he was an upright man. If I was not old enough for such penetrating appraisal of her, I slowly gathered all this from the expressed attitude of my parents, who admired and respected those people for their native integrity.

Her sisters' children called her mother, of course, and ran freely in and out of her house as though they lived there. By turns they did live with her, and how they vied for that privilege! She was their most popular relative. I remember her house: she had beds, tables, and chairs, a stove and cupboard, and a row of trunks—always a sign of prosperity in homes of that day. The trunks were filled with the kind of things dear to women, so that the *wit'ášna-ų* could at any time pull out a gift worthy of herself, and present it to a visitor. Yard goods, shawls, blankets, pretty patchwork quilts—star quilts were the finest—towels, aprons, and such purchasables. And also pairs of decorated moccasins in various sizes, beads in bunches of all colors, porcupine quills in paper envelopes (formerly in parchment), and skins of various animals (doe skin, calf skin, cow skin, and so on) already dressed to a soft and pliant consistency for easy embroidering. Moccasins were kept tied together by their long supple strings, the rawhide soles with tufts of hair, showing they had never been worn, on the outside, and the moccasin-faces inside.

I once watched the virgin sorting new porcupine quills preparatory to dyeing them with native dyes. By their pinlike tips she set them up in small bunches on the wool blanket over her lap. Then she picked out the tallest and coarsest quills for one lot, then the next size, and the next, until she had classified them all from longest to shortest, from heaviest to finest. Each size was for a different type of work. In the process she had rid the quills of hairs. It should have been tiresomely painstaking work, but she did it deftly from long practice.

People referred to the perpetual virgin—the only one in the whole region—with the veneration due to someone very special, which she was. My impression is that she did not go everywhere constantly. That, too, was in her favor and consistent with her role. An old men's adage was "If you behold a real woman, you must seek her out." A gadabout was no real woman.

That home was in fact one harmonious establishment, a veritable institution, with the three sisters in their three houses, the several children in all of them, and the single male head. It was a cordial and pleasant place to visit and I went there often, but after their fourteen-year-old daughter, who was my best friend, died, I did not go there anymore. I had begun going away to school by then, and the virgin died during one of my absences.

Though, as I have said, avoidance relatives of the same sex learn to be together after a time, they properly remain deferential. If son- and father-in-law are working together, neither tries to force his ideas on the other arbitrarily. One of them may offer a suggestion that is for the other's good. "T‘ɥkáši 'father-in-law', it is growing very warm. You better go in and rest. There is not much left to do." No arguments; no rollicking familiarity. Two women may sit and discourse together about common family problems—the children, the food supply, the plan for tomorrow—and so on, but in the same manner as that of son- and father-in-law. The subject of sex with reference to human mating is taboo between child- and parent-in-law. Nor do mother- and daughter-in-law, however long they have been together, venture to share their intimate desires, personal secrets, or private weaknesses. A mother-in-law is never a confidante. As at first, so always, there is a mutual inner aloofness.

Regardless of the kind of marriage, it is the kinship duty of parents-in-law to welcome a new daughter-in-law with respect. They knew already, in olden times, that their son was buying a wife, or that he and some girl had agreed to marry, and so they were prepared to receive the bride. Even if the marriage was an elopement—which did not have social approval—they still must show respect to the bride. Reproach would come from other quarters; it should not come from parents-in-law.

Sometimes the eloping girl came in the night after the family had retired. She remained outside, with wrap pulled up over her head, bashfully awaiting reception. When her presence was realized, some woman relative of the husband went out and led her in politely.

"We were all in bed. Sometime in the night two persons stole in and lay down in my brother's space without saying a word. We knew he had brought home a wife, so we passed the word around in whispers and one by one we went outside and found places to sleep in the tipis of relatives." In some such manner, privacy was quickly effected by a man's family, for even an eloping bride.

What I have been describing and illustrating is the ideal behavior of avoidance relatives, but sometimes child- and parent-in-law have a falling out. A thoroughgoing quarrel with harsh words volleying back and forth might occur between mother- and daughter-in-law, some women's dispositions being what they are. Such a quarrel between two men would be extremely rare—so rare, in fact, that I have no example of it.

If there was trouble between mother- and son-in-law, it was likely to be voiced by a woman of short patience who wanted to justify her irregular behavior by announcing the reason for it. The son-in-law said nothing back. Instead he kept far away, sometimes permanently. However, even the most patient woman might be driven to making this kind of outburst by her son-in-law's flagrant faults: he neglected his wife, he did not provide for his family, he drank too much, he was habitually unfaithful, he was heedless of kinship obligations, he was lazy, and so on. It was impossible to overlook such glaring failures forever by even the most long-suffering mother-in-law. Especially should her daughter be made ill through his neglect, she broke the traces with a vengeance, no doubt feeling that since she must break kinship rule, she might as well do it thoroughly. Such a woman was condoned by those who knew what she had endured a long time.

Open quarrels between father- and daughter-in-law were the least likely; I could even say they did not happen, because theirs was the one relationship not likely to deteriorate. Most men could accept an unhappy marriage of their son and make the best of it. "If that is my son's choice, what is there to say?" With that realistic attitude a father acts as he ought even when his daughter-in-law is far from his taste or her persistently improper conduct distresses him—as in the case of the warrior who remained impervious to his daughter-in-law's behavior, which gossips were spearing with sharp tongue. At all events, thanks to the rule that avoidance relatives of opposite sexes keep apart habitually, neither has the opportunity or leisure to observe any idiosyncracies or inadequacies of the other to be irked by them. No daughter-in-law is perfect in every detail.

If his wife complains to him that her relationship with their son's wife is not ideal and that it is the younger woman's fault, the father-in-law tries to iron out the trouble by reminding his wife of their obligation as avoidance relatives, and encouraging her to keep on being good to the alleged troublemaker. For usually a man is above taking sides and thereby abetting any difficulty toward an open break. Too often he cannot wholly sympathize with his wife's position because, unlike her, he has no close dealings with their daughter-in-law. She treats him impeccably well and that is all he knows. He remains optimistic as long as possible.

It must be said in all fairness, however, that most mothers- and daughters-in-law are proud to start their relationship correctly, and with the best of intentions to keep it so, and that a surprising number so succeed in maintaining the correct behavior and attitude always. They would rather not quarrel if they can help it, for once they do, it is nearly impossible to patch up their differences and resume their former association with confidence in each other.

The older woman is expected to be more lenient and forgiving because "she has lived longer." Knowing this she tries to endure in silence. Then it is up to the discerning powers of her son to sense the trouble. His mother is too loyal to him to upset his marriage, but sometimes an unprincipled wife does not hesitate to tell him that his mother is secretly hateful to her. This puts any man in a tough spot: he is devoted to both women and longs for them to be on good terms. He dreads the thought of offending one by defending the other. Each man must find his own way out of such a dilemma. If he and his wife are otherwise compatible, or if he feels that his mother is really at fault, he might change his residence. Otherwise the couple might separate after continued misunderstandings.

It is improper for respect relatives to address or refer to one another by name. Kinship terms are required instead. The parents of either spouse are always *t'ųkáši* 'father-in-law' and *ųčíši* 'mother-in-law' to the other. A child-in-law is always *t'akóš*. Since everyone has several fathers, including own father's male collaterals, and mothers, including own mother's collaterals, sometimes one must specify them. One may say "*t'ųkáši* who lives near the Missouri" and "*ųčíši* who was here this morning"—or some such designation. If in an extreme instance one must be even more exact and speak that father-in-law's name, one says reluctantly, *T'ųkáši Mat'óska* 'my father-in-law White Bear' if that is his name, never *Mat'óska* alone. That would be unpardonably rude. Likewise, when parents-in-law say *t'akóš* or *mit'ákoš* in reference, they mean the spouse of their child, but that child's collaterals also are *t'akóš*. So, in referring to them, they may specify, as in the case of those extra fathers- and mothers-in-law. They must not call them by name only.

Occasionally one may have a respect or avoidance relative who is unable to play his reciprocating role correctly. I once knew a woman who had such a father-in-law, one of her husband's other fathers. The old man was losing his mind, but she treated him as though he were entirely responsible, and never slighted him because of his deficiency. If someone joked about him in her presence, she came swiftly to his defense in anger. Any time that she saw him stumbling along in the offing, she said: "Go bring your grandfather in, he may be hungry." When the child returned leading him by the hand, she was gone, having set out some dinner for him. The old man accepted her marks of kindness as a child might, never asking why. Nor was he concerned about any return courtesies to a daughter-in-law. That made no difference. In Dakota kinship, as I have said already, one tried to uphold one's end at all events, and that was what she did.

The Joking Relationship

Collaterals-in-law—that is to say, one spouse and all that spouse's collateral relatives, on the one hand, and the other spouse and all his or her collateral relatives on the other—are permissibly informal in behavior toward one another. This is the joking relationship. These two groups exchange brother-in-law and sister-in-law terms indifferently, since there are no terms specifically meaning male and female cousins-in-law.

To the initiated the joking of collaterals-in-law is unmistakable. If a man and woman engage in trifling talk or speak curtly to or about each other in a mock fighting mood, tend to belittle, ignore, or treat lightly some serious act or statement of the other, it is obvious that they are brother- and sister-in-law. If two women tease each other by trying to make the other appear silly, in the wrong, or at a disadvantage, they are sisters-in-law. If two men treat each other in that way, they are brothers-in-law. The aim of joking relatives is to gain the advantage over the other somehow—and hold it. It is improper for other kinds of relatives to behave like joking relatives; if any did so, they would be completely out of line. They would be changing their regular behavior toward each other for something else, and by so much they would be unreliable Dakotas. It is not permitted to treat this relative one way and then unexpectedly change to another way.

Spouses are, technically, joking relatives in that they belong respectively to the two groups of collaterals continually squared to each other, but they do not desultorily plague or tease each other, being too at home together for it to be an exciting or particularly satisfying pastime. They remain, however, alert to take sides with one of their collaterals whom the other is teasing, criticizing, or disparaging—in fun or in earnest.

Joking relatives of opposite sexes are, so to speak, potential spouses, meaning that they are eligible to marry, other things being equal—that they are both free to marry and that they are mutually attracted. But whether or not they are free to marry or mutually attracted, they are potential spouses anyway in that they are father and mother or uncle and aunt to the next descending generations of both sides.

While not obligatory but only permissible, joking in this relationship has its uses. It offers an informal avenue of approach and a mood and atmosphere conducive to courtship, should courtship be the aim. For the joking sanction tends to break down reserve, weakening normal formality between the sexes and lightly invading personal dignity—all of which makes it a suitable prelude to introducing ideas of marriage, whether in earnest or for sport, whether in one's own, or a shy brother's or cousin's behalf. Proxy wooing is legitimate. Even a married man can do it for another. His wife accepts the matter casually and is not above putting in a good word herself to help him, by advising the girl being courted that here was a good opportunity for her.

Joking between men and women may be flippant, shallow talk; frothy, smart, pert, rude, and sometimes positively hostile in tone. Finally, where it is certain to be accepted and rebutted in kind, it may be even suggestive. However, such joking is determined by the temperament, taste, mood, and good sense of those engaged in it. That being so I cannot state categorically that all joking between collaterals-in-law must invariably be carried on thus and so everyone must joke. The problem of selection of a joking opposite, and of how much and what kind of jokes he or she will accept, are factors. Such joking is quite innocuous and decent; it attempts only to be clever enough to trap one joker by the other.

One informant gave the different ways in which her several brothers-in-law joked with her. The names are fictitious, of course. Frank, her own sister's husband, teased her often: she was lazy, slept late—an insulting accusation unless one was sick—was a poor cook, spoke out of turn before her avoidance relative, and so on. She countered by making fun of his broken English and accused him of being afraid of ghosts. Usually he wound up this mock tirade by saying: "Well, I see you dislike me. Never mind, So-and-so [naming a pretty girl] likes me!" This was her cue to say to her sister: "Jane, did you hear that? Here is your chance to get rid of him, for there is actually someone who likes him!" Frank had no designs on his wife's sister; nor was he trying to interest her in someone else, some shy younger brother. This was simply his way of passing the time of day by amusing himself in aimless joking until she lost her temper.

Another was Tom, a dignified man of sixty, a fatherly sort. He remained ready to do anything for my informant, who was a girl at the time, but without the flippant approach, which was unnecessary to him. Instead of trying to get a rise out of her, he took extreme care not to annoy or embarrass her, and he always called her by kinship term, hǫká, the man's term for 'sister-in-law'. Most men of dignity would not engage in futile levity with a very young sister-in-law, but preferred to behave more like a father or uncle to her, being closer to her parents in years, even though they belonged in her kinship generation.

George, another elderly brother-in-law, was as paternal but more sociable. He often chatted pleasantly with my informant and brought her current news and did favors for her, always courteously. He made more fuss over her little sister, "who always wanted him to comb and braid her hair because he did not pull it as our mother did when she was in a hurry." As he worked to get out the tangles, he would beguile her with folktales. "I am brushing your hair with slow, lengthening strokes to make it grow fast. Soon you will be a beautiful young woman with long braids."

Even among other men William was a silent man. Yet whenever he met my informant he would say as he shook hands, "Well, well. This time I failed completely to recognize. She is getting to be such an old woman!" She would counter with "Just what I was about to say of him. I thought it was . . ." naming the most decrepit old man in the village. Then they would laugh a little over their monotonous standard joke that varied slightly each time only in the wording. That was the extent of their periodic banter as joking relatives, and William would immediately become silent as they parted.

His brother Daniel was a vivacious, talkative, and friendly man whom everyone liked for his congenial ways. My informant knew him as a brother-in-law, being William's brother, but she had never had any dealings with him because he lived at a distance. However, one day at a rodeo she found herself back of him in the crowd, where, unaware of her nearness, he was exchanging some earthy jokes with two women of unsavory reputation. All three were laughing lustily when suddenly he turned and saw her. Stammering out in confusion, he said: "*Haká*, had I known you were near I should never have said what I just did to these two. It was not fit for your ears. I have shamed myself."

My informant was very young and enjoyed a blameless reputation. Even the most ribald joking relative honors that. Though Daniel obviously relished coarse talk with women who were hardened to it, he became suddenly respectful toward the girl who merited respect. Thus did men vary their behavior according to the joking relative they addressed.

One did not joke with every joking relative but only those amenable to joking and able to play fairly as joking opposites. It was primarily a matching of wits and a challenging of one another's sporting spirit. It was not fair to overdo in joking, but sometimes a mature and very self-assured woman found it amusing to say really cutting things to a male joking relative as though to see how much he could stand. Said a man about such a woman, "She doubtless means well enough but I'm afraid of her because I always come out worsted."

I would not give the impression that brothers- and sisters-in-law had nothing else on their mind but to joke, for that would not be true. Most of the time they conversed in a matter-of-fact way, and if things took a serious turn, as when a relative was suddenly ill or had died, levity was completely forgotten. In their common anxiety or grief, even joking relatives called one another by kinship term—always a mark of serious, respectful approach—and soberly discussed what ought to be done. It was in poor taste to try to joke with one who was mourning. He or she must be the first to joke again. An untimely joke got no reaction—but only the stupid or the callous would be guilty of that. Moreover, whenever one's avoidance relative happened on the scene, one stopped joking, and then his or her partner usually knew enough to respect one's need to be suddenly deferential. In rare instances a person refused to talk flippantly to a joking relative because he commanded general respect in the community. Thus, a certain Yankton consistently rejected the joking privilege with reference to one woman, saying, "I revere that sister-in-law." Similarly, a youngish Teton woman, when encouraged to make a saucy remark to a man of prestige who had recently become her joking relative, said: "Oh, I couldn't say that to him! It has always been my aim to do him honor." She meant that she would not capitalize on her new joking privilege to demean him.

These extraordinary cases were determined by the quality and position of the persons involved. The particular sister-in-law whom the Yankton revered was an acclaimed "perpetual virgin" of established reputation for purity. Being one who appreciated her quality as something good in the tribe, he would not belittle her station. Such a woman ought not to be discussed lightly, even though that was permissible to him. Thus the extreme informality of the joking sanction might give place to the highest deference, depending on the rank, character, and reputation or achievement of one's joking relative.

It is improper to become sexually intimate with a collateral's spouse, despite the almost unlimited freedom to banter words. Upon hearing the rumor that a certain man was being intimate with his brother's widow, one of his male collaterals remarked: "Indeed? Oh, well. She is ours anyway." His meaning needs explaining. Not all joking relatives—potential spouses—were theirs for the taking against their will; in every case they would have to be accepted first. He meant simply that an unattached sister-in-law was within their territory and might properly be courted by any of them. Such courtship might lead to legitimate marriage—or merely to intimacy outside of wedlock, which was always wrong, depending on the woman's own standard of conduct. He meant only that no kinship taboo was being transgressed.

When a wife's sister lived in her home, what might occur depended largely on the character of the husband. Even though he might joke with her as his sister-in-law and might go even to risqué lengths verbally if she was amenable to it, he had no right to rape any woman just because she belonged in the category of potential wives.

Quite probably it was to guard against such a possibility that, in olden times, sometimes the young sister-in-law was given openly and gratuitously to her brother-in-law as cowife to her sister. "That she may help her sister with the work" or "That she may hold the baby for her" were the euphemistic wordings. Child-tending was expressed by *hokší-oyúspa* 'baby-holding'.

Since to be married honorably and without premarital sex experience was of highest importance to a woman's subsequent life, a girl who, though docile, was without proper relatives to chaperone her, or a too-spirited girl who was proving unmanageable, might be thus placed in a married sister's care, often at the sister's own suggestion. Should the girl live there unwed, and should her brother-in-law prove to be unprincipled, the very thing feared could occur. It was safest to forestall such an eventuality and so to save the reputation of all involved by making the girl a cowife. In this way any likely union was legitimated beforehand.

The girl-wife lived somewhat as an eldest daughter of the family, acted as helper and companion to her sister, and played with the children while caring for them, until she was herself with child. Her sister advised and trained her, and the two wives stood together in any arguments with their common husband, the outsider. Within reason the auxiliary wife enjoyed a modicum of freedom. She did not, of course, run around freely, but otherwise she did what she was inclined to do and was not bossed by the head wife. Nor was she expected to cater to her. Each did her stint of the work, and their relationship as cowives was much the same as it used to be in their parents' home. Only their setting was altered. Their mutual affection was expressed in the same casual manner, with reference to everyday questions that did not matter one way or another, but in crises they stood together.

One elderly Teton woman spoke appreciatively of her own experience as a cowife. Upon the death of her mother, since her aunts lived too far way, her father gave her in marriage to her sister's husband. No doubt it was her sister's idea. At any rate, because she was only fourteen years old, her brother-in-law "being a good man" permitted her to live in a happy, carefree manner under his protection like one still unwed. He often said he accepted her because she needed care and shelter, and he humored her. If his wife asked too much responsibility of her, he would say: "Let some strong woman do that . . . She is still a child." Never once did he take down or lower his standard as a dignified, self-respecting man, "lest his friends think the less of him." It was not until she was nearly twenty years old that her elder sister sent her on a hunting trip "to cook for him," while she remained at home with the children, and the girl became a wife at last. The sister had planned everything for her.

Although joking relatives usually avoided hurting one another by carrying their joking too far, still, occasionally, a boisterous man teased a very young girl mercilessly, thus making her conspicuous at an age when she wanted nothing so much as to be unnoticed. He might amuse himself by trying to break down her excessive shyness. Shyness and modesty were encouraged by the elders, who were certain that a loud, aggressive girl was unquestionably on her way to ruin. The young girl might run off to hide, and perhaps cry there or only suffer in silence, until one of her women collaterals—perhaps the very man's wife—rose to defend her and put the talkative brother-in-law in his place with a few well-chosen thrusts. It was wise for young girls to keep out of a noisy brother-in-law's way.

Also, a certain type of woman enjoyed teasing a very young brother-in-law in that way at the age when he was quite as bashful and inarticulate as the girl, in the opposite situation. But at least he had a ready vocable that only men used to indicate vehement denial, *Hóȟ!* or *Óȟ!*, which means something like "Indeed not! Nothing of the sort!" One callow youth who was being teased romantically by a mature sister-in-law stammered out an angry *Hóȟ!* with each step until he had retreated out of sight in complete confusion. A woman who overdoes this kind of teasing will find her husband or some other of the boy's male collaterals coming to his aid. Among Dakotas everyone has champions: those relatives who are obligated by kinship to stand by them in such situations as this. No one need go undefended for very long.

A woman's formal gift to her brother's wife and a man's to his sister's husband are dignified gestures, since in reality they are made for honoring that brother or that sister through giving to their spouse. This practice is part of the pattern of giving to another in a relative's name. Consequently, no levity accompanies the gesture even though the actual recipient is a joking relative. It is lifted into the realm of serious, ceremonial honoring of relatives.

The everyday exchange of trifles and even valuables between joking relatives, however, is indifferent and blunt, in the spirit of enmity that joking relatives feign. It is as though the recipient were a nuisance for wanting or needing something that one has. The giving is done casually, to be quickly forgotten as something unimportant anyhow. Here, if you must have it—and stop bothering me!

An instance of reluctant giving under a joking relative's mocking importunacy may further explain this kind of giving. A man who owned more stock than anyone else in the community was once publicly challenged by a likeable ne'er-do-well, aided and abetted by his male collaterals, who liked to put their joking relative at a disadvantage. Pretending great hardship the challenger moaned, "Here I am, trudging the dusty countryside, while he has more horses than he can count. An exaggeration, of course. Why does he keep them? To eat themselves to death, no doubt!" This he said for the amusement of his hearers, who were familiar with such attacks on a brother-in-law, and appreciated the fact that he was being purposely unfair, since everyone knew that, far from stingy, the man was one of the most public-spirited and generous.

The man ignored the taunts for a time. Then, pointing out one of his ponies grazing nearby, he said, with proper exasperation, "Stop your howling and take that buckskin away—though he won't last long," meaning "You don't know how to own a horse, never having had any—soon enough you will be walking again!"

Undented by the implied insult, the happy-go-lucky recipient rode happily off. From a joking relative that was just so much persiflage. All he heard was his male collaterals' cheering over his success. It was all in fun. A joking relative who couldn't take such treatment was a poor sport, best left alone. Similar instances of women getting the best of a female joking relative, encouraged by the female collaterals, could also be cited.

The challenger must be pretty sure that no real hardship would result to the one challenged. Common sense and discernment governed here as elsewhere. That prosperous brother-in-law had many horses that bred themselves and fed freely over the land; only a few choice ones he kept for his own use and carefully tended. The others he gave away quite readily to anyone in actual need, so why shouldn't his poor brother-in-law, who must otherwise walk, get one, too?

Thus the joking sanction operates in one facet as a comic relief to the formal respect relationships. Lacking their obligatory character, it allows considerable latitude of personal expression.

The Omáwahit'u

Both individually and collectively, the fathers, mothers, aunts, uncles, and grandparents of one spouse are in *omáwahit'u* relationship with the corresponding relatives of the other spouse. The term applies to the relationship and is at the same time the kinship term of address and reference reciprocally. In some bands of Dakotas *umáwahit'u* is the alternate pronunciation. The precise meaning is not clear in either form, and the word defies analysis. Various informants have tried to interpret it, but what they say cannot be substantiated, satisfactory examples not existing, and so it must be dismissed as mere folk etymology.

The *omáwahit'u* must be classed with the other unrestricted relationships since it is without specially dictated rules of attitude and behavior. Nevertheless, it is customary for *omáwahit'u* to treat one another with a certain spontaneous respect characterized by mutual deference and caution. "*Omáwahit'u*, you can visit us so rarely. You must eat this particularly delicious meat," or, "*Omáwahit'u*, should you like to rest? Here is a nice place in the shade." In such ways they express solicitude mutually.

They are friendly, cooperative, and dignified whenever they meet. Normally they do not become chummy, no matter how well they know one another. However, occasionally, when two of them, both men or both women, are very old and find themselves living near their children for help and protection, they in time become cronies, if they are congenial. Two women might then enjoy sharing a small tipi, do their own cooking there, and entertain their own company. Living so closely they could drift into a casual familiar association and become more like sisters than formal relatives whose relationship began when their children married each other. In time they might joke and poke fun at each other quite freely and even scold and blame each other over trivialities as sisters sometimes do.

When I was a child, the aged but lively mothers of Chief Grass and his wife were inseparable. They maintained their own little tipi outside the chief's frame house, so that he could look after them. Many amusing stories of their highly irregular treatment of each other floated about. One was that they often played the Dakota game of chance with bowl-and-plumpit counters in their tipi, and could be overheard in many a long and heated dispute over points. But since the marks on the pits were so tiny that they were a strain on even normal eyesight, and the old women had very limited vision, none could have said which one was right, nor would any stranger guess that they were in *omáwahitᶜu* relationship!

As a rule each group of *omáwahitᶜu* strove to outdo the other in deference. Each tried to please the other by showing partiality to not their own child but that child's spouse, their *tᶜakóš*. If a married couple disagreed, it hardly mattered which one was technically right; his parents-in-law came promptly to his defense. Harmonious marriages offer little occasion for this, and yet even in trivial matters, in-laws take this position as a formality still, among those Dakotas who cling to old ways. It goes without saying, though, that if there is serious disagreement between man and wife leading to separation, naturally the relatives of each will rally to his side, and not to his spouse's.

The solicitous gesture works in reverse, too. A husband will reprimand his wife for what he deems her neglect, not of his people, but her own; and the wife will in turn come to the defense of his relatives, if she thinks he is neglecting them. It must be quite plain now that this diagonal kind of reciprocal deference between spouse and in-laws is but another phase of the formal concern for avoidance relatives discussed earlier in this chapter.

9

Formal Relatives of Birth

The Hakáta

Once again we must discuss both formal and informal behavior. This time the formal is not consequent to marriage, but rather is a lifelong habit inculcated from earliest childhood. It is man's behavior toward female collaterals, sisters and cousins, and woman's toward male collaterals, brothers and cousins. This relationship between collaterals of opposite sexes is called the *hakáta,* and it is marked by mutual respect that may end only with death. Social approval is contingent upon the acceptance of all kinship obligations, but particularly those of the *hakáta* relationship.

There are specific terms for younger and elder brother, younger and elder sister, and male and female cousin, and those are always used in address and often enough in reference, too. *Hakáta* is for reference only, whenever the formal aspect is purposely stressed. Thus a woman might say to her daughter, "Put your elder brother's things there," if all she wants is to get the work done. But if she says "your *hakáta's* things" or "Do this for your *hakáta,*" one may rightly infer that she is once again hammering in the lesson of mutual regard that her son and daughter must learn for all time.

A girl must learn to put her *hakáta* first, and his needs and wants ahead of her own. She must be alert to help, comfort, honor, and hearten him, and enhance his prestige. All the while she must remain in the background and make no direct demands on him or claim his attention on herself, but he also is trained in the same way with reference to her. As a good *hakáta,* he must anticipate her needs and be sensitive to her wishes. Anything *hakáta* do for each other must be spontaneous and voluntary. They may not indicate a contrary preference but accept whatever the other would like. They may not compete; they may not try to change the other's mind or plan for their own advantage. They may not question the other's judgment. They may not argue. They must refrain from doing anything that might annoy the other.

Since this is the respect relationship in the family of birth, just as the avoidance was the respect relationship in the family of marriage, each must respect the other's person and courteously welcome the other's spouse. A *hakáta*'s choice takes precedence, however poor it might be. Now and then a girl accepted a man who offered to buy her "because my brothers need horses." But no instance occurs in my notes that a brother wanted horses so much that he compelled his sister to marry a wife-buyer against her inclination.

Correct *hakáta* behavior is exemplified in the following incident. When an Oglala Teton family was stricken with smallpox, they went off into the wilds and remained there until everyone was well who did not die from it.[1] The disease had spent itself at last and the survivors were preparing to return to the camp circle when a Crow war party raided their tipis and killed all but two adult sisters. Badly wounded and helpless, they, too, would have perished had not a man happened on the scene unexpectedly. He stayed to hunt for the women and protected them until they were well enough to travel, and then took them home.

Observe how they lived out there under the *hakáta* rule, for the man was a cousin to the women. He repaired their tipi and then made for himself a brush shelter, within call but at a decent distance, because *hakáta* never occupied the same tipi alone (i.e., without spouses). That simply was not done. They refrained from informal association, never passing the time in joking and idle talk. Only when a vital matter must be considered did they confer, and then their talk was brevity itself. For *hakáta* must not change under any circumstances whatsoever but must observe the same strict formality wherever they were. In this most extraordinary situation, as always, their isolation offered no excuse for deviating, else they would no longer be respecting one another. In other words, there was nothing remarkable in the fact that they never lost sight for even a moment of the fact that they were under the *hakáta* sanction. The narrator, who was one of those women, took this for granted and did not dwell on it. The cousin brought them through the trying time with irreproachable propriety.

A man should be brave in war, generous at home, upright and manly among his fellows. Then his *hakáta* could be proud of him; he owed that to them. A woman should be chaste and should keep her name unassailable, by conduct so consistently careful that even idle gossip would have no basis. Then her *hakáta* would not have to be embarrassed by her.

When a certain little girl's brothers gave away horses in her name at her honoring ceremony, the *huká*, that fact served to hold her in check throughout her girlhood. "Whenever I was tempted to run around carelessly or go to the Night Dance, where I might invite gossip, my mothers said, 'Was it for this that your *hakáta* gave their best in your name?' Then I was willing to give up good times in risky places."

When a family decided to elevate their child's personal prestige through the *huká* ceremony, their relatives helped them according to their ability at the time by adding food to the feast and gifts for the inevitable giveaway, all in the child's name. Any gift from the child's *hakáta* would be a special honor. Those who became *huká* were expected to live under a compulsion for the rest of their life, for with that honor went the obligation to be exemplary persons—that is, to be always generous and hospitable. An old person was once heard to say, "I gave him my last, remembering what I am [i.e., a *huká*]." While a detailed description of the ceremony is not necessary here, I may add that a *huká* gave privileges to paint his face in a special way for all public appearances, by which he was instantly identifiable.[2]

I cannot translate *huká* by any specific term. Just exactly what it means is not known, but on the basis of other words in which that stem occurs one might say it means 'eldest', 'leader', 'foremost', 'of first rank', and so on. Quite possibly it is related to the idea of kinship, too. Compare *húku* 'his or her mother'; *hukáke* 'parents', and, by extension, 'ancestors'. Also compare the Santee word *hukáwaži* 'sibling'; *waži* 'one' occurs also in *ówažila*, already cited in connection with collaterals in this chapter. Then there is *hukáyapi* 'one designated to lead', a rare alternate for *wakíč'uža* 'camp circle magistrate'. In religious nomenclature the sun was addressed as *Hukáyapi-It'áča*, which might be translated as Leader of Leaders or Chief of Chiefs. Incidentally, this term is applied to the elders in the Dakota Presbyterian and Congregationalist churches.

Not only parents but also close relatives might choose to honor a child and assume all the responsibility of the ceremony, and not only children but also adults might become *huká*. My understanding is that it was never at the latter's own expense, however, but that of someone who wished to show them special regard. An old man said to me, "I was made *huká* twice, once as a child of six when my parents arranged for the ceremony, and once after I was a mature man. My nephew, who always pitied me on account of his mother, my sister, gave me that honor." It would have been most unseemly for a person to arrange his own *hųká*, since that would be pure self-glorification.

In mythical lore the *ptesą* 'albino buffalo' was a *hųká*. It was represented as the aristocrat of the Buffalo Nation. It is said that the glory and honor in killing a *ptesą* was comparable to killing an enemy chief in war. The rarity of the *ptesą* added immeasurably to their importance. I have also heard, though not officially, that certain Dakota bands would not kill them. This seems to be borne out by a story I heard very recently, only in time to include it here.

When a certain Yankton youth killed a *ptesą* quite by chance, the elders of the hunting party tied its feet to a stout pole, suspending the body. Thus they bore it homeward on their shoulders, with the solemnity of a funeral procession. The people wailed as though over the death of a relative, a friend, a human being. Later they all partook of its flesh ceremonially. Though this indicates a deep veneration, no explanation was given me, nor could I learn whether it was the custom to eat *ptesą* flesh in that way, or whether this single instance was a spontaneous display of respect and awe. It could be that those particular Yanktons would not kill a *ptesą* on purpose. If that were the case and the boy had done so accidentally, then this rite might have been in expiation, but that is only a guess.

The *Hą́-Wáč°ipi* 'Night Dance' requires explanation. According to informants, this was a late innovation, a product of the breakdown of morals consequent to the confusion of changeover from camp circle to reservation life. "Nice girls" did not go there because anything might happen to them in the dark. The oldest informants insisted to me that in ancient times all social dances and celebrations ended at sundown. There is little doubt that the *Hą́-Wáč°ipi* held a certain allure. Informants rated their contemporaries according to whether or not they were frequenters of the Night Dance: "She was a good woman, one who never attended the Night Dance."

Men were proud of a sister well spoken of. This was the silent hope of all men. Nevertheless, if a woman did misstep and everyone else was talking about her, her *hakáta* did not join in; for them it did not exist. Conversely, a sister rigorously avoided blaming her brother—even in her mind, apparently—if he was being accused of irregular conduct, because at all events *hakáta* must keep high their mutual respect and loyalty. When a baby was born out of wedlock and left at a certain woman's door "because her brother was the father," she accepted the little girl as an especially wanted niece and showered on her even more honors than many legitimately born babies enjoyed from less loyal aunts. It is said that she made feasts and gave lavishly in the child's name on many occasions, and arranged for her all age ceremonies as they fell due—with a defiance that said, "Let them talk! Any offspring of a *hakáta* is precious to me, howsoever it comes into being!"

Another woman, when forced to comment on a *hakáta's* involvement with a woman, verbally transferred the blame, "Well, after all, when so many [women] run after the same one, it is impossible to dodge them all!" A man said, when his *hakáta* bore a fatherless child, "Motherhood is woman's destiny. Bring my nephew here, I will raise him!" Thus cavalierly he dismissed the fact of his *hakáta's* guilt, and in accepting his nephew he reaffirmed his loyalty as something no power could shake. No matter how disappointed one might be in a *hakáta's* conduct, one must not selfishly resent and foster the hurt. One must instead intensify one's kinship devotion and so counteract the disappointment. That was the *hakáta* way at its finest.

Mutual affection and appreciation, and selflessly intense loyalty, motivated *hakáta* behavior. They were the proper attitudes, but they were not manifest in overt gestures or words of endearment because *hakáta* had been trained to avoid all physical contact except to shake hands briefly before a long separation or after a long absence. Though it was not forbidden them to exchange ideas or information if necessary, they did not sit alone together and indulge in mere chatter. They did not make journeys alone together, and in fact they shunned all occasions that might lead them into informal association. They did not look boldly into a *hakáta's* face or speak a *hakáta's* name.

All the foregoing was the passive side of *hakáta* expression. There was also an active side, manifested by an occasional exchange of certain specific honors. The most usual of these are listed as they come to mind.

1. A boy's first kill was for his *hakáta's* meal. He brought the bird or rabbit to his mother: "Mother, cook this for my sister." A girl's first

effort at fancywork, perhaps moccasins or some other item, was for her brother's baby. Such courtesies in childhood were encouraged as the promise of adult mutual honors to come.

2. It was a sister's unique privilege and obligation to honor her brother by giving his bride a ceremonial dressing and face painting. She, or several female collaterals together, placed a handsome gown with accessories on the new sister-in-law and spread a thin film of red paste over her face, to which she submitted wordlessly, for this was a solemn rite. If unable to provide a gown, the sister gave smaller gifts, but always with them a pair of ornamented moccasins as the major item.

Reciprocally, a man honored his *hakáta* by giving a horse or comparably important present to her new husband. He must do this whether or not the man gave promise of becoming a worthy husband—as much as to say, "Whatever is my sister's choice I accept." For he must not question her taste. Should the husband prove himself a failure, he stood confident to provide his sister with meat.

Within recent years a man who drank heavily and neglected his family caused a certain elderly man to say to his sons, "Do you not see your *hakáta*'s plight? Have you forgotten your duty in the matter?" But one of the sons replied indifferently, "That is his [the husband's] duty, not ours. If he were any kind of man he would look after her." They were taking a very modern attitude, but their old-fashioned father was not impressed by it. "Alas, what are we Dakotas coming to"—he shook his head—"now that *hakáta* no longer pity one another." Pity, as I have explained, meant to feel a kinship concern for.

3. A popular man's child might be presented with more than one beaded *p'óštą* 'cradle' from other kinds of relatives, and that was a nice, friendly gesture, but only his sister's gift to his child had social significance, for by it she was honoring her *hakáta* through his child. Old people sometimes inserted into their oral life histories: "I was immediately placed in a *p'óštą*, for my aunt was the best artist in the camp circle." It was their way of saying, "My people were alert to all the kinship niceties, obligations, and privileges. That's the kind of family into which I was born."

In his own time the child's father would give a worthy gift to his sister directly, or to the *níča* 'needy' in her name, which was an even greater honor.

4. The crowning honor to a woman by her *hakáta* could be conferred only by a successful warrior who, immediately upon returning in triumph, presented her with a trophy representing his feat of bravery. Then it was the woman's prerogative to bear it on a tall standard in the victory parade and dance. If she was not in the camp circle—perhaps married into another at some distance—then his mother-in-law or his mother carried it, since carried it must be. Everyone knew for whom they were substituting—namely, the warrior's absent *hakáta*.

Reciprocally, although anyone who felt so moved might give in the warrior's name at the ceremonial giveaway, that was the special privilege of his *hakáta*. Many women, wishing above everything else that her brother's or cousin's name be extolled and his prestige enhanced, gave and gave, with something close to orgiastic recklessness. "I left myself bereft of all decent possessions," said one, "when my only brother returned victorious from the warpath, bespattered with blood, having sustained a severe wound." This is a very characteristic kinship boast. A woman was justifiably proud to suffer temporary poverty for a *hakáta*'s sake.

Whenever a warrior was slain in battle, emotion compounded with grief and glory mounted to its highest pitch at the giveaway. As his riderless horse, daubed with black earth down the face, was led by in procession, his sister hurled a reddened stick into the crowd while calling out in a near cry, "There goes a horse for the *níča!*" As a sublime climax she might add, weeping, "High Eagle [naming the dead warrior], the *Kúšni* gives it!" One slain in battle was called by the euphemistic name *Kúšni*, the 'Nonreturning'. When women gave in a living person's name, they modestly allowed the herald to announce for them, as a rule, but this deliberate calling out of a brother's name was a willful breach of the taboo against enunciating a respect relative's personal name. For now it was all over. Now that her *hakáta*, formerly honored inarticulately, was dead and gone, what did it matter that she waived her lifelong observance of the rule? Anything— anything at all—to glorify him!

Gifts given for the *niča*—anyone who lacked—were undesignated. Whoever got the stick got the gift it represented. George Sword, the Oglala Teton who recorded in Dakota many ancient customs, described such a scene:[3] "Orphan boys and destitute old women scrambled together shamelessly to get the stick. If they disputed seriously over it, the drummers, who sat where they could judge who had it first, were the arbiters. The massed spectators fell back in great confusion to avoid being hurt."[4]

There was nothing mechanical, nothing cut-and-dry, about this interplay of *hakáta* honoring: no deadline for returning a compliment, no avid measuring of deed against deed, gift against gift, for their comparative worth. The giving was important primarily as a symbol of mutual regard. When and if one was able, one gave in return. Years might pass in the interval. Voluntarily, from long training, one acted from inner necessity and not in response to outside pressure—and acted with seeming randomness.

Suicides are reported, which were caused by a flagrant disregard for *hakáta* respect. One should rather die than live on as one dishonored by a *hakáta*. One story is of a Santee boy who shot himself on the spot because his elder sister—whose approval he had taken for granted, as he had a right to do—ordered him publicly to get off from her horse, which he was about to enter in a race. "My sister cares more for a horse. Henceforth, let the horse be her brother!" so he exclaimed and then fired. "But," said the narrator, "that was not the thing for the boy to do either." A maturer man would have quietly slipped off to war, with the private intention of letting himself be slain. He would not have dramatically destroyed himself, to make his *hakáta* regretful. He should have left it to others to censure her, because one must spare one's *hakáta*, at whatever price. *Hakáta* had been taught to give the best and expect the best, to and from one another.

A Teton youth managed it better. He, too, had been shamed by a sister's inconsiderate treatment, but, said the informant, "he secretly donned his best clothes and applied his insignia of the *Iyúptala*, a young men's society, and rode leisurely away—only to shoot himself out on a distant hill." The sister "suffered from the concerted feeling against her for failing as a relative, until she finally removed to another community far away."

The term *Iyúptala* had appeared once or twice in my materials, but I found only one informant who could say what it meant. It was, according to him, the name of a loosely organized youth society among some of the Teton bands. Its sole aim was to engage in pranks, and its members were those youths who had outgrown childhood games but were not yet interested in male pursuits, war, women, and hunting.

"Organized" is not the word. The *Iyúptala* was unofficial, unorthodox, and its membership was entirely haphazard. As some turned to maturer interests and dropped away unmissed, there were always others who were ripe to join its ranks. Not yet faced with serious duties, the *Iyúptala* found their life of irresponsibility a diversion. Their pranks, which were innocuous enough, were tolerated much as are Halloween pranks, because nothing could be done about them anyhow.

Their chief delight was to steal fresh meat off the drying racks after a communal hunt, thereby confounding its owners, some of whom were their own mothers. "We planned our attack carefully," said my informant. "First we went *tȧwéya* 'scouting' to spot those racks where good pieces of jerked meat were hung up to dry. Shortly before the time to *natá* 'attack' we diffused throughout the camp circle and lingered near the game we had each spotted earlier. The *wónase* 'communal chase' was accomplished suddenly." This was done so simultaneously that the hue and cry of women upon discovering their losses was heard all around at once, but the boys did not betray themselves by running off. With their loot concealed under their robes they stayed around the women, occasionally expressing sympathy for them, or watching them taking it out on the dogs. Much later they drifted one by one to a prearranged place in the wood where they supped on fresh boiled meat and recounted many hair's-breadth escapes. But the *Iyúptala* were not willfully destructive, they carried no grudges, nor were they obligated to steal food in a society that made a fetish of hospitality. All they sought was the thrill of getting away with it.

My informant said he was once a member. "When we planned an attack, we always indicated it to one another by signs, the style of our dress or face paint, which no one else would know." But he hedged when I asked for details, so I knew he had forgotten what those signs were. Perhaps they were changed from time to time anyway, like codes. From his choice of words it was clear that the boys were playing a game imitating both war and the chase.

The term *Iyúptala* does not appear in my Yankton or Santee material; it would be *Iyúptana* in Yankton dialect, and *Iyúptadȧ* in Santee. One Yankton recalled a prank one boy and his companions once played that was typical of their activities and closely parallels the nature of *Iyúptala* pranks. In this instance they stole potatoes. When the government first planted a vast field back of the new Yankton agency, the people showed no interest in it, but in the late summer, the word got around that "there is something new growing there and it is said it tastes good."

Upon hearing this a group of young boys, who must correspond to the Teton *Iyúptala*, crawled on their bellies for a half-mile to get some of it by stealth. After digging furiously in the twilight and stuffing their shirts above their sashes all they could contain, they crawled miserably back, for the things were hard.

The joke was on them. Early next morning the crier went by announcing that the new food had been planted for the people and was now ready, and that they might dig all they wanted. "If you like the taste of it, you will want to plant it in your gardens next spring," the crier shouted throughout the encampment. All Dakotas ate a wild tuber called *bdó* in Yankton, *mdó* in Santee, and *bló* in Teton. For the Yanktons this was their first introduction to the white Irish potato. The native term *bdó* was promptly applied to it.

Those Yankton boys had no more sense of guilt from "stealing" potatoes than had the Teton *Iyúptala* from "stealing" meat. All food was freely shared, and in those days wild game and growing things were still for the taking. The only feeling was no doubt one of elation from accomplishing a difficult feat successfully.

In *Iyúptala* the stem is *ptá*, a bound form. It is a neutral verb and denotes 'torn condition'. *Í* is a preposition, *yú* an instrumental prefix denoting 'by hand action'. The diminutive *lá* indicates that this is a small matter (i.e., not real; not serious). A fairly close translation of *Iyúptala* would be 'meat torn for fun'.

Sometimes people committed suicide not out of shame but out of loyalty. For example, back in the early days of reservation life, a Mrs. Elkhorn—a pseudonym—received from her cousin a fine span of horses, of which she was very proud because they were a *hakáta's* gift. Shortly thereafter the Native policeman brought a summons from the agent for her to come in. Since the giver belonged to an adjoining reservation, the agent merely wished to ascertain whether the transfer of property to his jurisdiction had been in accordance with government regulations, which had already begun to interfere with kinship obligations, their very existence, let alone their influence on social life, being not so much as suspected.

It might quite well have been according to regulations, but the matter was never determined, for Mrs. Elkhorn's immediate reaction was a firm no. She simply would not go there to discuss a *hakáta*, or his actions. Here was a delicate emotional involvement. Realizing this her husband tried to make light of the summons. "Why, of course. *Č'į tók?* 'Why not?'" And to the policeman, "*T'ǫháši* ['male cousin', man speaking], tell the 'father' [agency superintendent] we shall be in directly. Everyone must visit our 'father' at least once. It is nothing." Then he went out to prepare the team and buggy, though he could see that his wife was not getting ready. But, as he went, he noticed her marching determinedly toward a little log storehouse back of their home, and heard her muttering to herself a vehement equivalent of "Over my dead body!"

Outside the bolted door he pleaded and reasoned with her for a long time but got no answer. At last he went after his nearest neighbor, my informant, and together they broke down the door, after due warning. As each had privately feared, there she was, hanging from the ridgepole quite dead.

Those who still lived under the traditional *hakáta* compulsion understood her tragic act perfectly. Mrs. Elkhorn was not going to answer any questions about her cousin, lest she incriminate him unwittingly. It was best for her to step out of the picture at once, thereby closing the subject irrevocably before it could be considered.

She did not reason this out step by step, but from force of habit she acted instantly for the good of a *hakáta* by taking the only course that would insure him absolute protection. Then no man could taunt him for taking back his horses, since there would be no living recipient for them. As for herself she would not have to live on in shame because a *hakáta* gift had been unceremoniously taken away from her!

These three instances show quite plainly, I think, that the primary aim of collaterals of opposite sexes was to keep unmarred that most sensitive of Dakota relationships, the *hakáta*—compared to which the mere loss of one's own life was a negligible matter.

For his own best social development, everyone needed *hakáta* with whom to practice the necessary lessons of respect, loyalty, interdependence, and all the rest. It was good to grow up with *hakáta* and forlorn to be without any. Conscientious parents, aware of this, sometimes assumed an artificial *hakáta* relationship for an only child through the social kinship system, discussed in a later chapter.

By purest accident I stumbled upon the following illustrative situation one day, simply because, as is my habit, I sat down on the ground beside a very old woman and engaged her in conversation. It is not infrequently rewarding to do so; some of my richest material is picked up that way. I did not know at first that she, with several others, was waiting for the priest to arrive at the remotely situated chapel to hold a funeral, and that she was the chief mourner.

"He [the deceased] was my 'chosen' brother," she volunteered, and was silent for long moments. I thought she was through. And then: "My parents found him for me because I had no brothers near, but if we had been born of the same parents we could not have been better *hakáta*."

Piecemeal, with long intervals of silence, I got her story. One must sit relaxed and without too obvious eagerness and tense waiting. Old people talk best if they are not pressed. It is well to make an occasional comment and ask very few direct questions, particularly when meeting with someone new. A transcript of our talk would fill several pages, allowing much space for the silent intervals.

She said that the government had broken up the *t'iyóšpaye* and scattered the related families on individual allotments and theirs was the farthest away from any of them. Her parents yearned for their relatives, but more than all else they were concerned that she, their only child, was being deprived of *hakáta*. To them it was no compensating advantage that all they owned would be hers alone, without having to share it. She would still be "poor."

So her mother selected another only child in their vicinity and made for him a pair of handsome moccasins and took them to him. "My daughter Žitkážila 'Little Yellow Bird' has made footwear for her brother Tʿašúke Óta '(Owner of) Many Horses'." Though she had made them herself, this was a manner of speaking that was understood. The mother of Many Horses was very pleased and wasted no time in causing him to make a return gift to his new sister.

From that initial exchange the two sets of parents conscientiously maintained their children's relationship by doing the honors for them, and teaching the proper attitude and conduct between *hakáta*. Whenever the children met, they diffidently shook hands as instructed—and no more. They did not play together but with their own playmates, boys or girls. The purpose of this manufactured *hakáta* relationship was something apart: it was to implant in their young minds a proper awareness and a habit that would last always. The children would enjoy the fruits in the future and by degrees appreciate the full impart of their distinctive relationship.

That was what Yellow Bird and Many Horses did. In time they were entirely accustomed to their roles and alive to their mutual obligations, having been told times without number, "So ought brother and sister regard, and do for, each other always," and "Those who disregard their *hakáta* duties soon disregard all other relatives, and are thereby a reproach." As they were able, they assumed their complete roles and relieved their parents of that responsibility.

Had they not been made brother and sister at that impressionable age, they might have grown up selfish, and never know the challenge and the assurance of help and comfort that was inherent in the *hakáta*. They might have been total strangers all their lives. But, as it was, according to the old woman, they had lived a lifetime respecting and honoring each other proudly. Now he was dead and she was here waiting to wail for him at his burial, apparently without remorse. She ended her story by saying, "I never neglected to *úšila* 'show compassion and kinship concern' for my brother; nor did he for me."

Ideally, brother and sister married spouses who also were in *hakáta* relationship already, but if those spouses had been total strangers, they automatically became related in a quasi-*hakáta* relationship, that being the proper status for them according to the Dakota kinship system. Thus, whenever Yellow Bird and Many Horses with their spouses camped side by side, the restrained behavior between the actual *hakáta*, Yellow Bird and Many Horses, was approximated in the behavior between their spouses, in that they did not get together alone and chat informally, but kept at a respectful distance. While their spouses were not obligated to carry the *hakáta* duties to the extent of honoring each other's names, sometimes they did even that after they had been related formally long enough to learn to appreciate the other's flawless *hakáta* respect, despite the fact that their bond was artificial. The "sister" was likely to do this publicly, lest the gossips think she was secretly interested in the "brother." She wanted her contented acceptance of the assumed relationship to be unmistakable.

This arrangement reduced to a minimum the danger of the pseudo-*hakáta* behaving informally together and perhaps going so far as to fall in love and become intimate, as they might if they were no relation. Thus they were constrained by *hakáta* rules as much as were their spouses, the actual brother and sister. This is a very interesting and important device of kinship and must be understood as such. It would be fatuous to claim that it worked in every instance. I only mean that this arrangement was an optimistic provision against any easy occurrence of improper behavior between the spouses of *hakáta*. Of course, no safeguard is absolute, human frailty being what it is. Nevertheless, I must say that as a rule most people treasured their reputation. The exceptions were few, when kinship law ruled the people.

I have to say finally that no small part of that drive compelling collaterals of opposite sexes to keep their standard high was due to their parents—now old and infirm, or perhaps no longer living—whose relentless nurturing of their children's beginning relationships (not alone the *hakáta*, but others, too) had brought them to full fruition and enjoyment. Thoughts like this, inextricably bound with the memory of devoted parents, were what made the *hakáta* way of life a precious heritage and kept its qualities tender and undying. They are the intangibles that cling to this day, impelling the Dakotas to give and give, unmindful of their own needs, with a recklessness that is irrational, improvident, and "stupid"—judged by the standards of an encapsulating culture in which self-interest is the dominant aim. Many are learning that now, and undoubtedly it is a good thing, if they are to survive.

The foregoing discussion had to do with *hakáta*, both of whom were adults or were children. What happened to attitude and behavior between an adult and a child in that relationship? The answer is that the adult's attitude of respect must be correct from the beginning, but of necessity his behavior might be modified to meet the child's needs. Respect might be indicated by gentle and considerate treatment and protection of the child and by the use of the kinship term in both address and reference, and never by the careless use of the child's name. Only gradually is the precise formalized behavior assumed, as the child comes to understand and accept it and is able to reciprocate it.

Three illustrations are available. One informant complained in retrospect of the fact that her French father and Teton mother had children in such rapid succession that, as the eldest, she could not remember when she did not have a toddler to take care of, because another baby was on the way. Being well trained in the *hakáta* tradition, she had no trouble in dealing with the boys gently and cautiously so that they grew up respecting her in turn.

Her real problem was the youngest, a boy, who became her sole charge, their mother having died at his birth. He was entirely dependent on her alone and for that she came to love him with a special compassion and yet she never *mothered* him by fondling and petting him. His mother's sisters and cousins, like his other mothers, gave him what fondling and petting he experienced, and that was right. But from the outset she *sistered* that little brother, for he was a *hakáta*. Her inbred sense of correct attitude and behavior forbade any maternal stirring over him, for how could she mother her own father's child? That for her was out of the question.

My informant married at eighteen and was already the mother of twin boys when she took charge of this brother. Her handling of him was different, and he was never confused with his little nephews. As soon as he no longer needed her direct physical supervision, she avoided touching him. When he became girl-conscious, she simply did not "know." *Hakáta* properly kept out of one another's romances. Thus in every sense her attitude was perfect.

Whereas she was correct in both attitude and behavior toward her other brothers whom she also helped to foster, it was never quite possible to conform her behavior strictly to the letter toward the brother she had cared for entirely. Whenever he came to her with his problems and plans, she sat alone with him in the house or out under the shade, and they talked leisurely while he ate the food she set out for him. She could do that because of the great disparity in their ages and because she had raised him from the day of his birth. Yet, despite her semi-informal association with him, she never joked nor colluded with him, never teased him, for that would not be dignified for brother and sister at any age. Certainly the subject of sex was completely out in their conversations, for that simply was not fitting for *hakáta*. Her attitude was fixed for life from the outset; her behavior was in accordance with his needs as a child, and later as a young householder finding his way to mature responsibility.

The second example is as follows.

My aunt and uncle had their home close to ours but I did not see my cousin often because he was away a great deal. And when he came home he took no notice of me and I did not bother him. Yet he never forgot to bring something nice to his mother, my aunt, and say: 'This is for *hąkášila* ['my little cousin', the term for a man's little girl-cousin], so I knew he was aware of me.

One day while playing *iglák-ománipi* [traveling and making camp, living there a short while, then striking camp and moving again; little girls would travel over a fairly large area while playing thus, sometimes getting out of sight of home, unintentionally], my playmates and I quarreled violently and so they left me sitting by the tipi, which was mine, and crying. Then my cousin rode by and stopped. Learning what had happened, he said, "Come on home, you must not stay here alone," and at the same time he hurled out a looped rope and caught my tipi around its "neck" and then rode on, dragging it after him, poles and all. I followed.

Later he scolded my mother and aunt for letting me stray out of sight where anything could happen to me. They were pleased to be scolded because that showed how much concern he felt for a *hakáta*. If I started to wander off after that, they always called me back, saying, "Do you want us to be scolded again?"

These two incidents involved *hakáta* living daily in the same *t'iyóšpaye* group, but if two who lived far apart came together for a very short while, automatically the adult assumed the usual way of a *hakáta*, for people always knew how to act and think toward each new relative and automatically assumed their proper attitude and behavior, as I have already said.

At a Fourth of July celebration, related families came in from their respective allotments and lived cooperatively in a *t'iyóšpaye* group for two or three days. At one such group the following occurred. While the men sat off yonder, talking and smoking, the women were happily cutting up fresh meat back of the tipi, and the little relatives were playing everywhere, the water wagon stopped by and the driver began bailing out water from his barrels and filling the row of pails and kegs set out for him. At such gatherings the entertainment committee usually sent a congenial man around to dispense water as needed by the campers, but this man was not congenial. Why so glum a man should have been picked for a social task was not plain. Though he lived with the proverbial chip on his shoulder, he was especially hostile at this time because an ugly rumor was circulating about him, which time proved true.

Nervously he snarled out without warning: "Get back, *Í Ȟčí!*" 'Torn Mouth'. He had coined the cruel name for a child with a harelip deformity who had evidently stood too near. Thereupon, a certain youngish visitor from a distant reservation who had been lying flat on the grass listening to the older men's talk sprang to his full height and began moving with grim determination toward the water man while uttering *ȟná-ȟná* sounds that betrayed rising indignation. The old men warned him in a chorus to control himself; the man was not worth a brawl.

Already the name caller had leapt into his wagon and was flogging his team to a hurtling run across a deep-furrowed field, with loud crashes resounding after him in regular succession. The water from the open barrels splashed tall in glistening spears against the late July sun, the barrels themselves dancing at crazy angles all the way. After putting on the impromptu show for the entire camp circle, he was seen no more at that celebration.

Now, why did one particular man feel called upon to avenge a wrong to one particular child? The truth was that he was that child's cousin, and although he never saw her before—and perhaps never again—it was his kinship obligation to champion a *hakáta*, and that he would do in no uncertain manner. Afterward there was no further need to pay special attention to her; she was simply one of the many children playing about. It was the principle that mattered; it was more than personal.

In Dakota life it was necessary, both socially and economically, to maintain the *t'iyóšpaye's* integrity—at whatever cost to the individuals comprising it. It must be united and it must be strong. To make and keep it so, there seemed no better way than for relatives of birth to stay together, and, whenever they must be separated, to keep together in sentiment still. To this day the Dakotas have not lost the habit of hankering for absent relatives and being happiest when reunited. The more relatives together the better, however difficult the financial strain might be.

The core of strength lay elsewhere than in the marriage relationship, despite the fact that, more often than not, husband and wife were held together permanently by a strong affinity, enduring loyalty and devotion, and a remarkable respect for each other's wishes and judgment. Even so, they remained separate in the final analysis, with deep roots permanently elsewhere. They did not become relatives, in the kinship sense.

I have to insert here a story about a small boy who suddenly became fascinated by the sound and variety of kinship terms and spent one evening quizzing his mother on them. Pointing out to different passerby, he would ask, "And that one—what is he to you?" (i.e., how are you related?) Finally he asked, "And my father—what is he to you?" "*Takúwayešni*," she replied quite simply 'He is nothing to me'. "He is only my husband." The bewildered child burst into tears. "Well, then, is he nothing to me either?" "Certainly," she told him. "He is your father; you are his son." She was not deliberately teasing her child; she was instructing him on kinship.

The mere fact of marriage did not tear a man and woman out of their natural setting and thereafter and forever fuse them into a self-sufficient mystical union that would shut out their own relatives of birth. To the old-time Dakotas that was as impossible as it was spurious. It was not their concept of marriage. A marriage that excluded family relatives would be inimical to society; it would destroy *t'iyóšpaye* integrity and, in the end, tribal structure.

Therefore, since marriage was not a natural state, it could not of itself give to the group that strength and stability necessary. However, the married were in no way relieved of the responsibility of generating in their children an unwavering collateral loyalty and interdependence, for those were the cohesive agents for holding the *t'iyóšpaye* together.

The key word was *owážila*, which means 'one and the same'. All collaterals were one in substance, one in source, like identical developments from a single multisplit embryo, many forms out of one material from a common matrix. That matrix was the parent for true siblings: the common grandparent for all lateral siblings and cousins. A single root of generation and of growth was thus implied. Collaterals were one; they belonged together always. There was the logical center of group strength. Consequently, they must keep unified through an unremitting insistence on their caring deeply for one another. It is reported that a certain ancient patriarch regularly admonished the collaterals, "Children, hold firm together always, for you form the *t'ič'ák'ahu* 'ridgepole' of the *t'iyóšpaye*." *T'i* is a classifier for dwelling; *č'ak'áhu* 'spine'.

The all-absorbing aim in training the young was just that: to keep the "ridgepole" strong and enduring. It was no problem to train boys only or girls only. Left together in free association, they grew up unrestricted by no special rules, beyond those within the framework of ordinary social amenities that all people should obey. As long as they did not go counter to tribal usages and sanctions, they were within bounds. In a momentary flare-up, boys were reminded that they were *owážila* and therefore strife was unbecoming to them; girls were told, "Be kind to your sister, for you are one."

Training boys and girls with reference to one another posed a problem that demanded extreme watchfulness and delicacy at all times. It was no less essential that a sense of oneness be inculcated to become something that would operate nearly automatically. Yet, from the time boys and girls became aware of their physical differences (which could be at an early age), it was unwise to allow them to be informal, since informality must lead to familiarity and familiarity could lead to incest—a grave threat where boys and girls must live together within the limited confine of the tipi. However, as a safeguard, barriers were raised early and high, to remain inexorable forever: barriers in the form of kinship rules of attitude and behavior, which, of all such rules, were the most stringent.

After all, what those rules asked was quite achievable: that collaterals of opposite sexes think and act toward one another as they ought—and in no other way. The rigid training toward this end so fixed a habit that it became actually agreeable. A woman could only think, "He and I are *hakáta* and that is all we shall ever be, and it is right." So braced, she accepted even the stranger who appeared on the scene as a *hakáta* and behaved accordingly as soon as she knew he was a remotely situated "brother." He might be handsome and most desirable as a husband—but he is not for her. The thought must be forgotten, or, rather, not permitted to enter her mind in the first place. It is eternally out of the question; it would be debasing to toy with it even momentarily in a daydream. The stranger, too, was under the same obligation to control his attitude and behavior toward her and to hold to the same fixed position. It was a mutual responsibility.

Since even an accidental look could be noticed by others and an improper attitude surmised, *hakáta* must never look directly at each other or study the other's facial features, body, or dress, but must instead be alert to realize one another's presence obliquely and proceed to act and think as they ought. This also was the case in that other respect relationship in the family of marriage, already discussed, the avoidance relationship.

Because these rigid rules were imposed early, any chance for brothers, sisters, or cousins to develop absorbing personal and exclusive friendships was blocked before children could be discriminating, before individual preferences could bud. Mannerisms that might ordinarily attract or repel were not critically noted. Any appealing feature, like an alluring smile or a cute way of talking—such as delighted lovers or amused joking relatives—passed unnoticed between *hakáta*. From the beginning they were trained to accept one another, as it were, sight unseen.

Since competition was discouraged at the same time that property—that most likely would cause a family strife—was made almost valueless in comparison to the prestige of a flawless *hakáta* relationship, collaterals of opposite sexes had little reason to quarrel, even as children. Moreover, because it was made wrong for them to associate informally together, it was simple enough for them to remain polite to each other.

Generally speaking, correct *hakáta* behavior was automatic by adolescence and in some instances earlier. Certainly, young adults could play their respective roles with a precision and adroitness that left little room for criticism. I can hardly overestimate how absolute their tacit cooperation could be. In explaining it minutely, I know I risk making it seem close to an obsession, too extreme to be mentally healthful. But by no means was it an obsession, claiming the forefront of the mind and crowding out all other considerations. As a matter of fact, it was entirely automatic to sit properly, speak low and seldom, conceal one's moods, hold one's self in abeyance, and, if practicable, move away smoothly at the first opportunity from a *hakáta*'s vicinity, with or without offering a plausible excuse. A man might say to no one in particular, "It must be time to water the horses," and so walk away. A woman might express concern over a truant youngster and go out to hunt for him.

This too was true: if to move away would be too conspicuous and might cause one's *hakáta* to feel that his or her presence was an inconvenience, it was possible to stay in the tipi simply by, as it were, turning on the correct mechanism. Then one could pay full attention to the general talk or sit musing on one's private interests elsewhere, and never make a false move—like setting a reliable clock and then forgetting it, certain that it will run without close watching.

All of this will seem unwarranted and perhaps even silly to those outside the culture. Yet it must have its rationalization in the needs of the past from which it developed. For instance, what could be so terrible in a sister's innocent glance at a brother, or vice versa? There is no explicit answer; but we are free to guess. When men hunted on foot, skins were got with only the severest hardship and consequently were scarce. After the shelter had been fashioned and one robe apiece allotted to each member of the family to serve as wrap by day and couch by night, one may imagine that there was precious little left. Clothing could hardly be plentiful nor amply cut. Skirts must be short and skimpy, now and then a breechcloth somewhat less than adequate. Under such conditions one must habitually avert the eyes or keep them on the ground, lest one behold accidentally what one ought not. Particularly guarded must one be if a respect relative was present, concerning whom even a fleeting thought of sex was a kinship sin. That was one facet.

Perhaps some other way, with less drastic disciplines, might have been just as effective, but this was the Dakota way. On, as it were, a principle of stress and counterstress, it seemed to be continuously pulling the two sexes together spiritually and at the same time holding them apart physically, with an unremitting power exerted equally in both directions. It as much as said that collaterals must keep close together for group strength; males and females must keep wide apart for group morality. By means of those inflexible rules of attitude and behavior the danger of impropriety was all but nullified. At the same time, by means of tribal approval with loud applause over every honoring act between *hakáta*, their will to stay loyal and interdependent at all costs was whipped up everlastingly.

In a woman's mind all her male relatives were neatly boxed, as are all female relatives in a man's mind. She knows who they are, in which box they belong, and how she must think and conduct herself toward them severally. There is no other sanctioned way. In the following list, *hakáta* are starred once, avoidance relatives twice, and joking relatives three times. The other relationships, those without specifically dictated rules of behavior—the "free" relationships—are not starred.

Many of a woman's relatives may never cross her path. If they do she already knows exactly how each kind must be treated and regarded, and automatically she assumes the right attitude and behavior, which is then a purely mental process without emotional involvement, because the new relative is as yet a stranger, actually. Attitude becomes a matter of feeling only as she comes to know that relative for the kind of person he is. Then

WOMAN'S MALE RELATIVES	MAN'S FEMALE RELATIVES
Grandfathers	Grandmothers
Fathers; uncles	Mothers; aunts
Brothers and male cousins*	Sisters and female cousins*
Sons; nephews	Daughters; nieces
Grandsons	Granddaughters
Fathers-in-law**	Mothers-in-law**
Sons-in-law**	Daughters-in-law**
Brothers-in-law***	Sisters-in-law***

she may learn to appreciate, "pity," love, and admire him as he earns those sentiments. But from the outset she must be respectful to any brother or cousin. I use a woman for illustration, but it is the same in a man's case.

I have minutely explained the *hakáta*, to which this chapter is assigned, but in all other relationships the obligation to act consistently remains. Thus, a woman may meet a stranger who is in father relationship to her who falls far short of her own father in looks, prestige, personality, intelligence. That makes no difference. She may no more be rude to him or disdain to accept him as father than she would think of falling in love with him.

This question of attitude and behavior in the Dakota sense is sometimes mistakenly explained as being "strictest toward blood relations and diminishing in proportion to those more distant." The truth is that attitude and behavior belong with the kinship term. They are a fixed triad and may not properly be dissociated. One who fails to express them altogether harmoniously is unsatisfactory as a Dakota relative. What does taper off with distance is the emotional quality of attitude. Tapering off, too, is the obligation to honor a relative tangibly—that is, with gifts to him or to others in his name. No distant relative asks that of one, but only that one's attitude, thinking, and behavior toward him be regular, so that he can reply on it.

Thus, in the last analysis, what kind of person a relative may be matters least. It is one's own duty toward relatives that matters. That is why conscientious Dakotas still make it a point to find out at once how they are related to a newcomer so as to assume the proper role and not blunder. Within recent times a little girl asked:

"Mother, is that stranger my brother?"

"No. Why do you ask?"

"Because he treats me as though I were his sister."

The new man in the community happened to be her father in social kinship, yet the child was not far wrong in supposing him to be a brother because he was a naturally cautious man who always behaved as though he were everyone's respect relative. The point to observe is that even a child, provided he or she was properly trained in Dakota kinship, could analyze the attitude and behavior of others toward him or her, and feel responsible for his or her own reciprocal duties. All Dakotas with even the most blithe and slapdash good sense manage to sober down before respect relatives, the *hakáta* obligations being the most compelling.

10

Informal Relatives of Birth

Although other family relationships are not as restricted as the *hakáta* is, their permissible informality does not result in random and unpredictable behavior. The various kinds of Dakota relatives still have their customary ways of treating one another. This chapter describes the reciprocal behavior patterns between collaterals of the same sex, between uncles and aunts and their nieces and nephews, and between grandparents and grandchildren. The parent-child relationship does not require separate treatment here, since it could only repeat what comes up constantly in nearly all chapters, and especially in the material to be presented in later chapters.

Collaterals of the Same Sex

Superficially, this relationship parallels the joking relationship in the family of marriage in that both are informal, in some instances to the point of "rudeness," but the aims and moods are not the same. The alertness of joking relatives to gain and hold the advantage and a readiness to banter to that end are absent among collaterals. They, the latter, are completely relaxed, being so used to one another that they incline to be rather desultory. They make no effort to gain the advantage, and when they lose it, they are indifferent about it. Under normal conditions what one says casually the other ignores just as casually. One may bluntly ask for something the other has, and be as bluntly refused—and no feelings hurt. This often happens regarding trivial, unimportant requests. Where the request is made out of an obvious need, then of course the response is quick and generous. Being *owážila* 'collaterals of the same sex', they care deeply for one another, under their sometimes brusque manner, but they are ordinarily not demonstrative.

This is the normal way of collaterals of the same sex. One who deviates from it by ignoring a real need is open to criticism. On this point we have the following story. Late at night a woman in premature labor sent word to her neighbor, a classificatory sister, for the loan of her car in order to reach the hospital speedily. But the sister demurred so long, not sure whether or not to let her new car go, that meantime the sick woman bled to death. That sister was notoriously selfish, and was also inordinately proud to be the first car owner in the community. In addition, she was partially deaf and might not have grasped the urgency of the matter. The tribal reaction to her behavior was very bitter. "What a way for a sister to do!" people said. "She always manages to hear what she wants to hear! She simply did not want to lend her car to her sister in need! She has caused her sister's death!" Perhaps they were right and she did not want to hear the request.

About trivial requests I have the following. When a certain woman received a handsome blanket from her *wašé* 'special woman friend', her younger sister fingered it idly and said, "My, I like this very much. Why not pass it on to me?" To that the elder sister replied, "I should like to own it for a while!" It was her way of refusing. The girl, who did not much want it anyway, shrugged and remarked, "Stingy—as usual!" and walked away. The whole matter was unimportant. She had expressed a mere whim and her sister had ignored it as such, and then affected not to hear the last remark calling her stingy. Yet if that young girl had been in dire need of a blanket to keep her warm, she would hardly have needed to ask for it.

Under pressing need a collateral's food or utensil may be taken in her absence. Even horses and wagon might be borrowed in that way, without prior permission. In one instance a woman came to a vacant tipi in the woods and blithely moved in with her children, telling them: "This is your mother's tipi so it is all right. We shall live in it until your father can come for us." So it was, for the tipi owner was her sister in social kinship, and a close familiar.

In olden times, I am told, there was one exception to this free borrowing. Outer garments, wraps in particular, were uniquely owned and might not be worn by other collaterals—or anyone else—except in an emergency. They might be given away, and then the new owner could wear them without criticism. Regarding a shiftless family in a legend, the people were quoted as saying, "And they even allowed their children to wear one another's wraps!"—a cutting remark directed at the family that did not provide distinctive suitable wraps for their girls.

Collaterals may correct one another without reticence and may warn without special care to be tactful. "By the way, this is being rumored about you. If it is true, you had better mend your ways!" More often than not—though not invariably—it is the elder who warns the younger. It is customary to act indifferent and casual even though profiting by the warning finally. Only rare is one who resents interference from any quarter. Said one informant, "My sister needed to be told and I was the logical one to tell her and yet I hesitated because she was always so touchy." Thus, sometimes even collaterals must take individual temperament into account. Of a petty woman, her sisters said tolerantly among themselves: *Čᶜuwé wačᶜįkᶜola sᵓá kᵓų̇, ųkókᶜiyakapiktešni yé!* 'Elder sister is given to pouting, so let's keep this from her'. The diminutive ending -*lá* denotes tolerant affection as for a child. While humoring her puerile trait, the sisters tacitly admit that she is not their equal to that extent, by that -*lá*.

The permissible good-natured "rudeness" comes out in various ways. For instance, regardless of a disparity in their ages, sisters may refer to or address one another by name, usually nickname, most of the time. A child, the youngest of three sisters, may call her adult sisters by name and it is no kinship offense; it is an indication that fundamentally they are peers. As peers they expect to act independently, yet they must be ready at any time to rally against the outsiders, the joking relatives who are their continuous opposition.

My feeling is that Dakotas generally are chary of compliments because it is "ridiculous to be fooled." A person naive enough to believe a compliment at once and to be obviously pleased by it is laughable. Only the simple-minded are excusable for failing to distinguish between it and a sincere compliment. Such persons are sometimes joked with mercilessly, and showered with more and more flattery to see how much they will accept.

When a reasonable man is overpraised he tells his friends later, *Mayéčᶜača wačᶜį*, which may be freely translated as "He tried to get me going; he tried to make me fall for his line." This cautious attitude must be back of the usual negative reaction to sale talk as we have it in white society. The very language indicates a dread of being taken in. For instance, if someone makes a sizable purchase, his friends are very likely to ask him: *Tóna ų̇ nignáye só?* 'For how much [money] did he trick you?' The phrase is almost a cliché. "He" is the seller. Even when the transaction was quite fair, and the questioners know it, they still pretend to doubt it.

Quite possibly the treatment collaterals gave one another trained them to be both skeptical toward compliments and jealous for their dignity.

Ridicule and loss of dignity were the besetting fears. To avoid them one very soon learned to maneuver himself with skill, among his own kind, while growing up and out in the world when he was an adult.

One more thing must be said. Collaterals did not spend their time waiting to pick on one another. If anything they were so matter-of-fact together that often enough they did not bother to comment, and at serious times they were mutually respectful. Many mature men and women collaterals were always serious together. What I have tried to show is only the way they were free to act and talk. Their "rudeness" was nothing to resent, really, as between sisters, or between brothers, so at home together that no formality was needed.

What may seem like rough treatment of collaterals by collaterals, or indifference, or "rudeness" at times, is actually nothing but a kind of in-training. Despite all that they are governed by certain loyalties. One very important loyalty is that a collateral's spouse, being an exclusive possession, must be respected as such. Properly, there is no trading of that one theoretically unalienable possession: the spouse. I mean *properly*. While it was true that in the camp circle such an offense was particularly censurable, it would be fatuous to suppose that it never did happen. Perhaps it is safe enough to say that it happened less frequently when the controls in the old life were strong.

The manly course for one wronged by his own brother or cousin was let him have the unfaithful spouse and step aside with stoical dignity, but not every man was equal to that. The classic example of such manliness would seem to be someone named Íyą Tʻó 'Blue Stone'. When he lived is not said, but his name and deed persisted long after his time. The story goes that Blue Stone had long been aware that his younger brother was attracted to his wife, but he kept his own counsel until one day he invited some upright men and feasted them in his tipi, his wife serving them. Afterward, as they sat smoking and talking, he suddenly told his wife to uncover her roll from herself. "It is only bedding, thrown over my things," she said. "Uncover it," he said again quietly. She did so, and there was his younger brother whom she had hidden there. Calling his friends to witness, he declared, "If this is how it is, very well. Henceforth these two are man and wife, but I am still his brother, so I shall never go near *his* wife!" He left both his tipi and his wife to his younger brother. Blue Stone's coldness and decisiveness under this circumstance, "the hardest for a man to endure," was what made him an outstanding example, it is said.

With considerable emphasis informants tell that in camp circle life no well-brought-up girl had illicit affairs or became pregnant outside of wedlock, and that this was due to the fact that in the better families daughters were protected and chaperoned constantly, while being repeatedly impressed that they must so conduct themselves as to "bind the mouth of idle gossip." If such a girl was improperly accused, she could always prove her innocence by staging the secular rite known as Virgin's Fire or Maiden's Fire—a dare to her accusers to step out into the open with their testimony. Or she might prefer simply to deny the charge so that her elder relatives, mothers and aunts could with assurance track down the rumor to its evil source.

The girl who did neither was questioned by a female collateral of maturer years rather than by mother or aunt, whose halting, disappointed, and shamed manner would be painful to both herself and the girl. A sister's probing was more direct but less embarrassing. Point blank she would say, "Is this a fact?"—meaning, if not, you have only to say, the sooner the better for us both. With sisterly candor she expected the worse as a challenge to the girl to clear her name speedily, if she could.

Collaterals to this day give and expect the same impartial care to all their children. A woman leaves home with an easy conscience if a sister or cousin remains behind. No need to exact a promise: "Can I rely on you to look after my child?" The implication of doubt that she wouldn't unless she promised was an insult to her. Why wouldn't she automatically do her duty! When had she ever failed in it?

Mothers and aunts might train their girls in skills and social duties, mothers might admonish them about morals abstractly and grandmothers concretely through legendary situations, but the real education would seem most possible in the free and easy climate of collaterals. Here all male or all female collaterals trained themselves and one another—quite unaware of an aim but simply following the haphazard give-and-take pattern for their kind—until by adulthood the majority were prepared to take real rebuff from the outside world. Here was their proving ground, where mock samples of it were good-naturedly handed out. But occasionally there was one who never learned to take it, as in the case mentioned above of the woman given to pouting whom her sisters organized to protect by keeping disturbing facts from her.

Sex education was acquired mostly by absorption of facts from the casual conversation of elder collaterals, but they did not set out to inform the adolescent in their midst. They simply discussed whatever subject arose, without whispering at certain points, but also without a specific aim to instruct. This was on the premise that references to sex escaped the young anyway until they were old enough to be curious and receptive to it. Quietly and in their own time the young would think their way through. Because of such indifferent exposure, it was nearly impossible for the young adult to go into marriage in total ignorance. Among the Dakotas, "Why didn't someone tell me?" would be a laughable question. From observation of animal life and from comments of collaterals, anyone with normal intelligence could grasp the subject—and did.

But the young resented and were embarrassed by too-pointed information. Said a woman informant, "I never liked that woman. Just because she was in sister relationship to us girls, she always talked too plain." Then she added, "As though we could not think for ourselves." Obviously that too-zealous teacher was a disagreeable exception. Certainly, no married woman—unless she was crazy—would analyze and chart her own marital experience in detail, not even for illustration. Public discussion on sex in relation to human mating was always improper because it must involve personalities. That was beyond the pale because it impinged on the cardinal rule that marital intimacy is the secret between self and spouse.

If sex education was indirectly and incidentally given, courtship education was starkly plain and forthright. If a girl needed criticism on her behavior toward men, where else could it come from but the blunt elder sister? If her technique was poor, if her conduct was unconventional, if she was too obviously eager for masculine attention or let any pangs of lovesickness show, those weaknesses in her might be ridiculed by an elder sister, in order to shame her into more maidenly demeanor and finesse.

As adults, collaterals being equal in status, they maintain a mutual hands-off attitude. This was not a deliberate policy consciously adhered to, but rather the inevitable result of their training. Being all alike, all one, in the *owáǧila* sense, one might not try to rise superior and lord it over the rest, for theoretically they were equally responsible. The pertinent phrase in this connection is *Įš hé iyéke č̣į.*[1] The idiom does not lend itself to easy translation. Perhaps "It is *his* business—he is on his own" comes closest to it. There was actually respect for one another's judgment, wishes, and plans behind the extreme matter-of-factness that appeared on the surface. Only if one's judgment or plan of action was plainly unwise and hurtful might a collateral venture to dissuade him or her, but to try to forbid or control arbitrarily was to doubt his capacities, and that was wrong.

This is not to say that everything was sweetness and light between collaterals in every instance; on the contrary. Occasionally two brothers or two sisters had a thoroughgoing quarrel, and people shook their heads and said, "Too bad, for they are *ową́žila.*" But quarrels needed a severe provocation, since the average Dakota prizes his dignity above nearly all else and would shrink from making a spectacle of himself over something of small importance.

The following incident provides an example. When a certain young woman married her elder sister's former husband, the sister fell on her in a rage at a public meeting, and a fiery struggle ensued that finally led to hair pulling. That sister was not jealous, for she despised the man who had dealt her so much misery, and felt well rid of him. The rub was that her younger sister had, in her opinion, showed a flagrant lack of loyalty by marrying the man instead of taking sides against him with the injured wife, as collaterals were expected to do. The on-lookers' pleading with them to stop had no effect until the naturally quick-tempered elder sister broke the other's arm.

A case of extreme loyalty also was reported to me. The informant related it as follows:

One day I unexpectedly came upon a giveaway ceremony at the instant that my cousin's name was being lauded in song because one of his *hakáta* had just given away a horse in his name. Well, I was his *hakáta*, too, and I was not going to be outdone. So in a moment of elation I, too, gave away a horse in his name and thus enhanced his prestige even more. I had acted rashly. The horse I gave was not mine but my sister's, and her finest at the time.

But when I confessed what I had done, my sister was noble. "That was all right . . . I would have done it myself. The important thing is that our cousin was honored. So forget it." But I never forgot it, and when, years later, I received a fine pair of horses, I gave them to my sister. In that way I not only repaid her but also, by the second horse, showed her how much I appreciated her.

It was customary, insofar as it was possible, to make the return gift more than equal to the gift received rather than the precise equivalent of the first, though usually not in such excess as here. The margin in the first giver's favor was a symbol of the other's surprised delight over having been singled out and honored with a gift. Relative monetary values did not enter into this. A horse, to symbolize one's appreciation of another's unexpected attention to one's child, rather than in return for the gift moccasins to him, was not unheard of. It all depended on the circumstances, and the persons involved.

There remains for discussion the relationship of adult and child collaterals of the same sex. This has particularly to do with the training small children received from elder sisters, I shall explain this with reference to females; it is practically the same with males.

From the beginning the child was playfully encouraged by her mothers and aunts to be independent of and a little pert toward her women sisters and cousins. They in turn pretended to be disdainful of her. The elders might pit the child against those adult collaterals until they succeeded in making them angry in fun, and then they took sides with the child against the "attack" by those collaterals. Or they might say, "Let me make you look pretty . . . hold still, now . . . your sister Zičá ['Squirrel'] never looked as pretty as you because she would not let anyone wash her face or comb her hair when she was little!" "Here's a fine new gown for you! Did your elder sister have anything so handsome?"

Such remarks were usually made in the elder sister's hearing so that she might defend herself and perhaps disparage the child in "angry" terms—whereupon the mothers and aunts argued promptly back in the child's favor. It was a harmless game of words in which the elder relatives acted for the child until she should be old enough to give and take with her collaterals.

The following instance is typical. One day the elder sister Zičá was looking over the family album while sitting in the tipi of one of her mothers. "And who may this be, with its mouth wide open?" she asked. "Is it perhaps some hungry birdling?" The mother affected a pout. "Why, daughter, how can you say that? You know very well that it is a picture of your little sister, taken only a few days after she was born." And then she added a characteristic defense. "But make fun of her all you like, now while you may." *Tókša léča hé namáhel iyéniyikte čį!* 'By and by she will be stepping on you and pushing you down out of sight', meaning, "Before long she will be far above you!"

Thus a child began to learn the customary way of collaterals. She was taught saucy sentences to repeat to this or that elder collateral, when they were pat, and was encouraged to call sisters and cousins by name rather than kinship term so that she never knew just when she began being in a sense their equal. Yet she somehow saw the inherent magical power of the kinship term to elicit a kind response to an earnest appeal. She learned to say with indifference, "Here comes *Zičá* again!" But also she knew when to say, "*Čuwé* ['my elder sister'], please take me with you," if she wanted very much to go. Of course her elder collaterals called her by nickname, too, most of the time, but should she be gravely ill or should she die, then they would speak tenderly of her as *mitʼákala* 'my little sister'.

With this kind of buildup, with the help of her mothers and aunts—and even grandmothers sometimes—the child had little cause to be in awe of women collaterals. Yet at times those sisters could change into stern monitors in order to intimidate her into proper behavior. If she grew hysterical and ignored her mothers' gentle efforts to quiet her, one stern look or one ominous word from a woman collateral sufficed to cool her down. Some children seemed to invite this unwelcome rebuke more than others by getting too cute or too smug from lenient treatment. A sister's feigned irritation then scared them down somewhat.

Some elder collaterals once invented a derisive nickname for one child on the way to being spoiled. Because of her Oriental-like eyes they called her *Očíkčikʼayela* 'Tiny Little Openings', to counteract the excessive petting she enjoyed. It worked, too. The uncomplimentary name effectively deflated her self-importance. It was gradually dropped when she reached the shy age and ceased to be annoying. When a spoiled child is being brusquely corrected by elder collaterals, her parents and others protest mildly, as a gesture to comfort her, but they actually welcome it, realizing that she needs sternness as well as gentleness. They protest only to reassure the child that she does not stand alone against the menace, so that she will not be permanently scared.

Little Tiny Openings was not really a bad child, and only a nickname was needed to correct her faults, but for a wilfully obstinate child, sometimes one of her women collaterals took it on herself to act as her *wókʻokipʻeka* 'one to be feared'.[2] This was a highly specialized office that, once assumed, must be sustained as long as the child had need of it. A *wókʻokipʻeka* had the perpetual air of expecting the child to be naughty. Mothers relied on that. They were glad enough to be able to "make a fear" for the child by saying, "Don't cry! I think I hear your sister *Zičʻá* or whatever her name outside. If she hears crying, she might scold us!" The "us" was intentional.

Any normal child outgrew his or her dread of a *wókʻokipʻeka* just as he outgrew any other fears and belief, after he was old enough to realize their lack of a valid basis. Then the once-feared elder collateral gave place to a friendly and helpful person with whom to enjoy give and take on more and more equal terms, and the backing of elder relatives ceased to be necessary. One could now stand on one's own feet.

The truth is that a relatively few needed the monitorship of a *wókʻokipʻeka*. I had one; my sisters did not. However much a small boy might need a scare, it was never a sister's place to supply it—nor a brother's, for a girl. *Hakáta* obligations prevented them. Out of respect they must not be stern with a collateral of opposite sex, however badly the child was acting. They must still treat him gently and, if necessary, resort to some ruse to beguile him—buy or promise him candy, or take him to some place or something that interested him.

Adult brothers' best tool was ridicule, perhaps the most effective of all. If the small boy cried, they laughed at him. "Here's a little girl crying!" If he was afraid of the dark or of animals, they called him "yellow" or, rather, its equivalent, for the idea of cowardice being yellow is not Dakota. If he clung to women's skirts, he was called *wíyą* 'female', and that was the most unkindest cut of all, for even very small boys wanted to be men. Little wonder, since from the time they comprehended speech they were regularly reminded by fathers and other male relatives, *winíčʻa yé ló* 'You are a male'.

Much skill and tact were essential in the role of *wókʻokipʻeka*, and most adults displayed good judgment, so as not to frighten a child too thoroughly. For instance, they ignored him at his worst if the proper relatives were not present to support him. However, the *wókʻokpʻeka* threat was something that any smart child could cope with by either improving his conduct on the spot or escaping to the sheltering arms of some mother or other relative. Under a woman's shawl was sanctuary. Not all adult collaterals cared to be feared, but should a mother, unable to control her child by gentler means, call on them, they served at once, even if half-heartedly. The bonafide *wók'okip'eka* was a deliberate volunteer in every sense of the word—a tireless altruist, dedicated to seeing the job through.

Aunts and Uncles, Nieces and Nephews

These relatives tend to give deferential attention to nieces and nephews, which is a projection of *hakáta* respect into the next descending generation. Aunts give such attention more promptly and articulately than uncles, and there is a valid reason for this difference, which will shortly appear.

A woman does not hesitate to scold her own or a female collateral's child even while dressing his injury. She chides him for perhaps his disobedience or carelessness, which has caused his trouble. Whatever the cause she blames him.

But just let a *hakáta's* child suffer a similar hurt and she turns mellow on the spot. Ignoring all such possibilities as that her nephew is a persistently disobedient imp or that his own stupidity brought on his mishap, she purrs over him sympathetically as she takes care of him. Never a word of censure. Worst yet, if her own child is standing near, she turns on him. "And as for you," she says, "this might never have happened if you had not led your cousin there!" Or, lacking a whipping boy, she contrives some other excuse for shifting the blame from her brother's child. It is not that she thinks less of her own child, but that she wants to hang the blame on something or someone else than on her nephew. His feelings and his dignity must not suffer if she can help it!

What about the child so unjustly blamed? Far from being resentful, he takes it in his stride. He is used to this peculiarity of his mother where his cousins are concerned and knows from experience that it does not mean a thing. He does not need sympathy, for he has his innings, too. His aunts—this very cousin's mother included—always rush to him if he is in trouble, and scold their own children for indirectly causing it, just as his mother is doing. He is sure of them, but he is also sure of his mother's love for him, despite her scolding. Why not play along with her, by taking her scolding with good humor? That is the way he takes it.

It does seem that mothers are inclined to be more severe with their own children if their aunt is near, as though they relied on her to take the edge off their scolding—which she does invariably. I actually heard a sorely tried mother say to her child, "Look here, don't drive me to scold you. Your aunt is not here to take up for you!"

Certainly aunts and uncles were not preoccupied with watching to see what happens to a nephew or niece, to the neglect of their own children. In the *t'iyóšpaye* camp, each woman kept generally to her own lodge and there devoted herself to them; today individual families are usually scattered on their own allotments, and do not know how their *hakáta's* children fare. After all, the parents can be trusted to look after them tenderly! It was and still is only when related families live together for a short time that situations arise in which parents chide their children and aunts and uncles take up for them. It is an old pattern.

It is equally true that these relatives will voluntarily go out of their way to comfort a *hakáta's* child, as in an emergency. When one three-year-old boy ran over hot ashes and burned his feet severely, his aunt hurried there as soon as she heard the news, leaving her children with their other mother, her sister. She and her husband camped outside and remained until the child was well. Never admitting tiredness, she dedicated herself to amusing, humoring, and caring for him. Most important of all, she anointed and massaged the feet gently every day, "so that the scars would not heal all drawn together." The mother was grateful for her help but she had no illusions as to why she was doing this: because she was *hakáta* to the child's father. The mother knew that she would do the same for a nephew or niece.

It was usual to accept a favor from a *hakáta* with quiet appreciation indirectly expressed by a deed. When that same lively child was again playing too near the fire, his father warned him by saying, "Take care, son, your aunt is too far away at this time. You can ill afford another burn." That was subtle thanks, spoken in the presence of his male guests, who would be sure to tell their wives—who would be sure to tell his sister. They did, promptly.

The reason why men did not hurry to the side of a child who was being scolded was that it was the mother, their *hakáta*, who was scolding, and they would not appear to go counter to her in any way. Afterward they usually managed to make the child happy to make up for the tears. They might take him on their horse and go riding, or walk with him or her to the water and let him wade or skip stones on the surface — a favorite pastime for children. Or if a store was nearby, they might take him there and buy him candy. It was no rare sight for a child to be returning home, holding on to his uncle's hand and clutching a paper sack of sweets with his free hand, a smile on his tear-stained face, his recent bad time forgotten.

In numerous big and little ways, uncles and aunts made children happy. If they must gently reprove a child, it was only to warn them of danger. Stern reprimand was the parents' province; theirs was to cushion the blow. Their attitude and treatment of nieces and nephews was impartial; it was the children themselves who gradually turned to one or the other — boys to uncles and girls to aunts — in a companionship that was always dignified, as they became members of different generations. Aunts and uncles did not behave like children, and children did not want them to. Mutual respect was important. In olden times it was most likely to be an uncle who took the boy on trips and excursions, and if the boy ran away and joined a war party, it was his uncle who looked out for his safety and saw to it that he was not abused in any way. An aunt was the traditional chaperone when a girl wanted to look on at the dances. Because aunts and uncles could be relied on to be ever ready to meet children's needs, and were loyal to the last, naturally enough they were very popular adult relatives to be with.

An illustration of their faithfulness is the following incident in one woman's life story. Having married at an exceptionally early age, she was having her first baby before she was seventeen, and that was fearful and confusing enough. But added to that was the girl's anxiety over the aged grandfather who lay dying in the tipi next to hers. All night long her mother shuttled between the tipi of birth and the tipi of death, torn by conflicting obligations: a natural pull to her daughter in labor, and a kinship duty to a dying avoidance relative whom she highly respected. So there were intervals when the girl might have been alone in the dark, had not her aunt remained with her to the end. This she did with undivided attention to the girl, although it was her own father who was dying. It was the way of uncles and aunts to deprive themselves as though they had no preferences, for the sake of a niece or nephew.

In return thoughtful adults esteem their aged aunts and uncles, and treat them with compassion. A young woman while home on vacation from a fairly well-paid government job told me this situation: "My poor aunt was about to lose her place for nonpayment of taxes when I got home. But I am paying them for her, at least this once." The amount represented a considerable part of the girl's monthly stipend, and her paying it now was not going to solve her aunt's problem permanently. She knew that. Yet she was evidently impelled by the memory of her aunt's tender care and devotion to make this typical kinship gesture. It was emotionally satisfying to her.

One might ask, "What was the use?" But "At least this once" meant everything fine in Dakota kinship. The question of practicality did not enter; nor did the fact that the woman's own children were not helping her, were not concerned. Neither did her father criticize them—he was their uncle, remember—although he must have regretted their lack of filial conscience. All he wanted was peace of mind for his *hakáta*, at least for a time. Tomorrow was still tomorrow; next year's taxes were far away. He was proud of his daughter for appreciating her aunt enough to do what he was without the means to do. The woman, for her part, had not complained but had borne her hardship in silence, for one ought not to worry a *hakáta*. Thus, father, daughter, and aunt were conforming to pattern, even though the aunt's own very modern children were living their own lives somewhere else and looking out for themselves, unmindful of their mother's plight.

Dakota parents, far from worrying lest the altogether pleasant treatment by aunts and uncles alienate their children's affections, welcomed it as a further safeguard for them. A dying woman said, "I go in peace. My children still have their aunts and uncles." A sick man told his young daughter, "Č̓úkš, when I am gone, stay with your aunt always. Do not try to live with your mother and a father 'who is not your father.'" He knew that his wife was morally unstable by nature and would soon remarry without considering the effect on her child. It was important to him that the girl grow up without tensions and wound to her spirit, and that his sister would provide the environment where she would receive first consideration, as a child ought.

Yet for all this, aunts and uncles are not wholly indispensable and cannot always satisfy a child. They know that. When a girl in the mission school became gravely ill during her parents' absence, it was her aunt who hurried there. In lucid moments the girl would moan, "T̓úwí 'aunt', I want my mother . . . where is my mother?" Then the patient aunt would stroke her hot brow and say, "You shall have your mother very soon now, t'ožą 'niece'. I have already sent her word. I will be right here until she arrives."

The mission school ladies marveled at such selfless devotion to another woman's child. "What a kind, tireless woman Cecelia is!" They were unaware of the invisible crisscross of reciprocal kinship obligations that held the Dakota close—obligations that, from their being habitually accepted, supplied the fabric of a cherished way of life.

Any conscientious woman of any race will gladly take care of the sick for a few hours to help out. But Cecelia's dogged devotion to a niece was driven by something far deeper than mere humaneness, and that was what the ladies did not suspect and Cecelia had neither the inclination nor the English fluency to explain to them. Many fine things in Dakota life their well-meaning friends do not know exist, and so they do not look for them.

There are difficult situations in a boy's life when the most attentive uncle is useless, when only a father can help. There are times when a girl needs nothing less than the tender embrace of the woman who bore her. An aunt does not give this. It is not for her to fondle a brother's child and press it with passion to her breast, as though she were its mother. She can only stand by, ready to help if needed. Thus, aunts and uncles are no substitutes for parents, finally, nor do they want or try to be. They will do their all to make a niece or nephew happy, but they will bring child and parent together speedily, if that is what the child asks for, and then step aside. It is the particular role they assume as a matter of course even though it is not strictly demanded by kinship law and could therefore be only casually and intermittently played, without impunity. The majority thus, nearly unconsciously, project in a modified way their habitual respect for a *hakáta* to his or her child. This is really one more honoring of the *hakáta*, and, incidentally, the child benefits.

In this, as in all the other kinship situations I have described or shall describe, the ideal, customarily followed by well-meaning people, is presented. That does not mean that everyone acted ideally, or Dakota society would be utopian, which it was not. Always there were exceptions who had never been properly trained in kinship duty, and therefore grew up unmindful of others. It is not necessary to dwell on them.

One question about Dakota kinship that puzzles non-Dakota is "Who are brothers and sisters outside the family unit? Who are cousins?" I have to alter one answer to this, given in a book by a non-Dakota. He says, "Children of brothers and sisters are siblings; children of cousins are cousins."[3] That, of course, is quite wrong. The answer hinges on the sexes of the related parents. Let me put it concretely.

If your father and mine are brothers or cousins, or your mother and mine are sisters or cousins, then you and I are siblings. If your father and my mother — or your mother and my father — are collateral relatives (i.e., hakáta), either cousins or brother and sister, then you and I are cousins. In other words, only cross-cousins are cousins in Dakota kinship; parallel cousins are siblings.[4] The quoted statement above might be amended to read: children of collaterals of the same sex are siblings; children of collaterals of opposite sexes are cousins.

Grandparents and Grandchildren

Here is perhaps the ultimate of freedom to be demonstrative, for there are no direct or indirect controls, no reason to inhibit or lessen a natural desire to be demonstrative. The ideal grandparent may be no more devoted and patient, no more self-forgetful and alert on the child's behalf, but whereas an aunt or uncle was cautious and formal toward the child of a respect relative, a hakáta, the grandparent could pet and fondle the child of his child, and openly call him by endearing names as much as he or she wished. His affection was explicit; that of aunt or uncle was by action in the child's favor.

Grandparents' attitude remains constant. They regard an adult grandchild as still a child. Of course all grown men and women must observe the rule of modesty, even before grandparents. However, a woman may sit alone all day in the tipi with her grandfather, and may even recline in her own space, or go to sleep. Meantime, like a sentinel, he sits in his space across the tipi, smoking in silence with eyes shut, thinking of the past and paying her no direct attention. But she would not dream of undressing in his or any man's presence.

Grandparents are invaluable as the child's last line of defense: his final resort, his sweet refuge. If his parents seem to correct him with too much sternness, the grandparents are there to soothe and sympathize, happily submerging their own desires for his sake, and providing him asylum. They tell the parents that too harsh or arbitrary discipline is hurtful to one still "fragile and unripe." Children need very delicate handling, they insist.

While they scold thus out of one side of the mouth, out of the other they murmur comfort and reassurance into the ear of the child held close in their arms. Parents, of course, are not cowed by the scolding, but the pattern is to leave the child alone and, so to speak, drop the charges against him. The grandparents will simply talk to him and straighten him out in their usual, gentle way.

Right may be unequivocally right and wrong wrong, but not even for that will all the family side together against a member, no matter what he has done. There are always some who are obligated by their particular relationship to stand by him. If they cannot justifiably condone him, they quietly ignore his fault. For a bewildered child this affords a priceless haven where he may recover himself and regain his dignity, unobserved and unforced.

Grandparents have their standard words of admonition. *Héč°ųšni, t°akóža, tuwéni héč°a héč°ųšni yé* 'Don't do that, grandchild; nobody does that', meaning, "It is not properly done." A man inserts *yó* after the first word and *ló* after the last; that is masculine speech. This admonition may seem feeble and ineffectual, but unless a child is too hysterical to listen, its very gentleness soothes him into compliance. It is the correction children learn to expect of grandparents. Thus, when a terrified woman cried out in panic, fearing that the child might cut himself with the sharp knife he held before she could reach him, "Put that down at once!," he became frightened and cried a long time. His confidence in grandmothers had been rudely jarred. She had been momentarily too loud, too peremptory, too ungrandmotherly to be understood. It took considerable explanation of the reason before he was finally appeased enough to depend on her again.

This was a major blunder. Ordinarily grandparents' unvarying nature gives children every reason to expect favorable response to their wants and needs. A youngish woman recalled the following incident:

Our school allowed us to go Easter shopping . . . I laid my purse, containing four dollars, on the counter while I tried on a hat, and when I came back it was gone. My folks could not send more money until the next month, they said. But that would be after Easter. . . . So I wrote to my grandparents and mentioned my loss. . . . Sure enough, by return mail I received a check for fifteen dollars from

my grandpa, for shoes as well as a hat. I just knew it would come. . . .
My grandparents never failed me.

Grandparents had a part in training the small child. They taught him
kinship terms, and the duties he owed his various relatives, and also had
a part in his moral and ethical education. This they gave by an indirect
method, through legends and myths from which they drew appropriate
lessons. While the old man related the age-old amusing tales about the
incredibly tricky *Iktómi*, whose only aim was to deceive and ensnare, the
grandmother injected an occasional comment that helped the child to
learn right from wrong. "He is very bad, that *Iktómi*," she would chuckle.
"He does things that 'are not done.'" Then she would add, "But then,
Iktómi is only an *ohúŋkaką* [something idly told, hence a myth]. He is not
a real human being." *You* are a human being, so do not imitate him, was
the implied lesson.

With obstinate loyalty grandparents remain uncritical of small grandchildren's faults, and of their morals as adults. Let others criticize! Thus,
when a girl bore a fatherless child, her shocked and disappointed mother
ordered her out of the home, but her grandparents gathered up mother
and baby and took them to their home and there lavished all care and compassion on the girl—and never a hint of blame. The thing was done, why
harp on it? The old man went to the neighbors to find milk for the baby
without apology or visible shame, concerned only with the vital issues: a
grandchild in need, an infant hungry. This closely parallels what an aunt
or uncle might do except that, being more able, they would probably buy
milk; if they lacked the means just then, they would borrow money, thus
assuming the responsibility. This would keep the matter on a respectable
level. Grandparents cast personal dignity to the winds if necessary, and
beg if they must, for a grandchild's sake.

Only the other day, while this chapter was being written, an elderly
woman went to a church office to arrange for the baptism of her unmarried grandchild's baby. The very young acting secretary filling in the card
asked tactlessly, "Father's name? . . . But this is a fatherless child, is it not?"
The woman, without a change of expression and with eyes downcast,
replied softly, "No. The baby does have a father. We know who he is." The
fact that there had been no legal marriage was gently ignored lest any

further discussion lead to criticism of her granddaughter. Of course, the baby was duly baptized.

In compelling gratitude for such selfless devotion, most adults are very tender with their aging grandparents and keep them in or close to their own homes. However, it is also a fact that a shiftless grandchild will go to them as a last resort, sure of an eager welcome. If a granddaughter brings with her a worthless or sickly husband and several children, they, too, are welcomed. Often old people are better off with their small monthly check from the sale of heirship land in which they share, or with a pension. Such money is turned over to the grandchild: "Take this and feed your family; buy shoes for the children."

The old couple will leave their cabin or tipi and retire to a makeshift dwelling outside. They will happily surrender their bed and sleep on the ground. An incurable compassion for the adult grandchild, who is ever a child in their eyes, leaves them no choice but to behave thus. They can be very easily imposed upon by the thoughtless, for they will not defend themselves. A well-meaning outsider who tried to defend them against such imposition is likely to be resented for a meddler. I have seen that happen.

Some people are naturally selfish — even grandparents. Rarely, however, are both man and wife alike callous toward their grandchildren. If one is remiss, the other is almost certain to be extra-dutiful. Once when such a grandmother, forgetting her own notorious record in her youth, mercilessly berated her grandchild in public for similar tendencies, the girl called back at her, "If I am bad, you set me the example!" The dreadful quarrel that followed was nearly unheard of. Any departure from normal kinship behavior was always censurable, and in this instance the burden of blame was on the old woman, as indicated by the comments on all sides: "Who would quarrel with a mere child on equal terms — let alone a grandchild!" "Poor girl, she never knew the affection of a 'real' grandmother!" "Here is a battle between enemies — not relatives!" Meantime the old man tried to do two things at once, comfort the girl, who was weeping violently, and curb his lawless wife whose steady stream of abuse had broken the girl down.

Aside from such exceptions, it seemed to be the nature of grandparents to shower affection on any and all whom they called grandchild — many being outside their t'iyóšpaye, in social kinship only. The ideal grandparents were soft-spoken, adoring, selfless, and patient. One often heard a man or woman say, "Childhood was sweet and easy for me, I was 'grandmother-raised.'" And men have quipped on their deathbed, "Oh, am I to die? Good! So much the sooner I can be with my grandmother again!"

As the crowd dispersed, immediately after the committal at an old Teton woman's burial, one man exclaimed poignantly, "*Hehehé! Hehehé!* 'Alas, alas!' Now am I entirely abandoned. No longer do I have an *onáp'e!*" The word means 'refuge': *ó*, locative prefix indicating place, *nap'á* 'to run away from danger'.

This was not literally true, for the man was one of the most self-reliant and able in the community and had never had to go to this particular woman for sympathy. But she, being the last to survive of all his own grandmother's female collaterals, had symbolized for him the quality of grandmothers. He meant only that he had nothing remaining of that spiritual haven, that little Eden, that grandparents provided. Nor was his forlorn outcry a reflection on the treatment given him by his other relatives, of whom he still had a goodly number but no more grandmothers. All who heard him understood and sympathized, for they, too, had had grandparents and remembered them well.

In times of stress, need, or danger, Dakotas sometimes exclaim, *Uçí, hiyú yé!* 'Grandmother, come and rescue!' They also say, *T'ukášila, tók'i yaúpi huwó?* 'Grandfather, where are you?', or *Tók'i ilálapi hé?* 'Where have you gone?' Such rhetorical outbursts are reminiscent of grandchildren's reliance on those relatives while they lived.

The Dakota child seemed to be well braced on all sides to save him from being either spoiled or abused. Whenever his elder collaterals casually picked on him beyond his ability to hit back at them in fun, then his parental, protective elder relatives rose to defend and shield him against them. If the parents, aunts, and uncles were proving too much of a shield, until he was in danger of remaining a baby overtime, those collaterals promptly challenged and ridiculed him, and so they spurred him out of that pampering situation.

Even an only child did not lack this training, for all his classificatory brothers and sisters were his correctives. Thus, if a boy of seven or eight, while acting babyish around his mother, became suddenly aware of an elder sibling laughing at him sneeringly, with eyes only, he recovered himself and became speedily independent. No words needed be said.

Finally, if he was being corrected too severely by a sorely tried parent, there was his unfailing and ultimate refuge, his grandparents. With them he found complete safety, where he remained to regain his bearings and turn into a good boy again, quietly. Parents did not invade his refuge; they knew what it meant in their own childhood to be sure of that resort. They accepted the muttered criticism from the grandparents whether it was deserved or not. Nor did those grandparents flinch from scolding even a child-in-law—only less directly than they scolded their own son or daughter—on their grandchild's behalf. Here was something bigger even than that inexorable law of avoidance respect! Always such a breach of kinship rule was justifiable, if for a child's sake.

11

Relatives of Social Kinship

The polite exchange of kinship terms of address is the outward and visible sign of mutual understanding and acceptance of one's obligations to the other. As such it is the indispensable preliminary for a successful association. At the same time it seems to bespeak wordlessly the other's good will. In that sense it is a prayer.

It is no accident that the verb *wač̇ékiya* means two things that are unrelated on the surface, for actually they are one in essence. The verbs are 'to address by kinship term' and 'to pray'. Only by the context—whether it is secular or religious—may one know which meaning is intended.

When a man says *Wač̇éwakiye s'á*, speaking secularly, he means that he always addresses people by kinship term, implying that he behaves as a relative ought to. Speaking religiously, he means that he prays regularly. Only by the context can one tell which use he makes of the word. I once knew a young woman named *Č̇ekéyapi*. For years I thought this meant 'one prayed to', which would seem to deify her, but it meant 'one whom others address by kinship terms'. It was a complimentary name for, in a roundabout way, it meant one whose conduct inspires others to act properly toward her: a good relative, faultless in her own attitude and behavior toward all.

One non-Christian informant used the word in both senses when he said, "At dawn I rise and climb to a hilltop and there I smoke—to be God's relative." The peace pipe ritual was called a *wač̇ékiyapi*. To him smoking his pipe ritually and acknowledging relationship to God were one and the same. "And when I leave I lay the pipe there as an offering to him. Hunt over the little knolls near my home and you will find a pipe on many of them." Then he warned, "But you must not collect them; they are God's property." I knew already that I should not; it would be like taking the sacred elements from a church altar.

Whether about to deal with man or with God, one must first establish kinship mutually acceptable, and that was to *wač̇ékiya*. The kinship approach was the open sesame, the clear channel for a two-way flow of friendship. Without that one dealt with the other in the dark, since what his motives were toward one, whether sincere or sinister, were undeterminable. Of only relatives, who knew their proper roles, could one be sure. Therefore, the solution was first to make the stranger a relative—thereby putting him on the spot—and then deal with him on that basis. Once he had accepted a kinship relationship one might be reasonably sure that he meant well. By the same token, one showed one's own good will toward him.

Certainly no Dakota preoccupies himself with all this. He establishes kinship as a matter of course. He does not first analyze his need for a kinship relationship or scheme to safeguard himself against strangers by artificially arranging it with them. The practice is accepted without question. Indeed I have never heard anyone explain it minutely or enumerate its advantages for himself. It is too integral a part of Dakota life to be seen objectively, as is also the idea that it is normal for all who have daily association or the most tenuous of connections to be specifically related.

On that premise, and with sublime optimism, the Dakota enters into social kinship where kinship through birth and marriage end. As he addresses his new acquaintance as father, sister, uncle, or else, he says in effect that he is prepared to think and behave as a son, brother, nephew, and that he presumes that the other is prepared to do the same. It is his statement that he will not default and that at the same time he feels certain, from the other's reciprocal term, that he, too, understands his role and that he, too, will not default. With such double assurance, the beginning association has a reasonable chance of success.

Formal adoption, publicized with a feast and some ceremonial gift-giving, was something other than the simple establishing of social kinship, which alone is under consideration here. This might be effected in either of two principal ways. It might be based on a mutual acquaintance, who would of course be a relative of both persons. Or, lacking that link, it might be fabricated out of whole cloth. By either means two complete strangers whom circumstances throw together might adopt each other informally and assume some suitable kinship relationship. This has the effect of drawing them together and making their association smooth and homelike. Otherwise, as between strangers, it must remain distant and tentative, and a little suspicious—a thing intolerable to the Dakotas.

But, alas, no ideal is consistently flawless in practice. Even the most ardent first avowal of kinship may prove unhappy. Every instance must be a separate act of faith. Even so it is well to expect the best at the outset. Most people accept social kinship with proper intentions, as a matter of custom. They welcome all the relatives they can have because they function best socially in an atmosphere of kinship, where everyone is "something to them" (i.e., related to them in some specific way).

The intangible tissue of Dakota kinship is made up of innumerable interconnections, a vast network that takes in all relatives of birth, including even the most remote, if only they can be authenticated, as well as all relatives of marriage. This means not only the relatives consequent to one's own marriage but also to all of one's relatives' marriages, for among Dakotas all relatives are shared. For example, the mothers-in-law of all my collateral relatives automatically become my mothers-in-law. One need not marry to acquire parents-in-law, or sons, daughters, and grandchildren; one shares such relatives through one's collaterals. The person acquired by marrying that is exclusively one's own is a spouse, but the spouse becomes a sister- or brother-in-law to one's collaterals.

Thus the Dakota is well provided at birth with relatives of all kinds. From there he adds more and more as he grows up and his acquaintance widens with each new marriage in his family.

But if he were to restrict his dealings to these relatives only, he would be excluding many neighbors from his social life, and would limit his scope of activity. However, through the social kinship system, he is enabled to extend his relationships to include everyone he knows, for the sake of better, more uniform group action.

The unlimited use of such intimate family terms as father, mother, sister, son, and the rest does not in the least water down their emotional content when applied to close and actual relatives. At first acquaintance such terms were a formality between social relatives, serving only to ensure a mutual acceptance of the obligations pertaining to them. However, such relatives could in time be treasured as "real" relatives because of their loyalty and devotion. I am reminded of four sisters who remained loyal and devoted to an elderly widow, and she to them, as sisters-in-law, although the elder woman's girlhood husband, who had been their social kinship brother, had died years ago, and the widow had been married and lost two husbands since then. She counted heavily on them, and she was important in their social life. They thought so highly of her because of her qualities as a sister-in-law that they always seemed more aware of her, and closer to her, even than to the wives of their own brothers.

The manner of "new" grandparents was and is immediately more articulate—that is, without any initial formality. I do not know if this is due to a lifetime of practice in dealing with numerous grandchildren, or whether to a mellowing by the years that results in an immediate acceptance of all youth as grandchildren—an automatic heart-opening to any and all who relate themselves to them. For example, at a gathering, my brother took me to meet the fine old man Little Warrior, who took part as a boy in the Custer battle. "He is my grandfather," my brother said. "He belongs to my parish. I want you to meet him, he is full of stories." So we went to him where he sat under a tree with his wife. "Grandfather, this is my sister, who . . ." The old man's tone and manner became that of a real grandfather. It was petting tone, a gentle, tender tone, as he reached out: *Háo, háo, tʿakóža kú wó; lél íyotaka yó. Mitʿákoža! Mitʿákoža!* He led me to a space between him and his smiling and equally cordial, though less articulate, wife. The warmth of affection in the air I could almost feel by touch. I had always been their prize grandchild, one would have supposed. No need to ask why I had come, what I wanted of them. They were ready to give all. I felt actually close to those two human beings whom I had never laid eyes on before.

His greeting was significant of total welcome. *Háo, háo, tʿakóža!* 'Welcome, welcome grandchild!' *Kú wó!* 'Return!' *Lél íyotaka yó!* 'Sit down here!' Then the exclamations 'My grandchild! My grandchild!' It is the *kú* that is significant. It is one of various directional verbs with fine distinctions. They constitute a whole grammatical problem too involved to discuss here, but the following must be said. The more technically correct verb would have been *ú* 'come' (this way); come for awhile from the place you belong; come for a visit, on an errand, or whatever. *Wó* is a man's sign of the imperative mood. Deliberately, Little Warrior used its companion form, *kú* 'return'; come home, here where you belong. It meant I had a kinship right to be there; I had immediate claim on all the grandparental ministrations I required, along with all their other grandchildren. It was an indescribably comforting choice of words.

He had not waited for any explanation as to why I had come, what I was after. He interrupted the moment he realized that as his grandson's sister I was one more grandchild to be treated as such. His instantaneous acceptance, generous to overflowing, was typical: so warm, so unstilted, so selfless.

This has happened to me before, many times, though never so dramatically. Nor have I ever detected any initial caution, any momentary fear of possible rejection. Whether one accepts grandparents or not, they accept one as a matter of course. Little Warrior did not act; automatically he assumed a grandfather's attitude and began living the role with complete sincerity—and enjoying it. So how could I reject my role? It was too irresistible. Now I had another set of grandparents. The more the better.

By its very nature, the family of birth remains constant and so does the family of marriage, as a rule, even after the two who married and brought their two families into relationship have died. But social kinship may be altered for a valid reason by "mending kinship," as the saying goes. An example of this is the story of an Oglala Teton woman who married into the *Húkpapʻaya* band and went north to live among that people.

There she expected to find many relatives of marriage through her husband, and through them to make social relatives of others. Ordinarily that would take time. However, she no sooner arrived than a host of women came to greet her with gifts and food, and each one addressed her by kinship term. As is proper she addressed them with the reciprocal term— *mother* to those who called her *daughter, niece* to those who called her *aunt*—and so on. She was mystified by it all until the women explained that they were adopting her as a social relative in place of the wife who died, to whom they were related in these various ways. It was a thoughtful gesture intended to make her feel immediately that she belonged, but it was neither customary nor obligatory.

The new wife might have graciously played the roles expected of her, but she was a woman of self-importance who at once resented what she saw only as a compliment to the dead wife rather than to her. Later she was mildly appeased when one of the women came back to "mend kinship" by saying, "Your predecessor was a daughter to me, and that was why I called you daughter. Now I know that you and I are actually cousins." Then she carefully traced their blood relationship to a common ancestor several generations back. Remote as was the connection, it was genuine. The old people who kept track of such matters attested to it. Thereafter, the two newly found cousins functioned in the usual way of collaterals of the same sex, and the Oglala woman found herself well integrated into the community much sooner than she had dared hope—through her cousin's many local relatives.

Perhaps my own experiences will best illustrate the two ways of establishing social kinship. As I approached the most easterly situated Santee community, near Red Wing, Minnesota, for field study, I grew more and more disturbed by misgivings. I did not know these people and they did not know me. I, a Yankton, would have to feel my way with tact as a total stranger.

As I had feared, I found myself at a decided disadvantage in the head man's presence because he knew no English and it is always awkward to converse in Dakota without kinship terms of address. At last we shook hands, I with a stilted "How do you do," and he with a noncommittal *Háo*, which, by the inflection, was as much a question as a greeting. Who may you be? What on earth do you want here? All the while we were both inwardly jockeying for position because we were uncertain of the other's motives, being total strangers.

Through a jerky and nearly one-sided conversation with long intervals of silence, I struggled along desperately until I mentioned that my father was Philip Deloria of the Yanktons. "You mean you are *Tʿípi Sápa*'s daughter?" It helped that he knew my father's Dakota name, even though he added, "Of course, I know him by name, though I have never met him." No relation there. However, groping for a straw, I told him that a young Santee with a first and last name like him had lately become my father's associate in the ministry. At last the head man's interest was aroused. Leaning forward he asked animatedly, "What are they to each other?" That is, how are they related? I said, "As brothers."

Then it happened! A new and wonderful light came into his eyes, a light of recognition. Here was no stranger! Here was someone he could place. A Dakota relative, his daughter. "I know of whom you speak. He is my own brother, my father's brother's son!" With that all need of further parrying was gone. Swiftly he crossed the room, once more with hand extended— but how differently! *Haó, haó, čʿų́š!* 'Welcome, welcome, daughter!' The Teton *čʿų́kš* becomes *čʿų́š* in Yankton and Santee dialects. We shook hands warmly. *Até* 'father', I acknowledged him. It was very good to be relatives and no longer strangers; to be linked in the great interrelationship of Dakota, the *wič'ótakuye*, which may be invoked anywhere any time that two Dakotas meet who know how to establish kinship and feel the need of it.

The essence was this: when my new Santee father called me *č'įš*, he gave me the assurance that his attitude and conduct would be that of a Dakota father, and nothing else; when I called him *até*, I as much as said, "I am quite aware how a Dakota woman must think and act toward one she calls *father*. You may count on me to act accordingly." Thus, every time two Dakotas exchange kinship terms, they virtually enter into a covenant.

At that instant I was in, for I was automatically related to everyone in that small community through the head man, my father. His wife, her sisters, and her cousins were my mothers; their husbands were my fathers; his daughters were my sisters. Their children were my children, their grandchildren were my grandchildren, and so on. I did not meet and talk with every one of these relatives. I and my interlocutors knew and played our parts well, from habit. I never expect to return there for field work, but if ever I saw them again, kinship will not have to be established; that once was for all time. Even if my acquaintances had all died, I could still arrive at consistent terms with their children and grandchildren—if we were still speaking Dakota. I still hear after long intervals from the eldest daughter of my father, who speaks English. "Dear Sister," she begins her letter; my reply is in kind.

It was unspeakably comforting to belong. The old people, upon learning the purpose of my visit, volunteered much valuable information regarding their former life. The eldest woman there, whose keen faculties belied her years, was a particularly rich source of knowledge of ancient customs no longer generally known. It was she who gave me the legendary account of marriage by capture. Being my father's sister—I do not know how close the relationship—she was my aunt. We had several talks together, which were politely and cordially punctuated all the way with *t'ųwį* 'aunt' and *t'ožą* 'niece', but not every single utterance need be so prefaced. That would be overdoing it. In dialogue usually the opening sentence as one begins to speak again in his turn requires it. One learns to know the right times to speak the term naturally.

This was an instance of establishing kinship through a mutual relative, a social kinship relative of my father, a real brother of my new father. If he had been related only through social kinship to both fathers, it would not have disqualified him. The important fact was that he was the valid kinship link I needed.

Now for the other instance. One summer I daily interviewed a youngish Oglala woman at Pine Ridge who was not related to anyone I knew. It was my first visit; I have made many relatives there since then. We were compelled to converse only in Dakota because she knew no English, and again it was too formal and distant to be natural, without a kinship relationship. Evidently she felt herself at a disadvantage, too, for she remarked on the second day, "Too bad we are 'nothing to each other.' I guess we have no one in common." Then she said later, "I never had a sister." She must have had many, at least classificatory, sisters; everyone has. She meant that she was the only daughter of her parents.

That seemed like a good opening for me, so I said, "Well, I shall have to be your sister." But I laughed as I said it so as not to seem presumptuous, in case that should not be her idea. Apparently it was, for she agreed eagerly. Right off, then, we began calling each other by kinship term. I said čʼuwé 'my elder sister' and she said mitʼą́ 'my younger sister', and as though by magic we were instantly at home with each other. This was a case of establishing kinship without a mutual relative. It had been fabricated out of nothing and yet it was warm and pleasant all the same. Again, as in the Santee community, I was suddenly no stranger to her mother and others who came while we held our talks, and again I was accepted as a relative through my new sister. At a celebration some six years later, someone in the crowd tapped my shoulder lightly. Mitʼą́, she said and extended her hand. It was that sister.

My impression is that women, even if they are to be together only temporarily, manage to become relatives very soon, whereas men are more deliberate. Women preoccupy themselves with questions of kinship. Directly a newcomer appears on the scene they ask one another, "Say, how are you related to him or her?" and often they are guided by the reply in deciding on a suitable relationship connecting themselves to the stranger. Unless men know that they are going to be permanent acquaintances, familiars, they simply borrow the pact-brother term kʼolá 'friend', which in reality designates a special friend, and exchange it in the free and easy manner of casual companions—much as cowboys of the west say "pard" or "pal."

The term kʼolá is a specific one belonging to the institution known as kʼolákičʼiyapi, a kind of pact-brotherhood term like *fellowhood* in the writings of early ethnographers.[1] No formal ceremony, such as sealing the pact with blood, was required. The relationship was quietly entered into, by mutual agreement, by two men of standing who admired and respected each other.

A *k'olákič'iyapi* was no light and transitory matter; it was for life and it was lofty and idealistic. Each must forget self in the other's behalf. Each must defend the other with his very life. If they lived in the same camp circle, they felt compelled by their relationship to go to war together. "Where my *k'olá* goes, I go; where he falls, I fall. His danger is my danger." Men have died in battle to keep their *k'olá* safe. They were like brothers, but they did not use the two brother terms, *mišú* 'younger brother' and *č'iyé* 'elder brother', for that would indicate a difference, and they were peers. They called one another *k'olá* instead, and that was admirably right. *K'olá* implies coequality in all respects.

It was also an extremely difficult relationship, whose mutual responsibility must remain on a par. At all times both *k'olá* must be ready to hold their own, fulfill their respective duties properly, and be on the alert to give aid and comfort to the other, while guarding against putting extra burdens on him. A *k'olákič'iyapi* was the proudest and most self-confident of all relationships. The tribe welcomed a *k'olákič'iyapi* formed by men of character and prestige, knowing it would last, as something good for society. For, by the very fact of their successful association, *k'olá* gave proof that they could be relied on in any tribal venture or emergency.

From all I can gather, true *k'olá* relationships are conspicuous and impressive, but infrequent. The term *k'olá* is common simply because it is borrowed and loosely applied by others. Male collaterals often use it informally rather than the actual brother terms, as they also use *č'ékpa* 'twin'. Men sometimes coax their child-brother into proper behavior by calling him *k'olá*, as though he were their equal, grown-up and manly. It pleases the child and challenges him gently to behave so.

Two more substitute terms of address may be mentioned here. They are *kič'úwa* and *wašé*. These were, I am told, originally courting terms, in a sense. That is, the first term was exchanged between two young men, the second between women or girls. *Wašé* does not admit of satisfactory analysis, now, and could be a corruption of a lost, original term. A variant, *mąšké*, heard in certain regions of the Teton country, is just as obscure. There might be still other variants that have escaped me.

Kič̓úwa literally means 'to chase, on another's behalf'. It is nominalized as a term of address and reference, the idea being "pursuer-for-another." If two young men were interested in two girls who went about as chums, the men, in *kič̓úwa* 'relationship', also teamed up in dual pursuit. Though perhaps still green at the game of courtship, they might confidently address each other as *kič̓úwa*, in a sly and devilish way, as men equally able to hold their own gains and also help the other. Strictly this implies a closer, more secret association, but sometimes male collaterals will speak of one another casually as *kič̓úwa*—the habit stemming no doubt from the old-time custom of courting by proxy.

Even a mature and settled family man might apply the term to a young brother or cousin, particularly a callow youth who is excessively girl-shy, with the aim of instilling courage in him. It is as though he was saying: "We two are blades of equal charm and daring—what woman could resist us!"

Still looser application of *kič̓úwa* might be made by a high-ranking man with reference to a tribesman of little consequence toward whom he feels kindly. This would tend to bring the two men closer, equalizing them in a sense, though not really so. The lowly man, perhaps one with a physical or mental handicap that keeps him in the background, would no doubt feel more sure of himself because of his important friend.

A case in point may help. At one time a group of fun-loving collaterals of standing in their community began desultorily to call a certain timid little man their *kič̓úwa*. No doubt they were sorry for him and wanted to pay him special attention, but also they got fun out of the incongruously applied term. At all gatherings they remembered to seek him out of his obscure position and bring him to the fore while he held back, reluctant to be made conspicuous. "By the way, where is our *kič̓úwa?*" "Hasn't he arrived yet?" "Oh, there he is!" "Come sit with us, *kič̓úwa!*" They would drag him along with them. Grinning from embarrassment, he would sit among them, looking a little out of place. But after they were seated, his *kič̓úwa* did not engage him in conversation or compel him to make a speech. They just let him be one of the fellows.

The crowd began to play along with them. "Here, make way for their *kič̓úwa!* They are calling for him!" So they would form a lane and let him through. The men who started this never missed an opportunity to pick up anything he said or did and announce it in glowing praise. "Thus said our *kič̓úwa!*"—as though it were brilliantly unique.

They were in for a surprise. In time their exaggerated attention had its effect, for the formerly unpretentious little man actually bloomed out — after he was sufficiently cured of his backwardness. He became something of a specialist in trapping small game and began earning enough from their pelts to meet the simple needs and wants of his family. His sense of inferiority had been overcome by so much, particularly because his skill was being recognized and his advice sought. Plainly he had been less stupid than timid all along. What had started as a simple greeting was surely tongue-in-cheek and had its by-product in a fuller life for him. Ever afterward he was loyalty itself and could have died for any one of his *kič̇úwa*. Because he stuttered he never talked very much; but he became a productive and useful man.

A *wašé* was first of all a confidante. While it might be very useful and exciting to have a *wašé*, it was only for the time being. Then it was unsafe, for, once the girl chums had married and gone their separate ways and their common interest waned, they could never be sure that their girlish foibles would remain a permanent secret. As dignified wives and mothers, they were uneasy in the other's company, lest an overenthusiastic outburst in reminiscent mood by one of them betray the other. "Oh, do you remember when you . . ."

It is easy to understand why such exclusive, romantic friendships were rare. A Dakota woman generally kept her own counsel, particularly in matters of the heart, and acted as though free of their domination. Many women have lived and died with their big romantic secret undivulged. It is definitely not a Dakota trait, anyway, to confide personal matters to all and sundry, indiscriminately.

The term *wašé* might also be used in a serious way — that is, without its romantic flavor. If two women, not relatives by blood, took a liking to each other because they admired and respected the other, they sometimes decided to be special sisters. Then they were said to *wašékič̇iya* 'be *wašé* to each other', but they used the regular terms for younger and elder sister, not *wašé*. They treated and regarded each other with more consistent courtesy than is usual among women collaterals, who could be very gentle and kind at serious times, but were casual and seemingly indifferent ordinarily. Because this *wašé* situation involving dignified women in essence resembles the *kʻolá* situation of a pact brotherhood, it is easy to believe that this was the original relationship, and that gradually the term was borrowed by romantic young girls and perhaps parodied. It is most unlikely that serious-minded and conventional-acting women would borrow from young girls a term first employed flippantly, but no informant could say this was so.

Women who were *wašé* exchanged fine presents whenever they met, at tribal reunions, for example, or at state-wide church convocations, in later times. Although they did not make oral promises of lifelong devotion, such relationships lasted. However, their program of systematic gift exchange might diminish as the women became increasingly enmeshed in family and home responsibilities. Also, as they grew older they found it easier to stay at home than make long and tiring journeys to meet. Even so they kept each other in their memory and continued to send an occasional message or gift by travelers going to and from.

I learned about one *wašé* relationship between a woman and a little girl who was one of her cousins, in a certain community. The young woman was in her late twenties and the child was around five or six. It was she, now in middle life, who gave me the story. The casual *wašé* relationship lasted perhaps four years and then the young woman died of tuberculosis. Doubtless it was to take her mind off her malady that she amused herself by it, and that her father and his two wives aided and encouraged her. Even after she died, they continued to bring a gift to the girl, as though from her *wašé*. This might be a special delicacy or perhaps an especially pretty pair of moccasins, or a rare piece of doeskin. Sometimes a year or more went by before they again brought a gift in their daughter's name. The informant said that the daughter had some schooling and was a faithful church member, while her two mothers and father were the most conservative family in the community, tenaciously clinging to old customs in the face of rapid change going on all around them.

If they were that faithful to ancient ways, they no doubt derived satisfaction out of acting for their daughter as though she still lived. They would feel they were "keeping her ghost," for the primary reason for ghostkeeping was to perpetuate the dead by extending his or her participation in human activity through vicarious hospitality and generosity, even after his death, and thereby keeping his memory alive. My informant said the young woman's father and her own mother died first, leaving the other mother alone, and that she continued their program as long as she lived, in a limited way. "She died while I was in high school at Haskell [Indian School, in Kansas]. Of course, my folks gave her presents too, and took care of her when she was sick."

In the early 1930s I was acquainted with a *wašé* situation of this serious type but have never heard of another since. Even then it was something of a rarity. Both were married women of middle age, one a Sisseton and the other a Teton.

One other use of the term *wašé* might be mentioned, although it was not intended to be serious or permanent. Just as those able men adopted a shy and diffident man as their *kič̓úwa*, sometimes a young woman of prestige amused herself by announcing as her *wašé* a cute little girl who struck her fancy. Then, since mere words were never enough, she promptly validated the relationship by giving the child a noteworthy gift, perhaps even a horse. Such a gesture was bound to delight the child's parents, who lost no time in causing her to make a creditable return gift. Thereafter, for some years, there might be an occasional exchange, until the child was old enough to be interested in her own age group and its activities. In these lighter uses of *wašé* and *kič̓úwa*, they take their point from their inappropriateness because of the disparity of ages, standing, or attributes of the principals. The relationship, adopted in a playful spirit, might be so carried on for a time.

In modern American life perhaps we can afford to be exclusive and selective in our associations and not ally ourselves with our neighbors purely on the basis of proximity. Because of that we have no way of determining their attitude toward us—until it becomes manifest in a crisis. When calamity or bereavement comes upon us and they hurry to us with help and sympathy, we are surprised and touched. "I did not know I had so many friends," we say. In a sudden and unexpected way we *become something to each other*. In a manner of speaking, we are related—for a time at least; and we find it good.

But the Dakotas in their group living cannot afford to wait for a crisis to discover how they stand with one another. They make sure in advance, going on a kinship basis at their first meeting, so as to know what to give and what to expect of one another. While it is true that two persons might have a mutual aversion that keeps them apart, the majority follow the pattern docilely, and like it. As long as kinship relationships are normal, as long as the various relatives treat one another as they ought, they do not make news. The occasional flagrant offense against a relative, being aberrant behavior, alone has news value.

Kinship law in the past was well enough satisfied if people treated one another in accordance with its rules of etiquette, expressed by attitude and behavior; that was what the masses aimed to do, but there were natural variations in both directions. Some with an innate sense of human decency over and above were wont to go beyond the line of duty and treat even strangers as though they were relatives. There are stories telling of men of influence who bought back white captives from fellow Dakotas and returned them to their own people. This they did out of human decency, over and above the demands of kinship, and entirely on their own initiative. I have no way of knowing whether all such deeds were recorded properly as historical facts, but I do know how such men were regarded. One storyteller concluded: *Dak'óta okáǧe waštéȟče čį̇ hená héč'ape dó!* 'They were some of our finest type of Dakota!' He was proud of them. Other people, with less than enough heart, were wont to treat relatives as though they were strangers.

They still tell of a stingy old man who never gave anything away out of the kindness of his heart; who, when his own nephew's child craved eggs — his "last meal" — accepted the quarter offered as a gesture and in exchange blandly singled out one egg from his hoard. Was not that fair? Did not a chicken cost a quarter? It did in those days. Then was not the egg from which it grew worth as much? He probably reasoned so, but the people were astounded. "He was always stingy — but this is too much! His own relative dying . . ." "He can't be human, he does not act as a Dakota! After all, what is an egg?" Only those of his relatives who were obligated to defend him offered feeble excuses: "Alas, my uncle [or whatever the relationship] was marked from birth to be so. He is helpless." "Do not condemn him. After all, he is old now, he too will soon die. Here, take this quarter." Only the old man, oblivious to the furor he was creating, was unperturbed, still hoarding his eggs happily.

On very extraordinary occasions two unrelated persons must deal together in a purely business way, as strangers who would shortly part for good. If both were naturally unselfish, they were likely to be more interested in the other's getting the best of the bargain — so accustomed to holding back in deference to relatives as kinship law required, that they did so automatically, even with strangers.

On the other hand, two equally shrewd men could engage in coldly impersonal barter unbecoming to relatives, and could drive as hard a bargain as might the proverbial horse trader, but they would not haggle, since haggling was contrary to the prevailing attitude that an avid interest in mere things was debasing. Because it was an insult to attempt to change another's mind except to dissuade him from an ill-fated course, the only effect of smooth sales talk would be immediate resistance to it. "Does he think I have no mind of my own? I'll show him!" Nor would Dakotas stoop to compromise. So, once they had taken their stand and stated their terms, the two remained transfixed and silent. To give in was ruinous to personal dignity and self-respect. Only attrition was left. The shrewd strangers stood their ground without further discussion — until the less determined gave in from weariness, or both walked away unyielding.

I have tried to show that kinship relationship was the very texture of Dakota life: that it was no detachable adjunct, but rather its very heart and at the same time its all-pervading, all-enveloping essence. One could hardly live among tribesman permanently free of kinship's sway, since one functioned properly in society only as a relative. Those who consistently obeyed its rules were the reliable and hence the good citizens of society. Theirs were the utterances in council that compelled attention because they were weighted with deeds of hospitality and generosity toward relatives. That was all the government there was; it was what men lived by.

Surely it was well to be brave, audacious, and heroic — though not all men cared for the warpath. It was well to be truthful and sincere, and in every way moral, and to keep one's name above reproach. Yet those were in a sense only selfish virtues, in that they redounded to personal glory alone. A man might have them all — and remain out of touch with his fellowmen, but to "truly live" (i.e., to live in relation to others), he needed also the social virtues demanded by kinship law. They were the indispensables of group living in t'iyóšpaye, band, and tribe.

In perhaps different words, I have said that the Dakota must think and behave in a prescribed way toward each person, in accordance with his particular relationship, but that did not make his life monotonous because the roles of different relatives were different, and there were many kinds of relatives to deal with. Their wide variety allowed him to gratify all natural impulses and moods by the simple device of turning to the kind of relative before whom he could do so, with impunity.

For detailed illustration take the woman's position. As an avoidance relative, she is careful to be unvaryingly courteous, self-contained, cautious, and reticent with reference to her parents-in-law, and to be ever the responsible adult when dealing with her other relatives of marriage. For a safety valve, she still has her fathers, mothers, uncles, and aunts, with whom she is free to relax from the restraining society of her in-laws. With them she can still enjoy being humored, petted—with words only—and gently chided. She need not conceal her fleeting moods, for they will not misjudge her by them. Momentarily she may act a little childish, even. She may pour out to them her petty annoyances or real troubles, and express her likes and dislikes frankly, and they will comfort and sympathize, advise and strengthen her. Thus, in a brief recreation of her childhood environment, she may recapture her careless childhood now and again. Then she is quite ready to go back to her in-law role once more.

With reference to her male cousins and brothers, her *hakáta*, again she is on her guard to be consistently correct in attitude and behavior, to be controlled and politely distant—if not physically, then by mental self-effacement. She avoids obtruding herself on them. Instead she bridles every instinct to be charmingly romantic, witty, and irresistible. In short she submerges the sex appeal she may be naturally endowed with, for that side of her is not for her *hakáta*.

Again, she does not have to behave in that manner toward all males, for there is one large group waiting, her joking relatives, with whom she is at liberty to assert her personality and femininity and to make full use of her wiles and wit. It has been said in chapter 8 that some persons are temperamentally disinclined to enjoy the joking privilege with the opposite sex, but if she is so inclined, then here is her field. She can well afford to inhibit herself out of respect for her *hakáta*, since she is free of all obligatory formality in the company of her brothers-in-law.

Another parallel: with her female joking relatives she spars in that eternal mock struggle permitted her. She puts her best foot forward while she tries to show them up at a disadvantage. They do the same with her, so it is quite fair. Yet, even though free enough, and all in fun, her role demands constant wariness and subtlety. For these, after all, are in-laws;

they are not her own flesh and blood. She must be watchful to keep within decent bounds and to sense their moods, lest she offend unintentionally.

When she wants to be completely relaxed and be her unvarnished self, she turns to her female collaterals. For with them she may be casual and even lightly rude, and can enjoy full freedom as their peer. With them she may show her feelings indifferently and without apology, her weaknesses and her conceits, which they already know as she knows theirs; with them she may just as well be by herself. No need to act to impress these women; no need of best foot forward. She cannot excite them nor they her, so why try? They are her kind; they grew up with her. There is hardly a flaw in her nature to be hidden from them. She can only be herself.

But again her mood changes. She would like to be very wise and parental; to be looked up to as one mature and capable and safe to be with; to be respected and relied on. So she turns to her sons and daughters, nieces and nephews, who are the collective offspring of her male and female collaterals. With them she deals in the same way that her own parents, aunts, and uncles deal with her.

Finally, when she craves the most selfless kind of comfort and loving, she goes to her grandparents. They will always put their own desires aside to attend to her, and it is very good, but if she receives their kind of attention, she may also give it, for—whether married or not—she has grandchildren, sharing with her numerous collaterals, and they look to her for such attention.

This is all quite theoretical, of course. The Dakota does not spend his days anticipating some approaching mood, and then dashing about in search of the proper outlet for it. He has other, more conscious interests and anxieties to occupy him. I have enumerated a woman's various kinds of relatives only to point up the range of choices that give her life variety of expression. There is a nice balance running through all this, so that no one role need be sustained too rigidly too long. Sooner or later— but unfailingly—there is available another kind of relative, permitting a change of roles. For each tension there is a compensating release. It is kind to the nerves.

Now perhaps I can say with a measure of truth that this more or less regular need to change roles makes of the Dakota a perpetual actor of many parts, without conscious or studied effort. Inured through practice from childhood on, he does not see those roles apart from himself but sincerely lives them all. The process is purely subjective; he and his multiple roles are one. So he changes from one to another rapidly and naturally, and with amazing deftness. If he has his wits in full, he rarely makes a mistake.

As a socially responsible person he may not indulge his moods without first considering his surroundings. His life is in constant reference to others. Hardly looking, he realizes who is present and what he owes that one in attitude and behavior. So, smoothly and imperceptibly, he goes from informality to formality, from frivolity to adult dignity, as different relatives shift about in his vicinity.

Only if he finds himself face to face with someone unaccountable in kinship is he momentarily at a loss, but straight away he proceeds to establish a plausible relationship with him. Then, back in character, he can once more carry on because things are normal again. He does not go into an act; he goes into character, and the action takes care of itself.

Since etiquette demands it, kinship terms of address are used instead of proper names, and their exchange represents a tacit guarantee of mutual good will. Perhaps their ultimate function is to regulate conduct. They are reminders of how to act, not only in the formal but in all relationships. How they could be effective even in doubtful situations is illustrated by the following incident, out of my own experience.

The July sun was setting in a blaze when, without warning, my car stopped on the vast empty flats two miles from the mission that was my home. I gave up trying to start it running again upon realizing the drain on the battery. Then I grew panicky as twilight closed in on me, remembering that no "nice girl" goes out at night alone. For here I was, stranded on the little-used wagon trail I had taken as a shortcut. So should I abandon my father's new Buick and start walking home? But something might happen to it. So should I stay with it all night? But what if a disagreeable stranger came along? Each pair of alternatives was one more dilemma.

Much as I needed help, then, I was more apprehensive than relieved when an approaching rider took shape slowly out of the dark. Against the lighter western sky I could see that he was someone youthful by the way he sat on his horse. He reined in at a short distance but stayed in the saddle, taking in my plight leisurely.

At last he dismounted and approached, with his attention only on the car. He jerked up the hood and stared at the machine, his broad-brimmed hat half-hiding his face. Suddenly, by the headlights, I knew who he was—one of those young men of the parish whom my father called *misų* 'younger brother' in social kinship—Father's brothers are fathers, remember. It was like a weapon thrust into my grasp out of nowhere to be able to say, "*Até!* What a relief! And I thought you were some stranger!" With that I began pouring out my story without any regard for coherence: I had planned to stay the night with my friends in town but had changed my mind. I could easily have got home before dark, but for this change of mind. Naturally my family were not on the lookout for me, unaware that I was coming. I had tried everything. What did he think was the matter? For a long minute he looked at me blankly, without a word. Then he turned to the motor and began to fuss with it.

Not until I was safe back home did I realize how I assumed the attitude of a helpless child relying on an all-powerful parent. That was funny, for the young man was no older than I—if as old. Somehow, the instant I called him *father*, I felt and acted as though he were my father. Kinship terms can make you do that.

When he had the motor purring once more, he spoke for the first time, pretty gruffly. "There . . . get in. Keep to a good speed or it may stop on you again." His next words were more kindly. "I will wait here until you turn in at the gate." The mission was in sight, then. As I shifted into low, he came up and grasped the windshield of the touring car, as though to steady himself. It was very easy to imagine he swayed a little. Had he been drinking? Was that why he was so noncommittal—lest he betray himself? In the next terrifying instant it flashed across my mind that he had not once acknowledged my *até* with the reciprocal term *čʼųkš* 'daughter'. Was it out of simple diffidence, because we were not really acquainted, or was it intentional? Even so I said, "Thank you, father. My father will be grateful that it was his brother who helped me."

With that simple utterance I neatly brought the three of us, my father, him and me, into a close, interresponsible family group. Kinship terms can do that, too. Don't think I was being amazingly clever, for mine was no cunning strategy. I had not chosen my words astutely, after first conniving with myself: you are away at school so much, maybe he does not know just who you are. If you make him realize who your father is, surely he must respect that! The truth was that I had neither the time nor the wit to scheme. The words just came, but their effect was to cancel out everything else and leave only the demands of our father-daughter relationship to assert themselves. He relaxed his hold slowly and stepped back to let the car move. *Hé įše tókˊa šní!* 'That was nothing!' He said, smiling a little.

I drove away fast — but not too fast to catch his paternal warning. "Don't you ever take a chance like this again. There are rough men about, you know!" He had to shout that last.

It was my first and last encounter with this particular brother of my father, but I had heard stories about him — none of them good. He was a rollicking carouser, a periodic inmate at the local guardhouse for engaging in brawls when drunk, which, according to the reports, must have been his chronic state. Worst of all he was a thoroughly heartless philanderer, the dread of all women with young daughters. If all of that was true, he should easily win the palm for the roughest of the rough men about against whom he had warned me.

All I know of him or shall ever know is that once he and I met on a deserted trail, all alone in the dark, and that he was nothing else than respectful and helpful, because that kinship term *até* reminded him of a father's obligation to protect a daughter in every way. He never did address me as *čˊųkš* but, nevertheless, he treated me like a daughter. That, under the circumstances, was quite enough for me.

The challenge to act nobly is inherent in the kinship term, but need I say that in the final test the response depends entirely on the character of the person addressed? Fortunately for me my *atéla* 'little father', for all his reputed wickedness, had it in him to accept that challenge. Those without enough training in youth were sometimes negligent in their relationships because the proper response in attitude and behavior was not habitual to them, like people who are only sporadically courteous — when they remember to be. Then there were others who willfully ignored the rules, because they intended to behave improperly and would not be restrained. Happily, my *atéla* proved himself not their kind. Like any other people, the Dakotas were of various natures and subject to human temptation, so it would be fatuous to idealize them en masse. What I have deliberately done was to select those situations that would illustrate best how Dakota kinship was designed to work, and how, as long as it did work correctly, it made for amicable group living.

12

Birth and Infancy

Human procreation was understood to the extent that a male element was essential, but that ova were equally essential was apparently not grasped. The male element and menstrual blood begat life and this combination was nourished in the womb prenatally. It was as simple as that. There were no beliefs about favorable and unfavorable periods for conception, but it was recognized that an initial and single union could be productive.

Children were expected as a matter of course, as the visible result of the marital state. When some wife was said to be with child, the people, particularly the old people, dismissed the news indifferently. "Of course; is she not with a man?" Only the unmarried woman with child made scandalizing news that was never entirely forgotten.

There was no invoking either barrenness or fertility, although the latter was petitioned for in veiled language, along with other womanly attributes, in the ceremony for girls known as the Buffalo Sing. Actual barrenness was regrettable but without stigma. One wife was not cast aside for another simply because she could not bear a child, provided that she and her husband were congenial. In any case, the absence of offspring was no absolute misfortune. Children were everywhere — sons, daughters, nieces, and nephews galore — for the childless couple to care for and enjoy.

"We had no issue," says an informant, not as something tragic but as simple fact. The need for someone to carry on the family name and inherit the family fortune did not exist in Dakota life, where there were no surnames to be perpetuated and where riches were not an end in themselves.

Childless couples often kept one of their small relatives with them as their responsibility and lavished on him such care and affection as they might have given to their own child. Dakotas were, as a people, completely at home with children from having always dealt with them in the family and *t'iyóšpaye*, as a matter of kinship obligation. The occasional exception who disliked children was regarded as abnormal, "unhuman." Nowadays they sometimes adopt legally some orphaned relative to whom they meant to will their land. The terms for legal adoption are two: *sutáya-t'áwapi* 'firmly theirs', because confirmed by law; and *č'įčáič'iyapi* 'made their child'. Adopted children know from the beginning that their own parents are dead and that they are being brought up by relatives, and they accept the situation without question. Since family relationships may not be changed, foster parents continue to call their child nephew, grandchild, or whatever. The adopted child is called *č'įkš* 'son' or *č'ųkš* 'daughter' only if he or she is the child of their collaterals of the same sex.

The subject of contraception by means of preventatives was dynamite. Reasonable persons would not dare speculate on it, however objectively, for fear of suspicion. "Why does she want to know that?" So strong was tribal sentiment against prevention—except by continency—that it would be suicidal to one's reputation to be known as dealing with anything of that nature. Aborticide, by herbs or other means, was a transgression of one cardinal principle: "Human life is the ultimate value." Another, related to it, was this: "Only the death of a human being warrants human tears"—so do not cry over the loss of mere things.

But if the subject of prevention was not for open discussion, now and then there were whispered rumors among women concerning someone's suspicious behavior. Thus, when a naturally uncommunicative woman was seen digging at a distance, using a crowbar such as old women used in digging *t'įpsila* 'wild turnips', she was immediately suspect. "There is not one *t'įpsila* on those pebbly hills; it is not that kind of soil!" The implication was that she could only be digging mysterious herbs for sinister reasons.

Again, when a young girl was summarily dismissed from a government boarding school, gossip spread the word that she was with child. When no child was born, they spread a new story: her grandfather in olden times was a clever herb doctor. He had doubtless bestirred himself to brew something for her. Such accusations were pure guesswork. Needless to add, in self-defense women went out of their way to avoid any activity that could be misconstrued.

The only sanctioned way of controlling births was by continency. "If a man loved his offspring—and every man should—then he must be willing to abstain in order to spare his wife through her pregnancy and until the child was weaned." Some made this a religious matter and used the ritual of the sweatbath to gain self-mastery. Or they preoccupied themselves with various activities away from home—the warpath, the communal chase, and individual deer-hunting—or at intervals they fasted alone on some distant butte, or took part in the Sun Dance and other such rites as demanded preliminary fasting and purification.

It is stated with considerable emphasis that those who lived on a high plane as a matter of principle were quite ready and able to wait as long as need be before cohabiting again, and that they waited with indifference, because "for strong men it was no particular hardship or deprivation." They even made a fetish of this. The high-class Dakota considered it beneath him to associate with loose women meanwhile. Should one slip into a clandestine affair, the affair itself was no blacker than the fact that his position in society was no longer quite the same. The gossip about him was bound to detract from his former self-assurance so that he would no longer be comfortable, however stoical he might appear to be. In the close-knit society of the camp circle, it did not take long for such gossip to get around, particularly if a prominent person was implicated.

Parents terminated their relations when it was a certainty that a child was on the way. "He is sleeping alone" was an indirect way of saying that the wife of the man in question was with child. A clean baby was taken as an indication that its parents had observed the rule of continency during its mother's pregnancy. One born besmeared with mucus was an indication that they had not. The midwives were the judges, but unless one carelessly or maliciously spoke of the matter, it was not known.

The milk of a pregnant woman was said to be poison. It lost its nutritive properties and became a watery fluid that made a baby sick, if fed on such impoverished fare. He became puny and fretful; "he lost control and dropped feces everywhere." There was an idiom for this condition. The child was said to be "rectum-killed," a reference to his lack of rectal control. The remedy was to wean him at once "prematurely." This "offense" against him by "abnormal, selfish parents" was deserving of censure; gossips made the most of it on the premise that "children should have first consideration—what is more important than a child?" "Parents should subordinate their desire for his sake."

A very dear child—boy or girl, Dakotas welcomed both—who had been wished for, and perhaps prayed for, or one who almost died at birth but lived, was often not succeeded by another child for some years, and such a child was humored in every way. If he showed no disposition to tire of his mother's milk, then by all means he should have it! To deny him what was deemed his right was unthinkable.

It can be truly said that the child of indulgent parents weaned himself, when he was good and ready. Very early in his life he ate all adult foods and then his mother's milk was no longer all-important. As long as he did not voluntarily turn it down, it was available to him. Often he nursed desultorily, only enough to wash down the dry food he had crammed into his mouth. It gave him enormous confidence. In afteryears it was one of the things to recall with pride. Occasionally an old informant manages to work into his narrative, "I nursed until I was four [or five] years old." I am expected to catch the import of that statement, and of course I do. He is saying, in effect, I was a child well beloved of my parents.

Because of modesty the woman with child did not want to direct attention to herself and would have been very unhappy if pregnancy rites were regularly held. They did not exist. However, impatient old people sometimes did honor to the coming grandchild by giving a horse or some other comparable item in the child's name at the giveaway—that is, "My coming grandchild gives this," they announced. One old man was so proud "to have a grandchild ere I die" that he celebrated prematurely by feasting all old men and women of his village and bade them wish the baby a safe birth and long life.

The pregnant woman had the growing sympathy and consideration of other women as she became increasingly unwieldy, but she did not expect to be pampered because of so commonplace an experience. Of a certain woman who wanted to be waited on, and made unnecessary demands, other women whispered an ironic comment that meant, "We have something unique here—the only woman ever to be with child!" Every woman expected to have children if and when she married. Neither blatantly joyful nor mutely bored by their condition, most women accepted it naturally and took it in their stride.

Unless something seemed wrong, it was not customary to make a woman's pregnancy the main subject of conversation. She might herself speak of it incidentally when talking with a woman relative but any reference to it by them was brief, and made only because it was necessary. If others were obliged to mention her condition, they spoke briefly and with delicacy. Even young girls, however thrilled by the prospect of a coming baby in the family, knew enough not to discuss it incessantly in public.

One girl told her chum in a whisper, though they were alone, because she must suppress her excitement, "I'll tell you something . . . but it is not to be talked about just yet. My aunt is going to have a baby!"

The male attitude was just as commendable and considerate. Fathers and uncles and by all means brothers and cousins, being *hakáta* to the pregnant woman, lived as though they were unaware. It was a proof of true masculinity to avoid womanish subjects, anyway. Only the old grandfather might be outspoken: "Our grandchild, being heavy with child, must suffer from the day's heat excessively. Old woman, why not do all her cooking for her from now on?" Yet even he subordinated the subject to something even more important: his granddaughter's comfort. To the old people, reticence for convention's sake grew less and less important.

Even the male joking relatives waived their foolery, once they knew, and slowed down their racy manner and gradually forgot to joke even impersonally, lest they forget themselves and say something tactless. As though in respect relationship, they avoided face-to-face encounters and long conversations with her, toward the last, in order to save her from self-consciousness.

Nor did young boys snicker at the woman with child, whether she was their relative or not. This was not one of the things to be ridiculed. Old men harangued on every conceivable subject and pregnancy came in for its due consideration: "Be kindly disposed toward the woman with child. She faces an ordeal that man can never know. With unparalleled courage she endures. If her function ceased, there would be no people." From such admonition, randomly given out and unconsciously absorbed, everyone knew better than to jest about so natural and vital a phenomenon. Only if one were crazy might one make fun of it. For responsible persons that was beyond the pale.

In olden times, whenever possible, a special tipi was set up for a birth, back of the home tipi and so out of sight of those who passed on the parade track around the circle. Probably the procedures and arrangements varied in certain details in accordance with local customs and usages. However, the following account of her own confinement as given by a Teton woman of the *Húkpap'aya* band should be at least representative.

In the tipi a couch of robes was placed on the ground, overspread with fresh broad-leafed sage. At the foot a log was laid crosswise against short stakes driven deep. This was for bracing the feet in severe labor. At arm's length were two more such stakes, one on either side, at shoulder level. These were for her to grip in order to steady herself. From two tipi poles a heavy bullhide strap hung, looping downward, to which she could cling or by which she might raise herself a little now and then for ease. Finally, a bit of porous driftwood was shaped like a large bottle stopper for her to hold between her teeth to avoid accidentally biting her tongue in a spasm of pain.

Unmarried young girls and children did not witness actual births, but were free to come in during the preliminary stages and entertain the patient for short whiles. Under pressing circumstances a mature unmarried woman might have to take full charge. Ordinarily, however, those in attendance were women who had themselves experienced childbirth. Most women in attendance were resourceful and calm and instinctively did the right thing, but one of my informants reported this: "My aunt [mother's brother's wife] was such an excitable woman that she exclaimed shrilly over everything, until her mother told her to be useful somewhere else." Certain women were known for their skill at midwifery and were in demand. Always the patient's own female relatives were also there to assist as needed.

To spare the patient's sensibilities, everything possible was managed under cover. Only if there seemed to be a complication did the midwife look; otherwise she knew by feel only. The patient tried—and generally succeeded—to avoid screaming. This was particularly important to her dignity. Since tipis were only skin deep, she did not care to be heard by people outside, some of whom might be chance passerby. Occasionally a woman in hard labor did scream, and nothing terrible happened. All the same it was preferable not to give way and attract attention. Self-control was always admirable, even under severest pain.

A stillborn baby was tenderly buried at once, usually by grandparents. The place was a secret they kept always. I believe it was an internment in the ground, but do not know for sure. I have a feeling that it was disposed of differently from the afterbirth of a normal delivery. Again it was the grandparents who took care of the placenta and umbilical cord. These they wrapped into a small bundle and left in the high fork of a remote tree, beyond the reach of animals. Nobody knew exactly where his own čʰekpá 'navel' was laid away, although it was nothing strange to see a tree with a birth bundle in it when roaming through the woods. It was wrong to unwrap such a bundle because of the mystery, the power, believed to be in it. Dire would be the penalty for doing so. The child whose *č̓ekpá* was desecrated by humans or devoured by beasts "might be deformed, or lack a mind, or might die prematurely."

The claim of old women that, in their day, labor was easier and of much less duration than now, is, of course, unprovable. If that be so, it might be attributable to the kind of life, demanding work, and activity until the last. One informant told how she walked in the line of the moving camp with intermittent pains that grew in intensity until she could hardly bear them, and how she left the line and went over the hill and there delivered her own baby, and then rejoined the line later in the day. "I left the line alone and came back with a baby in my arms — and no ill effects," she said.

In case a normal delivery was impossible, no attempt was made to remove the child by surgery. It was never the practice to cut a living body, not even to save it. The extent of surgery did not go far beyond the lancet and cupping horn to remove excess blood, which was believed to cause headaches. Any cutting would have to be done with empiric haste, in private, if done at all. There was no lore to go by. No medicine to dull the pain of labor is remembered, but only that brews were given internally to expel the fetus if the birth was delayed too long.

Nothing was said about pressure being exerted on the abdomen to hurry the birth, but if that was done, it was of course done by women. The scene of birth was not for men. Even the father remained outside then, ready in case of emergency. He entered the tipi only after it was all over and he was called in to see his child and wife. An experienced father took his new child and addressed it at once as *č̓įkš* 'son' or *č̓úkš* 'daughter', but a very young father could be so tongue-tied before all the women that he could not do this. One man, speaking reminiscently, stated that he was sure his firstborn died because he was too shy to welcome her into the family as *č̓įkš*. The baby resented it. This was a common belief, and twins were believed to be especially touchy.

Twins were believed to remember a previous existence and to be endowed during their early childhood with a superawareness denied to others. Their childlike naivete was an act; underneath it they were sometimes crafty and designing.[1]

Twins generally lose their awareness of a former association in the spirit world after they reach the age of reason and live on a practical level.

As adults they are no more unusual than the people around them. It is only as very small children that they seem to be sampling life on earth, always ready to depart if the surroundings and treatment given them are not satisfactory. A typical story reflects this idea.

Two four-year-old twin girls were overheard in earnest conversation. "I don't like it here." "Neither do I." "Well, then, why do we stay? Let's go back!" The terrified mother dropped everything else and devoted herself to keeping them happy and contented until they became too fond of her to leave; by then they were old enough to forget that "somewhere else." Always she was apprehensive lest they die in a huff over some imagined slight on her part. The narrator of this tale was entirely convinced that it was true. The lore on twins is nearly endless, but this is a fair enough sample. Nearly every informant knew some of it, from hearsay at least.

The umbilical cord was cut with a sharp blade at "about the length of a finger or somewhat longer" and tied with sinew. But, before even that, someone reached into the baby's throat to draw out any matter that might obstruct his breathing. This came to be a routine practice just in case, whether it was necessary or not. It was said that the woman who performed this duty thereby transmitted her own traits to the child— not physical, but temperamental traits. Thus an excessively plain woman might be asked because of her congenial and kindly nature, and given a present afterwards. Though only women did this, the virtues transmitted were those that any boy or girl would do well to have.

Babies were not bathed but instead were greased with oil and then wiped and their faces repainted with red ochre paste. Everyone, babies and adults, wore a thin film of this red paint as a protection against sunburn and chapping, particularly while on a journey. In summer, when the heat was severe, babies were held in shallow water warmed by the sun to make them comfortable, or they were sponged.

In an emergency birth anyone present must serve without previous invitation. Then, should the child later display a streak of temper or other undesirable trait, people said, "Blame it on her [naming the woman], she reached into his mouth!" Of course, the vital aim was to ensure easy breathing to the child. As far as I can gather, this idea of blaming or crediting the performer was not taken seriously. Perhaps it only gave an excuse to tease the woman who served under necessity. Today the idea is largely forgotten, most babies being born in hospitals. And how did the woman take the teasing? Once when a little boy was being crossly insistent, I heard someone say, "His cousin Nancy is to blame—she reached into his mouth!" Nancy (Chief Gall's daughter) said, laughing, "Fine! All the better for my *šič̓éšila* 'young male cousin' [woman speaking], he will hold his own. Just let anyone try to run over him!" There was nothing obsequious about Nancy Gall, as I remember her.

Interest in a new baby was general and the first question on all lips was *Tákula hé?* 'What is the little one?' Old people frankly indicated the baby's sex, but others wishing to be more delicate, said *hokšílala* or *wič̓íčalala*, 'little boy' or 'little girl'. *Hokšíla* and *wič̓íčála* are applicable to children of all ages, but the added *-lá* indicates the speaker's attitude of affection or pity or some such sentiment. For *-lá* seems to say, "The poor, dear, cunning, helpless little one," by connotation. If a name had been chosen tentatively by an overeager grandparent, and it was apt, the baby was called by it forthwith; later it was publicly announced, with a gift to the needy. If the name was long and descriptive, sometimes it was shortened into a single word or sound, and that was the child's *iȟʼál* 'not serious' name, or nickname. Names were sometimes proclaimed at the Sun Dance, at the time allowed for piercing children's ears for ear ornaments. This was a very important honoring ceremony for a loved child.

No instance was given of a baby's being born with teeth, but for one to be born with a caul was not unheard of. Some believed that a baby born with a caul was "almost a twin," which was what they believed also of one born with two spots on the head instead of one where the hair grew in a whorl. Such marks indicated a special endowment, a kind of prescience and supernatural awareness not given to all—the kind of endowment "separated twins" enjoyed.

The idea of monstrous births was not absent. In legends and rumors repeated around the campfires, listeners learned that "once upon a time a woman gave birth to a dog, they say." "A child was born with horns." "There was a little boy with the characteristics of a swallow. Though he was a deaf-mute, he always knew when a thunderstorm was in the making long before it was manifest in the sky. Out of his tiny swallowlike mouth he would emit bird cries and run madly about, flapping his bent arms like wings, round and round as swallows fly." "It is said that somewhere a woman born a *wówąke* ['something resembling something,' i.e., a monstrosity]. It was furry and had the face of a monkey, but almost at once it died, for it lacked any organs for eliminating body waste." To such stories people listened with muffled equivalents of *oh* and *ah*, as a sign that they were properly horrified.

Birthmarks were explained by the familiar formula "The mother was frightened by . . ." Whether that was a native or a borrowed saying cannot be established now. One woman related how a mouse jumped out of her rawhide box while she was rummaging in it and how she was so startled, "I must have clutched at my hip unknowingly. At any rate, soon after that the child I was carrying at the time was born with the perfect outline of a mouse imprinted on his hip!"

Unless a person was physically imperfect, crippled, or misshapen from birth, or an imbecile given to senseless blabbering, he was unnoticed if his outer appearance was not unusual. Because it was not popular to be garrulous, even a moron managed to live as a passably normal being. His deficiency might always remain inconspicuous. Only if he should be caught in a crisis requiring good judgment and swift action might he give himself away. Provided he worked at something useful, however slowly, and played his kinship roles tolerably enough, he would fit acceptably into a society where it was undesirable to be too aggressive, talkative, or competitive; where even the exceptionally endowed played down their talents rather than be conspicuous, justifiably bringing those gifts into full play only to save the situation in an emergency.

The relatives of a mentally defective person shielded him from the cruel remarks of outsiders by keeping him in the background, and they made allowances for him among themselves. He was no more blameworthy than a still unreasonable child, whom no sane adult would punish. If necessary to explain him to a newcomer, they said in regretful tones, *Mitʿákoža ečʿákel-witkótkokela* 'My grandchild is by nature foolish, stupid, irresponsible, abnormal'—harsh words, but softened by that terminal *-lá*, indicating the speaker's sympathy for one so limited. Paraphrased and with all connotations, the phrase seems to say, "My grandchild is thus because he was born that way and cannot help it, the poor, dear one. He needs your kindness; he has mine." Without the *-lá* the whole would be starkly devoid of feeling. It would be a blunt "He's crazy!" or that even more heartless vernacular "He's plain nuts!"

Dakota is rich in such particles as *-lá*, without absolute meaning as independent words, but giving color and shading to the speech. In straight, objective reporting they have no place, but are useful to the speaker who would convey not only facts and ideas but also his personal attitude and feelings concerning his subject. The renowned orator could sway his hearers by a skillful use of just such particles, as well as by tone, voice modulation, and pace, but even the most prosaic do very well with them.

It was unfortunate and inconvenient for a mother to lack milk for her infant, but she was not regarded as inadequate just for that. Artificial feeding or a wet-nurse met the need. The new mother's milk was not expected to flow promptly, as a rule, and in that case her first baby must be suckled by another woman with a nursing baby. Such a woman received a worthy gift from the relatives of the baby she took care of, for her favor was greatly appreciated by them. No manipulation to induce a flow is reported, but it is said that the baby was put to his mother's breast at certain periods, even though he got no milk at first. In time the milk came. Today a wet-nurse is hardly necessary, because bottles, nipples, and canned milk formulae are available and prove satisfactory. However, under normal conditions, mothers want and expect to nurse their own child. Not long ago a woman was reported to weep when the doctor forbade her for medical reasons.

The old-time "mother's gown" was made with the seam left open from armpit to belt on both sides so that the baby's head was thrust inside for nursing. The gown was very loose, sometimes only hitched together by string ties, so that there was plenty of room and air. The baby was fed at any time of day or night that he became restless. If he whimpered during the night, he was gently patted and soothed back into sounder sleep to the accompaniment of a little hummed tune, to prevent his waking up the neighborhood with his lusty cries. If he was hopelessly awake, he was quickly put to the breast. Any time a baby cried on and on, people asked, "But where is his mother? Why doesn't she feed him?" He carried the entire responsibility of regulating his diet. If he refused the breast, it meant that he simply was not hungry. His stomach was sole judge.

When animal skins were the only material for clothing, the newborn infant wore only a belly band, but he was kept wrapped and snugly bound in soft skins. His diaper was a bit of fawnskin so treated in the tanning (i.e., by smoking it) that it could be washed out and dried and still retain its pliancy. This piece served to hold in place the cattail fuzz gathered in the fall, which answered for absorbent cotton between the legs. When the baby cried and refused to eat, he needed changing. The soiled "cotton" was removed and a fresh quantity substituted before he was happy again. Pulverized rotting wood was sprinkled in all body creases to prevent or lessen chafing and heat rash.

It would seem that the Dakotas did not use the prairie puffballs for body powder as the Cheyennes did. They treated an inflamed navel with the powdery contents of a smaller pod found under withered grasses in autumn. Quite possibly the South Dakota pasque flower was also used for that purpose. This I infer from the fact that the pasque flower is called *hokší-čʼekpá*, which can mean 'baby's navel'; however, it can also mean 'baby's twin', likening the flower to a baby's face. The word *čʼekpá* has both meanings. The botanist at the State Agricultural College, Brookings, called my attention to another plant also listed as *hokší-čʼekpá* and suggested that both plants contained a certain astringency that may have supplied a styptic in case of bleeding.

Very soon the baby became active enough to pull his arms out of his tight wrappings by his own strength and then they were no longer bound with his body. Occasionally he was unwrapped and left free to kick and stretch as he liked. For the first several weeks he was carried in the arms in a tied, later pinned, package of oblong shape, and, wrapped or not, he was held on the lap when his mother sat with him. When he went into the second active stage, and was not wrapped except now and then, as for bedtime, he was carried about on the back of some woman, or his grandfather, held secure under the shawl of the one taking him about. He fell asleep at night while nursing, or while being carried about on someone's back. The mother's or others' rhythmic walk was like a cradle on rockers, and her monotonously hummed tune, whistled through the teeth, was a veritable lullaby that he could not resist. When he felt heavy and lumpy, the mother knew he had fallen asleep. Very gently she eased him off her back and onto his bed. Teton and Yankton babies were regularly carried facing forward. If once on a time the Santees carried children facing rearward, as old book illustrations show, I failed to verify that.

Babies were never forced, never made to sit or stand prematurely. When they began making strenuous efforts to sit up, they were encouraged and helped. If they kept toppling, what did it matter? That was only part of the business of growing up. After a while they had enough balance to stay seated. Then they were barricaded with pillows all around, which also kept them in position. Teething toys were given them to bite on or play with, but none with sharp edges. Most toys were of bone, wood, or deerskin stuffed with soft material. These were made in the shape of small animals such as lizards, turtles, and dogs. Turtles had a special significance and were the most common. They symbolized longevity for the child, and they were eye-catching, too, with bright designs worked all over the "shell" approximating those on real turtles. Each child's turtle was his own in a special sense, for, embedded in the stuffing was that bit of navel string that dried and fell from his body. As part of ceremonial dress, little girls wore their turtle as an ornament on the belt, in the back. If one wore two or three turtles in a row, the extras were her brothers', which she was displaying for them, since boys did not wear their turtles.

Soon enough the first tooth appeared and the baby cried from teething pains and struggled to cram his whole fist into his mouth. He was irritable then and vomited or suffered from diarrhea. "Ah, poor baby! He is making teeth now. Ah, well, everyone must make teeth at some time!" people said, petting him. His mother eased his pain by running a cool finger lightly along the gums where teeth were working through. No other precise remedy or help for this trying period was recalled.

The second stage began when the baby found a way to travel on his own, by creeping and crawling. *Waná slohéla* 'Now he is a little crawler' was the usual answer given those inquiring about him. From then on and until he "had his senses" he was continuously watched, lest he reach for bright embers in the campfire or harm himself in some other way. When he tried to stand, it was time to take both his hands and help him to stand for short periods. He knew when he had had enough and so he sank back down into sitting position. When playing with him, his male relatives crouched beside him and encircled him with both arms, as a banister to which he could cling while he moved gingerly around. No matter in which direction he might fall, the arms were there to catch him.

Careful families did not entrust a baby to young children to carry in their arms, considering them not strong enough to support his spine properly in the event that he threw himself vigorously backward, in high excitement or in a tantrum. Spine injuries resulting in a hunched back were too often due to such an accident, and the Dakotas had a dread of physical deformity. Babies who must still be carried were safe with only their adolescent brothers, sisters and cousins, or with adult relatives, of course. Girls liked to go down the line of tipis showing off the baby to admiring relatives and social relatives such as neighbors. Boys did not care to go too far afield with a baby in their arms.

Nevertheless, it can be said that most Dakota boys rather admirably accepted the baby placed in their charge; they did not balk at the task as a bother or because it was "woman's work." Babies were relatives, too, and kinship demanded that obligatory duties must be fulfilled graciously on their behalf as if they were adults. Every normal boy who had been properly trained in kinship knew that his small relative must be watched and kept from danger. Even when he was at the age to be reticent—and very manly indeed!—he saw nothing incongruous in his tending a helpless infant for a while. To be sure he was usually called on as a last resort, and he somehow contrived to serve out of sight of passerby, behind the tipi or the house, perhaps, but he did not desert his post, and that is my point.

When the baby tried to walk, a rope was stretched between two stakes a few feet apart, and he traveled what for him was a considerable distance by clinging to it. At this stage the small boy and girl finally entered the picture actively as "baby walkers," the assignment they had long waited for. The mother would tell them *Nisųkala mánik'iyapi* 'Cause your little brother to walk', and so, holding him by either arm, two children would happily and with infinite patience walk about with him until he grew accustomed to taking progressive steps. Thus he gained self-confidence in two ways: by clinging to the rope and going it alone, and by being walked by his brothers or sisters. One day he surprised himself by walking independently from one pair of arms to another. If the older children knew that he was able and strong enough but reluctant from fear of falling, they might trick him into walking alone by first interesting him in something shiny and colorful and then holding it at a short distance while urging him to come and get it. Soon he would be walking, then running about on sturdy legs.

From the beginning the baby was talked to in adult language regularly. One day a very young mother was heard talking in adult language to someone in her tipi while her callers halted outside, hesitant to enter. It was only her tiny baby, lying on a bed, kicking. She had been conversing—albeit one-sidedly—on practical matters just as though the infant understood.

This, too, may have a bearing. An informant said, "From childhood, my son was wise beyond his years and that was because of the way his grandfather talked to him." Then she explained that from the day of the child's birth, the old man sat down near him once a day and discoursed on every subject in completely adult language. What were the qualities of a good man; what were courage, and generosity, and hospitality; how indispensible was kinship; and so on. Sometimes he merely rehearsed war stories, in dramatic style and with vigorous gestures, while the baby slept on. He wanted somehow to imbue the child with wisdom and knowledge and a grasp of correct speech, acquired subconsciously, perhaps. In time the child understood.

Mothers sometimes talked meaningless syllables to babies when petting them, but, as a rule, adult speech was employed from the time children began trying to speak. This was important in Dakota because certain consonants have varying degrees of sound, each degree meaning something different. For example, there is medial *č*, aspirate *čᶜ*, and glottalized *č'*. There is *k*, and *kᶜ*, and *k'*. *Maká* is 'skunk'; *mak'á* is 'earth'. Distinctions must be sounded or the words mean something else than what is intended. Small children sometimes found aspirates and glottalizations difficult and made all sounds medial because they take the least effort. Also they reversed such clusters as *tp* and *pt*, *sk* and *ks*, and pronounced *s* like *š (sh)* in the wrong places. Nearly always the first words were *iná* 'mother' and *até* 'father'. Certain Teton groups encouraged the child to say *mamá* when he wanted to nurse, but I have never been sure that *mamá* is a native word. Perhaps it is borrowed from the English word for *mother*. Yankton and Santee did not so refer to mother's breast, as far as I can find out.

Certain baby words were traditional. *Wé* 'blood' was reduplicated *wewé* to indicate a pain or bruise. *Čí*, a bound form connoting smallness, was also reduplicated *čičí* to mean something the child feared. The mythical scare figure known as *hįhákaǧa*, a spirit in the form of an immense owl said to throw naughty children into its ear, was definitely a *čičí*. A worm, bug, or anything alive that was tiny was a *čičíla*. A fretful child was quieted by the warning "Shh! Don't you hear a *čičí* outside? Do not cry . . . or else!" The *čičí* was never faced openly, never defined, and perhaps its very indefiniteness contributed to its value as a scare. Any piece of fur was a *čičí* to small children. Many babies recoiled from my fox neckpiece, thinking it was alive, and they called it *čičí*. The elder collaterals who acted as the child's *wók'okip'eka* in order to control him was not a *čičí*. The distinction must lie between the known as the unknown. The elder collateral was after all a familiar, whereas the *čičíla* or *čičí* was strange and incomprehensible, something alive, real or mythical, whose behavior was unpredictable.

Káka, a purely fabricated word, meant something untouchable because loathsome. Feces is the stock example but anything messy and unpleasant was also *káka*. From *mní* 'water', *mnimní* meant 'I want a drink of water; I am thirsty'. *Pápa* means 'dried jerked beef', but to the child it meant any kind of food, 'I am hungry'. This word does not parallel *máma*, and neither has reference to a parent. *P'ápa* meaning father requires an aspirate initial *p'*, if written as a Dakota word.

These were standard words that small children taught their baby brother or sister, and adults understood them. Sometimes an original child made up his own vocabulary and insisted on it until people understood. One little boy said *k'uláč'iye* by which he meant 'Pick me up and carry me'. He said *lapótątą* when he wished to go riding in a horse-drawn vehicle. Such words defy analysis.

Abú-abú meant 'I am sleepy'. *Abú* was the singing syllable in impromptu lullabies, sung to children while they were gently rocked or swayed in the arms. A child whimpering in sleep was lulled back into sound slumber by easy taps on his shoulder in time with *abú* at each tap.

His daily routine varied all the time. Strictly speaking it was no routine, for he never lived by schedule. Time of this, time for that, was unknown to him. He wakened early and roused the family, demanding food. Then he slept and played according to his inclination; there was no attempt to prevent him or bend him. Even so the household did not revolve around him. Wherever his mother went, he must go — still eating, sleeping, and playing.

When he showed interest and made initial attempts he was encouraged to feed himself; to hold the cup while drinking; to carry food to his mouth without accident, and, as he grew older, to take off his footwear — with assistance at first. He was praised when he could do it alone and praised even more when he could put on his moccasins and finally distinguish right from left, which was not too hard after he learned that the inner sole was straight, the outer curving. When he could wrap the bands neatly and tightly around his ankles and could tie his moccasin strings securely, he had arrived. This was usually not until he was roughly six or seven.

Toddlers were called upon to perform very simple acts, like blowing out a match. Smokers held out their match for the smallest child to put out, until he took it as his special duty. And if someone forgot and extinguished his own match, the child cried from slight and had to be appeased.

Very early children were taught to dance to their grandfather's singing and rhythmic beating on his hand drum, and they were applauded with delighted laughter and hand clapping, which made them dance all the harder, to make their audience gladder still. They liked little dolls—anything shaped out of skins and swaddled like an infant would do—and hummed *abú-abú-abú* while holding it against their cheek and shaking their heads in time, "to put baby to sleep"—imitating the way they were put to sleep. Both sexes did this, often before they were two years old.

Soon enough they learned to make a verb of *káka* by accenting the first syllable, and then they were led outdoors. In time they knew where to go and took themselves. There could be no fixed place but whenever camp was made, it was always a vague *t'ilázata* 'back of the tipi' (i.e., out of sight of passerby along the parade track). The main thing to learn was not to *káka* indoors or where they could be seen. Bodily functions were regarded as normal, natural, and were not sedulously watched. A child of four knew when and where to go and managed without constant adult supervision, as long as he stayed well. Unless he was sick with diarrhea or was constipated and feverish, he did not draw attention.

Once burned he knew enough to fear the flames that had fascinated him before, if he was a child with average intelligence. Children around eight to ten years of age found it irresistible when playing together in the evening to reach a long stick into the outdoor fire until the tip was aglow and then wave the stick about in midair to describe curves, circles, and other shapes in the dark. "Stop that! Playing with fire will deaden your bladders and you will wet the bed!" was a fairly good threat since it was unpleasant to wake up in a puddle; but only a temporary one. The very next time that their elders sat talking outside at night, some daring child was sure to introduce that pastime again.

Until a child could understand reasoning, he was not punished or blamed and disciplined for his blunder. The treatment he enjoyed from his elders was altogether conciliatory. An adult who held a child responsible, as if he were mature and reasonable, proved himself to be immature and unreasonable. "He makes himself a child" was said of him.

Vices—crying without a valid reason, getting cross, making faces at other children or at strangers to indicate hostility, playing with one's own genitals, abusing the puppy (also the cat, in later times), playing with fire, kicking, or scratching—were all corrected by the standard formula

"Nobody does that . . . it is not done." But babies and very small children who did not yet understand words were not directly rebuked, not even with that mild argument. Instead their attention was quickly diverted to something else of more interest, with shrill exclamations that made them think it was very important and exciting. Or the grandmother or some other woman might snatch up a child who was misbehaving and fling him expertly onto her back, draw the blanket tight about him, and go somewhere else, to new scenes and new attractions, volubly enthusiastic about "something yonder that we must not miss!" — until he forgot to be naughty. His natural curiosity and his ability to sustain a mood, a grudge, or a peeve, for very long, were relied on to correct his behavior — and it did. To scold or moralize would be a waste of effort: this other was the way.

Later on, around perhaps at age eight or nine, children were sometimes given to pouting and had to be ridiculed out of that by older siblings of their sex. Very small children did not usually pout silently in that way because they lacked determination. Yet in some instances even ridicule failed to cure the pouting habit, and adults who pouted were known for it. *Hé wačʔíkʔo sʔá* 'That one is a habitual pouter' (so watch out!) Adult pouters were not pleasant to deal with; even their joking relatives must act gingerly toward them.

In handling a still unreasonable child, there was nothing in the mother's tone to generate fear of her. The typical mother played down the seriousness of his fault or mistake, and, as though she were mildly amused, she encouraged him to laugh it off as something not important and therefore not worth repeating. If he struck her, accidentally or in anger, she pretended to cry softly, her hands over her face. Then in contrition he tried to stop her by pulling her hands down and then embracing her to comfort her, as she comforted him when he was unhappy. It was not until the child had his full senses — meaning he could be reasoned with — that a sorely tried mother sometimes spoke sharply because he made the same blunder too regularly out of heedlessness, and perhaps hurt himself as a result.

I have said earlier that very small children and babies were applauded for walking, dancing, or singing, but the hand clapping diminished into almost none as they grew older. It would not do to bring them up too bold and self-assertive — as though they were alone in the world — since such traits did not fit into the *tʿiyóšpaye*, and finally into camp circle life, where deference to relatives was the ideal.

Certain portents were drawn from the unconscious actions of babies and very small children, who were half-believed to possess a prescience denied work-a-day adults. Earlier I listed some of these; for example, if a child cut off his hair—a sign of mourning—or played at burying, wailing aloud and being sorrowful, he was predicting a death in his family. Similarly, it was said that if a two- or three-year-old voluntarily brought in sticks for the fire in summer, or held his palms toward the flames as if he had come in from the cold outside, he was foretelling a severe winter ahead. If a male child was strongly attracted to a pregnant woman, her baby would be a girl, and vice versa. A variant, which seems to be more consistent with typical courtship behavior, is that if a male child acted bashful toward a pregnant woman, her baby would be a girl, and vice versa.

Instead of the hummed *abú-abú-abú* or the random tune whistled through the teeth for putting a baby to sleep, sometimes a song with sensible words was invented and sung to a familiar or an improvised tune, which amused him as he gradually understood the meaning. Such lines could be on any subject, often a quite silly one. An aged informant sang such a song that so caught her little son's fancy that he demanded it regularly for a while.

> The meadowlark is singing.
> He is saying horrid things:
> "Your little boy is naughty—
> He wets the bed at night!"
> The meadowlark is singing!

The child countered with his own version—"so cleverly!" she told me with an indulgent chuckle. "He sang, 'I hear him! I hear him! But, mother, the meadowlark is lying!'" was the meaning of his song.

Little children were led to believe that the meadowlark spoke fluent Dakota, knowingly. It delighted them that the lark seemed to say the very words that grown-ups fitted to the pattern and lilt of his song and imputed to him. If, happily, a lark was singing at the time that a child was fretful or naughty, it was a sure way to divert him. Some lines were invented on the spot, while others were standard. Of these latter perhaps the most universally known was *Ptéčʼíčala pʼí napį!* 'Buffalo calf liver rich and sweet'; *pʼí* 'liver'; and *napį* 'palatably oily', like sweet cream, for example, or broiled ribs dripping with rich juices, a great delicacy.

To distract the child completely, his grandmother might straighten herself to her full height from the task over which she has been bending, and turn her full attention to the lark. "Stop that! You make my mouth water!" she might complain. "Who can remember the taste of fresh raw liver anymore?"—meaning that there had not been a decent butchering in many days. Entertained by the undaunted lark and the old woman's losing battle, the child would usually forget to be naughty anymore.

As soon as he was able to hold things without dropping them, the baby was given a strip of lightly boiled buffalo or deer meat to suck on. The bloody juices were thought to give him strength, and likewise the meaty bones he gnawed on to "make teeth" and sharpen those already present.

Said an old man, "Our children were straight-limbed and sturdy and grew sound teeth because they ate animal flesh—nothing like the *čočó* 'mushy' breadstuffs and candies of today. Our native diet suited us. Nor did children suffer from bone disorders unless they had been hurt. Only very old people sometimes had bone pains that crippled them."

Many informants insist that the so-called children's diseases were unknown in their time, and that neither children nor adults took cold from ordinary exposure. If they got a soaking while on a journey and had to go to bed wet, they experienced no lasting effects. At the worst they might have a runny nose and a cough that lasted a short while, but without fever or aches. To this day "I have a cold" is expressed by an idiom: *Howáȟpa* 'I cough'.

Scrofula was an abhorrent scourge that, though not new, became alarmingly common at the beginning of the reservation period, but gradually diminished until perhaps 1925, when it became rare.[2] Mothers, believing it to be contagious, not inherited, were in constant fear of it for their children and tried furtively to keep them from playing with one who was afflicted by it: "Both my children caught scrofula from playmates, for it does not run in our family." Once it started scrofula had to be left to develop, since there was no cure for it. When finally it healed, after two or more years of oozing pus, there remained a hideous dark red-to-purple scar along the side of the neck below the jawbone, sometimes from ear to chin. In severe cases both sides were affected and disfigured for life. At first resembling an embedded egg, it grew in size and area and there was no checking it before it broke and became an open sore.

Even if contagious scrofula must begin somewhere. The theory was that it was caused by a mole. The name of the disease is *wahį́heya-ó* 'mole — to shoot'. If a person was accidentally within range when a mole surfaced, it shot an invisible poisonous dart that found its mark on his neck — and scrofula set in! Lest this vicious thing happen to them, children were taught to run away from places where moles had been burrowing and had left little ridges of dirt.[3]

Stomach upset, if not due to teething disturbances, was caused by unripe wild berries and fruits eaten without mother's knowledge. She would forbid it if she knew. The standard remedy was a certain white earth that was bittersweet and astringent — like alum — but was not unpleasant to swallow when mixed with water. This earth was allegedly obtained in certain regions of the Badlands of South Dakota, rather near Hot Springs, and was called *mak'ízita*, a contraction of *mak'á* 'earth' and *izíta* 'to emit smoke'. This is also the name of the White River, flowing through the Badlands. Mothers traded for this earth in small quantities, and managed to keep it on hand for their children in the days before doctors and commercial drugs were available. Even after that there was still faith in the efficacy of *mak'ízita*, and for some time there was considerable traffic in the powder.

For the most part, constipation was a seasonal ailment among children, during chokecherry processing time. They could not resist the cakes of mashed cherries spread out to dry in the sun, unmindful of the dire warning, "Stop eating that! Or we shall have to dig you out with a stick — the broken seeds will block your passage." This was an allusion to one of the more vulgar *Iktómi* tales, telling of a day when the trickster cheated someone out of his berries, and then ate so many of them that he became sick and had to operate on himself.[4]

Bruises were left to nature for healing but swellings were treated with poultices of various kinds made by crushing juicy plants and leaves that were known to be effective, or by rubbing with various brews. Just which plants, or which herb brews, seem no longer clear. Some, at least, were the herb doctor's secret, which he alone administered, with or without incantations. "Call So-and-so," friends advised. "For this particular ailment he alone has the cure." In other words, he was a specialist.

Many seasoned warriors were skillful bone-setters, from practice on fractures sustained on the warpath. When my little sister broke the ulna of her left arm during an all-Dakota celebration far from town, I watched an old warrior take care of her. He split soft pine into little sticks, hitched them together parallel, by means of interlacing cords, and so fashioned a protecting case that he put around the arm, after first working gently, with sensitive fingers, to fit the broken ends together. As soon as possible, my father rushed the child to a doctor, who felt of the injured spot and then said, "This was set by an expert. Let it mend as it is." All he did was replace the emergency case with one of plaster. In a few weeks we could not tell where the break had been, unless we felt for it, so straight was the bone.

Although no superstition attaches to this, if a child cried at bedtime from growing pains, his mother or someone else beguiled him by carefully mixing in her palm a paste of ashes or dirt with her spittle, and then finger-painting a lizard or turtle crawling realistically up the aching shin. "There, now, go to sleep. He will cure you in the night." Partly from the soothing cool application and partly from faith in its promise, the child slept. By morning he was ready to go again at his usual lively pace.

It is said that in ancient times, severe burns were quickly healed if fresh buffalo dung was spread over the affected parts, evenly. But this could hardly have been the regular treatment, since it would be the rarest of coincidences for someone to be burned while buffalo lingered in the vicinity. It had to be buffalo dung, and it had to be still moist, I was told.

Perhaps I was eight or nine when I first heard of treating a burn with fresh buffalo manure, but I had forgotten it until informants spoke of it not long ago. When we camped overnight at Cheyenne Agency while on a trip across the state, someone told my parents that a young girl was very sick in a tipi nearby, so my mother went to see her and took me along. It was proper to visit the sick even if they were strangers.

The girl had been very severely burned. She lay across the honor place, her entire back and one shoulder freshly bandaged. The old grandmother who watched by her told my mother, "The white holy man [government physician], he is very kind, but whenever he changes the wrappings, my poor grandchild suffers terribly! Oh, if only there were fresh buffalo dung to be had, for then it could be left on and she would recover quickly!" My mother said some kind words and left a money gift and we came away, but we heard later that the girl died shortly after our visit. I remember that scene vividly and the old woman's words. I remember the girl's father's name, too. It was *Zuzéča-wakpá* 'Snake River'; this could mean a meandering river, snake-like.

A final bit of primitive doctoring that came to my attention was too remote for even the oldest informant to vouch for. He told it as myths are told, with the quotative ending *keyápi* 'so it is said', implying, "but don't hold me responsible for it!" Incredible and unsponsored though it is, I give it now.

If a festered finger did not heal, it was treated by a toad. Not any toad, but one that had first been set apart by the holy man who painted him with ceremonial red paint, and made a relative of him. Then he addressed him: "*Mitˁákuye* 'my relative', I implore you to heal this finger!" Then, while the child slept, his finger was inserted into the toad's mouth and the toad sucked and sucked on it, and then, when he had drawn out all the poison, he left it, limp and wrinkled but well rid of the "badness" so that the healthy tissues could heal.

A gift of gratitude was then saddled onto the toad's back before it was turned loose to hop away into the grasses. The giving was the ceremonial necessity; the gift would soon drop off, tied loosely on so it would. Perhaps it was a tiny piece of red buckskin, or, better yet, since moccasins rated second only to a horse as the appropriate gift, perhaps it was a miniature pair of moccasins. I have no comment to make about this except to say that it could be mythological, a fragment out of context.

Mothers were wrapped up in their children and played charmingly with them when alone in the tipi. If other children were present, they paid attention to them all. Because all the *tˁiyóšpaye* children, the collaterals' offspring, looked to her for help and comfort and reassurance, a woman was careful not to seem to shut them out by hugging her own child passionately to her heart unless he was a mere baby and was fretful and needed loving. More than once I have observed a woman momentarily lost in fondling her child with natural delight—only to turn at another woman's child standing near and make over him next.

One particular mother who was putting her child to bed first whispered endearments into his ear while he listened with a happy grin. She even lapsed into his baby lingo, which delighted him all the more. Because she was deliberately being "naughty" with him by resorting to something usually avoided, it was great fun to him. "This my little son is very bad," she said with a scowl, while tickling him for his merry laughter. "I shall have to spank him!" Whereupon the child obliged by rolling over on his stomach while she dealt him some light taps on his buttocks, and it was a high joke between them. When someone entered the tipi unexpectedly, both mother and child came to speedy order.

In such ways Dakota children enjoyed a great deal of private mothering and found cozy the gentle warmth that surrounded them. Apparently it was enough to last a lifetime. When a certain old woman was being unkindly treated, she remarked, *Etáš tók! Iná éka č‘áš t‘emáȟila k’ų́!* This idiomatic phrase means 'Who cares?', or 'What of it? Enough for me that my mother loved me!' It meant that any slight by someone less significant was beneath the speaker's notice.

Gradually from his mother's behavior toward others, the child came to see that he did not have exclusive claim on her; that she owed various duties and kinship courtesies to others, too. And so, whenever they were present, he waited. Nor did he expect lavish kisses all the time, for kissing was an event among the Dakotas. It represented excessive joy, relief, or grief over some crisis barely passed.

In her life story, a woman described her nearly unbearable anxiety when her little girl became lost in the wood during berrying time: "When the searchers found and restored her to me, I could not contain my joy and relief. I had to caress and kiss her repeatedly, for a long time."

Another woman related the following:

When the military ordered her people of the *Húkpap‘aya* band to be floated down the Missouri to Fort Randall as prisoners of war, with Sitting Bull, she was about eight years old: "Late at night my mother woke me. She did not say why she was trembling. She only whispered, '*Č‘ų́kš*, put on all your [calico] dresses, one over another, as quickly as you can in the dark. I will return soon and take you to your aunt.' I did as she said.[5]

We stole inside the stockade and hastened to the log house where my aunt lived with her husband, the trader. It was not easy to dodge the sentry, but we managed it safely. As she was leaving, my mother pressed me tight to her breast and kissed and kissed me, all over my face and head, and seemed unable to stop. *T‘ewáȟila k’ų́!* 'How I loved her, my own!' she kept murmuring, but she did not stop.

I never saw my mother again. By morning the entire camp had vanished; and, everywhere, those who for various reasons had been allowed to stay wailed as for the dead. This I realized when I was older and could think: my mother knew I would be safe with my aunt. So she gave me up and went forth alone into the unknown. She died at Fort Randall shortly after arriving there.

What I call kissing was expressed as *i-ipút'aka* 'mouth pressure against'. The lips were gently pressed on another's cheek or forehead in tender caress. Such a kiss was accepted passively. A child might enjoy this display of his mother's love but he was not obligated to reciprocate at the time. When he, too, felt moved to kiss his mother, he pressed his own lips on her cheek.

The cooperating, mouth-to-mouth kiss was not required, nor—or so I was told—was it conceivable until it was learned through outside contact. At first sight it was a silly and disturbing thing that white people did; but gradually it was accepted for one more alien peculiarity, as more and more instances of it were observed. Especially shocking was the prolonged, empathic, and unabashed kiss of screen lovers. Now, I think, practically everyone is quite used to seeing it in motion pictures, but I recall a time some years ago when we invited a woman from the hinterland to her first movie. Very soon she became so ill that we had to leave. Later she apologized and said, "For no reason [i.e., no crisis], all they did was kiss and kiss with mouth hard together. It was senseless." She had failed to follow the story being unfolded and was only nauseated by such "unwarranted" behavior.

13

Preadolescence

Until the Dakota child was *wač'įksapa* 'wise in his mind, aware'; until he could *wíyukča* 'think', specifically, 'reason'; until he could remember and profit by his experiences, he was humored, fed, clothed, and kept from bodily harm, and very little was required of him in return. Being still unreasonable he was neither blamed nor punished; he was not struck, then or later. I speak here of the ideal treatment of children by the vast majority of people, though it must be realized that occasionally a careless woman struck her children. Such a woman incurred general disapproval.

The preadolescent had no duties until he assumed them voluntarily, and no formal training to speak of. He was given no moral or ethical reasons why he should or should not do thus-and-so. He was only told, "Nobody does that; it is not done." The only systematic training given him was in relation to those about him. Almost before he could talk, kinship terms and duties were relentlessly insisted upon by his elders. The terms first, and, gradually, the specific duties those terms indicated were implemented, for it was essential that he see everyone in proper relation to himself. He might be impersonal with animals, but not people. The baby was told, "Shake hands with this one, for she is your aunt" (or whatever the relationship), and his little hand was held extended for the aunt to take as she addressed him by kinship term, "Oh, my little nephew!" Thus he unconsciously absorbed the terms and the obligatory attitude and behavior appertaining to them severally until they became an automatic response.

The child was praised each time he made the right kinship move, even if by accident, and he was promptly set straight if he made a false one. Everyone helped him, even chance callers. Three incidents illustrate this practice.

1. Two elderly sisters stopped to pet a two-year-old boy on his grandmother's back and one of them exclaimed, "My, my! How fast our little *t'akóš* is growing! Before long he will be riding horseback!"

They called him "son-in-law" because he was a classificatory brother to their daughter's husband. The child replied with the one complete sentence he had mastered. *Tᶜaló makʾú pó!* 'Give me meat!' An instant chorus of protest went up from all the women within earshot. "Oh, no! This is all wrong! A *tᶜakóš* must hunt and bring meat to his *učí-ší*—not ask them for it!" They pretended to be surprised and horrified.

2. Some years ago a young boy announced, "Sophie is so good to me that I want to marry her when I grow up." Again the hue and cry from the women: "For shame! No one marries a *hakáta!*" Sophie was not a relative of birth but the boy's sister in social kinship, who lived in his home. The very idea was preposterous, particularly because their two families had always been very close friends. All of this was implied in the women's exaggerated cries.

3. A man napping under a tree was wakened by a child's shrill scream nearby. He rolled over and eyed the situation drowsily, until he saw the trouble. The child's playmate, a somewhat bigger boy, was hogging the improvised swing, while he screamed for his turn on it. "Hey!" the man called out. "Let your little uncle have the swing next. That's no way to treat a relative!" With that he went back to sleep. He had done his bit to correct a slight kinship difficulty, even if he was indifferent about the effect of his advice. Some adult had to interfere and he was the only one nearby. That's how it was: a universal concern among all responsible adults.

Dakota children were guarded closely. If parents left the young alone for long it was extraordinary behavior on their part. Always there was some relative to keep an eye on them. In addition, certain precautions were taken to insure their safety, just in case. For example, many parents tattooed their child to insure for him a safe passage to spirit-land when he died. This was, apparently, based on the vague notion that the old woman guarding the *wanáǧi-tᶜačʾáku* 'ghosts' path', the Milky Way, allowed only such as could show her a tattoo mark to proceed. All who could not do so she pushed off the path, to fall through space and wander bodiless over the earth.

No one is tattooed anymore; the custom died with the belief. When I was a child I used to see such marks on the faces of old women. Always there was a dot smaller than a dime on the exact center of the forehead and a trifle above the eyebrow line. Sometimes there were also one or two very fine lines, rarely more, down the chin. The marks were blue or reddish purple, and appeared nowhere else on the face. I cannot recall any marks on men's faces, but one chief I knew very well had a small broken ring the size of a half-dollar tattooed on his left wrist—like a camp circle.

Other families provided their children with a *maȟpíya tʻóla* 'little blue sky', tied with a red thong to their forelock or around the neck or wrist. The thong was first soaked thoroughly so that it would dry in a knot permanently. The little blue sky was a safeguard against all danger but especially against becoming lost. It was not removed until the child was old enough to take care of himself. Little blue skies were of many fantastic shapes, no two alike, and were said to be made mysteriously by certain old women endowed with supernatural power.

Such women were very rare, perhaps never more than two or three within the entire Dakota nation at the same period. One hardly dared ask how they worked and with what materials. Even if not actually feared for the secretive and forbidding creatures they were, they were certainly reverenced for their allegedly witchlike skill. Parents gave important gifts for one little blue sky, no bigger than the first joint of a baby's finger. A horse for one was not exorbitant, seeing what it would do for their child.

A six-year-old girl from the hinterland was once entered at our mission school wearing a thing tied to her hair. It was said to be a *maȟpíya tʻóla*, and, if so, I have seen one. It had the texture of glass and looked as though it had been dropped from a crucible in a molten state, to harden into any chance shape as it fell. She would not remove it, but she allowed us who were her friends to examine it. As I recall, it was quite black, but, when held up to the sun, it glowed an exquisite blue of highest intensity. Incidentally, the little girl cried every time she had to walk up or down stairs, and finally went home, still wearing her amulet. The *maȟpíya tʻóla* was a novelty by 1910. It went the way of many other cultural elements, with the breakup of camp circle society. Today the native term is scarcely known, much less its specific meaning. My information on its alleged manufacture is scanty enough.

One woman reported:

I saw a *wakáȟkala* 'elderly woman' being led toward a small black tipi set well back from the circle so I left my play and followed. She was bent almost double and walked facing the ground, but now and then she cast her black eyes actively about from under mannish, thick, and bushy eyebrows in a way that was frightening.

The younger woman who led her along settled her inside and tied the doorflap securely and weighted it with logs. Then she stepped back and waited until dense black smoke poured out from the top of the tipi and the *wakákala* could be heard singing—not a real tune but more a moaning, as if in agony. Thereupon she turned and saw me. "Go away, grandchild," she said. "This tipi is *wak'á* 'holy', and the old woman, too, is holy. She sings for power to make *mahpíya t'óla*. She wants to be alone, so go far away." I went. *Wakákala*, the name for the mythical witch woman already mentioned, was often applied, as here, to strange old women whose motives were obscure and might be sinister.

In ancient lore, it is said, the sky was a deity under whose endless view nothing was really lost. It is thinkable that the *mahpíya t'óla* amulet was relied on to guard little children who still did not know their way around because, by some magic, it was actually the sky—in epitome, as it were.

There were also those who pinned their faith on a tiny sacred bundle. A veritable religious relic, it was worn on a string around the neck. A holy man was asked to make it and was paid handsomely for his work.

One man told how his bundle saved the lives of his mother, himself, his elder sister, and the baby on her back. While journeying on foot from one camp circle to another, they lost their way under an overcast sky and wandered over the trackless prairie, until they were exhausted and their water supply gave out. Suspecting that they were walking in circles, the boy planted an arrow before they went on one day, and found it not far from the place where they stopped for the night. This so alarmed his mother that she said to him, "Son, take off the thing your father [a famous diviner] placed on you, and do with it as he taught you. If ever it can help us, it is now."

The boy took off the sacred bundle and struck it to earth four times very slowly, and then the party staggered on. The sky had cleared meantime, and the sun blazed hot on them, but at least they could retake their bearing. Presently a cloud formed in the west "no bigger than a man's hand," and grew rapidly as it approached. When it was overhead, it showered on them so generously that they caught enough water on skin to refresh themselves and continue their journey to safety.

The narrator of this remembered that he was eight years old, but he could not remember when or how he stopped wearing the bundle. No doubt his father removed it when he was satisfied that his son was capable enough. "I never thought of unwrapping it to examine its material content." It was so very holy; he might set free the imprisoned power and leave himself unprotected. He understood that a tiny thing charged with unlimited potency was the core of his bundle but he never saw it. Maybe it was a bit of little blue sky?

There might have been other material safeguards also, which are no longer remembered; none came to my notice besides these that I have described.

But, after all, physical protection was not the only important consideration. Tribal prestige was just as essential, and it was never too early to begin ensuring that for the child. This was done through ceremonial giving of gifts and feasts in the child's name, thus making that name count. Then, in after years, people would say, "There is a man!" (or woman), meaning, there is one whose very existence benefited others. Even should he one day be pitiful, infirm and alone in the world, his reputation would command the respect of the tribe. That was his family's goal for him.

One of the earliest feasts given in the child's name was for his ear-piercing rite, at which time his real or serious name, as opposed to nickname, was publicly announced. A horse or other present of comparable worth was given to the high-ranking man chosen to perform the rite, again in the child's name. Always the lobes were pierced and sometimes the helices, too, for good measure, thus leaving no doubt of parental devotion. To reach adulthood with "white" ears—that is, untouched, clean of holes—was to be pitiable, as one who just grew without loving attention. To lack relatives to honor one was to be poorest of the poor. Conversely, to possess dutiful relatives concerned with building up one's prestige was to be rich, even without owning many things.

Children had their way, unless it would be harmful to them. Arbitrary orders were not given merely to exact blind obedience. From the time they could be reasoned with, the why of each rule or command was explained to them. If still unreasonable small children insisted hysterically on having their way and must be silenced before their crying and screaming could disturb the neighborhood, they were deliberately lied to, or threatened with something they had learned to fear. "He was in such a tantrum that I had to 'make a fear' for him to get his attention."

They might be told, "Hush, that sounds like your sister [or brother, if the child were a girl] coming. How cross she gets when you cry. But she can't hear you yet, better stop before she gets here!" "Shh! listen to that commotion outside? It must be the híhá-kágá going by looking for naughty children. Be still, or he will throw you into his ear!" Then, when the child stopped crying to listen and wait for the worst, his mother, or whoever was trying to control him, put him instantly at his ease by calling out, "Tell that híhá-kágá we have only good children in this tipi. Go away, Owl spirit! Find other children, off yonder somewhere!"

As previously mentioned, the híhá-kágá was conceived of as a spirit in the form of an owl, with an enormous ear into which he threw naughty children. In the legend the defiant culture hero finds himself there. Already it is filled with the youth of the land. The hero slashes his way out with his magic blade and sets the other prisoners free. For this he is given the chief's daughter for a wife. There are several variants of this tale.[1]

Should someone enter at that instant, he said to the mother, "Do not fear the híhá-kágá. Since he heard no crying in this tipi, he passed swiftly on. Already he is several tipis down the line!" With a sigh of relief, the mother said to her child, "Ah, now we are quite safe, and we shall be all night because we will be quiet!" Grown-ups went along with the child, acting scared to bolster him with the assurance that he did not stand alone, that he could feel secure. In this little play, a brief deception was useful. It seemed the only right method of managing babies and small children. Always the child's naughtiness was made unimportant, while his "goodness" was stressed positively, until he was persuaded that he had been a pretty good boy (or girl) all the while, and since the approval was so pleasant, he determined to continue being good. In this way his fault of the moment was casually neutralized and he was spared from shame. Even outsiders, sensing what was going on as they entered, cooperated, for everyone was familiar with this standard technique for dealing with very small children who could not be reached through adult reasoning.

In more recent times they were told, "Look! There comes a white man collecting school children! Hide, and keep still, or he will take you far away.

Many die there!" Or they said, "If the *atéyapi* [the 'father', i.e., the reservation superintendent] hears of this, he will put you in jail!" I may point out that "The Great White Father," that grandiose name for the president in many news stories, is not a Dakota term. The term is *t'ųkášilayapi*, which, in its way, is an even more impressive title. For it means 'grandfather,' whereas the local superintendent is only a father. The terms imply hierarchical authority based on relative wisdom and power. A grandfather, being older and hence wiser and more experienced, was a cut above a father.

Universally feared was the mythical witch-woman called *Wakąkala* 'Someone Full Of Years,' an eternal and durable old woman whose special aversion was naughty children. They had better be good—or else! This character, known only by name, caused children to be wary of old people who were strangers, since any one of them might turn out to be the *Wakąkala* herself, if not her male counterpart!

There were also local scare figures. One was *Sióko*, whose very name held the children of two contiguous reservations consistently in line. Another was an innocuous old man named *Kahązi* who was the terror of small boys in a certain region. They identified him with the old man of legend who avenged an insult to him by releasing water from his body that drowned all the people.[2] Though too senile to realize the dreadful role attributed to him, poor *Kahązi* remained powerful even long after his death. This is the flood story, in which an old man avenges an insult by puncturing his testicles and creating a flood that drowns the people. Little boys were controlled by the warning that if they were naughty, "*Kahązi* could start another flood!"

Children had no reason to fear their grandparents, on whose love and selflessness only they could rely. Sometimes an obstreperous child was quickly brought to terms by the acting of some playful old woman who was a stranger to him. Suddenly she might scream, "Oh! Oh! Hold me, hold me! *Ak'é tókeča amáu wé!*" 'Once more I am becoming "someway"'. This meant she was about to have fits. She would moan, rock, and roll her eyes frighteningly—all to good effect. Meanwhile, all the women present would pretend to be scared of her, and exclaim, "Oh, yes! Hold her, somebody!" The child was sure to stop short, stare at the extraordinary sight, and then fly to his mother or some other relative for safety—and remain very still from then on.

I saw a scene like that. At a feast, when a four-year-old boy's hilarity mounted to hysteria as he darted repeatedly out of his mother's arms and went tumbling over the orderly feasters' feet, an old woman rasped out, "*Háu! Háu!* [a meaningless vocable expressive of misery]. Pity me, you people! Pity me! 'It' is coming over me again! I shall be *tókeča* ['someway'] in a moment. Unless," she added slyly, "unless that very active little boy rushes some *t'aspá opémnipi* 'wrapped apple' to me!" "Wrapped apple" was the name for pie, because the first pies introduced were apple. The women urged in mock fear, "Hurry! Get wrapped apple for her, quick! Before she gets 'someway' again!" The terrified youngster hung from his mother's skirts, imploring her to hurry with some pie. From the food to be served, the waiters laughingly handed her a cut. The "silenced" old woman munched it happily, suddenly restored. Of course, it was the child who was silenced.

His mother gathered him into her ample shawl and sat whispering in his ear while he stole an occasional glance at the old woman, out of the corner of his eye, to make sure that she had been really appeased. "The old woman was upset, because you were naughty. She is all right now, because you are good," his mother said. "You better remain good—or she might frighten us all again!"—as though the entire company depended on him to keep the peace by behaving properly.

But such scenes were never prolonged. They ended the instant that the child created a countersituation. I have never known a normal adult who did not laugh at the memory of his fears at such a time as this, or who developed a trauma from it. Children outgrew their early fears as well as beliefs after they could see them for what they were. Soon enough they took sides with those adults who scared younger children into compliance by the same method. They even got fun out of it, as much as to say, "Give them the works! We had to take this. They'll find out, as we have, that really there is nothing to it!" With some condescension they adopted the same line to control a fractious younger sibling "who still did not know any better" but would, in time. The thing was an endless tradition. Little girls would "make a fear" for their doll; but, lest they be thought too harsh, would at the same time give grown-ups a knowing smile that meant, "It is all right, I am only fooling her. She has been naughty!"

After children were amenable to reason, the Dakotas lied or equivocated to them hardly at all. There must be an invincible dividing line between fact and fiction, and children soon learned that myths and fairy tales were a thing apart. Even weighty matters were confided to a child old enough to grasp them, without prettifying or glossing over them.

When a six-year-old lad stood staring at his grandmother's expressionless face as she lay in her coffin, and then asked, "But why is grandmother sleeping so still?," he was given the stark truth. "She is not sleeping. She is dead." With an indifferent "Oh!" the boy walked off, satisfied with the answer. He was not yet ready to ask further about the mystery of death. Had he been ready, had he inquired for details, he would surely have been told as much as any adult knows about it.

One man once said to his nine-year-old son, "Since you ask, I will tell you. I will never lie to you. But get it straight; you are old enough to understand it." He ended by warning, "Guard this well. For it is the kind of thing 'not to be told.'" Thus even secrets were confided to a child responsible enough to keep them.

Preadolescents, because they did not understand the tragic side of a *heyók'a* ceremony, were particularly delighted with the antics of the clowns as they publicly made fools of themselves in an effort to appease the thunders. But for a normally controlled elder relative to act suddenly crazy was very upsetting to them. They expected consistently adult dignity from their elders. One woman told how it shocked her to come by accident upon a scene in which her own mother and aunt (father's sister) were tangling bodily in an effort to wrest some trivial item from the other, until both were laughing and rolling on the ground. They were young women, but to her they seemed too old for such conduct. "I hated it," she said. "For a long time I secretly disliked my mother for having forgot herself, rolling around like a child."

On the whole life was a paradise for the young, until from inner urge they assumed responsibility. Everyone worked but they. Nor was their indifference a matter for grave concern. They simply were not ready— that was all. Some even idled from preference and remained motionless and abstract for short periods, amid the hurry and bustle of life all around them. Even then no special notice was taken of them unless they were in the way and must be asked to move to one side. The extreme understanding and patience of oldsters with this characteristic of their preadolescents was remarkable; apparently they were not disturbed by it.

If he suddenly decided to work a little, he was not therefore expected to take over the whole task and complete it. For the novelty of it, a girl might fill her own tiny bucket at berrying time while her mother filled large pails. Or she might, if she liked, go after *t'įpsila* 'prairie turnips' with her grandmother and perhaps enjoy spotting the familiar plants for her to dig—for a little while. When the grandmother sat down at last to peel and braid the white tubers by their long taproots into a rope to dry, she might, if the mood struck her, pick out the smallest ones and braid them. They were hers to keep, for decoration or for provender when she played at camping, or for giving away to one of her friends. Her berries also were hers to do with as she liked. If in a generous impulse she added them to the family's store, she was praised and thanked, but they were not demanded of her. Her brother was usually engaged at vigorous play, or off on his pony with other young boys. He, too, had the same freedom to be idle or to work.

What I am trying to say is that children were left with a minimum of obvious direction and interference. There seemed no need to devise activities and more activities to keep them interested and busy. How could grown-ups know what would interest a child at any given moment? And why must he be everlastingly "busy"? It was as if the grown-ups agreed to "let him be . . . when he wants to do something, he will!"

A parent who worked his young children in order to lighten his burdens, who kept them relentlessly to a given task, was scorned, or at least ridiculed. If he were a man, he would not depend on a child. Especially were menial tasks spared the young lest they be overwhelmed at the outset. Soon enough they must shoulder adult burdens; why make them do it prematurely? Yet if a girl wanted to make something, new materials were provided her, as far as possible. She probably would ruin them, but what of that? Next time she would do better. Should she wish to make tiny moccasins for her brother's new baby, what could be more fitting? Was it not per peculiar privilege to honor a *hakáta* through his child? She was praised for assuming the kind of thing she should want to do all her life. To start young was all to the good.

If her brother asked to go hunting, by all means let him! The rabbit or edible bird he killed with his blunt arrow was ceremonially served to her. "Here. This you shall eat, for already your brother is looking out for you!" But should he come home empty-handed, it was a grave mistake to speak of his failure, lest a premature sense of obligation wear him down.

If a child was entrusted with a vital errand, for want of a maturer messenger, he was first carefully instructed to perform "like a man." The implicit challenge was for inspiring him with a sense of adult trustworthiness. But he was not expected to sustain the role beyond its immediate necessity.

When he at last displayed a sense of duty, without coercion, it was a happy thing—like the first bloom on one's favorite plant some morning unawares. Till then, however, no sly hints or artful talk were employed to induce it. "Your poor parents have to work so hard . . . Wouldn't you like to help them?" Children were not impressed by that until they were ready. On the other hand, one who behaved irresponsibly after he knew better was reprimanded by a parent: "These things you should see and do, without being told. You are old enough to 'think' now."

One winter evening I called on a family camped below the mission and sat talking with the women near the entranceway while several men carried on their own conversation at the honor place. Suddenly the seven-year-old son of the family came up from behind the men, and ran his hands lightly over his father's shoulders. Then he carefully spread a blanket over them, before he went back out of sight to resume his play, whatever it was. On his own initiative and because he felt cold near the tipi wall and supposed that his father was cold, too, he had first investigated, made sure, and then done something positive about it. His father murmured, *Haó, čʿį́kš!* 'Thank you, son!' and continued talking with his guests, but his mother and aunt exchanged amused and happy glances. Their little boy had just then commenced to "think"!

I have already said that very small children must be controlled by little scare devices, but as soon as they outgrew that stage they knew how to be seen and not heard when guests sat in the tipi. From one another they learned decorum. The desire to be like their own kind forbade their drawing unnecessary attention to themselves because "that was not done." When only indulgent relatives sat in the tipi, children felt free to be themselves. When there was company, they played contentedly together in a little group away from the center of conversation—or sat whispering their common interests—and never disturbed it. They managed to say and do funny things and still suppress their mirth. Or, rather, they laughed heartily, but voicelessly. Only their squinting eyes and shaking shoulders betrayed them, their hands covering their mouth. Anything to be quiet and inconspicuous!

Generally speaking, children were quiet and orderly when there were visitors, as I have said. Occasionally, a daring youngster in a devilish mood deliberately tried to make the others laugh by making funny faces and saying funny things, and sometimes by throwing comical shadow pictures on the tipi wall by various hand and finger positions, but a mother did not single out the guilty child and make him conspicuous. Instead she addressed the group impersonally, as though she did not know who was making the noise. "Shh! Be quiet, children, and try to hear something!" She meant that they could learn from the men's conversation if they would but listen.

If that did not curb the trouble, she resorted to another device: vicarious scolding. She rebuked her own child though he might be quite innocent, as though she believed he was at fault, so as not to embarrass the unruly guest. He thus had time to readjust to more acceptable behavior, unnoticed. Most children, once they were old enough to understand their mother's real aim—to restore quiet and at the same time spare the offender—cooperated by taking the reprimand casually. Sometimes it was nobler to accept an injustice temporarily, as a matter of expediency, than to insist on personal rights immediately and all-righteously. The same device was used in training very small children. When they realized that an older child was taking the blame for what they were doing, they gradually learned to conform to proper public behavior, though not a word was said to them.

Since boys carried about little clay or bone animals almost as standard equipment so as to be able to play with them at any time, anywhere, in the tipi they massed their buffalo and "rode" out after them on "horses" held fast between first and second fingers, which were the rider's "legs." With abundant imagination, and flexible wrists, those tiny horses were made to buck, rear, and balk realistically. The boys could stage a lively communal buffalo hunt in pantomime without growing boisterous enough to disturb the adults present. Just as quietly little girls kept busy at string games—cat's cradle—or at "embroidering moccasin tops" by pinning bright flower petals in pleasing designs and color combinations onto large sunflower or grape leaves, with stiff grass for pins. Sometimes they shaped the tips of the nearly triangular leaves of the cottonwood, and then pinned the sides together to form tiny "tipis," which they placed in camp circle formation, and there caused proportionately little "people" to carry on the social life they knew so well. They made these figures of skin or rags, or used plain sticks. In these and other ways, and with the simplest of materials, Dakota children unobtrusively entertained themselves, when it was needful to be quiet, but they could also sit idle and listen to the talk.

If for the Dakota child there was a time to be quiet, there was also a time to laugh. When they were outside in a group by themselves, they played noisier and livelier games with complete abandon, where they were not being watched doing it. Being natural mimics they got fun out of imitating people, or acting out scenes from folklore spontaneously, by "scene-living" them. Or they played standard dramatic games, some with singing. There is no room to describe them here, but one special favorite seems to have been called *Takówe šúka miyéč̓astaka hé?* 'Just why did you whip my dog?' As the one who was "it" came round the ring of players asking the question, they must invent reasons: because he bit me; because he tore my moccasin, right here; because he stole my meat; because . . . Unfortunately, the climax is no longer remembered. I found no trace of riddles or puzzles. My feeling is that they were not of interest or that perhaps they simply did not exist. I may be quite wrong about this. There were puns, plays on words, however; but only among grown-ups. Most puns were devised with a sting, for fun or censure.

In random talk much laughter and wit marked the comments or the good-natured but spirited arguments, provided no respect relative was present. When a connected story was being told, it was no less rude to interrupt or be inattentive than it is to whisper or move about during a musical recital or any such program today.

If a grandparent or a professional storyteller was relating a myth, the only permissible utterances, at each longish pause, were *Haó* from the men and boys and *Há* from women and girls, which showed that they were listening with interest, or that they had not fallen asleep, if the session took place after everyone was in bed, as was often the case when a grandparent was relating *Iktómi* tales. However, it was not rude to chuckle softly at the amusing passages, and a good storyteller, like a good actor, allowed time for laughs.

If a noted storyteller was sojourning in the camp circle for a season, he was invited, feasted, and given presents, that he might tell stories especially for the benefit of the children of the *t̓iyóšpaye*. Then, since it was their hour, planned for their instruction as well as entertainment, any archaic or obsolete words or expressions, or unfamiliar allusions, were parenthetically explained to them. Instead of one of the rarer myths or the long novelistic tales with a culture hero as protagonist, the winter count might be recited by the professional. Certain men could name three hundred years in order without a flaw because they had phenomenal memories; that was how they become professional.

If any of the terse descriptive names of the years caught the children's special interest, the narrator digressed long enough to relate the incident behind it. For example: the year name *Mat'ó wą kič'í wanít'ipi* 'they wintered with a bear' referred to a year of more than usual hardship from cold, famine, sickness, and many deaths. Indeed, it was so severe that a bear sought shelter in a tipi and spent a season as guest of the family! That always delighted the children. *Paháta-i wą ktépi* 'one who "went to the hill" was slain' was allegedly the year of flagrant sacrilege, committed by marauding enemies who killed a Dakota at prayer on a distant hilltop and left him lying prone over his altar. Such a ruthless transgression of the tacit intertribal law that guaranteed safety to anyone fasting for a vision was unequivocally *the* incident of the year, it was said. A real winter count teller knew the stories as well as the year-names. *Paháta-i* was the figure that referred to either a scout sent to the summit, to scan the landscape beyond for signs of danger, or one who stood alone on a lonely peak to fast.

Some of the names allegedly referred to events so old that they are all but legendary. It is a fact, moreover, that some incidents, which were regionally significant but not generally important, became local year names. That was one reason why the winter counts of different bands were not in complete agreement, or so I was told.

The young were instructed not only by myths and legends but also by pictographs, painted on the dew curtain, or on the summer curtain hanging only across the rear of the tipi. They might depict scenes of camp circle life in the past, from which social history could be learned, or perhaps some incidents of major importance in the life of an illustrious relative. One man said, "It was my uncle's deeds that were painted on our *óžą*, 'dew curtain'. How he struck first coup, how he killed his first buffalo, how he met the Crow delegation coming to sue for peace, and suchlike events in his life. In all, I should say there were 'ten or nine' such pictures."

I want to point out that the Dakotas usually named the larger number first, as in the foregoing example. When the ancient Prayer of St. Chrysostom was translated into Dakota some seventy years ago, the Native translators expressed the line "When two or three are gathered together in Thy name" as *Tohą yámni káiš nųpa ešá* . . . 'When three, or else [only] two, even so . . .' It is excellent Dakota idiom. When my informant spoke of his uncle's laudable deeds, "ten or nine," he meant "possibly there were ten; at any rate, I am safe in saying there were nine."

Dew curtains sometimes illustrated customs from the past: a shinny game, target practice with bow and arrows, a courtship scene, a spirited buffalo hunt, and suchlike subjects. It is recalled that for some years there was a wave of enthusiasm for beautifying the new home in the old-time way. People went visiting just to see a newly completed mural. Feasts were given in honor of some important ancestor whose deeds had inspired the pictures. Surely here was a futile last effort to keep alive the pride, glory, and excitement of bygone days, now slowly dying before the people's eyes—if not already dead.

When frame houses with walls in flat paint displaced the log house, those murals on muslin disappeared rapidly. That was a pity, for they were excellent conversation pieces. A capable interpreter of pictographs could entertain all evening by going into the details of each scene in order, and answering questions. Thus, for the children especially, they furnished a new kind of story hour—with visual aids. Unfortunately, they were short-lived.

I have said already that children were left with a minimum of obvious direction and interference, but in one particular they were constantly watched and subtly channeled into the right direction for their sex. Girls must be women some day and boys men. To that end they were directed that they might become a universal woman or man. The girl who persistently used masculine speech after she knew better was not one to be copied. A boy who was attracted to the gentler domestic games of girls was a special worry to his family because it was believed that one who affected womanish ways was in danger of impairing his normal development as a male and might become a *wįkte*—the most tragic of fates. A man-child should be masculine, through and through.[3]

At a memorial feast for a little girl, the weeping mother gave out many gifts, randomly, without stopping to decide which was most suitable for whom. As a result the eight-year old grandson of Chief Gall received a complete set of play dishes in a blue willow pattern. The boy was delighted with their texture and color, but for his mother they created a dilemma. She did not want him to have any such domestic toys: boys did not own dishes! At the same time she would not order him to give away what was his own. However, he himself solved her problem neatly. When my mother and my little sister went to call on his mother, he went outside and paced the yard in deep meditation, and then came back in. "I am a boy and dishes are not for me; but she [pointing to my sister] is a girl, so I want her to have them!" His mother was visibly relieved. Without her interfering with her son's possessions, the danger of his growing up a sissy had been so simply averted.

Any predisposition to stinginess was checked at the first sign, because "only those who lacked generous relatives grow up stingy." The logical inference from that was "one's generosity is proof of one's upbringing." Quite possibly the tribal characteristic of indifference to material possessions at least partly stemmed from this attitude. Thus it was as much a matter of family pride to be liberal as to be ethical. Nevertheless, sympathy was very real, too. "He needs it; I have it. So why not give it to him?"

This is not to say that property was scorned. Even children owned substantial things individually. If at birth they received a horse or other valuable gift, it was carefully guarded in their name, even though they had no immediate practical use for it. "That is his," parents said again and again, thus indicating their respect for his sole right to it. Haphazardly, children made new acquisitions, too. If the child claimed something, however idly, like the newborn calf or colt, or the new wagon or tipi, his parents let it be his and would not dispose of it without his consent. If it was sold, they hardly thought of deflecting the proceeds from his personal use. Often enough they found it a convenience to be able to say, "Alas, it is the child's, and he sets great store by it." No prospective buyer would press them further after that.

A woman informant said:

When our mare foaled I said idly, "The little horse is mine." I did not really want it and promptly forgot that I had claimed it. Yet, though I was only a child, my parents let it be mine. "White Fawn's horse," they would say in speaking of it. After I went to school, our new white neighbor brought my parents to the agency boarding school to ask my permission, for he wanted to buy my horse. I said yes, so he started to pay my father, who said, "It is the girl's money. Give it to her." The buyer poured thirty-six silver dollars into my lap.

I bought dress goods for my mother, tobacco for my father, candy and toys for my little brothers, and shoes for myself. I sent a nice present home to my grandparents and kept what remained. My folks wanted me to keep it to spend. Later I bought gifts and sweets for my best friends and their relatives in the school, and enjoyed that money because of all I could do with it.

On the other hand, if on impulse the child gave a valuable thing away, his parents usually let it go the first time he did so. It would be a grave risk to curb his inclination to give, since generosity was a quality all should develop. One informant recalled sadly, "My little boy had already told his playmate that he wanted to give him his little red calf, but I withheld it. Small wonder then that he promptly sickened and died." As a result she blamed herself forever.

Any responsible adult would manage by some subterfuge to avoid taking a valuable gift proffered him by a child. One man said, with ceremony, "This is mine now, since you have honored me with it. Very well, then. Since I am leaving on a journey shortly and cannot stop, I wish to make you a present of it because it is the finest thing I own at the moment." The child was pleased and satisfied. He and his friend had just enjoyed the privilege of giving and receiving, and that was the heart of the matter. Alas, not all recipients were so scrupulous. Some have been known to take advantage of a child's unconsidered generosity with loud, effusive thanks, before the gift could be questioned by anyone.

Occasionally a child was given to calling any chance passerby to come in and eat, imitating his parents' extending of hospitality. Again, the thoughtful person would say in effect, "This is indeed an honor, but I am on an important errand just now. Another time, perhaps." This spared the mother who would otherwise be obligated to make her child's invitation good, ineptly extended though it had been, but if someone deliberately accepted, he compelled her to cook and feed the passerby in her child's name. Homeless and irresponsible old people were the most likely ones to do this, always so eager for a good meal. Without shame, they used flattery. "Oh, surely now it will be a choice meal that I eat. When a boy-beloved invites, there is no stinting." Few mothers could withstand the obvious challenge, even if they were not pleased.

As a rule old people lived with their children or other relatives, but in every locality there were bound to be a few without permanent homes, either because they lacked living relatives or their disposition was such that they were not satisfied anywhere for long. Those were the ones who sometimes overworked the hospitality obligation by praising blatantly someone who fed them well, as though to shame less liberal women into doing likewise, or by complaining about the heartlessness of some, with the hope of stirring pity in others.

Gradually, however, children learned to consult their parents privately first, after understanding something of the art and the intricacies of the institutional giving that was part and parcel of social life, and after catching the spirit of it: "I give you this gift, because it is worthy. But it is not the thing itself I give; it is what it represents: that I wish to honor you. Now the thing is yours to do with it as you wish."

Indeed, it was nothing extraordinary or insulting to be given something one had once owned but gave away, after it had gone the round at its own unhurried pace, honoring many. One woman I knew was happy to be formally presented with a gift that turned out to be one she gave away years before. Out of pure interest, she asked around and was able to trace its course from one owner to another throughout the intervening years. It gave her a great deal of satisfaction.

Largesse, and the lordly manner of dispensing it, were the aim and pride of the Dakotas. Whether they could afford to give or must deprive themselves was beside the point. Needless to say, avidity was a contemptible trait; those who worshipped possessions were the queer people. Once, such a woman contributed a sack of dried sweetcorn with unwonted readiness when collectors came by in behalf of a starving family, but when she discovered her mistake, she was almost in tears. Finding her remaining corn moldy and unfit, she cried, "What have I done? This was what I meant to give. Instead, I have given my best corn away!" She was too overwhelmed by her loss to detect the sarcasm beneath the teasing of her male joking relatives: "What a pity! One should always give the worst and keep the best for oneself!"

If tipis had attics, they would be empty. It was senseless to keep things no longer useful or in excess of one's needs, just for the sake of owning them. Anyway, such a practice was incompatible with the mobile way of life. One who clung with tenacity to everything he ever got, and wanted more and more, was said to be *waglúhahaka* 'to have the habit of keeping things'. The idiom lent ridicule—even opprobrium—in regard to one with this undesirable trait. The terminal *-ká* is a suffix that, in this usage, somehow makes the trait a freakish propensity.

From all this it should be understandable why Dakotas as a people were not souvenir hunters, or collectors either, although keepsakes were treasured for their sentimental value. My informant was sharpening his wife's knives while we talked, and at one point he said that the whetstone in his hand once belonged to his grandfather and went on many a war-path with him.

From the beginning children were trained to respect the belongings of others, and warned not to open a container that was not theirs. A woman on a visit with her two- or three-year-old would whisper to him, "No! Let that be; it is theirs [meaning not yours], so do not touch it. That is not done," if he so much as touched the fancy tying strings of a beaded or painted bag that caught his eye. In time the idea that "it is theirs" was as good as lock and key. Indeed, it was the only equivalent, for there was no such thing as a real lock and key.

But I had a delightful playmate once who was a true investigator. Her curiosity over the white man's goods was boundless. When she came to play with me, if the missionary supply closet stood open, she dived energetically into boxes and things for whatever she might find, her eyes gleaming with anticipation. She wanted nothing to keep. Once her curiosity was satisfied she was ready to play, leaving everything scattered about. My mother would reprimand *me*, but she and I knew I was not at fault. That did not educate Julie, nor did the nickname Julie *Wóblečes'a* 'Julie who regularly opens and scatters things,' which her elder women collaterals fastened on her, shame her into reforming at once, though she gradually did as she got older. It was her good-natured but peculiarly irresponsible mother who annoyed other women by this gap in training her child. Julie investigated at other homes, too.

Julie was still my favorite playmate because she was the most original, imaginative, and interesting of all my contemporaries. She could think up new ideas faster than we could carry them out before she had to go. They sometimes led us into trouble and even danger. At least there was never a dull moment when Julie came. We were perhaps eight or nine years old, old enough to "think."

Because a desire to own things was underdeveloped, and because they knew that what belonged to their parents was as good as their own, if children fancied it enough to claim it, thieving and filching were unnecessary and offered little temptation. If a very small child stole, it was only cute; soon he would know better. If an older child did so, he was not being properly trained—a reproach to his parents—or he was mentally slow, and unable to "think." Yet even for him, friendly outsiders found excuses. So it was when two ten-year-old girls stole brown sugar from the tipi of the Sans Arcs chief Čʿasmú 'Sand', when the government issued it for the first time. The amused comments on all sides had entirely to do with the girls' ingenuity in packing the sugar solidly in empty baking-powder cans and burying it. "How cute of them!" people said. "Think of caching it for future enjoyment, as surplus foods were cached long ago!" The incident was regarded as a quaint diversion and not the ominous sign of a criminal tendency. No ethical or moral principle was thought to have been violated.

After all the attention focused on them, the shy girls doubtless wanted never to steal again. Their mothers scolded them, a bit more shrilly than necessary, both out of embarrassment and a wish to indicate their disapproval publicly. "Yú!" they snapped. "Aren't you old enough to think? How could you take what was not yours?" But outsiders laughed it off. "Čʿąhą́pi zí, 'yellow sugar' is such a novelty! Who could resist it?" "Children crave sweets, naturally. So why blame the little girls?" "After all, it is only food. Who would deny food to the young?" Best of all, Chief Sand exclaimed with a flourish, "Take the entire sack to them! Far be it from me to withhold the stuff so that children must thieve for it!" He had it delivered to their tipis. One last item: the community wag dubbed that year "When Minnie and Lizzie stole sugar," declaring it to be without dispute the outstanding event of the year. That closed the episode.

Since all Dakotas, being relatives, owed one another a certain respect and consideration, only a person who was a little crazy and hence socially unreliable would think of filching, but there were some like that. According to reports, there was once a lively old woman nicknamed Little Ragged Tail who stole anything within reach, as though she could not help herself. At the same time that she was received everywhere as a relative, women warned one another, "She is heading this way again. She must be hungry, *úšika!* ['poor thing!']. Still, better keep your eye on her, or, with superhuman cunning, she will pick things up the moment your back is turned." She came to be a byword. "Dear me, where is the knife I put down a moment ago?" And then the quip "Little Ragged Tail must have come and gone—while I blinked!" To be accused of stealing was not only to have one's morals questioned but also to have one's upbringing slurred. The indignant retort "Why would I want to steal? I who was liberally brought up?" was a thrust at the accuser who, in the speaker's opinion, never had anything.

Not every child was favored by fortune. Orphans, with only a helpless old grandmother to care for them, were the underprivileged, in the Dakota sense, because they lacked able relatives to honor them and thereby raise their social prestige. With neighbors sharing meat with the grandmother, she was able to feed and shelter the orphan in her meager abode—and that was all she was able to do for him, materially. Because she could not clothe him well, he was likely to go about untidy and shabbily dressed, though occasionally some kindly woman gave him new moccasins to replace his ripped and torn pair, or a badly needed garment or robe.

However, such thoroughly unfortunate children were few at any given time because nearly always there was some able relative to look after them, rather than an aged grandmother. Certainly this drab description would not apply to the orphaned child of a large *t'iyóšpaye*, where the several relatives, if they did not actually pamper him, were nevertheless inclined to bend over backward in compensating him for his lack of parents. Group pride as well as individual kinship obligation compelled them. More than one informant has said, "My parents died when I was an infant, but I had relatives," meaning that he was well brought up anyway; meaning that they concerned themselves to make his name and standing important; meaning that he was not a "nobody."

In contrast the favored child was, by Dakota standards, well nurtured, adequately dressed, had his own pony, and so on. Personal neatness was indicated by oiled, smooth hair, braided tidily; by carefully applied face paint; by suitable attire; and, most essential, by proper footwear. Moccasins should be whole, worn with the bands wrapped snug about the ankles and firmly bound with their long supple strings of deerskin—because of its stretchability—which accommodated to the necessary play of the ankle. Other kinds of skin were too constricting because they did not give, and were used only as a last resort. Incidentally, unkept hair and moccasins worn with ankle bands flapping and strings broken and trailing were signs of delinquency. A robe apiece was essential to favored children, after they were no longer small enough to be carried inside the mother's shawl. Proud families aimed to provide ornamented garments.

One particular necessity was a regular examination of the child's head, to inspect his hair from time to time, because he could all too readily catch lice from some less-favored playmate. It was not disgraceful but admirable to engage a lice-hunter for him—usually a woman with thoroughness and good eyesight, and infinite patience. Contrary to the assumptions of casual observers, there were fastidious families who kept clean of lice, though shiftless people wore them quite indifferently. This made hospitality to them something less than carefree. Even so, kinship law required that one might not receive some comers and reject others, since all were relatives, real or social.

Once when a government school matron called all Dakota children lousy, indignant mothers disclaimed the charge and, in blasting tones, berated those who had earned them this blanket criticism by their lack of pride: "*My* child caught lice from *your* child because they were made to sleep in the same bed at school. *My* child never knew what it was to be lousy until he went to school. *We* in our family do not tolerate lice."

Family neatness was indicated by orderliness in the home and skillfully packed goods when traveling. Some groups were so consistently trim that trimness marked them as a *t'iyóšpaye*. Others could be as extreme in the opposite direction. I was told by a Teton informant that the respectable name *Waǧáǧeča* originated as a derisive nickname for a notoriously untidy group. "In the line of march, their section could always be spotted at a distance because of their poorly tied goods, which came loose and hung in strips, blocking out the daylight at [seemingly] regular intervals." The stem *ǧaǧéča* describes an alternation of solids and open spaces, or, as in this case, of opacity and light, like a picket fence, and also perhaps latticework. Certainly the thoracic region of a skeleton would be *ǧaǧéča*. Obviously the name was a deliberate exaggeration.

"Children should be gently reared, and protected against hard knocks while they are still *štukála*," an old Teton said, deliberately using the term for 'unripe, soft, damageable,' which has specific reference to vegetables. He went on to develop his analogy this way: "Strike a squash while it is *štukála*, and the wound will mar its surface for all time. Strike it after it has grown a hard coat and the blow will glance off and leave no scar. So it is with people," he concluded.

In other words, the sense of security engendered by a sheltering childhood environment was deemed better than any disciplinary device that required or permitted normally serene and loving elder relatives to become momentary tyrants, whose unwonted behavior could only shock and confuse a child and weaken his confidence in them. It was their invariability that anchored him, "because they cared for him." That was the proof. Certainly they could not keep him in blissful ignorance of hard things ahead in the world of men. Indeed, they prepared him for it. "We shall be gone, but you will be a man, and able to stand up to rebuff." But it was not for them to give him occasional foretastes of life's sterner side. That was the province of collaterals of his sex, who created their own world of brusque give-and-take by which they good-naturedly trained themselves and one another to take it.

Old people say, "Yes, I have met with hard times, cruelty, and craftiness in my time—but not while I had my relatives" (i.e., fathers and mothers, aunts and uncles, and grandparents). To the end they look back gratefully to the brooding care they experienced in childhood, and they sometimes boast, "My relatives gave without stint, in my name, so that many benefited from it." Of course, those who had faulty parents, or lacked relatives altogether, could not make that claim.

Yet, when they underwent an honoring ceremony as small children, they wore elaborate dress and played their role without visible sign of excitement or vanity. Should a grateful beneficiary come back to thank them by stroking their faces gently, which was the proper gesture, they submitted with a passivity close to boredom, as to something that must somehow be endured momentarily. Dakotas learned young to take things with composure and stoicism. Indeed, it was laughable to be wildly exuberant over personal good fortune, since others did not share in it. Only very small children, still self-centered, were pardoned for that bit of naivete. Restraint and not exuberance was the becoming quality. The only time I think everyone rejoiced with abandon was on Armistice Day in 1918; everyone felt equally liberated from the evils of war forever. To this day the countenance of even the preadolescent is more than likely to be sober in repose. Smiling over nothing was the mark of a fool.

Already at this age, children knew that relatives must be considered since it was the one matter consistently stressed. Thus, if for want of an older person children were called on to wait on a relative, as a rule they performed creditably and without rebellion. One woman took her small boy out of a group game and placed him in charge of a sleeping infant. "Watch here beside your little son, until I get back. I shall hurry back. Scare the flies for him or he might waken and cry." The baby was the boy's elder brother's, hence a son to him.

With his eyes he participated in his playmates' game at a distance, and laughed softly at their antics from time to time, while his short arm, scaring the flies, moved quite mechanically to and from above the infant's face. He stuck to his post until he was relieved because he had learned that a father does not desert his son. Many children led their blind grandfather on a round of visits to their cronies in the camp circle, and waited outside with a forbearance far beyond their years until it was time to lead the grandfather back home.

The well-trained child was a *wahwála* child. This term, meaning 'tame' and 'tractable', refers specifically to domesticated animals; idiomatically applied to people it means 'peaceable, considerate, and noncontentious in all relationships'. It was the admirable way to be. Some of the most *wahwála* men at home were reputed to be fierce in battle. It was one mark of the chief or head man. It is hard to picture a leader without it. For Dakotas were not led by the arrogant and domineering.

Mothers warned their child before sending him out to play with a new boy in the community, "Be careful now. Play *wahwáyela* [adverbial form]. *Takúyaye séče.*" 'He may turn out to be a relative to you'.

Not family prestige, not fine possessions or fine clothes, only likeableness determined the choice of a playmate. A boy from a superior family might prefer some wretched-looking orphan on that basis. In that case his family respected his choice and were kind to the boy. An informant in speaking of his childhood with only a needy, though loving, old grandmother, said, "She could not do much for me, but I had a happy childhood, and, besides, I had a friend. It was his clothes that kept me warm, his food that kept me filled."

There was such a friendship in our community when a boy of good family teamed up with an impersonable youth of doubtful paternity.

The two rode, hunted, and fished together until the poor boy's untimely death, an incongruous but congenial pair. The first boy's parents called the other čʼį́kš 'son' and looked after him as though he, too, were their son. Moreover, they valued him, knowing that their own son was safe in his company. Such a boy played a voluntary "Fides Achates" role, which made him even more valuable.

Upon entering his own age and sex group for the first time, the waȟwála child might be diffident, but he was not hostile. It was not required to show one's mettle immediately by picking a fight with someone in the group. One only incidentally proved it, by perhaps defending a younger member against the bullying intruder bent on teasing him for fun. Nor was it required to exhibit some special talent or proficiency in order to gain entry. The show-off was never popular. The group's cool reception of him was enough to make him mend his ways—or get out. Their thinly veiled attitude was readable: "If he is that good, let him go elsewhere to show off; we have not asked him."

Sex and gender, being natural and ever present, were taken in stride, because adults did not deny them out of existence for a while and then magnify them into a preoccupation. The subject was mentioned whenever necessary so that children took it for granted, but this was in regard to animal life only. The breeding of pets and stock was a commonplace, anyway, and their anatomical terms were familiar. However, human mating for which there was a separate term was not for casual, public discussion, whether there were children present or not. Out of regard not only for the persons involved but also for their respect relatives, who would be offended on their behalf, there was universal delicacy about the subject. Here and everywhere the interacting kinship obligations had a restraining effect. Even in private conversation between two responsible persons, mutual respect compelled them to employ tactful euphemisms. If an old person came out with the subject in frank language, nothing was made of it—as though it had not been said at all.

Courtship was strictly for young people of the proper age, but because they sometimes stood in pairs talking where they could be seen, wherever a man could "catch a woman," it was not surprising that children sometimes acted out the traditional courtship hour in their play. Fast Whirlwind, the Teton, said:

We little boys of eight to ten years sometimes cleared a circular spot in the tall weeds and there acted out the Sun Dance and other holy ceremonies, which we were forbidden to do. Girls our age did not play with boys. But if we could persuade them, we brought smaller girls out to supply the female chorus to our dancing and singing ...

And sometimes we played at courting them. We held our wraps loosely about them and began, "Ahem! [clearing the throat for a significant utterance] There is something I want to ask you. Will you marry me?" They shook their heads a decided "No," and tried to get free. But most of them liked the game well enough. Only a few cried real tears and ran home. "I shall tell my mother on you!" they said.

Such games, like homosexual practices, were never tolerated by the mothers, who watched their children closely and kept them together according to their own sex, after they were aware of differences between boys and girls. One informant remembered that her mother used to warn her about a certain girl, "Do not play with her. 'They say' she does bad things. She will teach you." The informant went on, "If that girl came to play 'family' in our little tipis, my mother always called me home."

When little girls played at camping, they were all mothers with their dolls, and carried on women's conversation. If they must at the same time keep an eye on their small brother, he became their eldest son, or a nephew, who "took care of the horses." He was never a husband, for that would be a kinship offense. The husbands were all myths—off to war or out hunting, and only referred to in conversation, for they did not really exist. Said one woman, "When he [her husband] gets home ..." and to her babies she promised, "Don't you cry, now. Soon your father will be coming home with meat!" This was the proper way to play "family." Whether all children played as they were supposed to, when adults were not around, was not reported.

Fairly or unfairly, a child suspected of homosexual tendencies could get a reputation that would follow him into adulthood, and reflect on his negligent trainers. Concerning one girl who was shunned by others on the insistence of their mothers, the story was that at birth she was a male, but that when the diaper was changed the first time, there was a female instead! Some sinister power had wrought an external change—but she was still a male and therefore not safe for girls to play with! Fantastic as this may sound, that girl suffered from it even though there was no proof that she "played dirty." She died from tuberculosis before she was married, but was by no means adverse to men or marriage, as any normal girl.

Boys could sit a horse in many cases before they could walk. They rode in front of an adult relative whose arm held them secure, and in that way they acquired the feel of riding swiftly. By six or seven years of age many owned their own ponies, with the necessary trappings, and learned to ride with an adult riding beside them, their horses walking at first, and only by degrees quickening their speed. By nine or ten they rode together, all boys, and egged each other on, faster and faster, until they were entirely at home on a horse. Then they were away most of the day, returning only to eat or sleep. But not always to eat. The rule of hospitality took good care of them, wherever they might be at mealtime. For when a mother called her boy in to eat his meal, she expected his friend, too. One who fed her own child only, and allowed his playmate to wait outside without eating, would be acting very strangely.

Trick riding was not systematically taught but came naturally. Filled with daring tales of men riding into battle and the buffalo hunt, and familiar with exciting scenes of young men breaking wild horses and doing glorious stunts on horseback, the boy could hardly wait to get into action, and when he started in, he rapidly gained proficiency without conscious striving. His elder male collateral relatives urged and cheered him on, and challenged him to "play the male" regardless of bumps and tumbles. At this stage he was more susceptible to their urging, being attracted strongly to horses, anyway, than to the suggestions of his womenfolk that he wait a while longer.

Girls also rode, but they usually started when they were around nine or ten. Many rode exceedingly well and could go at a fast speed without falling off, but trick riding and horse breaking were not proper, being strictly men's work. Both girls and women rode astride. If side saddles were formerly used, I find no trace of them. Womanly modesty demanded dignity in mounting. They led their horse to a rock or bank out of sight, to avoid being seen in awkward movements and positions while clambering on. When seated they laid a narrowly folded shawl across the lap to hang down on each side and conceal the legs and ankles somewhat. Divided skirts were not used, but the elongated side gores of the old-time buckskin gown were a token effort toward the same end, both in walking and riding—that is, to keep the legs at least illusive.

Swimming also came by doing as did everything else that called for motor coordination. Learning was purely imitative—no minute, step-by-step analysis. Small children bathed with the women, but, soon enough, the boys preferred to go with the males to a different place or at a different time from the women's. Certainly boys of nine and ten were too old for mixed bathing. Both boys and girls learned to swim underwater without disturbing the surface any more than necessary, in order not to betray their direction—a practical accomplishment in case of enemy pursuit.

Girls entered deep water feet first and did not dive from the bank. Boys and men dived mostly from a half-kneeling position, the so-called Indian dive. On the whole there appears to have been no special interest in diving for its own sake, no striving individually or competitively after style and form. I could not discover any standards for that. If once there was a right way, I do not know of it.

In general, competition for personal excellence was unimportant. One might almost say that the emphasis was less on being first than on not being last. In impromptu footraces boys shouted as they made a dash for the goal, *Eháke kį hé wíyakte ló!* 'The last one in will be a woman!'—girls in their races said, *Eháke kį hé ištá ošášakte!* 'The last one in will have red eyes!'—and so they ran, fast enough not to be last. If a runner dropped out because he was so far outdistanced that he could only be last, he was not derided for giving up. To keep on running would seem pointless. Sometimes two, who were hopelessly behind, simply walked in together, laughing, and panting. The joke was on the boy who ran, supposing those two were back of him! The whole race was for a pastime, anyway, not something that must be run with do-or-die determination. To be top man was not worth the struggle.

Only in organized games, like Dakota shinny, did individual players give their all in order to win. The necessity to bring success to their team as a whole, and good fortune to those betting on it, were their justification. At such times nothing else mattered, not even relatives. This was brought out nicely by the informant who said, "The [shinny] players went for the ball with a mad determination to win. Whenever it was knocked into the crowd, people fell back in waves for fear of being struck. They knew that the sticks were being wielded by men who were temporarily not themselves." In other words, one had to be a little crazy before one forgot to be deterred by kinship obligations, or so it would seem.

When the shinny game *t'áp-kašpíčapi* 'ball advanced by causing it to jump' was played on the common within the camp circle, little children were safe from being trampled on, in case the ball should be knocked out into the crowds watching, because they had their private grandstands on their tipis. They stood on the laced-up part of the tipi, one higher than the other, and were able to see above the spectators; with one hand clutching a lacking pin at shoulder level, and the free hand waving and cheering the players; and with feet braced on lower pins. This scene was pictured on a mural that I saw, such as I described above.

The system of betting must be explained, for though it was true that individual persons placed their own bets, still it was in a sense a group affair. Before a serious, planned contest, for which the two halves of the camp circle recruited teams from their own side to represent them, the bets were collected, first on the challengers' side, in a huge buffalo robe. They might be quivers with bow and arrows, moccasins, ornaments, knives, blankets, and such things, all of which made acceptable stakes. When the collectors approached the other side they shouted *Iyákaška-waú wé ló!* 'To tie onto I come!' Those who were so-minded came running out with the things they were betting. First they looked over the bets from the challengers and tied their particular item to the one there that they would like to take a chance on owning. Thus all the bets were finally tied in pairs. After the game they were all carried to the winning side, where the owners claimed their things plus whatever was tied to them. It was customary for losers to accept their loss coolly, and that was where good sportsmanship was displayed. I have already emphasized the fact that one should let any possession go if it was timely, "without the pulse quickening" in regret. The least sign of regret would be mercilessly ridiculed by one's boisterous joking relatives.

It is said that a woman's game was something to watch. For, once unencumbered by the inevitable wraps, they sped across the field and were gracefully agile. *Ičázop-s'é*, said one informant, meaning 'like a line (quickly) drawn', which was his way of describing their speed. This is equivalent to the English "like a streak." At a Fourth of July celebration some years ago, when portly women demonstrated the ancient game—with obvious effort—an old man sighed: "Our Dakota women were lean and graceful in the old days. Alas, they have lost both their shape and their speed—and little wonder! Our life today is so changed that none of us live actively anymore."

Women players went after the ball with as much zest and zeal as did men players, and were just as dangerous when recovering it from among the spectators. Then their single aim was to win for the sake of their team and for their half of the camp circle. Even kinship considerations must stand by.

In summary I would reemphasize the following ideas. Infants and very young children were fondled and held lovingly in the arms. As they grew more and more self-sufficient, physical contact lessened in proportion. Excessive petting, squeezing, mauling, and indeed all playful manhandling of them, and certainly kissing—without a reason—were things the child did not normally expect from even the most devoted parents, just as he did not expect whippings. An occasional sharp rebuke from a tired parent, or even a shove because he held back when he ought to step lively, were things the child accepted and was callous about.

He did not really fear his parents because they gave him little cause to be feared. The average Dakota parents were no hostile brow-beating symbols of discipline and arbitrary authority. They did not need to be, for they had an age-old, ready-made system to fall back on, a system that allowed them to be gentle all the way. When the still unreasonable child would not respond to their conciliatory approach, the illusive mythical scare was the sure remedy. When he was old enough to see through that sham, it was time for his special one-to-be-feared to bring him to terms, either by speaking stern words in mock anger or by simply assuming a certain austerity that the child dared not take lightly.

Yet even that was no absolute threat. A smart child quickly learned how to cope with it. He could change his conduct on the spot or, with more dignity, do so gradually and unseen under the shawl of mother, aunt, or grandmother, taking sanctuary while she whispered to him, "That's right, do stop crying. We shall not be scolded then." Mutually agreed-on strategy, rescued and rescuer quickly nullified the threat. For as soon as the child ceased to be naughty, his one-to-be-feared ceased to be cross, and turned to other matters. (But just let him hear further crying or fussing!) What really happened was this: stern sibling and lenient oldster played into each other's hand to the same end, and somewhere between their respective methods, the child got his training—painlessly enough.

Without forcing him parents nevertheless made it seem praiseworthy for him to be independent as soon as he might normally be. Their delighted approval of his progress was a spur. Soon enough he was insisting on dressing and undressing without help. A father took his little daughter along—if she asked to go. He led her about—if she placed her hand in his. He was just as happy if she got along by herself, showing she was developing self-reliance. A mother welcomed her small son each time he turned to her and gave him undivided attention and affection. She knew and accepted the fact that her boy of eight or nine would be quite satisfied to leave her side and venture out among his own kind, when the time came for that.

The typical Dakota child was not demonstrative, because his parents were not. He was quiet and self-contained, because they were. Even when they petted him they did not pester him with repetitious questions like "Do you love me?" "How much?" "Say it again! Again!" He was not asked to declare his feelings, but he was so treated as to assume the feelings of others toward him: "I have always placed my child ahead of all other considerations." "What are mere things to me in comparison to my child?" This last was said by a woman just before she served her guests at the feast she was giving in her child's name. Thus nothing was pointedly required in exchange for the warm environment created for the child; enough that he basked there in total contentment.

If he gradually developed an appreciation of his parents' love and on his own initiative began reciprocating it, without doubt he or she would grow up to be the kind of son or daughter who would not neglect his aging parents. Regardless of whether or not he gave such promise, he was loved anyway, simply because he was their child. Nor was he ever told, "Now, remember. It was I who brought you into the world. You owe me thus and so in return." Especially for that favor, children were never held accountable.

The Dakota was allowed to stay a child as long as it was right for him. He was not weaned and hurried out of his childhood stage before he was able and ready. Once his legs could support him, his parents were proud to let him go. Once he was on his way, they seemed to follow him, figuratively one step behind and with arms extended in case he fell, fearful of touching him otherwise. *Caution* was the watchword in handling the young.

14

Adolescence

From about twelve years of age, the young were no longer treated as children to be tricked or intimidated into good behavior but were reckoned as personages to be respected as reasonable young adults on their way to full maturity. Something like subservience was suggested in the parents' habit of deferring to their adolescents, of holding their own inclinations in abeyance for their sake. The young did not demand this; they did not have to. They accepted it simply as something that inhered in the nature of parenthood. It would operate in them when they reached parenthood, and in their children and their children's children, ad infinitum.

Subordinating one's children on the plea that "I must think of myself; I have my own life to live" was an aberrancy. For one's children *were* one's life. Self-abnegation for the sake of offspring was automatic behavior, inherited by parents from parents, and transmitting to children, in an endless chain, by precept and example. Filial devotion could not be expected solely on the basis of physical parenthood. It must first be generated in the child by an unswerving devotion to him.

There were parents who failed their children, to be sure, and were still treated kindly in their old age. "He ran away from us when we were little," said a woman of her father, "but after all, he is our father and we must 'pity' him." Thus, without earning it, they sometimes enjoyed it anyhow. There were also unfilial children, because they lacked the sense of fair play and gratitude to repay in kind. But it is safe to say that self-denying parents and grateful children were the rule.

Like a plant that must be nurtured with extreme delicacy, the Dakota adolescent as an unpredictable complex was to be nurtured with tact and sympathy. There are stories about adolescents who ran away and became lost forever because of hurt feelings over something that in a few years would have seemed trifling.

The classic example is the Standing Rock legend in its various versions. Perhaps the commonest is the one that says that an adolescent girl once ran away into the wilds because of hurt feelings and was permanently lost. After a long search she was found in a sitting position, in the midst of a vast prairie, with her little pet dog perched beside her—both facing west. But they were of stone.

Things were made easier for the young during these trying years by the simple tactic of avoiding direct attention to them. For instance, nothing was said to the boy when his changing voice occasionally got out of control, or when a girl became listless and dreamy almost overnight or suddenly took endless pains with her appearance, or was irritable if compelled to speak when she wanted to be silent and unobtrusive. Then, should an elder brother ridicule the boy's cracking tones or an elder sister exclaim impatiently to the girl, "Pay attention to what you are doing. What ails her, anyway. Is she in love already?," both were privately reprimanded by their parents. "Son, do not embarrass your brother. It is right that his voice is deepening." "Daughter, spare your sister's feelings. She is past the age to be spoken to as a child."

It was not customary to ask direct questions of anyone; in fact, it was discourteous. One might skillfully draw out what one wanted to find out, but it must be skillful indeed. The other person must volunteer the exact information if he chooses; otherwise he did not. This refers especially to secrets, not such trifles as "Do you know if the visitors have left?" One who asked leading questions boldly, and as a habit, was said to be *wawíyuğe-s'á* 'regular questioner', and it was not a compliment. *Wóyake s'é* 'regular teller of things' was not a compliment either, for one known to tell secrets freely was to be avoided. *Waslóslol-kiyįktehčį* 'bent on knowing everything' also was an undesirable title to have.

The adolescent girl was usually too diffident to fight back at her elder sister's ill-timed raillery, so instead she went off alone somewhere out of sight and perhaps cried there. If a mother or aunt knew of this, she went out to comfort her and bring her back. The boy had one advantage denied her. He could always escape on his pony and stay away all day. After dark he crept back into a tipi, where his mother or aunt would be sure to feed him without questioning him: "Well! And where have you been all day?" Even if she had missed him, she did not say so. Grown-ups did not pelt their adolescents with needless questions or talk small talk to engage them in conversation. They knew it was unwise to make them conspicuous by compelling them to speak. If and when they must speak, they would voluntarily do so.

I once observed a boy of fifteen as he sat eating in his aunt's tipi. He kept behind her, half-hidden from her guests, with whom she chatted pleasantly, just as though she had promptly forgotten him after giving him his supper. Yet, at the precise instant, she reached behind her and took the empty bowl, with attention still only on her guests. They said nothing about the boy either. Though she betrayed no sign, she knew exactly when the boy had finished eating and slipped away. It was one of the smoothest instances of sympathetic humoring of the young that I ever saw.

If very old people sometimes spoke out ineptly, it was only because they were so proud of a grandchild growing up that they could not keep silent. One old man boasted loudly to his crony, "Just see him now, my son's son, yonder. Almost as tall as his father, and his voice! Deep as a man's!" The poor boy quietly melted out of sight. Old women could blunder just as badly, for the same reason. This, too, I witnessed.

During a per capita payment for tribal lands, each person promptly claimed his check when his name was called, as requested, in order to expedite the proceedings. When one girl's name was called several times without result, the official was about to lay the check aside, when from a wagon in the distance an old woman called out, "Why don't you get it for her instead of standing there čʼą̇ sʼé? You know that our grandchild is bashful now!" Čʼą̇ 'wood, tree', sʼé 'like', a common simile for inert, motionless, unresponsive. She was scolding her spouse, somewhere in the crowd that jammed the porch where the checks were being passed out, but, even more, she was proudly informing the public.

It was normal for a fourteen-year-old Dakota girl to be conventionally bashful. But that her grandmother should broadcast the fact so blatantly was characteristic of grandparents. The sympathetic Dakota official waived the in-person requirement by handing the check to the grandfather without a word—and without smiling. Meantime the girl sat passive in the wagon box with her shawl pulled over her head, as though all the commotion had nothing to do with her.

The days of childish, imitative games were definitely over. Boys now tended to associate only with males and girls with females. During the day they were mostly with special friends of their own sex and age, but the well-trained girl did not sleep away from home without a chaperone. If she spent a night with her cousin or a classificatory sister, the woman of the tipi, being an aunt or a mother, was responsible for her as much as for her own daughter. She made sure that both girls were safe, and, whenever necessary, she took the usual extra precautions to guard their virtue.

Women guarded their girls extremely when it was necessary by binding their bodies from the waist down in a blanket or with things. If, for example, it was rumored that a stranger was in the camp circle who was said to be a feeler in the dark for young girls' bodies, mothers did this, it is said. Such a lewd character might pull up the anchoring pegs of the tipi and reach in for them as they slept. Since, ideally, young girls were kept from all male contact, just the mere effort of the man would be a contamination of them. Then the elder women slept near the wall and placed the girls inside. There is a story of a woman who laid awake all night with knife in hand, and struck the hand reaching in. Next day the man was identified by a deep gash across the back of his hand and was driven out by angry men. To have the reputation of *wótʿatʿa sʾa* 'given to feeling around for something' was to be the lowest of men.

For boys the rule was not as stringent. Often enough they slept at home, too, but if several were riding far out at nightfall, they slept on the ground under an open sky, like warriors, to harden themselves to it. Only the *tʿiyókitąhela-ų* 'dwellers between tipis' slept in anyone's tipi where they happened to be. The idiom referred to persons without kinship relatives, or to newcomers in the camp circle who had not yet related themselves to some local household. Sometimes the term was slanderously applied to mean "homeless, no-account," but most often it was used in its literal sense. Thus, if an outsider said, "I am still *tʿiyókitąhela-ų*," he meant he was still undecided whether to stay or go.

The normal adolescent having reached the age of understanding was ready for serious admonition. A reliable Santee woman informant reported that her mother first of all advised against her and her sister's listening to gossip. "Go not alone into other people's tipis for there you might hear *tókʿen-čiči iápi.*[1] That may be an old woman's pastime but it is not for you." If a visitor approached, she sent her girls outside. "She is coming to talk with me [or he is coming to talk with your father] and she might forget herself and indulge in gossip. When she leaves you may return." *Tókʿen-čiči iápi* is a strictly Santee idiom that means 'to talk as one pleases, idly, without respect for the truth'. The Teton and Yankton term is *wóaiye* 'talking over someone'.

The mother listed the qualities of a "good woman" as follows: the good Santee woman is faithful to her spouse and devoted to her children; she is industrious and skillful in the womanly arts; she delights in being hospitable and generous; she is a correct relative; she thinks much and says little; she does not gad about. Most important, she is chaste; she has no "deeds." *Oḣʼą* 'deeds' in this usage refers to unsanctioned sexual affairs. "Without chastity, all the other fine qualities are not enough to earn the name 'good woman,'" the mother told her girls.

Regarding marriage, one father told his son, "Treat your wife with 'pity' [compassion] for a woman is not a slave. But choose her with care. If after all you find her unfaithful, let her go! Men scorn one who is content to endure the shame brought on him by a false wife. 'Was she the best he could get?' they sneer. 'And can he not find another woman?'" The father glorified giving: "Give adequately, give worthy of yourself—or do not give at all. Give abundantly and with glorious abandon. Do not give half-holding-back, timid of your own private security, as though you pinned your faith not on men but on mere things. Better to give and have nothing left than to be stingy. So let gifts flow freely out and they will flow freely back. If everyone gives, everyone gets. In the endless stream of giving, this is bound to be so." These ideas were almost sure to be advanced by aged haranguers on tribal ideals.

He, the father, was contemptuous of men who concerned themselves with perishables, those who furtively restricted their wives' dispensing of hospitality and their giving of their own womanly possessions. Such petty men were not real men, he said. Finally, he emphatically lauded continence as a moral and physical value. Overindulgence of appetite and passion was hurtful and sapping, he said. A man could lose his senses that way. Only by a nice moderation could one remain strong and able to endure. "Remember these things, son. And so live that you need never 'drop your head' when men look at you," he said.

The father here is a composite of many fathers, and the foregoing is my collection of fathers' words as quoted to me by sons. Of course this does not mean that every father was a penetrating thinker and wise counselor. To the question "How did your father talk to you?," one man replied tenderly, "My father was a kind, good man, but he was a man of few words. It was my grandfather who told me how to live."

To this day the average Dakota respects his children as though they were his equals. When a boy ran off from school, his father welcomed him without question. He told the Native policeman sent out to investigate, "Nephew, your cousin has not said why he left school. If he likes, he will tell me, and if he chooses he will go back." The father would not force his son. The boy was entitled to his own feelings and reasons, and he respected them.

The wording "Nephew, your cousin . . ." in addressing the Native policeman is so typical that it deserves comment. The important thing was to draw all concerned into closer kinship relationship. Perhaps the policeman was only a social relative, and not close. Nevertheless, by calling him nephew, the speaker unconsciously (for this was not intentional simply to win his tolerance for the boy) reminds him of the regard owing to an uncle and shows him that the uncle feels his reciprocal duty toward a nephew. "Your cousin," he says, not "my son," and by that he again tightens the bond between cousins. This custom, this device, makes kinship more important than any other consideration. Always the tendency was to draw Dakotas nearer to one another in the wič̣ótakuye 'universal human kinship'. A woman said to me the other day, "Daughter, your grandmother is very feeble now. It will sadden you to see her." She was talking about her own mother, but she did not say "my mother," which would cut me off from them both. Kinship relationships produced warmth and comfort. "You belong with us." Reminders of them had both their spiritual and practical effect. The policeman could hardly take a domineering attitude toward a cousin, an uncle's son, just because he was wearing a badge. There were gentler ways of dealing with people. I could not but feel affection and sympathy for my aged social grandmother, and closer to one who called me *daughter*. That was how Dakota kinship worked.

Fathers did not nag or admonish incessantly. Said another informant:

When I was a boy, my father sat me down and talked seriously to me about once a year, going over the same things until I knew them by heart. I was sixteen when he called me in for another session, but I said to him: "Father, I am not a fool. These things you have told me so often that I can never forget them. Why do you repeat them year after year?" I was afraid he would be offended but instead he was gratified. "Son, son," he said. "I hoped you would say this to me one day. Very well, then. Remember that I shall never rehearse these points again." And my father never did.

However, there were times when a father must give preemptory orders, as in an emergency. *Mak'úla's* father once did so, but not without first explaining his reason. One wintry dawn during the boy's teenage years, he roused him roughly. "Wake up, son, wake up! Buffalo are nearby. The chase is about to start. Jump on that swift pony and get into it, you are old enough now. Come, come! Women may stay warm in their beds at a time like this, but real men must go forth! Males may not shrink from striking their skull to the hard ground now and then!"

So *Mak'úla* entered his first communal hunt in a raging blizzard and returned triumphant with a buffalo calf, his first major kill. It was the reference to his maleness that challenged him. To be compared to a woman was the worst possible insult, whose effect was to drive many boys into assuming a man's role regardless of danger and possible death. Even as small boys they were reminded from time to time by fathers and grandfathers, *Winiča yé ló!* 'You are a male!' As already explained, they were argued into good behavior by their male collaterals, or dared to take risks "because they were male." If a small boy cried, they remarked, "Here is a girl crying," and that was enough. Courage and endurance were thus inculcated and induced.

The boy approaching physical maturity seemed not to go through the awkward stage. It was a help to him that his people treated him with that peculiar blend of respect and inattention already noted, and that adolescents were not required to remain in adult company at home. Consequently, even if he felt himself all arms and legs suddenly, he did not act clumsily out of self-consciousness. He was quite free to ride as he pleased and spend much time with only boys his age who also were experiencing normal changes from child to adult manhood and there take his bearings out of sight. Whenever he must be at home, his caring for the family horses as they grazed on the hillsides was a merciful chore away from observation.

People sympathized with a boy's needs during these teen years and accepted the fact that he was away regularly. Nevertheless he was a constant cause of parental anxiety since what could befall him was unsure. They forebore to pry into his activities, only hoping that he was safe and relying on his good sense. If he allowed himself to be provoked into a fight, he might kill or be killed, even if accidentally. In more recent times he might get drunk and be jailed; he might be implicated in some crime and sent to the penitentiary. The possibilities were all but endless. Yet they were kept pushed into the background, and only the faith that somehow he would pass this period unscathed as stoutly held.

The incarceration of human beings was but one more of the white man's oddities. There was no term for it in Dakota. Since only animals were sometimes forcibly held, the term for imprisonment is a borrowed term, *kaškápi* 'to be tied fast'. It was an inconvenience, but no disgrace — an indignity also, of course. Friends did not have to say in an undertone and with blushes, "He is tied up." One woman camping at the agency explained quite naturally the reason for her stay. Indicating the children, she said, "Their father is tied up just now. When he is untied, we shall go home." A boy who returned from the penitentiary was received as joyfully as if he returned from school. His absence had been the grief, but now, at last, here he was! A feast of rejoicing in his name was in order. All his relatives were happy. Kinship once more took precedence. His guilt, if he was guilty, was regrettable, but, unless he had taken a life, mere imprisonment for a duration did not make sense. What did make sense was repayment for a life with a life. There was precedent for that. There was nothing for the relatives but to accept the inevitable consequence with resignation, in that event.

By the time the boy was sixteen or seventeen — the age necessarily varying with individual development — he was ripe for at least a tentative interest in courtship. Then he might pair off with some close companion, often his cousin, and together they might test themselves out in shy experimental skirmishes in pursuit of girl chums who furtively attracted them up to a point — and then ran away: a game that the young of both sexes played with so much subtlety that to all appearances they had no slightest interest in the other!

Since a double standard was an established fact, no boy was checked on, gossiped about, or questioned regarding his movements. Perhaps he was quite innocent, or was actually engaged in a secret affair. "What of it? After all, was he not a male?" Since there was no specific turning point to be publicized, as there was for his sister, and since there were no puberty rites as such, each boy was at liberty to find his own way into full manhood, at his own rate and in his own inconspicuous way. This he did, if he was average.

The following story, with embellishments, was sometimes told for a laugh when congenial men sat talking. I do not know whether it is fact or fiction, but, at any rate, any boy who would be so frank about something that most youths kept adroitly hidden would be acting queerly indeed. If not a bit abnormal, he must be at least belatedly naive.

A boy of seventeen began to act sullen, moody and stopped riding with his companions. Instead, all day he laid in a vacant tipi with "forehead pressed to earth and buttocks high," until his father was compelled to question him. "Son, is something bothering you? Tell me. I am your father, I will stand by you." A long silence, and then a mumbled, "Yes, there is, father. I want to get married." The man was relieved. For a long time he had been disturbed by the boy's lack of a natural interest in girls. "That is great news, son!" he exulted. "It is only right for a man to want a woman. But, tell me, who is to be my daughter-in-law?" Another silence. Then the boy spoke into the ground, "I do not know."

Even were he intimate with some girl, the fact would become manifest only if she was with child and named him as the father of it. Then the blame was on the girl for "running wild and being free with herself." Doubtless her relatives would try to shift the blame onto him, but from the beginning the public largely tended to gloss over his share of the responsibility while it never entirely forgot the girl's misstep. In such a situation in a legend, the boy was killed by the girl's uncle for wronging her, but that would be a rare occurrence.

Fathers talked earnestly with their sons and advised them to avoid any such serious involvement. Although courtship for sport was more or less sanctioned—it could not be effectively prohibited, anyway—elder men disapproved of it. It is said that warriors in particular were against premature courtship for the youthful brave, believing that it could dominate him and hinder him in his pursuit of war. One legend tells of a budding warrior whose promising career was cut short by an alluring woman. His struggles to keep to his chosen course, and his final fall with attendant tragedy, furnish the conflict and climax of the tale.

Any self-restraint must be self-imposed. It was up to a man to decide what he wanted most, and to keep his entire attention on getting it. There was no public notice of or praise for this; it was his own private glory if he succeeded.

However, according to the informant Standing Bull, there existed among the Yanktons a secret society called the *Wimnášni* whose sole condition for membership was to refrain from dealing with women until the four feathers were won, signifying four major deeds in war. Then, as a full-fledged warrior, he might think about courtship and marriage. *Wimnášni* may be paraphrased as "innocent of all taint or influence of womankind." Since the society was exclusively for those who chose the warpath, it would seem that one who disqualified himself must be dropped. However, that point was not clear; nor was it clear whether men who had kept the rule long enough to win their feathers retained membership after marriage, on the basis of their record. My feeling is that they did, but perhaps not. The term *Wimnášni* does not appear in my Teton and Santee material. There may have been similar societies by other names, which have escaped me.

Unlike her brother, who moved into manhood status in relative obscurity, a girl's turning point was no private matter. Case histories would seem to show that the first catamenia appeared somewhat later than is normal today. The ages given were from fourteen to seventeen "winters." These ages may be safely moved back one year, however. The Dakotas counted the winters rather than full years so that one who was born in the autumn was said to be "two winters" old by the second spring. One woman gave her age as seventy, and then explained, "But I was born into my first winter," and she counted that also.

The three usual terms for the catamenia are all euphemisms; *išnátʿi* 'to live alone', *tʿákayąka* 'to sit outside' (i.e., away from the family tipi), and *wakʿą* 'to be holy'. Those who would be even more delicate in their speech said *tókʿeča* 'to be someway; to have something the matter'. The first two terms, used indifferently, were secular terms. The last—no longer heard except as a deliberate archaism—was a religious term to be used only in reference to the doctoring work of medicine men operating with supernatural sanction.

The girl with average intelligence was able to accept the new experience and bridge the transition into womanhood without emotional upset, for she was no stranger to the phenomenon. She had heard mention of it regarding girls older than she, had seen the hasty preparations for their ceremonial withdrawal from home, and was present when women discussed it as one more item in the day's news. And so the girl, even if she was embarrassed by the publicity in her own case, realized that all Teton women had it to endure as their common fate.

Her elder women relatives, mother and others, worked to make it as easy for her as possible by secluding her in a private tipi that they quickly erected at some distance back of her home in the camp circle. It did not have to be a new tipi expressly made for her; any good, smallish tipi would do, and it might be used as an ordinary abode afterward. By that I mean it was not regarded as sacrosanct or as ceremonially unclean from having housed a withdrawal period. Its significance was temporary. On a carpet of pungent sage, blankets and pillows were laid, and water and plenty of good food provided, for this was no fast. For the girl it was in most particulars no different from living at home.

The only special feature was that at the honor place a small hole had been dug "about an arm's length down," and she was caused to sit directly over it so that lifeblood and earth might commingle, both being equally holy and symbolic of fecundity. Theoretically it was the first flux that was not for indifferent disposition. The observance was sometimes postponed until the second period under necessity, as when a camp move was coincidentally in order.

The girl remained nearly immobilized in her tipi, but she did not literally "live alone." No man would knowingly enter there, for a girl in retirement was in sanctuary. Even so her mother and other women relatives took turns staying with her, lest she grow introspective and moody by day or frightened of the dark by night.

She was encouraged to keep busy at fancywork: porcupine quill work, traditionally, and beadwork in more recent times, as European beads became available. If she originated interesting designs with her many-colored media, so much the better, but she was not under pressure to work in silence or without let-up. She stopped to rest, eat, or talk with her companion, and she was not hidden from view. In fair weather the tipi entrance was flung wide open for air and she could be seen at a distance, bending over her work, or sitting, or reclining, as she pleased.

Her visitors were women. They brought her special delicacies and sometimes sat down a while to talk sociably to entertain her. They were required to talk pleasantly of light matters and never of the immediate occasion, lest they embarrass the girl. It would not do to center the attention on her by magnifying what was but a natural process old as womankind.

Moreover, it was required to keep the atmosphere placid and normal, and free of anything untoward—gossip, anger, cruel comments about people, and so on—to the end that the girl's mind might become accustomed to only pleasant ideas during this, her most sensitive and impressionable hour. Her companion of the moment must be alert to steer the conversation into safe channels in case the visitor should be careless on this point. The utmost care was taken in all details to carry the retiring procedure through successfully because of the supposed effect of menstruation not only on the girl herself but on other people, too.

Though the reason was not precisely stated to the girl, according to informants who spoke from their own experience, this necessity was based on two rather vague but persistent folk beliefs. One was that a menstruating woman possessed a temporary power, a *wak'ą́*-ness, which was a threat to the medicine man, whose doctoring would be less effective should the two powers clash, but the medicine man's power did not lose to the menstrual power without a struggle. The opposing forces warred within the patient and caused him to worsen—or even die. No woman would willfully cause this to happen, but it could. She had no control over her power.

That being the belief, the young girl must remain in seclusion during her first flux and not go randomly among people, some of whom might be under religious treatment for their ills, so as to be impressed at the outset with her share of this responsibility of women. She must learn to be careful, for she would be a periodic threat to the sick throughout all her fertile years. Catamenial power was not for healing, as it is said to be among some other tribes, nor was it a conveyor of individual blessing to those who came to be touched by the menstruating girl. No one came for that; it was not that kind of power.

The *Wíyą-Núpapika* 'Two Women' was a double-natured spirit, about which everything seems always to have been extremely vague. Though no informant would take the responsibility for the following notion, nevertheless it was said by those of old that this dual personality lurked about the retiring tipi offering the girl a choice, the good half trying to inspire the girl to become a "good woman" and the bad half luring her into becoming the opposite. The girl who docilely obeyed the rules of retiring thereby made the better choice. The one who broke the rule and ran away from her tipi thereby made the wrong choice and was destined to live forever under the bad nature's control. As its devotee she would incline toward a futile, pleasure-seeking existence and lightly transgress the rules of propriety whenever they got in her way. Restlessness would mark her life.

Perhaps I ought not to put in concrete terms what was never clear to the laity, but, from all I can gather, I infer the following idea. No girl who was constantly accompanied could run away, and, consequently, whenever one did so, her women chaperones were censurable. "They do not love their daughter," it was said of them. "They are not real parents." "They are themselves restless women who seek pleasure and prefer it to the sacrificial task of staying close to the girl to help her through." "Like mother, like daughter." Thus were good and bad women made, in a succession down the family line, or so it was believed.

The work of the *Wįyą-Núpapika* shaping a girl for life was an awesome, elusive matter better left indistinct. Indeed, no woman who underwent retiring was able to tell me that she was informed of the sinister possibility in case she should not keep the rules. The Two-Women was not even mentioned to them. My feeling is that the subject was restricted to sacred lore in which only a few were versed, and they did not divulge such lore randomly, I am told. The *Wįyą-Núpapika* appears in some of the older myths as an incidental character whose ambivalent influence on innocent maidens, for weal or woe, must certainly be the basis for the belief relative to the retiring custom.

It is reasonable to suppose that families who were negligent or were too poor to arrange a retiring period allowed their daughter's initial experience to go unmarked. But the conventional majority, and certainly the able *tʿiyóšpaye* composed of self-respecting families, made it a matter of routine to have all their daughters properly inducted into womanhood via the retiring custom. Generally they gave a feast in the girl's name afterwards, and now and then a family went even further by arranging for the expensive *Tʿatʿąka-Walówąpi* 'Buffalo Sing', a strictly Teton ceremony. It was highly religious, and too involved for adequate presentation at this time.[2]

Subsequent periods did not require a "sitting out," but if a woman wished to be quiet for the few days, her flux was a valid excuse. Then she enjoyed a retreat without any religious implications. Many settled *tʿiyóšpaye-tʿípi* had a small tipi or a dome-shaped hut, resembling a sweat lodge, which stood back of the home tipis for the various women who might care to use it. Two or three whose periods happened to coincide might sit out together and do fancy work there without interruption. The group was informal, sociable, and free of anxiety because other woman relatives automatically cared for their children and families. They brought out food unless the women chose to cook for themselves. The few days of respite prepared them to go back at the end of their period and resume their several home duties.

One woman told of trying to finish some intricate work on saddlebags to be given away at the pending feast, and how she found that sitting out offered her the best chance to finish them on time—which she did. The rule always applied: women were *wak'ą́* during their flux, and could complicate a religious healing and must therefore stay away from the sick.

Fast Whirlwind, an Oglala informant, said of his father: "He had very sore eyes but was being treated by a holy man so that he was certain to be healed. But, alas, one day he walked, with eyes well banged, into an *išnát'i-t'ípi* where three women were doing fancy work. One of them, who knew of his treatments, called out a warning, 'Uncle! Go back! Do not enter here!' But already it was too late. He went blind right then and remained sightless the rest of his life."

Presumably there had been an instantaneous clash of powers and the medicine man's power had lost.

For this alleged clash of powers there was a specific term. The woman's power was said to *ohákaya* the medicine's power. Literally, the word means 'to cause to be blocked or tangled' (*hehʼáka* 'elk', from *hé* 'horn' and *hʼáka*, a stem meaning 'something many-branched, of hard material', like branches or horns). The verb *ohákaya* would thus seem to suggest branchlike things interlocking in conflict and impeding a cure.

The other belief was that whatever a person unconsciously overdid during some emotional crisis became a fixed habit that operated like a spell from which he could not break free. Bereavement if normal grief was mixed with shock as from an unexpected death, and the experience of a first menses, were typical crises that could so dominate as to make one forget everything else, including what one was doing.

Very well, then. If habits could be so nearly instantaneously formed, then by all means let them be *good* habits! Here was the ideal opportunity:

make the most of it by managing the retirement properly! So the girl was caused to hear only agreeable talk, that she might be habituated to it—and shrink from gossip and ugly speculation about her neighbors. She was kept calm and unruffled, that she might always prefer composure to excitability, dignity to unseemly behavior. She was encouraged to do fancywork, that she might prefer to idleness. She was allowed to retain her maidenly reticence, that she might not become a tiresome chatterer. She was given repeated occasion to extend hospitality to her women visitors, that she might be habituated to hospitality "from supernatural compulsion." Finally, she was impressed with the importance of staying in her tipi, that she might not become a gadabout.

The sitting out might be physically uncomfortable but it was not unbearable and would soon be over. In the meantime those desirable traits and virtues for the Dakota woman were supposed to stick as lifelong habits. Though only time would tell if they actually did, it was worth a hopeful try. There were no explicit "Thou shalt nots" and indeed no formal instruction at all. Only the occasion was created, and the atmosphere kept conducively placid—and that was as much as could be done. From there on it was up to some undefined, inscrutable, and invisible something, which was trusted to produce miraculously an ideal woman.

At the end of the period the girl went back home, after she was well purified and rubbed dry with sage leaves and dressed in a fresh gown. Only women attended her in the darkened sweat bath, and they worked by feel only, out of regard for her nakedness. For, even before her maturity, she had grown far too modest to be seen nude by anyone, not excepting her own mother. Not even her female collaterals, for all their permissible informality, saw her so. For that was one of the things "not done." The three instances of exhibitionism in my Dakota material have to do only with mentally afflicted persons who were, of course, not aware of themselves.

Women bathers took extreme measures to avoid being seen naked, particularly by men. They entered the water wrapped in a blanket, which they tossed to the shore after they were well immersed. Finishing their ablutions they either called or reached for it and emerged from the water completely covered. It was a kinship sin to see a bather of the opposite sex, and so men and women bathed at different times and at places out of sight. Even so one could never be sure that some evil-minded man was not stealing a glimpse from behind the rocks or bushes. To impress young girls of the importance of modesty, it was even said that a woman clumsy enough to let herself be seen might as well yield herself since she had nothing left to conceal—an extreme view of the matter.

After such teaching it is small wonder that reservation girls, whose reticence was still pronounced, suffered shame when they found they must bathe together under open showers at school. To this day, after several generations of school experience, many still manage to shield themselves with some light garment while showering. Furthermore, they are careful to look the other way, out of consideration for their schoolmates, lest they embarrass them.

The custom of enshrouding the body in a robe in all seasons was doubtless for concealing body curves in public. Men were embarrassed rather than excited by a revealed female form in public and looked quickly away. If it aroused them they would not let themselves show it, because that simply was not done. Since only a crazy woman could deliberately exhibit herself and no man wanted such a one, even the most lustful would not leer and ogle at such a sight. Of even them it was true that "too great a departure from the normal excites aversion rather than admiration." Some of the most modest-appearing women were women with unsavory reputations. Yet their quiet demeanor in both movement and repose was a thoroughly convincing act. No stranger could spot them in a crowd by flashy dress or loud manners, for, however loose their morals might be, they knew that voluptuousness was no bid for masculine attention.

The withdrawal custom has long been obsolete. Only the oldest informants could describe it in detail out of their own experience. It died out because changing conditions made its proper observance unfeasible. One especially upsetting innovation was the off-reservation boarding school, to which girls were taken as children and returned after two or three years as mature young women. "But without any teaching to mark the change," one woman complained, "it is not surprising that our girls no longer have good habits." Many older people regarded "the schoolgirl manner" as too loud and aggressive to be "womanlike."

Once again this description is my attempt at harmonizing the several Teton accounts given me. Nothing so complete was obtainable from the Yanktons and Santees. My own understanding is that if they also formerly gave the subject as much public emphasis as did the Tetons, it was further back in their history, before the disintegrating effect of culture contact was felt by the Santees first, and then the Yanktons—long before it was felt by Tetons. What I give here is reasonably accurate in essentials, although it omits a few slight local variations of no significance. It is in the main representative of the general Teton picture, coming as it does from four of the seven bands of Tetons—the Oglalas at Pine Ridge Reservation, *Húkpap'aya* at Standing Rock, *Sič'áǧu* (Brules) at Rosebud, and Sans Arcs at Cheyenne River.

It was regarded as improper for a girl to be courted until after her menses started, and this rule, it must be noted, was admirably respected by all well-intentioned men. Only a man who was *witkó* a 'fool', lacking in good sense and indifferent to people's low estimate, might try to flirt with a girl who was still a child, or talk to her in a way calculated to awaken her interest in sex. But for the rest, such behavior was completely out of keeping. One informant reported: "In the twilight one evening a man caught hold of my wrap and asked in a whisper, 'Tell me. Are you ready to be courted?' Since I had not yet 'sat outside,' I replied no. At once he let go of my wrap and said, 'Very well. But I will come back'. After two years he did come back, and I married him."

The ability to conceive and bear a child was correlated with the catamenia, but enlarged breasts were explained by some women to be the result of emotional reaction to petting and necking. A malicious aside from gossiping women was "Surely she is allowing herself to be fondled. Why else should her breasts be so large, young as she is?"—a gross injustice to the naturally roly-poly girl who developed early, but who might be quite innocent of the implied charge that she was being improperly free with herself. It has been reported that, formerly, to forestall any ugly speculation about them, many young women in their twenties, if still unwed, bound their bodies to appear flat-chested as proof of their innocence.

The art of elusiveness was the average adolescent girl's outstanding talent. She managed to keep generally out of sight and even when she must help her mother out in the open, as when packing or striking camp, she maneuvered herself in such a way that she could disappear smoothly if she was being steadily watched. One moment she was there, the next she wasn't. If she came back to resume her work, it was a safe guess that the one who had driven her away by simply looking was no longer there. If she went to other work out of sight, some understanding woman relative took over what she had been doing, without comment. She had done the same thing for the same reason, in her time. The girl did not first give her watcher a stony stare to indicate annoyance, and then dash for cover as though a bear were at her heels. On the contrary, she moved with such deliberation and casualness that he could not flatter himself as having made any impression. All her movements looked plausible.

No young girl was assigned to menial work and held to it but instead was left free to be useful in her own way. Her elders let it be so, sparing her just as their elders spared them when they were young. Thus, haphazardly and without excessive concentration or pressure, she acquired those techniques and skills that she would need to have in her own tipi. On her own initiative she cooked a meal and fed her family in the mother's absence, and if company came, she served them. This she did at first as a novelty but in time she felt responsible to relieve her mother occasionally, and ended by taking her turn with the work of the home.

All the while she was growing more and more self-conscious from an awareness of the opposite sex. *Sču* is the term. This romantic affliction, common to both sexes with reference to each other, plagued them pleasantly and often excitingly throughout their later teens. After once married it was conventional behavior to be matter-of-fact, and leave *sču*-ness behind. Sedate composure was the proper decorum for married people. To be flirtatious, though married, was to be unstable. This might not be surprising in the very young, but a mature person who acted giddy, who habitually walked and talked with affectation, was ludicrous. "See how *sču* she [or he] acts—at her age!" That was the inexcusable part of it. Since one would not be *sču* at one's (intimate) spouse, such behavior hinted at probable extramarital interest, and that was improper.

There was a giggling stage, in preadolescence, when a girl was not yet sure how to behave. By the time she was around twelve, her growing dread of being conspicuous controlled and cured her of that. Like girls the world over, she laughed and enthused freely—but not in public. Only when she was with her own age and sex group did she let go. At this stage a baby or small child was a boon, because it enabled her to express herself by fussing over him. Thus, if baby-tending had formerly been a prosaic duty, now it suddenly turned into a coveted privilege. Since people noticed a baby, while who was holding him was of secondary interest, he gave her an excuse to go about in public with him, letting him have the attention while she, as it were, hid behind him to divert scrutiny from herself.

For at the public gatherings, "nice" girls did not mingle indifferently in the crowd without an obvious reason. If suddenly they went with directness and purpose, it was to deliver a message for an adult or to relieve some woman of her cute baby. Any mother was grateful for the respite, while the girl legitimately moved about with him, because he needed to be amused, or because friends here and there called for her to bring him that they might pet him.

Lacking a reason like that, she remained quiet in her place, a little back of mother, aunt, or elder married sister. Such maidenly diffidence was the bulwark against aggressive men and, no less, against the community gossip (alas, usually a woman!), whose self-appointed mission seemed to be to watch young girls with an eagle eye in order to detect from their most innocuous action a hidden motive to be "bad." It was no wonder that they did not flit hither and yon aimlessly! Their mothers' admonition "If a man is really taken by a certain woman, it is for him to devise a way to see her, so do not parade yourself!" was another reason for them to act guardedly.

All normal fathers no doubt adore their children, but they may demonstrate their love in only the way that is socially acceptable. The Dakota father's love for a daughter who was no longer a child was shown through a respect close to reverence for her person as well as her personality. In the first place, it was unthinkable for men and women to romp and roughhouse together, not even if they were joking relatives. That was "not done." Certainly, then, if a father was informal toward his daughter, the only effect was to dishonor himself and confuse her. Did he cease thinking of her as his daughter? Then he must have gone crazy. That could be the only explanation.

So, fathers and daughters kept their distance, but, indirectly, fathers managed to make a daughter happy. Some even went to foolish lengths for this. It is told of one man that he left his garden at its most critical stage and took his family to the week-long celebration at the agency, simply because their sixteen-year-old daughter had planned on going all winter. "She might be too unhappy and even make herself sick if we did not go." That was to him the best of reasons. When they returned, of course, the garden was beyond saving, and that was too bad, but to have disappointed the girl would have been far worse.

Confident of their father's weakness for them, some girls, though by no means all, tended to be touchy. Their tears were their unfailing weapon:

father could not abide them. They cried if he unintentionally disappointed them, but they did not make a scene by exploding in public. Instead they stole off somewhere and wept quietly until they felt better. If the father learned of his blunder, he was all contrition and hastened to make amends. One man told his wife, "You will have to tell her not to ride the bay. He is too wild, it is not safe, but I dare not forbid her, lest she cry!"

Men seemed unable to keep from buying extravagantly for their daughters, never questioning the wisdom in paying too much for something impractical they seemed to desire. They were more sensible when buying for their sons, who must learn spartan ways, but mothers with subtle insistence looked out for their sons' wants so that in the end sons and daughters enjoyed equal attention. Parents would not arbitrarily say no. Instead they seemed to anticipate with a sixth sense their children's undeclared wishes and longings. Hardly would the latter need to tease them for anything. For the normal adolescent was too discerning to expect what was plainly beyond his parents' ability to obtain. Only as much younger children did they sometimes cry for the impossible, being still not fully reasonable.

One informant remarked, "No decent man would live all alone with a young girl, even if she was his daughter. Such things did not look right." It was a fact that fathers were happiest if they could leave their motherless daughter with one of her aunts or mothers (i.e., mother's sisters or cousins). For she needed a woman's chaperonage and counsel, and a certain sympathy and comfort that no father could give. If she was old enough to be courted, certainly he was not the one to supervise her conduct, since a daughter's femaleness was completely outside her father's province. This fact would make it shockingly irregular for him to pry into her courtship and—even more—to tease and pester her with jokes about her suitors. Insofar as a man would think of doing that, he would be stepping out of character as her father, and that would indicate that his attitude was not what it ought to be. The only relatives who might permissibly tease a girl about her courtships were her female collaterals and her male joking relatives. No one else. This would give the daughter the right to distrust a father whose behavior did not conform to the behavior that was proper for Dakota fathers.

The father's correct attitude and behavior in regard to his daughter's romances was exemplified in the following incident:

A drunken youth of no special importance in the community once followed a dignified man all over town, shouting from time to time, "I am going to marry your daughter. What do you say to that?" He had never dared speak to the girl but was indulging in bravado. When the man could no longer ignore him, he stopped and said, with admirable restraint, "My daughter is not a child. She makes her own decisions. So do not come to me. I have nothing to say." (He had plenty to say, but he could not say it: "My daughter, indeed! You no-account fool!") So he said the only thing a Dakota father could say, rather than seem to forbid her marrying. To be sure of maintaining the correct manner of fathers, a man was best off in not knowing. When his daughter decided to marry, that was soon enough for him to know officially. If she sought parental advice, father and mother conferred in private, but only the mother gave her their opinion.

Sometimes, however, a father was rightly disturbed because his daughter wished to marry a man who was, in his opinion, unworthy. He discussed the matter in private with his male collaterals, who were the girl's other fathers. Should they agree with his position and be able to back up their opinion with concrete evidence, one would say, "Brother, it is said on good authority that he was married to a fine girl where he came from, but he treated her cruelly and finally left her . . ." Then the man's wife might speak to her daughter in warning. Better still if their elder married sister did so. For she would pull no punches in enumerating the unworthy suitor's glaring faults, since sisters did not stand on ceremony with one another. An enamored girl might remain unimpressed and perhaps eventually elope with the man anyway, but her father would have quietly gone as far as he could to save her.

Open and violent objection could be misinterpreted by those who, without having all the facts and reasons, were quite ready to indulge in disagreeable speculation about him. Did the man object to his daughter's marrying? If so, why? The very inference would be shameful. So it was, according to reports, when a certain white man kept his young daughter tied up so the story ran, because he did not want her to be courted. His Dakota neighbors thereupon turned suddenly away from him. For, from their premise, there could be but one explanation of such behavior: the man was indecent. He wanted the girl for himself!

Elsewhere I have said that sometimes a girl was given gratuitously to some able man, often her brother-in-law, to be a cowife with her sister. This was to insure protection for the girl who, lacking suitable chaperonage, might otherwise get into trouble. Sometimes parents selected some very desirable unattached man whom they wanted for a son-in-law and proffered their daughter to him, but these were extraordinary situations. Also, sometimes a girl was bought with horses and other valuable gifts. Then, ostensibly at least, she was left to accept or reject the offer. The ideal attitude of parents was, "Let her decide, since she alone is involved."

Should a mother object to her son's intended bride, the same sort of criticism would fall on her, but it was not in the tradition for a Dakota mother to keep a grown son tied to figurative apron strings. She would blush to announce, "My son does not care for girls; he says I am the only sweetheart he wants!" However, she could not say that even if she were insane because she could not ideate what was quite alien to her thought patterns while she was rational. Instead she openly encouraged her son to take a wife, saying, "Son, how happy I should be caring for your children! Oh, before I must die may that come to pass!" And she would praise some eligible girl in his hearing and enumerate her assets and admire them one after another, hoping she would thereby awaken his interest in her.

The Dakota mother did not weep because her son married, but instead she welcomed his bride proudly and showed her kinship respect and courtesy—overdoing it all a little—to show that this was what she wanted for her son. In a manner of speaking, a man's marriage was his mother's justification. One woman I knew gave a big feast and there selected a dozen or more prominent guests, asking them to "please shake hands with my daughter-in-law." Then, as though they had done her a great personal honor, she gave them all fine presents. Of course, every guest shook hands with the bride anyway, but she arranged for this ceremonial hand-shaking in the bride's name. It was an extra gesture.

In the light of the foregoing facts it should become understandable why, on the whole, young people were fairly free from parental interference, supervision, and, especially, vicarious participation in their romances. However, it was not unheard-of for a girl's mother to be so violently opposed to her daughter's choice that public opinion no longer mattered. It is told of one woman that in her frenzy she broke the traces, and went about hurling invectives and cruel epithets in the direction of her daughter's unworthy suitor. "The likes of him! How dare he aspire to my precious daughter? Who does he think he is? That . . . that *t'iyókitạhela-ú!*" would approximate the things she said. By *t'iyókitạhela-ú* 'dweller between (and not in) tipis', she was in effect calling him a nobody.

Meantime the young people slipped away and were married by the justice of the peace in a nearby town. As it turned out the joke was on her, for the young man proved himself an exemplary avoidance relative. He missed no opportunity to help his wife's people and do them honor—perhaps even pouring it on, in retaliation—while all the time he carefully avoided getting in their way. In time they became the envy of others with less punctilious sons-in-law. In complete surrender the chastened woman voluntarily recanted. "Oh, the things I said about my *t'akóš!* Now every time he honors me, I am more ashamed than ever!" she would say, hoping her words would get back to him. She could not say it directly because of the respect rule never to talk to a son-in-law. Perforce she herself became a model mother-in-law.

Women were as concerned over their sons' welfare and happiness as fathers over their daughters' and they also tried to please them. Doubtless out of regard for a young son's manly independence, they expressed their devotion in subtler ways. Sons accepted their mother's ministrations confidently, as something they could always rely on. Because they were not surprised they did not say much. It was simply the way of a mother: she could not help herself.

However, in old age, men expressed their appreciation of their mothers, and marvelled aloud on their constancy. Said one:

Homákšila k'ų́hạ ạpétu ál-átaya maníl šų́k-wíh'ạwak'iyį ná h̃tayétu-wakú č'á č'ạté waštéya wakú ečé. Tók'eȟča hạt'éhạ k'éyaš ak'é iná eč'ų́kapįšni p'etíčagla ụwéya yuhá amákip'e-yakį́kta slólwaye čí ų́. . . . Wašį́ska wíčahiye-zí ų́ káǧapi k'ó k'alyá mígnake s'á k'ú, tóhuweni tákuni hehą́yạ oyúlwašté watį́kte šní.

This is full of nostalgia. A free rendering would be:

In my youth, when I returned home each evening after grazing the horses all day somewhere alone, I always rode home happy. For I knew that no matter how late there would my mother be again, without fail, sitting beside her fire waiting for me, with food ready. . . . Never will anything taste so downright good as did the salt pork and soda biscuits she kept warm for me.

Something akin to this sentiment was expressed by a man over sixty when his only surviving mother—youngest of his own mother's collaterals—was brought down from Canada "to see my son once more before I die." Out in the shade mother and son sat all day on a blanket spread on the ground and talked of the many incidents of his childhood which she remembered vividly, and recalled their relatives—long since dead—who cooperated in nurturing him lovingly. He could not get enough of it. Oblivious to the immediate, transported to another day and setting, he relived his youth, when life was sweet.

So close he sat to the tiny, fragile old woman in order to catch her every word, that when his wife brought out their dinner she remarked teasingly, "Well! No matter how glad, he does not need to crush her!" But his answer was in dead earnest. "Let me be for now. I have starved for mothering these fifty years!" In this, his last auxiliary mother, he could sense his own mother's attitude toward him.

But she varied her behavior from the conventional, in the way of very old people, who often bypassed the stringent rules they once obeyed as a point of honor. Apparently she, too, had starved for a son, and she did not hesitate to gaze searchingly into the man's eyes with frank affection as though he were her little boy, and stroke his shoulder now and then. He did not return her caresses—it would be wrong for him—but he sat placid and did not shy away from her.

There is no denying this was extraordinary behavior toward a mature man, even if he was a son, but so was the occasion extraordinary. As a rule Dakotas might not veer with impunity from the prescribed attitudes and behaviors that, as already explained, were scrupulously observed by the law-abiding majority. Even parents and their grown children of opposite sexes were governed by the tenet that a man's arms are for a wife only, and a woman's for a husband only, and then never in public. Anything to the contrary was considered close to scandalous.

For example: one morning many years ago, a young girl was found dead in her bed. This gave her family an almost unbearable shock, because she had never complained of being ill, though she was always listless. While they were wailing inconsolably—and their neighbors were "helping them to wail"—the girl's nineteen-year-old brother came in and went straight to his prostrated mother and took her in his arms to comfort her.

The impulse to comfort her was natural, but what he did was an unheard-of thing. However, he was quickly condoned. "The boy has been away at school so long, it was inevitable that he picked up foreign customs. White people do that." But the woman had laid herself open to censure for accepting her son's unwarranted embrace so passively! She need not push him roughly away—there were other ways. She could have risen and gently left him to go to some duty. The fact that she was distraught at the moment was no excuse. Womanly conduct should be automatic, whatever the exigency! Such were some of the murmured comments, later on.

But at the moment no notice seemed to be taken of the matter. It was a characteristic of the Dakotas that they took in a situation in its various details without apparently "seeing" it. In that way this, too, registered, and it came up for rehashing whenever two or three close women friends passed the time of day in confidential talk. If some were inclined to be lenient, none could deny outright that the mother's behavior had been improper in the extreme. Incidentally—or so it seems to me—it was women who made much of such slips of conduct and talked of them critically. Men usually let them pass without comment, unless they were forced to express an opinion: "Well, yes. I suppose it was irregular."

One last facet of this parent-child relationship remains. I am strongly tempted to skip it altogether, rather than risk giving it unintentional emphasis. For actually what I have in mind is without substance and consequently lacks a name. To say that it is "a voluntary surrender of position, for a definite purpose" is to be wordy without clarity. Intangible and elusive as it is, perhaps it is better described and defined.

As their daughters near adulthood, in some instances even earlier, many women seem to fall back into second place. Privately they still hold the reins; they coach their daughters behind the scenes concerning the new duties and responsibilities awaiting them. But in public one acts absurdly confused over some simple problem until her daughter must set her straight on it. Then she submits happily, proudly. In one such case, the mother said resignedly to her friends, "Well, I suppose I am just getting old and foolish." She and they knew that she was far from old, far from foolish; that she was in fact one of the most astute and able women in the community.

This would seem to be the final phase of a mother's training. All along she had been pointing out what was morally right and socially correct—not so much by incessant preaching as by occasional comments on women's behavior; she had said, "What that one did was right; what this one did was improper for a relative." But now that the teaching must be put to practical application, the mother deliberately created artificial situations in which she was volunteer guinea pig so that her daughter might sooner learn to assert herself, take the initiative, and acquire adult good sense in practicing on her. This might well be called the Dakota woman's special self-sacrifice for her child's sake.

Thereafter, she inclined to defer to her daughter. *Mičʼŭkši iyómakʼišni čʼá* . . . 'My daughter forbids me, and so . . .' was a typical maternal boast. Always this was in the mother's interest as in the instance I observed once. "I am not going again," a woman said. "My daughter says no, because she feels that I am being imposed on." Just as if she could not see that for herself, and must be saved by her daughter!

Another instance was as follows. An illiterate woman was about to sign papers drawn up by a white man who wanted to lease her land when her daughter came upon the scene and stopped her. "Wait," she said. "This could be to your disadvantage. You do not know what those papers say." The docility with which her mother took her advice was plainly affected. Later she told some women, "How stupid I am getting to be! Why, just the other day I was going to be 'blue-thumbed' on a paper I did not understand. But, as usual, my daughter saved me in time! She is very wise and learned." *Napʼáhŭka tʼó* 'blue thumb' meant a signature, as on a document. To this day, though the number of those who cannot write at least their name is lessening all the time, the idiom stands.

It was sheer self-praise. As much as to say, Behold the product of my training: a mature, self-assured young woman with much wisdom and learning. "I, her mother, must look to her!" For even if her daughter was not so wise and learned, her mother wished to have her show up well—at her own expense, any time it was necessary.

In their own way, fathers sacrificed, too, though never so selflessly or completely. At one annual gathering of a men's state-wide society, the eldest delegate blocked nearly every motion, thinking them too radical.

At times he even heckled the youthful new president—something nearly unheard-of—in a voice that resounded throughout the ample meeting place.

He would ask, "Eh? What was that?" When the new motion was explained to him, he would snort, *Hóȟ!* a man's word equivalent to "Oh no! Surely not *that!*". He would go on, "Of course you are all mere lads—but try to think! Think! In my day men were thinkers!" Then, leveling his cane in the direction of the chair, "When your father was our leader, he used caution. His judgment was never rash."

Out of respect for age, the president would not argue or call him to order. Instead he appealed to the old man's son privately during recess. "Brother, speak to our father. You can see we are not getting anywhere." The boy called his father to one side and was heard to say to him, "Stop it, old man! You do not see the new problems we have to meet in these new times. In your day things were simpler. *Kaǧíyaye kištó wą!* 'Can't you see, you are hampering him!'"

Smiling wryly the old man came back to his seat without a word. Later, when he was asked to comment on something he at first pretended not to hear, he rose with a grunt—he was a rather unwieldy man—and, petulantly, he began. "Of course, I can see you are rapidly moving towards the cliff. But go ahead, boys, go right ahead. Kill yourselves if you like. As for me, I'm not talking anymore. Amos is sticking up for his brother and scolding me." It was his indirect way of showing pride in his boy's first assumption of manly authority—even though he squirmed under it, a little.

It was never easy for the male to surrender irrevocably. In all my material I have no instance of a father's deliberately sticking his neck out in the precise way of many mothers. But at least this much can be said of them: most Dakotas are proud and eager to concede to even adolescent sons the full status of men. Men as good as themselves.

Afterword

Philip J. Deloria

For those who have studied the writings of Ella Deloria, it has become something of a truism that she was deeply invested in kinship. She insisted on its importance in her 1944 book, *Speaking of Indians*, and in many of her other writings. The description of and praise for kinship relations proved to be a reliable, and much appreciated, aspect of her public speaking and educational career. No doubt some part of that interest stemmed from the methods of ethnographic fieldwork of the era, which often began with elaborate chartings of individuals and their kinship networks and ended with theoretical and comparative work on kinship that dated back to the methodological innovations of Lewis Henry Morgan.

It is quite clear, though, that Ella Deloria's focus on kinship grew mostly out of her own kinship experiences, both as a child growing up in Dakota and Episcopalian communities *and* as an ethnographer enabled and constrained by her kinship relationships to her collaborators. Here, in *The Dakota Way of Life*, one finds her rich and full account of Dakota kinship: the detailed range of its possibilities, its behavioral mechanisms, its cultural meanings, and its social functions. These were the ways of being that structured Ella Deloria's own thought and action, visible not simply in the accounts of her "informants," but also in her own ethnographic and personal experiences. Those experiences are given shape in the use of personal anecdote and shared story, which helps bring these pages to life and gives us a taste of Ella's own unique voice.

Ella Deloria was also shaped, and shaped herself, in relation to the world of Columbia University anthropology, and, in particular, her mentors Franz Boas and Ruth Benedict. Indeed, if Boas's hand can often be seen — as coauthor, for instance — in most of Ella's earlier writing, one reads *The Dakota Way of Life* and finds something distinct: an appreciation for the "culture and personality" arguments given form in Benedict's 1934

365

book, *Patterns of Culture*. Benedict wondered how individual and social development were linked to, and productive of, cultural patterns that existed on an arc of possible social organization and human behavior. For Ella Deloria the cultural patterns that defined Dakota life were to be found in the detailed kinship relations and behaviors described so thoroughly in this book.

Taking *kinship* and *culture and personality* as central organizing principles, one can see the way that Ella's argument developed over the course of this book. Though she did not separate the study into discrete sections, it does in fact fall into three. In the first seven chapters, she offers a descriptive account of "camp circle life." She is giving us the ethnographic content that will become grist for the kinship analysis that makes up the second section, chapters 8 through 11. A third section, chapters 12 through 14, draws from Benedict, tracing the development of the Dakota individual (a "personality," if you will) from birth through adulthood, observing closely the various mechanisms that shaped those individuals into a distinctively Dakota cultural and social subjectivity. Those mechanisms and that development explain the "camp circle" world, and thus return readers back to the first chapters and the descriptive elements of a Dakota way of life. If Ella never quite drafted a conclusion for the book, we can nonetheless do her the favor of thinking on and with these three sections and observing the ways that they do in fact form a unified whole and a sequential argument. *The Dakota Way of Life* is a book to study, for content, and to *be studied*, for its form and the mechanics of its production. In that sense the book and its fraught history offer telling insights into American anthropology, the rise of modernist forms of literary expertise and authority, the constraints on Native scholars such as Ella Deloria, and the "fictive kin" relations with figures like Boas and Benedict that both enabled and constrained her possibilities.

Ella Deloria spent much of her peripatetic career making the rounds between New York and South Dakota. Ella's September 1948 visit to Columbia University should therefore come as no great surprise—though it was her first visit to New York City in over three years. In her valise were two manuscripts: the novel that would eventually be published as *Waterlily* and the ethnographic study *The Dakota Way of Life*, sometimes known as "Camp Circle Society". Both projects had been underway for almost a decade. She had commenced the novel as it became apparent that her years with Franz Boas were winding to a close; the ethnography was to be the culmination of fieldwork undertaken during the 1930s.

Boas had mentored an amazing number of women anthropologists: Ruth Benedict, Margaret Mead, Gladys Reichert, Ruth Bunzel, and Ruth Landes, among others. Many (though not all) of these women were able to pursue higher education precisely because they had the financial resources to sustain their work. Ella Deloria, as she pointed out to Benedict early in their relationship, occupied a very different position, always working and always in need of cash. As Boas's fieldwork money dried up, Ella began to contemplate what would come next, hoping that it could more directly involve writing and research. After a slightly rocky beginning, she and Benedict had grown relatively close over the course of the 1930s, and, when Boas died in 1942, it was Benedict who agreed to help Ella make a transition from fieldworker into scholar.

Ella would always be something of a vernacular scholar—more than once she lamented not earning a PhD—but, in point of fact, she had received basically the same linguistic training as Benedict, Margaret Mead, and other Boas students. When it came to fieldwork, Ella insisted on a bicultural practice—and, by implication, the bicultural nature of her training. Always sensitive to kinship and hospitality obligations, she traced the development of her ethnographic skills not only to Columbia, but also to sessions with her father, who made Lakota connections for her, coached her on kinship behaviors, and helped her understand what kinds of questions could and could not be asked of people holding certain social roles or sitting in particular relationship to *her*. Bicultural practice and training could not also help but produce an equally bicultural literary style.

It was not inconceivable—to Ella, at least—that, even without Boas's guiding hand, she might achieve some respect and acceptance within the field. That acceptance, she knew, needed to translate into a reliable and remunerative position, perhaps even a career—if not in anthropology, then in church or Indian Service work, two related fields that she had long considered. In any case, she needed to move from acts of collection and translation, undertaken for someone else and consolidated in the occasional article or in coauthored publications like *Dakota Grammar* (1941) to original writing, scientific research in which she was the primary interpreter of the material.

And thus the two manuscripts she carried to New York City in 1948. The first, inspired by Benedict's advice to collect material on family, kinship, social life, and the role of women, was the scholarly work that she had promised to complete in fellowship applications to the American Philosophical Society. The second was fictional, a new rendering of her ethnographic research that took the form of a multigenerational women's story. *Waterlily* had been in Ella's mind, and quite likely her typewriter, at least since 1942, and possibly even earlier.

There seems little doubt that Ella Deloria had struggled with both manuscripts. Her first funding proposal for the projects dates from 1939, and, in the years following, she had been patching together an income as best she could while trying to stay focused on the manuscripts. Fellowship grants from the American Philosophical Society in 1943 and 1944 finally allowed her the financial support needed to complete the ethnography, and one can only imagine a rare current of optimism entering into her writing routine.

Those two years, 1943 and 1944, proved to be among the most productive of her career. In addition to working on *Waterlily* and *The Dakota Way of Life*, she also published a short but powerful apologia, *Speaking of Indians* (1944), written for the Episcopal Church. Benedict was looking helpfully over Ella's shoulder. In November 1944 she wrote Ella to discuss both manuscripts, promising to help get the ethnography "in fine shape for the Philosophical Society to publish." Ella's letters reveal her to be a strong writer, with a classical sense of language and a gift for turning a phrase. But, just as she had to refresh her Dakota-language skills and then learn to do fieldwork and to understand the conventions of linguistic interpretation, so, too, did she labor to acquire the editorial and structural skills of a long-form writer. Benedict promised to help her hone those skills and to connect her with the publishing world:

Mrs. [D. E.] Emery read your *Waterlily* with great appreciation. She thoroughly agreed with me that it would be appreciated and could be published. She made quite a number of suggestions, largely in connection with cutting the ms down to the usual size for such a book. We must get together and go over them, so that, when the war is over and publishers are taking books that don't have to do with the war effort, the manuscript will be ready to submit to them. There is no immediate hurry about this, though, for the first thing to do is to get your study finished for the Philosophical Society. There's one caution for your preparation of the manuscript for them, though: don't try to make it as long as you can; try to illustrate points you want to make with good stories, but don't think you have to expand the discussion just to make it long. (November 7, 1944)

Ella's writing troubles continued. Indeed, there is a kind of family folklore surrounding both the novel and the ethnography: that they were ungovernable tangles of story, proliferating across multiple drafts and confounding everyone who sought to untangle them, including Ella herself. Both Benedict and Emery seemed to hint that the works had gotten long and out of control, though one might wonder about the stylistic differences between Ella's expansive love of detail and the emerging canons of the publishing industry her readers tried to anticipate. What is clear is that Ella failed to complete the grant-funded projects in 1944. When asked to demonstrate her work to the American Philosophical Society, she presented and then later published the shorter piece, "The Dakota Treatment of Murderers," which, as we can now see, was part of *The Dakota Way of Life*.

She moved to Tampa for the winter of 1945–46 and reported to a friend that she had her notes and was working on a manuscript based on the kinship system, although she also worried that she had no grant support; money was now going to "practical research." In 1947 she reported being finished with *Waterlily*. And yet to another friend she observed, "I am nowhere near through." She seems, in these years, to have started up a sequel to *The Dakota Way of Life*, perhaps aiming to produce a more marketable "practical research" that would trace contemporary practices for the emergent world of applied anthropology. She gave speeches throughout the eastern United States, wintered cheaply in Tampa, and started work on a Dakota dictionary.

By 1948, though, she seemed to be getting close to finishing both her manuscripts, writing in June of that year from a new home base in Flandreau, South Dakota: "I expect to remain here until I finish my book, the story of the Indian girl who lived a century ago. It has been revised and I have only 80 more pages to copy. . . . In September I shall be returning East, and all summer I am going to work on revising another manuscript which has been edited for me at Columbia. It is about Dakota family life, in the past of course." It is not hard to surmise that the editorial hand at Columbia was that of Ruth Benedict, and that she was perhaps giving *Waterlily* some of her time as well. Benedict was actually not in residence in New York that summer, having gone to Europe. But she told Ella that she would return after Labor Day, that Ella should come back to New York, and that they would sit down together and finish off the book, which had now been adrift for almost four years.

Ella was not the only Native writer to struggle with editing and publishing. John Joseph Mathews (Osage) and John Oskison (Cherokee) saw their manuscripts rejected by both New York publishers and regional presses such as the University of Oklahoma. As writers they were caught in a moment of transition, as older intellectual leadership — often vernacular "armchair" scholars — gave way to a new cohort of cultural authorities, trained in the modern universities, brandishing credentials and newfound power. The combination of modernist expressive forms, supposedly concerned with innovation, and highbrow gatekeeping tended to push other modes to the wayside. Native writers faced particular forms of marginalization. Insufficiently "Indian" to be primitivist, insufficiently legitimate to be modern, they fell between the cracks. The American Philosophical Society's report on Ella's presentation of *The Dakota Treatment of Murderers* emphasizes what one might take as an unauthorized expressive style. It was warm, humorous, and story-centered, worlds away from either the confident colonial expertise of the Victorian or the brisk arrogance of the modernist authority. It makes perfect sense, then, that *Speaking of Indians* emerged outside of the mainline publications circuit, as a "church" book, and that Deloria felt the need to wonder what might have been had she possessed an advanced degree. These things offer contextual evidence for the challenges presented to her by the cultural moment, even by those she considered her allies and friends.

We should try, empathetically, to imagine Ella's frustration. And with it we must try to anticipate her excitement, her impending relief at the prospect of getting the ethnography out of her typewriter and out into the world. Given her continuing financial struggles, we should also try to imagine our way toward Ella's own hopes for *Waterlily*. "Pray," she would later write to a friend, "that my novel will come to the notice of the right editor, who can see its worth and appreciate its peculiar flavor.

I know it is good." Her judgment on both counts—the book's quality and "peculiarity"—proved accurate, if painfully so. All of the anxiety and possibility surrounding the book came to rest firmly on Benedict's shoulders. Ella arrived back in New York in mid-September, and she headed almost immediately for the university. "Upon arriving," she wrote, "I found a funeral going on at St. Paul's Chapel, Columbia."

And then the bombshell: "It was Ruth's! She had died very suddenly with a heart attack, which shocked everyone, because nobody ever suspected it of her." Ella had come to town to consult with the mentor who was going to help ease her into work as a writer-scholar—and found, as had so often been the case in her extraordinary life, the toughest of tough breaks. "That threw all my plans awry, and shook me up pretty badly," she later recalled. Ella retreated to Florida once again, set to work alone on the editing, and, despite her best efforts, failed once again to produce legibly "publishable" manuscripts. With *Waterlily*, she received turndowns from Macmillan and from the University of Oklahoma Press. And though Margaret Mead later stepped in to write an introduction to *The Dakota Way of Life*, offered some editorial help, and even transmitted the manuscript to the American Philosophical Society on Ella's behalf, the work, so long and labored in its gestation, did not see the light of day.

When *Waterlily* was first published posthumously in 1988, there was immediate acclaim for the work: it appeared as a (post)colonial ethnographic novel, an innovation in form excavated from an unjust history of nonpublication. *Waterlily* reminded scholars that Ella Deloria needed to be seen as a major presence in the historiography of settler colonial anthropology, and there was a collective sense of regret that the book had failed to find a sympathetic and visionary publisher during Deloria's lifetime, one able to step outside the matrices of modernist cultural authority that she confounded so well. Susan Gardner's literary historical scholarship offered detailed accounts of the book's writing and editorial process, and Maria Cotera's 2008 volume, *Native Speakers: Ella Deloria, Zora Neale Hurston, Jovita Gonzales, and the Poetics of Culture*, helped reveal how a number of women of color situated on the margins of anthropology and folklore turned to fiction as an effort to communicate their own scholarship. What *The Dakota Way of Life* reveals, then, is that the challenges Ella Deloria faced with *Waterlily* were of a piece. In addition to her own struggles as a writer, Ella—along with Oskison, Mathews, Hurston, Gonzales, and many others — confronted structural and institutional impediments to her work, which should be read as systemic rather than particular.

Few scholars have been as attuned to these challenges or as committed to rectifying them as Raymond J. DeMallie, arguably one of the most accomplished anthropologists to ever focus on the Great Plains. DeMallie — who appears as the author of an afterword to *Waterlily* — had been a close friend of the Deloria family since the 1960s. As a young scholar, he sought to learn from my great-aunt Ella Deloria herself. For many years he worked closely with my grandfather, Vine Deloria Sr., particularly on language and linguistics. DeMallie was a longtime collaborator with my father, Vine Deloria Jr., a relationship most notably visible in the important collection *Documents of American Indian Diplomacy: Treaties, Agreements, Conventions, 1775–1979.*

Growing up I can remember my father teasing Ray about anthropologists: they were both heirs and participants in a complicated genealogy that encompassed Ella Deloria and Margaret Mead, the sharp exchanges between Mead and my dad, Ella and Ray, Ray and my father, and Ray and myself (and perhaps, through the distant thread of early American studies, between Mead and myself). My dad would toss out witty, pithy jokes on the evils of anthropology, and Ray would sit, quiet and bemused, and then bring them back to the point and back to work. Later Ray proved a guiding light for me as well. I went dog shopping with him in Colorado and hiking in Arizona. He and my mom bailed me out when I collapsed on a high school camping trip, and he was a comforting presence during the low-key summer I spent recovering from mononucleosis. Ray gave me the opportunity to work briefly with him and Doug Parks at Fort Belknap, encouraged me to consider graduate school, and offered thoughts and corrections on my work out of his own voluminous knowledge. He treated me like a grown-up and serious scholar long before I had earned the right to either. Ray DeMallie was, quite simply, an extraordinary human being.

Long before *Waterlily* splashed down as a book, Ray realized the importance of *The Dakota Way of Life* and the necessity of untangling the tangles, merging the drafts together for maximum impact, and getting the work into print. He made the book a project and devoted himself to it for years — through health challenges, institutional negotiations, and the massive pile of work that Ray had set for himself. When it became apparent that he needed help getting the book across the finish line, he recruited Thierry Veyrié to bring it to completion, which Thierry has done admirably and well. The result is the densely descriptive account of family and social life before you, laced through with Ella's characteristic turns to narrative and story. As anyone who was lucky enough to hear her speak can testify, she was an extraordinary storyteller, with a gift for drama and humor that can still be glimpsed in these pages.

My grandfather became Ella's literary executor, and he had an understanding with Ray DeMallie. Ray was the chosen one, the person my grandfather trusted to do right by Ella, to whom he gave the task of bringing *The Dakota Way of Life* to the world. Ray promised to do just that. He was obliged to make the book happen, and Ray and Thierry together (along with Matt Bokovoy and our friends and colleagues at the University of Nebraska Press) were able to fulfill the promise.

In 1948 Ella Deloria lost Ruth Benedict at exactly the wrong time, and the loss must have been soul-destroying. This time around things played differently. We lost Ray DeMallie in 2021, and those who knew and loved him continue to grieve. But his commitment—to my grandfather and to Ella—is fulfilled with the publication of this book, closing the circle on a long-standing promissory note and a bit of disciplinary and cross-cultural redemption. That note was originally drafted back in 1944 by Ruth Benedict, who was in some measure stepping up on behalf of Franz Boas himself. I hope that somewhere, in a "camp circle" afterlife that looks thoroughly Dakota, all of them—Boas, Benedict, Mead; Ella, Vine Sr., Vine Jr.; and Ray DeMallie and Doug Parks—can join together with those of us who remain behind, at least for now, to celebrate the return, at long last, of *The Dakota Way of Life*.

Notes

Acknowledgments

1. All correspondence between Ella Deloria and Hiram Beebe is from the Southwest Museum of the American Indian, Los Angeles, California.

Presentation of Ella Cara Deloria

1. Philip Deloria was baptized on Christmas Day, 1870, and was ordained priest on September 4, 1892 (Olden 1918, xii, 14). Lodge groups, *tʻíyošpaye*, which Ella Deloria calls "camp circles" in this volume, averaged ten to twenty families. They were led by a recognized chief, the *itʻáčʻa*, who often inherited their position from their fathers, if they were qualified and received the consent of the band council (DeMallie 2001b, 734–35).
2. All correspondence between Ella Deloria and Franz Boas is from the American Philosophical Library, Philadelphia, Pennsylvania.
3. All correspondence between Ella Deloria and Ruth Benedict is from the Vassar College Library, Arlington, New York.

Introduction

1. The Santees and Yanktons called themselves *Dakʻóta*, while the Tetons used *Lakʻóta*. During much of the twentieth century, "Dakota" was the term used to designate all three divisions; the *Plains* volume of the *Handbook of North American Indians* used "Sioux" to avoid the confusion caused by using the name of a part to designate the whole. For a discussion of dialect differences, see Parks and DeMallie (1992).
2. Most Lakotas pronounce *Húkpapʻa*, but Ella Deloria wrote it as *Húkpapʻaya*. Deloria uses the diacritics ʻ for an aspirated consonant, and ʼ for a glottalized consonant. She provides more details on Dakota phonology in chapter 12.
3. Ella Deloria described the *Nakóda* "Tying" divining ceremony, the *Yuwípi*, at more length in chapter 3 of her "Assiniboine Report" ([ca.] 1933). A medicine man could be bound with ropes to get him to the divine. This ceremony required to prepare a fire and to build a tipi over it. One pole was erected upright so it went through the smoke vent, and offerings to the Supernatural, a drum, a whistle, and a rattle were hung at the top of it. The medicine man was bound with a long thong, starting with his fingers, then tying his hands behind him,

and finally winding the thong about him, around and around. He was laid in the honor place of the tipi, and everyone left him. Inside the tipi people could hear him sing, pray, and call on his helpers. Suddenly, the drum, the rattle and the whistle sounded and the pole started shaking visibly. One spectator said, "And then the *íyąškąšką*, 'rocks in motion' came down and I heard them fall." The medicine man started conversing with the stones, but his voice alone could be heard. At last, when he emerged from the tipi, he carried the thongs neatly coiled around his arm. He had been informed of the return of lost warriors and shared his divination at the council tipi.

4. According to Douglas R. Parks, "Until the mid-nineteenth century the Sioux [or Dakota] occupied most of present Minnesota, northwestern Iowa, North and South Dakota, and parts of eastern Wyoming and Montana and northern Nebraska" (2001, 97). The proto-Siouan homeland, the hypothetical region from which these languages may have originated, is the object of debate (104–5).

5. *Mak'úla* died in 1935. Ella Deloria wrote about him as she was traveling to Pine Ridge: "*Mak'úla* or 'Left Heron,' who was the best historian on Pine Ridge, and was 88, died just two weeks before I arrived. It was from him that I got many of my legends in the past, and much information on customs and the like. I miss him dreadfully" (August 25, 1935). According to her again, *Mak'úla* was also a source for James R. Walker: "It is definitely established that he was one of Walker's constant informants" (December 5, 1939). Three stories that Walker received from *Mak'úla* were published in 1983 (Walker 1983, 101–33).

6. Before the Dakota adopted the horse for travel, they used dogs as pack animals. Travois consisted in "poles fastened together where they crossed over a dog's withers, and sometimes with a small platform on the drag behind" (DeMallie 2001a, 7).

7. John C. Ewers investigated the history of the horse in the northern plains and found that the Assiniboines, according to La Vérendrye, who met them at the Mandan villages in present-day North Dakota, traveled without horse in 1738. La Vérendrye's son, however, took two horses back to the Mandan villages in 1741, which Ewers dates as the beginning of the trade in horses, through the Mandans, to the tribes southwest of the Missouri (1955, 4–5).

1. The Camp Circle

1. Ella Deloria used *migrations* to designate moving camp from one place to another, not in the sense of permanent moves.

2. The *wak'ą* is the Dakota spiritual concept of the supernatural. "Of all forms of life, humans were the least powerful, and so for the Sioux the important distinction was between that which was human and everything else. The universe was fundamentally incomprehensible; it could not be fully known or controlled" (DeMallie 2001c, 806). George Sword explained the concept of *wak'ą* as it relates

to mystery, ritual, and medicine in Walker (1917, 152–53). A general discussion of Lakota spiritual concepts can be found in DeMallie (1987, 25–43).

3. The Lakota Thomas Tyon shared with James R. Walker his experience of the *heyók'a*, partially quoted here: "The man who dreams of *Wakinyan* is called *heyoka*. In all their speech, the *heyoka* talk in opposites (*inzinhe-kta kinya eca-iyapi kin unwelo*). . . . The *Wakinyan* often command the man who dreams of them to do certain things (*wakinconzapi*), it is said. But some *heyoka* do not follow their commands closely and the *Wakinyan* will surely kill them. . . . They command him to commit murder (*tiwicakte xipi*), it is said. And if he does not do it, they will make him kill, it is said" (1980, 155–56).

4. Reverend Stephen R. Riggs, in *Tah-Koo Wah-Kan: The Gospel among the Dakotas* (1869, 66–69), characterized to the *heyók'a* as "the anti-natural god." Ella Deloria is probably referring to this description.

2. Law and Order

1. A synthesis of the Dakota practices to punish murderers was published by Ella Deloria in Deloria 1944b.

2. According to George Sword, "coup" or *kté* were war honors that distinguished different degrees of bravery on the battlefield. "The Lakota word *kté* 'to kill' was used metaphorically to mean 'count coup on the enemy,' and its primary sense referred to touching the body of a fallen enemy" (DeMallie 2001c, 805). Warriors recounted their coup to each other during formalized ceremonies of which Black Elk provided examples (DeMallie, ed. 1984, 34–36, 187–88).

3. Murder could also result from sorcery. The Stephen R. Riggs dictionary, cited by James Owen Dorsey (1894, 499) includes the entry ȟmúǧa, "to cause sickness or death, as the Dakotas pretend to be able to do, in a supernatural way; to bewitch, kill by enchantment" (Riggs 1890, 165).

4. The Home

1. James Mooney described sweat lodges in the following terms in 1890: "The sweat-house is a small circular framework of willow branches driven into the ground and bent over and brought together at the top in such a way that when covered with blankets or buffalo robes the structure forms a diminutive round-top tipi just high enough to enable several persons to sit or to stand in a stooping posture inside" (1896, 822).

2. Vine Vincent Deloria Sr. (1901–1990) was an Episcopal priest ordained in 1932 who exercised in several communities of South Dakota including at Pine Ridge and in Martin. He was a revered community leader committed to educational programs that could empower the Lakota youth and mediate the Native heritage and Christianity. Deloria became the Episcopal Church assistant secretary for Indian Work and lobbied against the Indian termination policies of the 1950s.

After this period of engagement in national politics, he returned to South Dakota and modeled the kind of cross-cultural leadership he did not find in the higher church institution (Deloria 2001).

5. Courtship and Marriage

1. Eight examples of *Iktómi* stories can be found in *Dakota Texts* (Deloria 1932, 1–46).
2. Mary Austin (1868–1934) was an American poet and novelist who wrote about Native American culture. This poem inspired by Dakota sentimental mockery was published under the title "Sioux Song at Parting" (1923, 79).
3. George Sword was an Oglala warrior, policeman, and judge who learned from the Pine Ridge agency physician James R. Walker that oral traditions regarding the Lakota way of life could be preserved by writing them. While at first George Sword relied on an interpret to translate and Walker to write, he later learned to write himself and published Native texts regularly in community newspapers. Some of the texts relative to Lakota ceremonies were published in English by Walker (1917, 1980) while some of the Native-language texts were made available by Ella Deloria (1929).
4. Elks symbolized Dakota masculinity. Thomas Tyon described *Heȟáka* as "The Spirit of the Male Elk [that] presided over sexual relationships" (Walker 1980, 121). Black Elk, for his part, described a ceremony in which he participated called the Elk Ceremony. In it six men serving as elks and four virgins prepared a ceremonial tipi. They painted themselves and then went to sweat together. The virgins came out of the sweat lodge first, followed by the men acting like elks. They then presented relics to the four directions, and the men returned to the ceremonial tipi, where they smoked the pipe (DeMallie, ed. 1984, 242–44).
5. The *huká* ceremony is one of adoption and mentorship. According to Walker (1980, 208–11), both men and women can take a *huká*, regardless of sex or age. The initiator can be the younger or the older person in the relationship. The elder in the *huká* relationship mentors his or her *huká* to be a good and true person and conduct a virtuous life. Deloria provides a description of the *huká* ceremony, as described by George Sword, in *Speaking of Indians* (1944a, 63–68).
6. This tale was published in Lakota along with a free translation as "Iktómi Takes His Mother-in-Law on the Warpath" in *Dakota Texts* (Deloria 1932, 8–11).

7. Death and Burial

1. Dakota rites and ceremonies were already a well-described academic matter when Ella Deloria wrote. She might be referring here to James Owen Dorsey's *A Study of Siouan Cults* (1894, 431–500) and to James R. Walker's "The Sun Dance and Other Ceremonies of the Oglala Division of the Teton Dakota" (1917).

2. It is unclear whom Ella Deloria is referring to here, but Alice C. Fletcher published a compelling ethnographic description of a "Ghost Lodge" ceremony that took place in 1882. After several months of ceremony, it was concluded by an exceptional distribution of gifts accumulated by the family of the deceased: "The men who receive at this time will save up their treasures and give them away at some future religious or secular festival" (Fletcher 1887, 306). On the Ghost Lodge, see also Dorsey 1889; and Curtis 1908 (99–110).

3. The Lakota woman Good Seat described ghosts thus: "There are two kinds of spirits. *Wanagi*, that is the spirit (*nagi*) that has once been in a man. *Nagi* (a spirit) has never been in a man. When *wanagi* is in a man, it is *woniya* (the life). When a man dies, his *woniya* is then *wanagi*. When a man is alive, he has his *woniya* (breadth of life) and his *nagi* (spirit). His *nagi* is not part of himself. His *nagi* cares for him and warns of danger and helps him out of difficulties. When he dies, it goes with his *wanagi* to the spirit world (*wanagi makoce*)" (Walker 1980, 70–71). Ethnographic descriptions of Dakota beliefs relative to ghosts can also be found in Dorsey 1894, 484–93.

8. Relatives of Marriage

1. A full-length version of the "Four Brothers" story, featuring such an orphan girl rescued by four brothers, can be found in *Myths and Legends of the Sioux* by Marie L. McLaughlin (1916, 179–97), but the miraculous growth in it concerns *Iyan Hoksila* 'Stone Boy' whom the girl rescues from the river. Another example of the motif of the miraculous growth in Dakota folklore can be found in "The Story of Iron Hawk," a boy adopted by Meadowlark, who makes him grow supernaturally (Beckwith 1930, 379–80). A version of this tale of Iron Hawk is available in the Ella Deloria Archive (Dakota Indian Foundation, Box 3, File 17, page 326). Stith Thompson found the story of the Blood-Clot-Boy, who often grows up in one night, to be one the most popular culture-hero tales in the plains region (1946, 335–38).

9. Formal Relatives of Birth

1. Smallpox began to infect the central and northern plains in 1831 and reached the high plains in the devastating epidemic of 1837–38. The mortality in some Native communities reached over 90 percent (Swagerty 2001, 258).

2. According to James R. Walker, during the *hųká* ceremony the initiates put red stripes on their faces while their *hųká* paint their bodies red. Other roles in the ceremony were distinguished by specific red paint patterns (1980, 223). Ritual implements were painted with different colors, but the meaning of the paint is a secret told to one who is made *hųká* (214). On the *hųká* ceremony, see also Densmore (1918, 68–77)

3. A medicine man and warrior, George Sword, born ca. 1847, was the only one of the traditional leaders to write a Native-language account of Lakota lifeways. Although he never received any western education, he learned to write from the published Native-language newspaper *Iapi Oaye*. About 1909 he wrote a series of texts in Lakota in order to instruct the Pine Ridge agency physician, James R. Walker, some of which have been published (Walker 1917, 1983).

4. This free translation appears to be of an excerpt of George Sword, text 9, *Wi-Wayak-wacipi*, "The Sundance," located in a ledger book included in the Dr. James R. Walker Collection, no. 653, a holding of the Library of the Colorado Historical Society (*Lena owa*, 190, 286–88). The original Lakota is included here: *Na can wanqu he sunka wakan ca karol iyeye ši ca cante parloka can kin icu nawan-wanyaka Najinpi el karol iyeya hecel lila winyan unšikapi na iš Hokšila unšikapi hena akiniglila ahiyayapi roka etanhan he tuwe tokeya icu kiciyasupi na he tawekiyapi ota šung oturan kiyapi.*

10. Informal Relatives of Birth

1. It is uncertain whether this final *čį* should be written as aspirated or not.

2. In the unedited manuscript, Ella Deloria wrote it as *wokokpeka*, in a chapter that had not received handwritten diacritics, but it is likely a contracted form of *wókʿokipʿeka* (*New Dakota Dictionary*, 2011, 680).

3. The editors have been unable to find the reference Ella Deloria is addressing in the anthropological literature.

4. Cross-cousin distinction was first identified to be part of a kinship system by Lewis Henry Morgan (1871). W. H. R. Rivers observed that the kinship terminology of the Dakota suggested that cross-cousin marriage might have been practiced in North America (1914, 49–55). At the time Ella Deloria wrote this ethnography of the Dakotas, many Americanist ethnographers looked for evidence to support or contest Rivers's hypothesis.

11. Relatives of Social Kinship

1. Ella Deloria is here referring to Stephen R. Riggs, *Dakota Grammar, Texts, and Ethnography* (1893, 196). He wrote: "One of the customs of the olden times, which was potent both for good and for evil, and which is going into desuetude, was that of fellowhood. Scarcely a Dakota young man could be found who had not some special friend or Koda. . . . They exchanged bows, or guns, or blankets— sometimes the entire equipment. In rare cases they exchanged wives. What one asked of the other he gave him; nothing could be denied. The arrangement was often a real affection, sometimes fading out as the years pass by, but often lasting to old age."

12. Birth and Infancy

1. For example, see "The Twin-Spirits," in *Dakota Texts* (Deloria 1932, 193–97).
2. *Scrofula* refers to the tuberculosis of the lymph nodes. The draining lesions are very much like an infected bullet wound and can leave large scars (Della Cook, personal communication). Tuberculosis was epidemic in Native communities at the beginning of the twentieth century (Hrdlička 1909).
3. The wound resulting from scrofula somewhat looked like the burrow of a mole: the swollen lymph node would be hot and tender, and one could move it around, more or less like a mole under the skin, and the channel it produced when it ruptured would be much like a wet, sticky burrow (Della Cook, personal communication).
4. The theme of *Iktómi's* gluttony is pervasive. Ella Deloria published a partially similar story in which *Iktómi* has a buffalo carry him inside his belly to cross a river. Stuck inside, as the buffalo had forgotten about him, *Iktómi* cuts him open to get out. He then has a feast on gooseberries and later invites himself to an eye-juggling contest with mice (Deloria 1932, 32–36). When many of the earlier Dakota stories were written, the ban on explicit content in the mail resulted in self-censorship from many ethnographers, which largely explains the absence of sexual content in the ethnographic record.
5. According to DeMallie (2001c, 812), 187 members of Sitting Bull's band surrendered at Fort Buford in the summer of 1881. Utley (1993, 246) found that 172 prisoners were taken aboard a steamer in April 1883 on their move to Fort Randall. Ella Deloria would have been familiar with Stanley Vestal's biography of Sitting Bull, which briefly mentions the hold on the Lakota chief and his band in Fort Randall as "prisoners of war" (1957, 237). Sitting Bull and most of his people surrendered at Standing Rock Agency, near Fort Yates, north of Fort Randall (Dickson 2010).

13. Preadolescence

1. More realistic stories featuring supernatural aid provided to a warrior have been published. "The Owl's Warning" is the story of a boy who is alerted at night by the hoot of an owl in a tree over his tent. He sees on the reflection of water in a bowl the face of an enemy preparing to attack him through the smoke hole of his tent and quickly shoots him an arrow that kills him. A wise man comments upon his return that the owl "brings a warning that danger is near or that danger is approaching "(South Dakota Writers' Project 1941, 57–61). Another story narrates the nightly scouting of Big Eagle in an enemy Crow camp. He finds inside a tipi an image of his deceased wife, sits by her side, and alerts his hosts of the imminent Sioux attack through sign language. He is later invited to marry the Crow chief's daughter and lives with them (McLaughlin 1916, 94–98).

2. A flood coming from a mythological character's body is a common motif in Dakota legends. In "The Warlike Seven" by Zitkala-Ša, Iya [*Iyą́*], 'The Eater' drinks up an entire lake so that his belly almost touches the sky. Iktomi, who was swallowed by Iya, decides to cut it open to attain the sky, and a flood that drowns the people of the village results from it (1901, 159–65). More fundamentally, *Iyą́'s* blood appears as an element of the creation of the earth: "To create *Maka, Inyan* [*Iyą́*] took so much from himself that he opened his veins, and all his blood flowed from him so that he shrank and became hard and powerless. As his blood flowed from him, it became blue waters which are the waters upon the earth" (Walker 1983, 107).

3. In contemporary literature *wįkte* might be referred to as Two-Spirit, but the Dakota concept refers specifically to male-bodied individuals who display feminine manners and occupations. This section, listed in the original manuscript as an appendix, was called "Transvestitism" and was published as such in 2007:

> This is a subject so distasteful to men informants that they would not discuss it with a woman, however objectively. But I was able to glean something about it from women informants and I give it here.
>
> Early ethnographers speak of *wįkte* by the French term berdache, from which we know that such persons were found also among other American tribes. My analysis of the word *wįkte* does not satisfy me and yet its component parts seem to suggest 'would be female'.
>
> The most famous *wįkte* in relatively modern times was *Wičʿíte-Waštéla* who was also the last, it is said. The name means 'Cute Little Face', which is obviously ironical for he was a comical-tragic figure. In frame, carriage and facial features he was a man; in attire and speech a woman, and a fastidious one at that. His skill in the womanly arts was second to few experts and he was gowned in his own handiwork, handsomely if gaudily. His coarse abundant hair hung in two long ropelike braids and were tied at the ends with feminine hair-ornaments.
>
> All references picture him as a pitiful paradox; ludigrous and ungainly in woman's dress, he moved with frightening masculine vigor; in a deep male voice he spoke with obsequious gentleness, using certain particles that distinguish women's speech from men's. His feminine mannerisms were perfect, but his air of pressuring himself to be accepted as a female because of them was never convincing. Known far and wide, for he was an incessant traveler, he would arrive for the annual Sun Dance with the camp circle where he had lived the past year and depart with another, there to stay the coming year.
>
> One informant remembered *Wičʿíte-Waštéla* as he appeared when visiting her grandmother whom he addressed as *čépʿąši* (term for female cousin, woman speaking). As a girl of nine or ten, she was so curious about him that she kept close to her grandmother in order to observe him. His face was

long and bony and his hands and feet were huge and yet at time she could forget that he was not really a woman. She especially recalled how he kept pulling his skirt over his knees, already well concealed, with exaggerated modesty, while he talked in a low, husky voice as he sat eating the food her grandmother set before him.

"How well I have feasted, čép'ąši!" he said upon leaving. "You must come to visit me next, I have plenty of good meat." The girl's grandmother thanked him, without any intention of going to the wį́kte's abode, which was a questionable place where no decent woman would be seen. In all respects the visit ended successfully, for the hostess acted the part expected of her. She was glad it was over and her guest was gone. For even if a wį́kte had no romantic interest in women, they often shunned him.

In 1951 another informant aged 86 told of seeing Wič'íte-Waštéla at close range on one occasion. The people, on a move to a new site, came to a narrow stream with steep banks, running swift and high after a cloudburst. Since they must go on, the men jumped over it and reached out to pull the women and children across while they jumped. But when they would help the wį́kte over, he acted like a shy girl too diffident to so much as grasp a man's hand even in this emergency. So while he postured and demurred he lost his footing and tumbled into the water. My informant said she disliked him intensely, a horrid sight as he thrashed and floundered about in his long woman's gown, until he was unceremonially fished out. This would have been around 1880, while the people were still moving about, for my informant was a girl of sixteen then. She never saw Wič'íte-Waštéla again but she used to hear about his actions and sayings. As far as she knew he was the only wį́kte living but was aware from old tales that there had been others in former times.

It is said that Wič'íte-Waštéla always pitched his tipi somewhat back of the circle or out beyond the entrance to it. Whenever he walked around and stopped at different tipis he was soberly received as a woman. If he was normally related as father, brother or uncle, he was addressed as mother, sister or aunt.

It is said further that a wį́kte would have a following of worthless characters who went to his lodge for a meal and for other reasons. In my time a certain old man was held in contempt because Hé ehą́ni wį́kte wą́ yúza keyápi 'They say that the once had a wį́kte for wife'.

The stigma affecting the wį́kte also appears in the following report: "He (the warrior) stole into an enemy camp and hid in a vacant tipi in order to steal horses after the people were all asleep, but late at night a woman entered and prepared for bed. His advances were not repulsed but he ran out in disgust upon realizing that it was not a woman."

For any male to be such as suspected of hidden proclivities in that direction was nearly as bad as to be an actual wį́kte. The awkward, labored way a man struggled with housework when his wife was sick or absent was only out of self-defense. Better to be clumsy than to be noticeably too adept, too at home at it, too much like a *wįkte*. Thus, ordinarily men were ashamed to be seen cooking or sewing, if their wife was present. One man who was expert at broiling ribs intact in one broad slab over an open fire always explained that he had to learn to do it out of sheer necessity while on the warpath. He wanted it distinctly understood that warrior and *wįkte* were incompatible terms.

Certain habits were characteristic: *wįkte* had a penchant for claiming event casual passerby as relatives, and whenever it was at all plausible they contrived to become "sister-in-law" to the men, which would give them one more opportunity to play a female role by exchanging banter with "joking relatives of the opposite sex." But lacking the finesse, judgement and good taste necessary, a *wįkte* would joke without restraint, boisterously and even ribaldly, much to the consternation of the man he was addressing in a mixed crowd. Men tended to avoid encountering such a character lest his loud remarks embarrass them.

Another habit was to invent nicknames for men, as they were inclined. If not simply laughable nonsense, these could be uncomplimentary or worse. He might fasten such a name on even the most sedate and upright man in the community, for no reason unless to spite him for his indifference. Several of those names were given me by women informants reluctantly. Some were quite harmless, some suggestive, and a few were downright lascivious. Vile nicknames no longer exist, apparently having died out when the last *wįkte* died. They were never applied by others, except by male joking relatives who wanted to bedevil one whom a *wįkte* had named, but this was in fun and in private.

Wįkte and others with other differences were not cast out but were accepted for what they were and accorded the treatment that was normally their due, with such modifications as were needed to suit their individual requirements. For at all events, a *wįkte* must be fitted—even on his own terms—into the universal kinship scheme, outside which a Dakota could live hardly as well as a fish out of water. He was still and always a relative entitled to his place as such. Incidentally, kinship rules and observances were taught and became fixed so thoroughly and so early in every child's life that a *wįkte* also conformed to them.

To that end parents and relatives were constantly responsible for steering their boys—and girls—in that path of development that was right for them, and were quick to detect and correct any disposition to veer from it in the least particular.

It was when a boy reached sixteen or seventeen years of age without showing any interest in girls that his parents became actively concerned to bring about the expected attitude in him. Some bought a wife for their boy with the hope that intimacy with a female would work the cure, which it usually did.

Not many years ago, one father went to great pains to arrange a marriage for his reluctant son of nineteen. The boy acted quite unconcerned, though he did not rebel at taking a wife but went through the ceremony and the accompanying feast quite obligingly; as though it were his father's show and he only a bit player in it. After the birth of his child, the marriage came to an end, only because he and the girl, literally foisted on him, found themselves uncongenial. Quite normally he wooed and won a woman of his own choice and lived happily with her, and their children.

14. Adolescence

1. The diacritics on *čičí* are uncertain.
2. The Buffalo Ceremony, or Buffalo Sing, was witnessed and described by James R. Walker. It is a rite of passage to the benefit of certain young women to promote their industriousness and hospitality. The ceremony is hosted by the parents of the girl. The officiant, preferably a shaman, prepares an altar with a buffalo skull and conducts the ceremony from dawn to dusk. During this elaborate rite, the officiant communicates to the girls the expectations of the Spirit of the Buffalo. A feast and giveaway, sometimes lasting several days, follows (Walker 1917, 141–51; 1980, 241–53). Black Elk also described the ceremony under the name 'Her Alone They Sing Over' (Brown 1953, 116–26). Ella Deloria herself described the ceremony in a section of the unpublished "Rites and Ceremonies of the Teton" manuscript.

Bibliography

Austin, Mary. 1923. *The American Rhythm*. Boston: Houghton Mifflin.

Beckwith, Martha W. 1930. "Mythology of the Oglala Dakota." *Journal of American Folklore* 43, no. 170 (October–December): 339–442.

Boas, Franz, and Ella C. Deloria. 1941. "Dakota Grammar." *Memoirs of the National Academy of Sciences* 23, no. 2: 1–182.

Brown, Joseph E. 1953. *Black Elk's Account of the Seven Rites of the Oglala Sioux*. Norman: University of Oklahoma Press.

Curtis, Edward S. 1907. *The North American Indian*. Vol. 3. Norwood MA: Plimpton.

Deloria, Ella C. 1929. "The Sun Dance of the Oglala Sioux." *Journal of American Folklore* 42, no. 166 (October–December): 354–413.

———. 1932. "Dakota Texts." *Publications of the American Ethnological Society* 14. New York: G. E. Stechert.

———. [ca.] 1933. "Assiniboine Report." Unpublished manuscript. Ruth Benedict Collection, Vassar College Library.

———. 1944a. *Speaking of Indians*. New York: Friendship. Reedited in 1998 with an introduction by Vine Deloria Jr. Lincoln: University of Nebraska Press.

———. 1944b. "Dakota Treatment of Murderers." *Proceedings of the Americans Philosophical Society* 88, no. 5 (November): 368–71.

———. 1954. "Short Dakota Texts, including Conversations." *International Journal of American Linguistics* 20, no. 1 (January): 17–22.

———. 1988. *Waterlily*. Biographical sketch of the author by Agnes Picotte. Afterword by Raymond J. DeMallie. Lincoln: University of Nebraska Press.

———. 2007. *The Dakota Way of Life*. Edited by Joyzelle Gingway Godfrey. Rapid City: Mariah.

Deloria, Philip J. 2001. "Vine V. Deloria Sr." In *The New Warriors: Native American Leaders since 1900*, edited by Dave R. Edmunds, 79–96. Lincoln: University of Nebraska Press.

DeMallie, Raymond J., ed. 1984. *The Sixth Grandfather: Black Elk Teachings Given to John G. Neihardt*. Lincoln: University of Nebraska Press.

———. 1987. "Lakota Belief and Ritual in the Nineteenth Century." In *Sioux Indian Religion*, edited by Raymond J. DeMallie and Douglas R. Parks, 25–43. Lincoln: University of Nebraska Press.

———. 2001a. "Introduction." In *The Handbook of North American Indians*, vol. 13, *Plains*, edited by Raymond J. DeMallie, 1–13. Washington DC: Smithsonian Institution.

———. 2001b. "Sioux until 1850." In *The Handbook of North American Indians*, vol. 13, *Plains*, edited by Raymond J. DeMallie, 718–60. Washington DC: Smithsonian Institution.

———. 2001c. "Teton." In *The Handbook of North American Indians*, vol. 13, *Plains*, edited by Raymond J. DeMallie, 794–820. Washington DC: Smithsonian Institution.

Densmore, Frances. 1918. *Teton Sioux Music*. Bulletin 61, Bureau of American Ethnology. Washington DC: Smithsonian Institution.

Dickson, Ephriam D. 2010.*The Sitting Bull Surrender Census: The Lakotas at Standing Rock Agency, 1881*. Pierre: South Dakota Historical Society.

Dorsey, James Owen. 1889. "Teton Folk-lore." *American Anthropologist* 2, no. 2 (April): 143–58.

———. 1894. *A Study of Siouan Cults*. Eleventh Annual Report of the Bureau of Ethnology. Washington, DC: Smithsonian Institution.

Ella Deloria Archive. Dakota Indian Foundation and American Indian Studies Research Institute. Accessed January 6, 2022. zia.aisri.indiana.edu/deloria_archive.

Ewers, John C. 1955. *The Horse in Blackfoot Indian Culture*. Bulletin 159, Bureau of American Ethnology. Washington DC: Smithsonian Institution.

Fletcher, Alice C. 1897. "The Shadow or Ghost Lodge: A Ceremony of the Ogallala Sioux." *Reports of the Peabody Museum of American Archaeology and Ethnology* 3: 297–307.

Gardner, Susan. 2003. "'Though It Broke My Heart to Cut Some Bits I Fancied': Ella Deloria's Original Design for *Waterlily*." *American Indian Quarterly* 27, no. 3: 667–96.

Hrdlička, Aleš. 1909. *Tuberculosis among Certain Indian Tribes of the United States*. Bulletin 42, Bureau of American Ethnology. Washington DC: Smithsonian Institution.

Lakota Language Consortium. 2011. *New Lakota Dictionary*. 2nd ed. Bloomington IN: LLC.

Lesser, Alexander. 1958. *Siouan Kinship*. PhD diss., Columbia University.

McLaughlin, Marie L. 1916. *Myths and Legends of the Sioux*. Bismarck ND: Bismarck Tribune.

Mooney, James. 1896. *The Ghost Dance Religion and the Sioux Oubreak of 1890*. Fourteenth Annual Report of the Bureau of Ethnology, 1892–93, Part 2. Washington DC: Bureau of American Ethnology.

Murray, Janette K. 1974. "Ella Deloria: A Biographical Sketch and Literary Analysis." PhD diss., University of North Dakota.

Olden, Sarah E. 1918. *The People of Tipi Sapa (The Dakotas): Tipi Sapa Mitaoyate Kin*. With a foreword by Hugh Latimer Burleson. Milwaukee WI: Morehouse.

Parks, Douglas R. 2001. "Siouan Languages." In *The Handbook of North American Indians*, vol. 13, *Plains*, edited by Raymond J. DeMallie, 94–114. Washington DC: Smithsonian Institution.

Parks, Douglas R., and Raymond J. DeMallie. 1992. "Sioux, Assiniboine, and Stoney Dialects: A Classification." Anthropological Linguistics 34, nos. 1–4 (Spring-Winter): 233–55.

Riggs, Stephen R. 1869. *Tah-Koo Wah-Kan: The Gospel among the Dakotas*. Boston: Sabbath-School.

———. 1890. *A Dakota-English Dictionary*. Contributions to North American Ethnology, Vol. 7. Washington DC: Bureau of American Ethnology.

———. 1893. *Dakota Grammar, Texts, and Ethnography*. Contributions to North American Ethnology. Vol. 9. Washington DC: Department of the Interior.

South Dakota Writers' Project. 1941. *Legends of the Mighty Sioux*. Chicago: Albert Whitman.

Swagerty, William R. 2001. "History of the United States Plains until 1850." In *The Handbook of North American Indians*, vol. 13, *Plains*, edited by Raymond J. DeMallie, 256–79 Washington DC: Smithsonian Institution.

Thompson, Stith. 1946. *The Folktale*. New York: Holt, Rinehart & Winston.

Utley, Robert M. 1993. *The Lance and The Shield: The Life and Times of Sitting Bull*. New York: Henry Holt.

Vestal, Stanley. 1957. *Sitting Bull: Champion of the Sioux*. 2nd ed. Norman: University of Oklahoma Press.

Walker, James R. 1917. "The Sun Dance and Other Ceremonies of the Oglala Division of the Teton Dakota." *American Museum of Natural History Anthropological Papers* 16, no. 2: 51–221.

———. 1980. *Lakota Belief and Ritual*. Edited by Raymond J. DeMallie and Elaine A. Jahner. Lincoln: University of Nebraska Press.

———. 1983. *Lakota Myth*. Edited by Elaine A. Jahner. Lincoln: University of Nebraska Press.

Whitten, Richard G., and Larry J. Zimmerman. 1982. "Directions for Miss Deloria: Boas on the Plains." *Plains Anthropologist* 27, no. 96 (May): 161–64.

Zitkala-Ša. 1901. *Old Indian Legends*. Boston: Ginn.

Index

camps (*cont.*)
  winter, 17, 30–31; police, 33–34, 48,
  343. See also *éyapaha* (camp crier)
Canada, 4
ceremonies, 23–26, 28, 29, 65, 68, 70,
  123–26, 134, 168–70, 179–80, 189,
  220–21, 222, 223, 224, 262, 263, 282,
  290, 304, 311, 315, 316, 329, 332, 350
Č̣ʼasmú (Chief), 326
cats, 191
čʼékpa, 270, 287–90, 293, 294
chaperones, 101, 105, 253, 340, 350,
  357, 359
charms, 309, 310
Cheyenne River, 4, 7, 134
Cheyennes, 4, 7, 19, 293
child-rearing, 55, 59–60, 93, 96, 213,
  232, 248–51, 255–58, 260–61, 293–
  305, 307–9, 311–37
Chippewas, 108
chokecherry, 175, 191, 302
Christian usage, 29, 138, 167, 172,
  175–76
čʼį́kš, 283, 288, 317, 331
čʼiyé, 270
cleanliness, 96
clothing, 132
clowns. See *heyókʼa*
clubbing, 25
collaterals, 12, 21, 65–68, 130, 148, 196,
  199, 202, 214, 215, 241–50, 260, 264,
  267, 270–72, 278, 283, 296, 304, 325,
  329, 333, 344, 352, 357, 358; of in-
  laws, 208–10; of opposite sexes, 72,
  74–75, 87, 119, 218, 228, 231, 235–38.
  See also *hakáta; joking relatives*
continency, 61, 283, 284
contraception, 283
corn, 19, 60, 324
councils, 45
coup, 44, 102, 320, 377n2

couples, 87–88
courtship, 8, 21, 40, 101–15, 118, 120,
  121–23, 148, 151–52, 209, 212, 246,
  270–71, 300, 321, 331–32, 345–46,
  354–58
cowives, 62–64, 115, 203, 213–14, 359
crimes, 39–40
Crows, 9, 10, 53, 219, 320
čʼúkš, 254, 267, 280–81, 283, 288, 305,
  363
čʼuwé, 242, 249, 269

Dakota etiquette, xv, xv–xvi, xxii, 11,
  13, 21, 29, 55, 60, 65, 66, 74, 88, 90–
  92, 95–96, 131–34, 137, 154, 195, 201,
  208, 211, 218–19, 230, 275, 279
Dakota Indian Foundation, xx, xxv
Dakota language, x, xi–xvi, xx, 1, 3, 11–
  15, 46, 76, 83, 96, 101, 109, 110, 128,
  137–38, 148, 176, 185, 186, 198, 220,
  227, 235, 243, 260, 265, 282, 290,
  296–97, 300–2, 308, 321, 325, 328,
  330, 340, 351, 372; expressions, 30,
  60, 113, 142, 156, 169, 189, 190, 243,
  247, 250, 257, 160, 281, 291, 299, 313,
  319, 335, 363; texts, 138, 243, 249,
  265, 275, 305, 334, 360, 364
Dakotas, 1, 3, 9–13, 38–39, 41, 42–43,
  46, 58, 61, 66, 67, 69, 73, 74, 81, 89–
  92, 93, 95–96, 102, 104, 114, 117, 118,
  126, 131, 133, 150, 156, 162, 163, 166,
  167, 172, 179, 196, 209, 215, 216, 221,
  223, 231, 234, 235, 238, 243, 246, 255,
  263–64, 281, 282, 293, 294, 305, 314,
  324–26, 329, 330, 343, 346, 361, 362,
  366
dances, 220, 224, 253, 298
death, 27, 33, 50, 60, 64, 117, 123, 135,
  151, 153–56, 159–71, 174–94, 218, 253,
  266, 273, 283, 306, 308, 315, 361; by
  lightning, 25, 191, 192; of children,

homelessness. See *t'iyókitȧhela-ų́*

honor place (*č'atkú* or *t'ič'átku*), 60, 83–84, 85, 87, 137, 144, 159, 168, 303, 317, 348

horses, 6–7, 20, 29, 47, 49, 54, 60, 73, 101, 111, 138, 141, 164, 169, 170–71, 242, 333; gift of, 70–72, 121, 123, 125, 144, 150, 161, 177, 201, 215, 219, 220, 225, 227, 229, 247–48, 274, 285, 304, 309, 322, 339, 359, 360

hospitality, 26–27, 37, 66, 69, 73, 88, 100, 115, 124, 151, 169–70, 171, 323–24, 333, 342, 352, 367

houses, 174, 216, 321

hųká, 70, 124–25, 220–21, 378n5, 379n2

hú-kȧǧo. See scarification

Hųkáyapi-It'ą́čą, 220

Hųkpap'aya, 3, 10, 20, 266, 286, 305, 354, 375n2

hunting, 18, 19, 22, 54, 60, 69, 133, 272, 283, 316, 332; territory, 4

hurdles, 48–49

Hurston, Zora Neale, 371

Iktómi, 103, 113, 129, 148, 258, 302, 319

iná, 13

implements (eating), 94–95, 97, 99, 242

incest, 38, 236

informants, 2–3, 4, 15, 25, 49, 62, 111, 151, 158, 168, 210, 216, 221, 226, 245, 285, 289, 301, 330, 349, 353, 365

insanity, 291, 326, 352, 353, 354, 359

intermarriages, 7, 8

Irving, Josephe, 50–51

Itázipč'o, 40, 63, 80, 326, 354

itúh'ą, 71–72. See also giveaways

Íyą T'ó, 244–45

Iyúptala, 225–27

jealousy, 38

joking relatives, 38, 129, 137, 143, 153, 186, 202, 208–15, 238–39, 241, 243, 277, 285, 299, 335, 356, 357

Kaháȥi, 313

kettles, 81, 148, 175, 177

keyápi, 2, 4–5, 50, 191, 304

kič'úwa, 270–72, 274

kinship, xiv, xv, xv–xvi, 16, 33, 64–75, 88, 125–28, 150, 161, 185, 192, 195–201, 215, 220, 230–31, 255–56, 258, 276–81, 282, 295, 311, 326, 327, 332, 335, 365–68; changing, xxi, 13–14, 41, 152, 231, 236, 274–75; terminology for, xxix–xxx, 207–8, 210, 233, 235, 267, 270, 296; relations, 8, 11–12, 21, 39–40, 42–47, 51–53, 55, 60, 62, 119, 121, 133, 139, 144, 195, 223, 227, 228, 229–31, 236–40, 242–43, 249, 254, 259, 262–70, 307, 343, 345; mending, 127–28, 266–68. See also *wač'ékiya*

killing, 45–58, 111; an enemy, 11, 45; within home, 11, 45, 51, 57, 58

kinnikinnick, 29

kissing, 305–6

Kitfoxes. See *T'ok'álas*

Klineberg, Otto, xii

k'olá, 151, 269–70, 272

Kúšni, 224

Lakota dictionary, xviii

leaders. See magistrates

left-handedness, 81, 91

lekší, 13

Lesser, Alexander, vii, xxiv, xxv, xxix

lice, 328

Little Crow, 140

Little Warrior, 265–66

loyalty, 62, 64, 70–73, 146–47, 151, 222, 244, 247–48, 264, 272

In the Studies in the Anthropology of North American Indians Series

Native Languages of the
Southeastern United States
Edited by Heather K. Hardy
and Janine Scancarelli

The Heiltsuks: Dialogues of Culture
and History on the Northwest Coast
By Michael E. Harkin

Prophecy and Power among
the Dogrib Indians
By June Helm

A Totem Pole History: The Work
of Lummi Carver Joe Hillaire
By Pauline Hillaire
Edited by Gregory P. Fields

Corbett Mack: The Life of
a Northern Paiute
As told by Michael Hittman

The Spirit and the Sky: Lakota
Visions of the Cosmos
By Mark Hollabaugh

The Canadian Sioux
By James H. Howard

The Canadian Sioux,
Second Edition
By James H. Howard, with
a new foreword by
Raymond J. DeMallie and
Douglas R. Parks

Clackamas Chinook Performance
Art: Verse Form Interpretations
By Victoria Howard
Transcription by Melville Jacobs
Edited by Catharine Mason

Yuchi Ceremonial Life:
Performance, Meaning, and
Tradition in a Contemporary
American Indian Community
By Jason Baird Jackson

Comanche Ethnography: Field
Notes of E. Adamson Hoebel,
Waldo R. Wedel, Gustav G.
Carlson, and Robert H. Lowie
Compiled and edited by
Thomas W. Kavanagh

The Comanches: A History, 1706–1875
By Thomas W. Kavanagh

Koasati Dictionary
By Geoffrey D. Kimball with
the assistance of Bel Abbey,
Martha John, and Ruth Poncho

Koasati Grammar
By Geoffrey D. Kimball with
the assistance of Bel Abbey,
Nora Abbey, Martha John,
Ed John, and Ruth Poncho

Koasati Traditional Narratives
By Geoffrey D. Kimball

Kiowa Belief and Ritual
By Benjamin Kracht

The Salish Language Family:
Reconstructing Syntax
By Paul D. Kroeber

Tales from Maliseet Country: The
Maliseet Texts of Karl V. Teeter
Translated and edited by
Philip S. LeSourd

The Medicine Men: Oglala Sioux Ceremony and Healing
By Thomas H. Lewis

A Grammar of Creek (Muskogee)
By Jack B. Martin

A Dictionary of Creek / Muskogee
By Jack B. Martin and
Margaret McKane Mauldin

The Red Road and Other Narratives of the Dakota Sioux
By Samuel Minyo and
Robert Goodvoice
Edited by Daniel M. Beveridge

Wolverine Myths and Visions: Dene Traditions from Northern Alberta
Edited by Patrick Moore
and Angela Wheelock

Ceremonies of the Pawnee
By James R. Murie
Edited by Douglas R. Parks

Households and Families of the Longhouse Iroquois at Six Nations Reserve
By Merlin G. Myers
Foreword by Fred Eggan
Afterword by M. Sam Cronk

Archaeology and Ethnohistory of the Omaha Indians: The Big Village Site
By John M. O'Shea and
John Ludwickson

Traditional Narratives of the Arikara Indians (4 vols.)
By Douglas R. Parks

A Dictionary of Skiri Pawnee
By Douglas R. Parks and
Lula Nora Pratt

Lakota Texts: Narratives of Lakota Life and Culture in the Twentieth Century
Translated and analyzed
by Regina Pustet

Osage Grammar
By Carolyn Quintero

A Fur Trader on the Upper Missouri: The Journal and Description of Jean-Baptiste Truteau, 1794–1796
By Jean-Baptiste Truteau
Edited by Raymond J. DeMallie,
Douglas R. Parks, and Robert Vézina
Translated by Mildred Mott
Wedel, Raymond J. DeMallie,
and Robert Vézina

They Treated Us Just Like Indians: The Worlds of Bennett County, South Dakota
By Paula L. Wagoner

A Grammar of Kiowa
By Laurel J. Watkins with the
assistance of Parker McKenzie

To order or obtain more information on these or other University of Nebraska Press titles, visit nebraskapress.unl.edu.